East Asia and Globalization

Asia in World Politics
Series Editor: Samuel S. Kim

East Asia and Globalization

edited by
Samuel S. Kim

ROWMAN & LITTLEFIELD PUBLISHERS, INC.
Lanham • Boulder • New York • Oxford

ROWMAN & LITTLEFIELD PUBLISHERS, INC.

Published in the United States of America
by Rowman & Littlefield Publishers, Inc.
4720 Boston Way, Lanham, Maryland 20706
http://www.rowmanlittlefield.com

12 Hid's Copse Road
Cumnor Hill, Oxford OX2 9JJ, England

British Library Cataloguing in Publication Information Available

Library of Congress Cataloging-in-Publication Data

East Asia and globalization / edited by Samuel S. Kim.
    p. cm.—(Asia in world politics)
  Includes bibliographical references and index.
  ISBN 0-7425-0935-4 (alk. paper)—ISBN 0-7425-0936-2 (pbk. : alk. paper)
    1. East Asia—Foreign economic relations. 2. East Asia—Economic policy. 3. East
  Asia—Politics and government. 4. Globalization. I. Kim, Samuel S., 1935- II. Series

  HF1600.5 .E17 2000
  337.5—dc21

                                                                00-034200

∞™ The paper used in this publication meets the minimum requirements of American
National Standard for Information Sciences—Permanence of Paper for Printed Library
Materials, ANSI/NISO Z39.48-1992.

Contents

v

Tables

Preface

At the turn of the new millennium, globalization seems to be sweeping across the world like a tidal wave, spewing new opportunities and new dangers to people's security, well-being, and identities in both developed and developing countries. As made manifest in the Asian financial crisis of 1997–1998, East Asia has become a vortex of globalization dynamics. The East Asian region is an especially interesting case for at least two main reasons. First, the role of the state is central to the globalization debate. Second, the region is comprised of states both large and small, effective and ineffective, adaptable and maladaptive, globalized and deglobalized (localized).

This volume seeks to advance our understanding of globalization in the East Asian context as well as various strategies for coping with the forces of globalization, especially in eight countries that have been selected as representative of the region. Eschewing both neoliberal "hyperglobalization" chant and neorealist "globaloney" castigation, the contributors joined in this project to integrate a broad synthetic analytic framework (chapter 1) with region-specific (chapters 2 and 11) and country-specific case studies (chapters 3 to 10).

Specifically, this volume poses and addresses three major questions about East Asia's globalization. First, it identifies the range of contending conceptualizations of globalization, albeit with some overlapping characteristics, that have underpinned East Asia's changing and contradictory views and attitudes toward globalization in the 1990s. Second, it critically probes the discrepancy between promise and performance—the myths and realities—of East Asia's globalization and the complex interaction of globalization challenges and East Asian responses. Finally, it looks at the impacts and consequences of globalization for East Asia's political, economic, social, cultural, ecological, and security development. These questions, which examine in particular the nature, challenges, responses, impacts, and consequences of East Asia's globalization, provide the focus and theme that the present volume seeks to address, with special attention to the developments after the onset of the Asian financial crisis in July 1997.

Although this is the first sustained analysis of the various and multiplying ramifications of globalization dynamics in East Asia, the editor and contributors make no claim that this represents the last word on this extremely important but highly contested subject. Nonetheless, we hope that the analyses contained in the following pages contribute to a better understanding of the forces of globalization affecting and reshaping East Asian development as well as set the study of globalization on a broader and deeper footing in coming years.

This undertaking has been the work of many, a collaborative effort from the beginning. A key catalyst in the preparation and emergence of the present study was an invitation that I received in early 1999 from *Asian Perspective* to serve as a guest editor of a special issue on a topic of my personal interest but also germane to a wider regional appeal. I quickly arrived at the theme of "Globalization in East Asia" as the primary focus of special issue, being both a topic at the core of my most recent collaborative project—*Korea's Globalization* (Cambridge: Cambridge University Press, 2000)—and an East Asian perspective that has been relatively neglected in post–Cold War years. In the course of carrying out the special issue project, I have received invaluable support, both substantive and editorial, from *Asian Perspective*'s Melvin Gurtov (editor-in-chief) and Su-Hoon Lee (managing editor). Without their sustained support and encouragement, the special issue would not have been possible. The eleven chapters contained in this volume represent revised and updated versions of the essays originally published in the special issue of *Asian Perspective* (vol. 23, no. 3 [1999]) and are used here with the publisher's permission.

In addition to thanking the contributors, whose revised and updated essays appear in this volume, I wish to express my appreciation to my graduate student assistant Ingrid Davis at Columbia University for indispensable logistical and managerial support.

Finally, Susan McEachern, our editor at Rowman & Littlefield Publishers, has been an invisible collaborator and invaluable navigator for the project. Special thanks are due also to Bruce Owens for superb copyediting to minimize stylistic infelicity and to Dawn Stoltzfus for efficient steering of the manuscript through the various stages of the production process. The usual disclaimer still applies: The editor and contributors alone are responsible for the views and interpretations and the errors that may persist in this volume.

Samuel S. Kim
New York

1

East Asia and Globalization: Challenges and Responses

Samuel S. Kim

Globalization has an immense potential to improve people's lives, but it can disrupt—and destroy—them as well. Those who do not accept its pervasive, all-encompassing ways are often left behind. It is our task to prevent this; to ensure that globalization leads to progress, prosperity and security for all. I intend that the United Nations shall lead this effort.

— UN Secretary-General Kofi Annan, September 3, 1998[1]

Globalisation not only pulls upwards, it pushes downwards, creating new pressures for local autonomy. The American sociologist Daniel Bell expresses this very well when he says that the nation becomes too small to solve the big problems, but also too large to solve the small ones . . . globalisation is becoming increasingly de-centered not under the control of any group of nations, and still less of the large corporations. Its effects are felt just as much in the western countries as elsewhere.

— Anthony Giddens, 1999 BBC Reith Lectures[2]

Globalization is creating new threats to human security—in rich countries and poor. . . . New information and communications technologies are driving globalization—but polarizing the world into the connected and the isolated.

— UN Development Program, *Human Development Report 1999*[3]

This report [*World Development Report 1999/2000*] seeks neither to praise nor to condemn globalization and localization. Rather it recognizes them as forces that bring new opportunities but also raise new or greater challenges in terms of economic and political instability.

— James D. Wolfensohn, president, The World Bank, August 1999[4]

With the clarity, simplicity, and apparent stability of the bipolar superpower conflict gone, nearly all states are subject to the twin pressures of globalization from without and localization from within. The Asian financial crisis (AFC) of 1997–1998 has put to rest claims that all the frenzy about globalization amounted to nothing more than "globaloney." In 1998 alone, three major discussions were held under UN auspices on the opportunities and dangers for the global community of globalization. For the first time that year, the UN secretary-general's annual report—a state of the world message—declared that the organization would take up the challenge of ensuring that "globalization leads to progress, prosperity and security for all."

At the turn of the new millennium, globalization seems to be sweeping across the world like a tidal wave, tearing everything in its pathway asunder. During the first half of 1999, the most comprehensive and definitive scholarly work on globalization, *Global Transformations: Politics, Economics and Culture,* a product of ten years of collaborative research by four leading British social scientists, was published. At the same time, the *New York Times*'s foreign-affairs columnist Thomas Friedman's *The Lexus and the Olive Tree*—a more popular and journalistic account of globalization as "revolution from beyond," or "globalution"—became an instant best-seller. It was translated into Arabic, Chinese, German, Japanese, and Spanish (but alas not French).[5] Even the BBC got caught up in the globalization debate when its Reith Lectures featured the prominent British sociologist Anthony Giddens, presenting five lecturers on globalization—from London, Hong Kong, Washington, and New Delhi—to live and Internet audiences who joined instantly in perhaps the first-ever global e-mail dialogue in a borderless cyberworld.

The second half of the year witnessed the UN Development Program (UNDP) and the World Bank turning their primary attention for the first time to globalization, presenting in their annuals—*Human Development Report 1999* and *World Development Report 1999/2000*—empirically rich and generally balanced accounts of its new benefits as well as its new threats to human security broadly defined. Then came the World Trade Organization (WTO) summit in Seattle in November 1999, triggering the single greatest and most negative storm over the management of globalization. In the coming years, East Asia will face a number of crucial issues, each of which, as the chapter-opening epigraphs suggest, will be a decision on how best to cope with the challenges and opportunities of globalization.

WHAT IS GLOBALIZATION?

Contending Schools of Thought

Like "security," "power," and "national interest," globalization is a highly contested concept.[6] Despite the burgeoning literature, there is as yet no dominant theory of globalization that commands paradigmatic status. The debates about globalization have remained largely simplistic, dominated by two extreme views. On the one hand, neoliberal proponents claim that globalization heralds the rise of a new post-Westphalian global order and the demise of the state system. On the other hand, neorealist and neomercantile opponents argue that all the talk about globalization is just talk.

Most neoliberal proponents take a Panglossian view, claiming that globalization heralds the emergence of truly open and integrated global economy, the rise of a new post-Westphalian global order, and the functional demise of the state system. According to this "hyperglobalization" school, social and economic processes now function at a mainly global level, and nation-states are no longer decision *makers* but decision *takers*. We are also told that the nature of international competition in the post–Cold War world has fundamentally changed. States no longer compete for control over territory and wealth-creating resources. Authority is said to have therefore devolved from states to multinational corporations (MNCs) and other transnational associations whose power has other sources. With the inner core of the state's authority over social and economic affairs so impaired by relentless globalization, it becomes a hollow or defective institution.[7] Paradoxically, the classical Marxist "withering away of the state" thesis that was revised to extinction in the former Soviet Union and other communist states has been brought back to life by the hyperglobalization school.

Indeed, the neoliberal school rests on the assumption that economics increasingly takes precedence over and dictates the course of politics. Economic globalization transforms the political and social affairs of interconnected human communities throughout the world. National economies are immersed in and perforated by a sea of transnational forces and actors that erode differences between and among nation-states. MNCs have already become truly global: able and willing to shift production sites in response to local conditions — thinking globally, producing locally. The claim is thus made that as a consequence of an integrated global economy, the castle of state sovereignty has been rendered an empty fortress. In short, the demise or, at least, the functional irrelevance of the nation-state is central to the hyperglobalization argument.

The critics of globalization, despite diverse political, methodological, and normative orientations, argue that all the frenzy about globalization amounts to nothing more than "globaloney." The "globaloney" school proceeds from two diametrically opposed starting points. Neorealist skeptics argue that there is nothing new in today's world economy and that the state is as powerful as ever. The populist-resistance skeptics argue that globalization already has gone too far at great cost to state sovereignty and social democracy. The argument that globalization is a threat to social stability, state sovereignty, national and cultural identity, and environmental protection has come from a wide range of competing interests, from cultural fundamentalists to neomercantile protectionists to environmentalists. Thus, we find the unlikely globaloney partnership of labor unions, environmental groups, hypernationalists (such as Patrick Buchanan in the United States), and billionaire businesspeople (such as Ross Perot and Sir James Goldsmith) united in railing against the North American Free Trade Agreement (NAFTA) and the WTO.[8]

From the old left of social democracy and the neo-Marxist *dependencia* school, it is often argued that the claims of diminished state capacity have less to do with the pressures of globalization and more to do with hierarchy and unevenness in state structure and policy. For example, Walden Bello, a leading *dependencia* theorist in the Philippines, argues that the answer to the unrelenting pressure of globalization controlled by the North is clear and simple enough: deglobalize or perish. The way out of chronic and continuing crisis afflicting the global South (the periphery) is thus the disconnection of the domestic economy from the global system controlled and exploited by the North (the center), that is, the South's reorientation toward greater reliance on internal markets.[9]

The problem with the *dependencia* argument—now joined by the radical populist resistance of the "globalization from below" school—is its seeming inability to point out a single country or economy that has shown this to be the way to economic growth or human development. To the contrary, the three most notable socialist antiglobalization projects in Asia all speak volumes about the penalties of self-reliance in an increasingly globalizing world economy. China's Great Leap Forward (1958–1962) campaign quickly turned into a Great Dying Backward, with roughly 30 million people—primarily the very young and the old—starving to death and nearly another 30 million lost who were either stillborn or not conceived. By most estimates, two to three million North Koreans, a whopping 10 percent of the population, have starved to death since 1995 in Kim Jong Il's "socialist *juche* paradise" thanks to his antiglobalization development strategy. India, the world's largest democracy, finally recognized the shortcomings of the self-reliance model and shifted from the unsuccessful policies of socialist antiglobalization, which it had pursued for four decades, to embrace a greater involvement in the world economy.

Viewed in this way, globalization is nothing less than an ideological fig leaf for a process in which governments have willingly abandoned many of the tools of governance and passed power from the democratically legitimated sphere of politics to the unaccountable realm of the market. A similar argument can be heard from conservative nationalists, from the Gaullists in France to Buchanan and Perot in the United States, who advance a more protectionist economic policy. Such a neomercantile defense of the state is often allied with a cultural politics of defensive and exclusionary nationalism.[10] As demonstrated in the recent collapse of the WTO summit in Seattle, globalization has become a magnet that attracts all kinds of antiglobalization groups in the United States: trade unionists, environmentalists, aid lobbyists, consumer rights advocates, and human rights activists. As a Chinese saying would have it, they all sleep in the same antiglobalization bed but have different dreams.

Popular claims in Europe and Asia that globalization is the same as American-ization have been dealt a lethal blow.

Theoretically, the most serious challenge comes from the neorealists, who are skeptical about the extent of globalization and the degree to which state power and autonomy have declined. They claim that recent developments fall far short of globalization and that the state is as robust as it ever was, with an impressive array of political options. Moreover, they contend, the contemporary state of in-ternational economic affairs is not without historical precedent. The postwar growth of international economic transactions represents "internationalization" or "regionalization" rather than the emergence of a truly global economy, and current levels of global flows are comparable to or even lower than those during the classical gold-standard period (ca. 1870–1914). Thus, the postwar growth is little more than a return to the status quo after the disruptions of the 1930s and World War II.[11]

A Critique

Both the hyperglobalization and the globaloney schools are misconceived, pro-ceeding from the dubious premise of globalization as an ideal end—a fully glob-alized economy—rather than as an ongoing process with its ups and downs. Globalization is on a continuum, with the local at one end—as in North Korea and Somalia—and the global at the other—as in many countries that are heavily dependent on foreign trade, foreign capital, and foreign direct investment (FDI) inflows. The either/or conceptions of globalization that underlie the current de-bates—suggesting that either a paradigmatic change has already occurred, herald-ing a new post-Westphalian global order, or that there is nothing new in contem-porary international life—stand on shaky historical and empirical grounds.

The problem with the neoliberal hyperglobalization school stems largely from heroic assumptions of costless adjustment in a hypothetically perfect global econ-omy. On the contrary, globalization remains incomplete, and global markets are not yet perfectly integrated. The collapse of the WTO summit in Seattle under-scores with particular clarity a duality in the globalization of free trade. We have come a long way from the protracted but successful conclusion of the Uruguay Round negotiations and the replacement of the General Agreement on Tariffs and Trade (GATT) with WTO, but there is still a long way to go to complete the glob-alization of free trade in all sectors. Nearly half the people in the developing world have yet to be fully integrated in the contemporary world economy, and roughly three-quarters of the world's population, lacking a telephone (let alone a modem and computer), are effectively outside an increasingly interconnected cy-berworld.[12] The world's financial regulatory agencies and central banks still re-main national in scope and location.

The neoliberal argument stereotypes and overgeneralizes MNC strategies, skating over the possible diversity of their responses.[13] Intrafirm trade engenders significant deviations from the ideal type of global competitive markets, and non-tradables remain a large proportion of national economies because intraindustry trade countries typically face less than perfectly elastic demand for their exports.[14] Moreover, the globalization of production has far outpaced that of trade in both value and scope. This is not to deny that MNCs have become the primary agents and catalysts in the increasing globalization of capital, goods, services, and manufacturing sites, nor that many people in "emerging markets" have been brutalized by the process, especially in the wake of the Asian financial crisis of 1997–1998.[15]

Competent states are not nearly as constrained by globalization as many of its hyperglobalization proponents would have us believe. States retain substantial autonomy in regulating their economies, social policies, and institutions in cases in which these differ from those of their trading partners.[16] East Asia is an especially interesting case since the region is comprised of states both large and small, effective and ineffective, adaptable and maladaptive, and globalized and deglobalized (localized). Even the revolution in communications has only weakened, not completely compromised, state control because "information does not flow in a vacuum but in political space that is already occupied."[17]

The significance of contemporary globalization therefore needs to be assessed in a situation- and country-specific way. It varies according to actors' respective resources, skills, and strategic choices or policies. Its impact on a state's power or role depends not only on the type of state but also on the state's globalization strategy. Far from making states functionally obsolete or irrelevant, globalization has in effect redefined what it takes to be a competent and effective state in an increasingly interdependent and interactive world. Globalization is a double-edged sword in this respect: It threatens both minimalist and maximalist states and provides an opportunity for competent and adaptable states.

Consider the case of the United States as a lone superpower in the post–Cold War globalizing world. As noted, globalization is not the same as Americanization. The United States is home to both the hyperglobalization and globaloney schools. Faced with the challenge of doing more and more with less and less, the United States under the Clinton administration and many other governments have sought to leverage scarce resources by forming coalitions with nonstate actors, such as MNCs, nongovernmental agencies, and global intergovernmental organizations such as the United Nations, the World Bank, and the International Monetary Fund (IMF). These coalitions help the United States "to work not only multilaterally, but multi-multilaterally, through several organizations and institutions at the same time."[18] Indeed, what really halted America's hegemonic decline and sustained its status as the only superpower, according to Thomas Friedman, was that "under the pressure of globalization America would slash its defense budget, shrink its government, and shift more and more powers to the free market."[19] Yet Americans are increasingly divided in their evaluation of (economic) globalization.[20]

States still command the loyalty of their citizens, still have control over material resources (one-third to one-half of gross domestic product [GDP]), and still define the policies and rules for those within their jurisdictions. World politics and the United Nations remain largely state-centric. Globalization has not rendered any state policy impossible, nor has it substantially erased state sovereignty. Instead, it has changed the payoff structure of certain state policies or strategic choices, especially those of states deeply enmeshed in the global system.

Thus, it seems more useful to explore the changes brought about by globalization pressures in terms of the shifting balance of costs and benefits. With the rapid growth of exit options for mobile (footloose) global capital, as shown in the recent Asian-cum-global financial crisis, most states have few viable options for defying the logic of globalization. One thing remains clear: Globalization has exerted pressures on all states to change their policies and institutions in certain ways, but the willingness and ability of states to adapt to the logic of globalization vary. In short, the neoliberal hyperglobalization school commits the fallacy of premature specificity and optimism about the benefits of globalization as well as about the demise of the putatively defective or obsolescent state.

The neorealist argument that the more things change, the more they stay the same, ignores the unprecedented scale, intensity, and rapidity of contemporary globalization processes in five separate but mutually interconnected realms: trade, finance, investment, production, and multilateral treaties and institutions. Each of these areas has been affected by rapidly falling communication and computing costs.

There are at least four major differences between the pre-1914 first-wave globalization and the contemporary second wave.[21] First, the end of the Cold War and the demise of the socialist challenge produced a reprioritization of the dominant issues in global politics. An event crucial to this transformation was the Uruguay Round and the eventual formation of the WTO. Second, the extraordinary advances in the communications revolution, interacting with financial and trade liberalization, have brought about rapidly declining transport, telecommunication, and computing costs, causing the natural barriers of time and space that separate national markets and borders to fall as well. Third, there was no such thing as the globalization of production during the first wave. In the 1990s, however, the globalization of production outpaced that of trade in both value and scope.[22] Fourth, developing countries, especially those in East Asia, are linked with developed countries and integrated into the global system as never before, this time as partners rather than as colonial dependencies.[23] The AFC has highlighted with particular force the ineluctable fact that East Asian emerging markets are now too important to the world economy to be relegated to the periphery. The combined synergistic effects of these momentous changes are evident in all aspects of contemporary life, not only in the economic area, as the world moves beyond international interdependence—the buzzword of the 1970s—to confront the new opportunities and dangers of globalization.

Global trade has continued to expand as a proportion of world GDP. Trade–GDP ratios increased to 15 to 20 percent—even higher for some developed countries—compared with around 12 to 13 percent for advanced industrial countries during the gold-standard era. If current trends continue, world exports of goods and services will reach $11.4 trillion, or 28 percent of world GDP, by 2005, nearly double 1998's projected $6.5 trillion, or 24.3 percent of world GDP, and up from a mere 9.3 percent twenty years ago. The volume of international merchandise trade is now about sixteen times what it was in 1950, whereas the world's total output is only five and a half times as great. When government expenditure is removed from a comparative calculation, the proportion of trade in relation to national economic activity has grown by as much as one-third. The intensity of trade has also increased as trade has risen faster than income. The services sector has more than doubled in the past decade to over $1 trillion annually, exceeding 20 percent of total trade. Contemporary international trade is more extensive, more entrenched, more technologically driven, and relatively cheaper to conduct than it was during the gold-standard era.[24]

Global financial flows have expanded more rapidly than world trade or income, with daily turnover in the foreign-exchange markets rising from $15 billion in 1973 to $820 billion in 1992 to $1.5 trillion by 1998 and still rising, from more than ten times the level of trade in 1979 and fifty times today. The volume of international banking transactions increased from $265 billion in 1975 to $4.2 trillion in 1994. The current globalization of finance capital is more extensive and intensive than in the gold-standard era, with more currencies and more types of assets traded more frequently at greater speed and in greater volume. Because of new tools of communication (e.g., the Internet, cellular phones, and fax machines), the infrastructure of exchange is more institutionalized and technologically more advanced.[25] The trend in the financial arena has been toward ever higher levels of global interdependence, putting governments distinctly on the defensive.[26] The Internet revolution continues to fuel a transition to informationization: a global information-based economy. Global FDI inflows and outflows, at $463 billion and $475 billion, respectively, in 1997, are nearly twice what they had been in 1990 and some sevenfold their volume in 1980. Even the AFC has not halted this trend, as the 1998 FDI inflows increased to $644 billion and FDI outflows to $648 billion.[27]

Without sacrificing their national identity, MNCs, with nearly 60,000 parent companies and over 508,000 foreign affiliates throughout the world, have come to play the dominant role in global finance, trade, investment, and production. Thanks to rapidly falling costs of transport and communications, MNCs account for about one-third of world output, 70 percent of world trade, 70 percent of patents and technological transfers, and 80 percent of FDI. In the late 1970s, the industrial nations invested $34 billion per year overseas. By 1990, that figure had reached $214 billion. The value chain of production can now be globalized, with different stages of the production process of a single output carried out in different parts of the world. With the exit options for MNCs making direct investments growing by the day, the balance of power has shifted in favor of mobile global capital as against both national governments and national trade unions. Indeed, one of the defining features of the contemporary global economy is the multitasking role of MNCs in trade, finance, and direct foreign investment; they play a much more central role today than they have in the past.[28] The ability of MNCs to outsource abroad in response to fierce global competition has not so much brought about an end of the nation-state as it has significantly changed the costs and benefits of particular national economic institutions and policies.

In sum, there is considerable evidence to rebut the neorealist claim that the contemporary international economy is not so very different from that of the gold-standard era. New tools of communication, new markets, new actors (state and nonstate), and new rules and institutions have all combined to fuel globalization dynamics. The scope, intensity, speed, sheer numbers, modalities, and impact of human relations and transactions have radically increased regionally and globally, eroding the boundaries between hitherto separate economic, political, and sociocultural entities throughout the world. As a consequence, more state, nonstate, and transnational actors are involved in more extensive and intensive transactions in more ideas, goods, and services than ever before. Falling telecommunications costs and protectionist barriers, the shift from virtually autarchic trade–GDP ratios to extensive participation by the United States and China (thanks to post-Mao China's reform and opening), the collapse of the COMECON (Council for Mutual Economic Assistance) system, and the subsequent liberalization of Eastern European centrally planned economies have all contributed to the emergence of a single, if not fully integrated, global system.

Defining "Globalization"

Much of the globalization debate, dominated by the hyperglobalization and globaloney schools, has been marred by tenuous conceptualization, ideological presuppositions and polemics, inattention to the full range of available empirical evidence, and above all overgeneralization based on the experiences and politics of Western industrial democracies. It is time to move beyond chant or castigation to a more specific analysis of the complex and evolving interplay between globalization dynamics and East Asian experiences. Before formulating an alternative notion and framework of globalization for this region-specific study, however, it is important to clear away some of the major misconceptions underlying the recent globalization debates. Globalization is not a singular condition, let alone an ideal end. It is not a linear, an irreversible, or necessarily a homogenizing process. Globalization can foster more globalization, to be sure, but it can also foster deglobalization in the form of a backlash.

Globalization does not inevitably signal the end of the nation-state or the arrival of a borderless society. It is one thing to claim the emergence of global

markets but quite another to equate such markets with a perfectly integrated
global economy, let alone a global civil society. Globalization is not the same as
"globalism" or "universalism"; it does not refer to values or structures.[29] This is
not to say that contemporary globalization cannot serve as a conduit for the rapid
spread of good and bad ideas or information and misinformation, nor to suggest
that contemporary globalization is all benign or without any polarizing and marginalizing consequences. Rather, the point is to spotlight the conceptual and
methodological dangers of eliding and conflating globalization with such normative concepts as globalism, universalism, and transnationalism. Above all,
globalization is more than a one-dimensional (i.e., economic) phenomenon.

For the purpose of such inquiry, I define globalization as *a series of complex,*
independent yet interrelated processes of stretching, intensifying, and accelerat-
ing worldwide interconnectedness in all aspects of human relations and trans-
actions—economic, social, cultural, environmental, political, diplomatic, and
security—such that events, decisions, and activities in one part of the world have
immediate consequences for individuals, groups, and states in other parts of the
world. Whether globalization is the new international system, replacing the Cold
War system as Friedman argues, is debatable. However, Friedman does capture
the two faces of globalization, viewing it as a dynamic but double-edged process
that is empowering more individuals, groups, nation-states, and corporations "to
reach around the world farther, faster, deeper and cheaper than ever before"
while at the same time "producing a powerful backlash from those brutalized or
left behind."[30]

Put succinctly, globalization is a worldwide revolution with far-reaching but
differing consequences for people's security, well-being, and identities. It is a
boundary-expanding or boundary-penetrating process, intensifying the levels of
interaction and interconnectedness within and among states and societies. This
boundary-expanding aspect of globalization has developed in tandem with a
mushrooming of communications facilities, economic and social interests, and
overseas markets that in turn foster still more globalization. The end of the Cold
War may not have given birth to this system, as Friedman argues, but it certainly
has accelerated the process. As a consequence, the separation between the local
and the global, between "domestic" and "foreign" affairs, has become increasingly blurred. For many states, including the United States, economic globalization is increasingly in the driver's seat. As President Bill Clinton put it in his
budget message to Congress in 1994 (cited by Gills and Gills in chapter 4), "We
have put our economic competitiveness at the heart of our foreign policy."

Perhaps the most salient feature of globalization is this intensification of domestic and external linkages. It is difficult to theorize about globalization because
its causes and consequences are interwoven, constituting mutually essential parts
of any theoretical (explanatory) approach. Consider the case of FDI: Is it a cause
or a consequence of globalization? The answer is both: The more globalization,
the more FDI inflows and outflows, and the more FDI, the more globalization.

Far from being a singular condition in a single aspect of human activity, globalization is a multidimensional process. As such, globalization takes place in all the key dimensions of contemporary international life, not only in the economic but also in the social, cultural, diplomatic, political, security, and environmental domains, albeit at varying pace and intensity. Globalization is not a preprogrammed or determinative process. Its nature and direction are shaped and reshaped by the dynamic interplay of objective (self-sustaining) and subjective (managerial) factors. The concept of globalization suggested here refers to an interactive and interpenetrating process that interrelates multiple levels and facets of modern life—economics, politics, society, culture, security, and ecology (see table 1.1). To understand the multiple cascading ramifications of globalization for East Asia requires careful examination of the differing patterns and intensity of interconnectedness in each of these domains.

Globalization and regionalization need not be seen as mutually exclusive terms; regionalization can take place at the same time as globalization, given the lower transport costs associated with geographic proximity. Rather than being viewed as contradicting globalization, regionalization is perhaps better seen as enhancing it, especially in the case of such trade-sensitive countries as those in East Asia. Even in Europe, where regionalization has gone further and deeper than in other parts of the world, the European Union has been a spur, not a barrier, to globalization. In the 1990s, more than ever before, regional and globalizing forces are mutually reinforcing: Both de facto and de jure regionalization are occurring on the one hand, and regionalization is fostering globalization by stimulating competition instead of protectionism on the other.[31]

This does not mean that any group, government, or MNC has actually accomplished complete globalization. Globalization dynamics stemming from the density and intensity of patterns of global interconnectedness generate a host of subnational (local), national, and transnational problems and stimulate the growth of multilateral regimes. However, those dynamics also fuel antiglobalization resistance movements.

EAST ASIAN GLOBALIZATION 101

The Diversity of East Asia

The starting point for understanding how East Asia is coping with the pressures of globalization is to recognize that the region's chief characteristic is its diversity. To begin with, even the global North–South, or center–periphery, divide is more blurred in East Asia than in any other region of the world. East Asia encompasses the world's poorest countries (Burma, Mongolia, Laos, North Korea, and Vietnam, with annual per capita gross national product [GNP] at or below $500) and the world's richest (Hong Kong, Singapore, and Japan, with annual per

Table 1.1   A Matrix for the Study of East Asian Globalization

	Conceptualization (1) Causation (2) Consequences	Pronouncements (1) Visions (2) Strategies	Performance (1) Extensity (2) Intensity (3) Velocity (4) Ranking	Impacts (1) Economic (2) The State's Role (3) National Identity (4) Societal (5) Security
Economic/ Science & Technology ⇕⇕⇕⇕⇕⇕⇕ ⇕⇕⇕⇕⇕⇕⇕				
⇕⇕⇕⇕⇕⇕⇕ ⇕⇕⇕⇕⇕⇕⇕ Political/ Diplomatic ⇕⇕⇕⇕⇕⇕⇕ ⇕⇕⇕⇕⇕⇕⇕				
⇕⇕⇕⇕⇕⇕⇕ ⇕⇕⇕⇕⇕⇕⇕ Social/ Cultural ⇕⇕⇕⇕⇕⇕⇕ ⇕⇕⇕⇕⇕⇕⇕				
⇕⇕⇕⇕⇕⇕⇕ ⇕⇕⇕⇕⇕⇕⇕ Military/ Security ⇕⇕⇕⇕⇕⇕⇕ ⇕⇕⇕⇕⇕⇕⇕				
⇕⇕⇕⇕⇕⇕⇕ ⇕⇕⇕⇕⇕⇕⇕ Environmental				

Note: The direction of the arrows in column one indicates interactive or influence flow.

capita GNP at or above $20,000). Five East Asian economies have made it into the IMF's *World Economic Outlook* classification of advanced economies: Japan in the major industrial countries (Group of 7, or G-7) subgroup and Hong Kong, South Korea, Singapore, and Taiwan in the advanced economies subgroup.[32] In

September 1999, the finance ministers of the G-7 established the G-20 for use as a permanent mechanism for dialogue between the G-7 and thirteen other "systemically important countries," including South Korea and China. The first ministerial meeting of the G-20 took place in Berlin in mid-December 1999.

Indeed, the defining feature of Asia is not common "Asian values" but linguistic, cultural, religious, and political diversity. However imperfect and unreliable, the Freedom House's latest (1998–1999) annual survey and ranking spotlight an almost equal distribution of fourteen East Asian countries on a "freedom rating," which combines political rights and civil liberties: "free" (Japan, South Korea, Philippines, Taiwan, and Thailand), "partly free" (Hong Kong, Indonesia, Malaysia, and Singapore), and "not free" (China, Cambodia, North Korea, Laos, and Vietnam) (see table 1.2). The Asian Gang of Four in global human rights politics—China, Singapore, Malaysia, and Indonesia—whose authoritarian political leaders have been most vocal in espousing the "Asian values" line, are multicultural, multireligious, and even multinational. The principal interstate division at the first-ever Asian regional preparatory human rights conference (held in Bangkok in March 1993 as a prelude to the UN World Human Rights Conference in Vienna in June 1993) turned out to be between democratic Japan, Thailand, Nepal, South Korea, and the Philippines, which assumed a more universalist interpretation of human rights, and authoritarian China, Indonesia, Iran, and Burma, which took a more uncompromising cultural-relativist stand.

The "Asian values," or cultural-relativist, line is further rendered dubious by other fault lines. One is between authoritarian Asian states and their human rights nongovernmental organizations (NGOs). Another is between and among those East Asian states that supposedly share a Confucian civilization: China, Singapore, Taiwan, Vietnam, North and South Korea, and Japan. Many of the bloodiest wars have occurred within, not between, such civilizations. Far from having a homogeneous Confucian culture, East Asia still embodies, albeit in attenuated form, a high degree of historical and national animus and fratricidal conflict—between North and South Korea, between China and Taiwan, between China and Vietnam, between Korea and Japan, between China and Japan, and so on. The most sanguinary armed conflicts have occurred in East Asia during the post–World War II period, more than in any other region of the world, with millions of human fatalities: the Korean War (three million), the Vietnam War (two million), the Chinese civil war (one million), and the Khmer Rouge genocide under Pol Pot (one million).[33]

Even in the post–Cold War setting, the security situation of East Asia is vastly more complex and volatile than any other region of the world. It is dominated by the twin pressures of globalization and localization, with little if any pan-Asian regionalism. Indeed, the security picture presents a rather unique combination of sui generis regional characteristics—high capability, abiding animus, proximity of the four major powers to the strategic field of play, and the absence of any multilateral security regime. For example, those characteristics underlie the differing

Table 1.2   Select Globalization and Globalization Performance Indicators of Eight East Asian Countries, 1997

	China	Hong Kong	Indonesia	Japan	Korea	Malaysia	Taiwan	Thailand
Competitiveness '99 (WEF)	32/59	3/59	37/59	14/59	22/59	16/59	4/59	30/59
Competitiveness '99 (IMD)	29/47	7/47	46/47	16/47	38/47	27/47	18/47	34/47
Internationalization '99 (IMD)	18/47	5/47	39/47	21/47	40/47	29/47	27/47	34/47
BPI Ranking '99 (TI)	19/19	n.a.	n.a.	14/19	18/19	15/19	17/19	n.a.
CPI and Ranking '99 (TI)	58/99	15/99	96/99	25/99	52/99	33/99	28/99	69/99
IGO membership '99, n=251	51	10	54	63	51	52	9	53
NGO membership '99, n=5825	1301	1116	1027	2124	1301	1052	982	1013
% of UN budget '99	0.973	n.a.	0.184	19.984	0.994	0.180	n.a.	0.167
# of diplomatic relations '98	156	n.a.	120	185	183	81	28	116
Political rights ranking '99	7	5	6	1	2	5	2	2
Civil liberties ranking '99	5	3	4	2	2	5	2	3
Freedom ranking '99	not free	partly free	partly free	free	free	partly free	free	free
# of 8 major UN human rights treaties signe d, '98[c]	6/8	n.a.	3/8	6/8	6/8	8/8	3/8	3/8
GNP $US bn	1,055	163.8	221.5	4,812	485.2	98	256	165.8
GNP per capita US$	860	25,200	1,110	38,160	10,550	4,530	13.198	2,740
Real GDP per capita (PPP$)	3,130	24,350	3,490	24,070	13,590	8, 140	13,800	6,690
Exports $US bn	207.3	225.5	60.1	456.9	168.7	92.9	122.1	72.4
Imports $US bn	166.8	232.1	60.7	432.3	171.9	91.4	114.4	71.3
Exports as % of GDP	23	132	28	10	38	80.4	43	38
FDI $US bn	45.3	26	5.4	3.2	2.3	3.8	2.2	3.6
Total external debt $US bn	146.7	n.a.	136.2	..	143.4	47.2	26.5	93.4
External debt as % of GNP	15	n.a.	62	..	33	48	9	61
Sovereign long-term debt rating '98	BBB+	A	CCC+	AAA	BB+	BBB-	n.a.	BBB-
Foreign tourism departures 1kp	5,061	3,445	1,782	16,695	4,649	20,642	n.a.	1,845
Television sets, 1kp	270	412	134	708	341	166	362	234
Telephone main lines, 1kp	56	565	25	479	444	195	370	80
Mobile telephones, 1kp	10	343	5	304	150	113	??	33
Fax machines'96 , 1kp	0.2	49.8	0.4	113.7	8.9	5.0	??	2.1
Personal computers, 1kp	6.0	230.8	8.0	202.4	150.7	46.1	??	19.8
Internet hosts 1/99 10kp	0.14	122.7	0.75	133.53	40.00	21.36	284	3.35
High-tech exports as % of Manufacturing exports	21	29	20	38	39	67	48.6	43
Total expenditure on R&D, $USm and ranking, n=47	5,813 13/47	403 37/47	187 43/47	130,126 2/47	13,522 6/47	195 42/47	5,445 14/47	277 41/47
HDI rank, n=174	98/174	24/174	105/174	4/174	30/174	56/174	n.a.	67/174
GDI rank, n=174	79/174	24/174	88/174	8/174	30/174	52/174	n.a.	64/174
GEM rank, n=174	40/174	n.a.	71/174	38/174	78/174	52/174	n.a.	64/174
% of Population below $2 a day	57.8	n.a.	58.7	n.a.	n.a.	26.6	n.a.	23.5
Unemployment Rate % '98	3.1	5.0	15.5	4.1	7.5	3.2	2.6	5.3
Armed forces '97 in million	2.84	n.a.	.284	.235	.672	.111	.376	.266
Defense expenditure $USm 97	36,551	n.a.	4,812	40.891	14.732	3,377	13,657	4,212
Defense expenditure as % of GDP 97	5.7	n.a.	2.1	1.0	3.3	3.7	4.7	2.5
Arms imports '96 $USm	1500	n.a.	800	2400	1100	200	2000	575
Arms exports '96 $USm	600	n.a.	10	20	20	5	10	..
# of global ACD treaties signed	11/13	n.a.	6/13	11/13	12/13	7/13	5/13	6/13
CO_2 emissions '96 mmt	3,369	23.1	245.5	1,169	408.7	119.3	n.a.	205.7
CO_2 emissions as % of world total,'96	14.1	0.1	1.0	4.9	1.7	0.5	n.a.	0.9
Average annual rate of deforestation (%), 1990-	0.1	..	1.0	0.1	0.2	2.4	n.a.	2.6

a=All data are as of the end of 1997 unless otherwise indicated.

b=The ranking of China for 1999 included Hong Kong.

c=The eight major UN human rights treaties are (1) International Covenant on Economic, Social and Cultural Rights (1966); (2) International Covenant on Civil and Political Rights (1966); (3) International Convention on the Elimination of All Forms of Racial Discrimination (1966); (4) Convention on the Prevention and Punishment of the Crime of Genocide (1948); (5) Convention on the Rights of the Child (1989); (6) Convention on the Elimination of All Forms of Discrimination Against Women (1979); (7) Convention against Torture and Other Cruel, Inhuman or Degrading Treatment or Punishment (1984); and (8) Convention relating to the Status of Refugees (1951).

n.a.=not applicable or data not available   00/n=number of total sample

WEF=World Economic Forum, Davos, Switzerland

Table 1.2 (cont.)   Select Globalization and Globalization Performance Indicators of Eight East Asian Countries, 1997

IMD=International Institute for Management Development, Lausanne, Switzerland
BPI=Bribe Payers Perceptions ranking of 19 leading exporting countries in terms of the degree to which their corporations are perceived to be paying bribes abroad.

CPI=Corruption Perceptions Index, ranking in 1999 of 99 countries	IGO=International Intergovernmental Organization
NGO=International Nongovernmental Organization	PPP=Purchasing Power Parity
bn=billion	GNP=Gross National Product
GDP=Gross Domestic Product	1kp=per 1,000 people
10kp=per 10,000 people	FDI=Foreign Direct Investment
HDI=Human Development Index	GDI=Gender-related Development Index
GEM=Gender Empowerment Measure	ACD=Arms Control and Disarmament
CO₂=Carbon dioxide	mmt=million metric tonnes
FDI=Foreign direct investment	

Sources: Adapted from the following: World Economic Forum, *Global Competitiveness Report 1999*, online at www.weforum.org/Publications/GCR/99rankings.asp; International Institute for Management Development [IMD] (Lausanne, Switzerland), *World Competitiveness Yearbook 1999*, online at www.imd.ch/wcy/factors/overall.html; Transparency International (Berlin), online at www.transparency.de/documents/cpi/index.html; *Yearbook of International Organizations 1999/2000* (Munchen: K. G. Saur 1999); United Nations General Assembly Resolution 52/215 (December 22, 1997); Freedom House, *Freedom in the World: The Annual Survey of Political Rights and Civil Liberties, 1998-1999*, online at freedomhouse.org/survey99/tables/indeptab.html; United Nations Development Programme, *Human Development Reports 1999* (New York: Oxford University Press, 1999); World Bank, *World Development Report 1999/2000* (New York: Oxford University Press, 1999); International Institute for Strategic Studies, *The Military Balance 1998/99* (London: ISSS, 1998); *SIPRI Yearbook 1998: Armaments, Disarmament and International Security* (New York: Oxford University Press, 1998); U.S. Arms Control and Disarmament Agency, *World Military Expenditures and Arms Transfers 1997*, online at www.acda.gov/wmea97/w97tb2.pdf.

responses of the international community to North Korea's nuclear and missile brinkmanship, as compared with the somewhat tepid and time-specific responses to the nuclear programs of several other threshold states, such as India, Pakistan, and Israel. In addition, East Asia is the only region where so many combinations and permutations of two-power, three-power, four-power, and even two-plus-four power or three-plus-three power games can be played on the regional and global chessboards with all their complexities and variations.

East Asian Notions of "Globalization"

All that said, however, it is possible to identify the range of contending conceptualizations of globalization, albeit with some overlapping characteristics, that have underpinned East Asia's changing and contradictory globalization views and policies in the 1990s. None of the East Asian countries in our select sample sees the retreat, let alone the demise, of the nation-state. Contrary to the hyperglobalization school, they see a strengthening of the state's role in meeting globalization challenges, especially in enhancing their competitiveness in the world economy. Korea's President Kim Dae Jung, for example, at his 1998 inauguration, pledged (although this has turned out to be honored more in the breach than in reality) that the signature of his administration would be the parallel pursuit of participatory democracy and a free-market economy. They are, he said, "two sides of a coin and two wheels of a cart" pulling Korea out of its current crisis to full recovery. Political reform in fact must precede everything else, namely, "a small but effective government."

On the other hand, with the possible exception of China, none of the East Asian countries in our sample embraces the neorealist line that the state remains as robust as ever or that all the furor about globalization amounts to nothing more than "globaloney." Most, again with the exception of China, do not view globalization as a value-neutral process of simply increasing interconnectedness; they see it as a transmitter of values, ideology, global standards, and organizing principles. For Kim Dae Jung, globalization is conflated with "universal globalism," which he described as resting on universal values such as "freedom, human rights, justice, peace and efficiency."[34]

Another common theme in East Asian conceptualizations, with the possible exception of Korea's multidimensional and multilayered thinking, is the almost unidimensional focus on economic globalization. Even Japan, with its enormous comparative advantage in cultural globalization, especially in the East Asian context, focuses mainly on the far-reaching and not always desirable effects of financial globalization on Japanese corporate governance and labor and financial markets. The Asian financial crisis has confirmed and amplified the legitimacy of such a narrow view of globalization.

In several respects, the contrast between Chinese and Japanese concepts of globalization is of great interest and relevance given their dominant position in the East Asian political economy. China holds a master key to the future prospects of globalization in the Asia-Pacific region in general and East Asia in particular. For most Chinese observers and policymakers, including President Jiang Zemin, globalization is conceived of in highly state-centric and state-empowering terms. Jiang admitted as much in his political report to the Fifteenth Chinese Communist Party Congress on September 12, 1997—two months after the eruption of the financial crisis in Thailand—when he stated that there is no longer an escape from "the globalization of economy, science, and technology." China, he went on, has no choice but to reform, restructure, and open up state-owned enterprises (SOEs) to "survival-of-the-fittest" competition if it is not to forfeit its "global citizenship" (read global power status). Indeed, some Chinese analysts see globalization as the functional equivalent of a Hobbesian war of all against all: "economic wars, commodity wars, technology wars, and wars over talented people—between developed and developing countries and among developing countries" (cited by Moore in chapter 5). Still other Chinese military analysts see globalization as the functional equivalent of "unlimited war." For a relatively weak country such as China to stand up to a powerful country such as the United States, it is strategically imperative to resort to compensatory devices such as terrorism, drug trafficking, environmental degradation, and computer virus propagation.[35]

At the other end of the conceptual spectrum, Wang Yizhou, a leading Chinese international relations theorist, breaks new ground in defining globalization as more than an economic phenomenon. It is an economic process, to be sure, but it is also a complicated political and historical process. "To each country, it is a 'double-edged sword' which can help break through brambles and thorns, but may also harm the user. In this situation, a new security concept should be established which pays equal attention to economic, social and political aspects." Security in the era of globalization "refers not only to 'safety' in the military and diplomatic senses, but also to economic and technological security, including financial, trade and investment security, the avoidance of big rises and falls, the ability to have stronger competitive methods and a grasp of information factors."[36]

The dominant Chinese conceptualization is not only state-centric but also one-dimensional economic globalization. While globalization has not changed the basic state-centric nature of world affairs or compromised state sovereignty, it has significantly redefined the economic and technological context within which the struggle for comprehensive national strength (*zonghe guoli*) takes place. Herein lies China's positive view of and dependence on MNC-led, network-based globalization. As late as February 1998, more than three months after the IMF responded to Seoul's call for a $58-billion rescue package, Korea Inc. still seemed to be the inspiration for China's attempt to restructure the SOEs into South Korean–style *chaebol* (conglomerates). Under the banner "grabbing the big, letting go the small," the state would try to establish an organic link between corporate revival and comprehensive national strength. However, by mid-1998, Beijing was forced to back away from this approach when the weaknesses of the *chaebol* were brought to light and Kim Dae Jung began trying to dismantle and/or downsize Korea's corporate leviathans.

Nonetheless, most indications are that Chinese reform-minded leaders still believe that the problems experienced by South Korean *chaebol* had more to do with management hubris and unsustainable financial arrangements than with their size. More broadly, as Moore argues in chapter 5, Beijing is trying to foster the emergence of a "global nationalism" as the shortest way to great-power status. Even more surprisingly, globalization is viewed for the most part as an "objective condition" of the world economy—a self-sustaining and spontaneous development—rather than as a manifestation of U.S. hegemony. Accordingly, Beijing seeks to establish a fit between two "huas": *quanqiuhua* (globalization) and *duojihua* (multipolarization). The two "huas" are said to have a reciprocal relationship, becoming both cause and effect of two "irresistible trends" of world historical development.

In striking and surprising contrast, Japan as an economic superpower defines globalization in highly defensive terms, seeing itself as victim rather than beneficiary. Unlike South Korea, where the term has been translated as *segyehwa—quanqiuhua* (China), *mondialization* (France)—in Japan the preferred term is *gurobaruka,* a straight transliteration of the English word "global" with the addition of a character that means "to change into." Unlike *kokusaika* (internationalization), which was the buzzword of the late 1980s, Japanese commentators have tended to keep the concept of globalization at arm's length. As Grimes suggests in chapter 3, perhaps this is because *kokusaika* was made popular in the 1980s, at a time when Japan was rising in world prominence, while *gurobaruka* has made its appearance in the more angst-ridden 1990s.

While in theory globalization can affect all aspects of the state and society, argues Grimes, in practice the main effects of 1990s-style globalization on Japan have been economic. "Globalization" is one of three main buzzwords, along with "internationalization" and "information society," that the Japanese media have popularized as a way of summarizing the forces driving the major changes facing the Japanese economy over the past fifteen years or so. Hence, the popular belief in contemporary Japan that *gurobaruka* is changing Japan in not necessarily beneficial ways seems closely keyed to and shaped by the depressed state of the economy in the 1990s. Indeed, there seems to be an emerging consensus that *gurobaruka* carries a clear and present danger of being imposed from the outside and beyond Japanese control. Japan not only views *gurobaruka* largely in terms of the dreaded "financial globalization" but also sees it as a threat to its economic way of life. Tokyo's *gurobaruka* angst underscores with particular clarity how Japan, the much-touted "reactive state," is not reacting fast enough to the changing logic and requirements of globalization.

Conceptually, South Korea's *segyehwa* is beyond compare. For good or otherwise, *segyehwa* became the self-styled hallmark and the self-designated litmus test of President Kim Young Sam's administration (February 1993–February 1998), the first civilian government in thirty years. Indeed, no state in the post–Cold War era has cast its lot with globalization as publicly as Korea did under the Kim Young Sam administration. Globalization has been touted as a matter no longer of choice but of necessity — globalize or perish. Indeed, *segyehwa* was meant to describe Korea's unique way of promoting political, economic, social, and cultural enhancement to reach the level of the most advanced nations in the world. The irony is that Kim Young Sam's *segyehwa* drive started with a bang but ended with a whimper, as Seoul's continuing decline in global competitiveness and the economic crisis of 1997–1998 made clear. Yet Kim Dae Jung has continued the globalization drive with greater vigor, even as the new administration has disbanded the Presidential *Segyehwa* Promotion Commission set up by the previous administration. Apparently, then, there is no escape from the payoffs and penalties of globalization, as the new leadership has been espousing the "five great reforms" as the only assured way to survive in the brave new world of infinite global competition. Put another way, the Kim Dae Jung administration seems to realize that the genie of globalization cannot be stuffed back into the bottle, even if it were desirable to do so.

Seoul's *segyehwa* drive inevitably became part of the politics of competitive legitimation and delegitimation on the divided Korean peninsula. Tellingly, North Korea lost no time in launching a war of calumnies against *segyehwa,* as if it were still a model island of autocentric and self-reliant development in a worldwide capitalist sea. That a country so mired in the theocratic trinity of Father, Son, and *Juche,* and economically barely able to survive, could be so vehemently opposed to globalization probably helped more than hurt Seoul's *segyehwa* drive.

Taiwan's leaders are of two minds about globalization, as White argues in chapter 7, because for them it contains two parts: "mainland China, which threatens them intensely, and the rest of the world, whose trade and potentially protective functions are welcome." Clearly, security and even "survival" loom large in Taiwan's globalization/localization dialectical discourse. Unlike South Korea, Taiwan's "globalization cum localization" drive seemed made to order for following a Daoist paradox: Talking less and less is really achieving more and more. It was in the boom years that globalization discourse gained prominence in Thailand, taking the place of the modernization mantras that characterized the early postwar decades. The Thai term for globalization, *lokanuwat,* became a buzzword, a neologism coined at the end of the 1980s meaning "turning with the world." However, the term served as a kind of magnet for a politically contested opportunity. For over a decade, according to Hamilton-Hart in chapter 8, globalization has been the subject of lively political debate in Thailand, between "globalizers" and "localists," with the globalization forces dominating Thailand's public policy. Although there is no agreement on the costs and benefits of globalization, both globalizers and localists agree that globalization is real and consequential and that it imposes constraints on the range of policy options available in Thailand.

In Indonesia, the world's fourth-largest and East Asia's second-largest country, globalization is generally perceived as an objective condition of contemporary international life that impacts on and shapes policy choices for state and nonstate actors. As in other East Asian countries, the responses of the Suharto, Habibie, and Wahid administrations to global pressures for economic liberalization, democratization, and human rights—three values closely associated with globalization in Indonesia—have varied and shifted in contradictory and situation-specific ways over time. Suharto neither embraced liberal capitalism as a positive force for globalization nor resisted it as a negative force. Instead, globalization was a useful tool to achieve his own political goals, supporting it when it suited his pursuit of power and plenty but resisting it when it promised to strengthen democratization and human rights. Unlike Malaysia, as Murphy argues in chapter 9, by the mid-1990s Indonesian state and society were ill equipped to cope with relentless globalization pressures. It had an open, deregulated economy that coexisted with a closed, patrimonial (crony) system. Unlike China, Indonesia used the "Asian values" argument to counterattack democratization and human rights, but without success. Although there is now an apparent congruence between the declared policies of the new Wahid government and the values and strategic choices associated with the logic of globalization, it is still too early to say whether it will follow the South Korean way or the Malaysian way of coping with the attendant pressures.

Malaysia stands at the opposite end of the globalization discourse. No East Asian state with the exception of North Korea—which is not represented in this volume and is off the statistical radar screens of all major yearbooks and annual reports—has attacked globalization as publicly as has Malaysia. However, there is far more here than meets the public eye in Malaysian prime minister Mahathir's antiglobalization attack. As Welsh argues in chapter 10, Mahathir's attitudes toward globalization have changed over time, in contradictory ways. While "globalization" was a common part of Malaysian political discourse in the mid-1990s, it was not until 1996 that Mahathir redefined it as the predatory integration of the world economy through the expansion of portfolio capital. Globalization became a threat to the power of the state in general and Third World states in particular. Only two years earlier, in 1994, Mahathir first used the term "globalization" to promote the expansion of capital markets. What accounts for such an about-face? There are at least two reasons, according to Welsh. First, globalization thus redefined became the scapegoat for the problems that Mahathir had brought about in the first place as the leading advocate of globalization in his country. The second reason had to do with a growing political contest with then Deputy Prime Minister Anwar Ibrahim for leadership of the Malay community. Despite the changes in attitudes toward globalization, the dominant Malaysian concept is similar to China's state-centric and state-empowering model.

EAST ASIAN GLOBALIZATION CATCH-22

Globalization has not generated a predictable set of policy responses in East Asia or a predictable set of performances and consequences. This is hardly surprising, for one of the defining characteristics of globalization is its rapidity and unpredictability. That no one foretold the momentous events and changes in world politics in the recent past speaks directly to the rapidity and unpredictability of the forces of globalization and antiglobalization in a world that increasingly is becoming both interdependent and fragmented.

Some Performance Trends

Still, for any state in a globalizing world, it is one thing to announce a policy and quite another to give it substance. The case of Korea is instructive in this regard. No East Asian country had such high-profile globalization policy pronouncements as Korea had during the Kim Young Sam administration, yet so little was achieved. Most ironic of all is that the single greatest gap between promise and performance lies in Korea's steadily declining world ranking. The so-called *segyehwa*-driven administration somehow managed to garner the lowest possible ranking in the "internationalization/globalization" input category, moving from eleventh place among the fifteen emerging market economies in 1993 to last place among the forty-six advanced and emerging market economies in 1998. Korea's global competitiveness ranking dropped from sixth place in 1993 to thirty-fifth place in 1998. To cope with the pressures of globalization is to make strategic choices about the basic structure and goals of the economy and the society. Such a choice is not only a matter of prioritizing one set of policy goals over another; it also involves both the speed and the sequence of reforms. The challenge is how to make such strategic choices in the face of conflicting international and domestic—"intermestic"—objectives and pressures.

It is worth noting in this connection that most East Asian countries in our sample are quintessential trading states with extremely high export–GDP ratios, ranging from 132 percent for Hong Kong to 10 percent for Japan (see table 1.2.). Those ratios are misleading in that Hong Kong is a small "city-state" while Japan's GDP is almost twice as large as the combined total of the remaining East Asian countries. Moreover, Japan has a huge domestic market. What is most significant is China's Great Turn Outward to the global economy, its trade–GDP ratio having more than tripled between 1978 and 1995. In addition, South Korea's trade–GDP ratio increased from 18 percent in 1960 to 69 percent in 1996 (and 75 percent in 1998), compared to 17 percent for Japan, 24 percent for the United States, and the world's average of 43 percent.[37] All in all, East Asian countries are extremely trade dependent compared with other regions of the world. This means that there is no exit from globalization that would not entail major economic, social, and political sacrifices. The strategic choice for East Asian countries is no longer, if it ever was, between exit and engagement; it is one of constant adaptation to the logic of globalization and quickening economic, cultural, and social product cycles.

Table 1.2 summarizes other performance indicators of globalization for the eight East Asian countries. The two major categories—the extent of global interconnectedness and the ranking of actual or perceived performance—cut across issues. Although no single indicator is sufficient, the performance indicators taken together provide a basis for making several generalizations. First, despite the large discrepancies between the competitiveness ratings of the World Economic Forum (WEF) and the International Institute for Management Development (IMD) due to the use of different criteria, Hong Kong, Taiwan, Singapore, and the United States have passed annual competitiveness sweepstakes with flying colors in recent years. That the United States (the lone superpower), Singapore (a ministate), and Russia (a failed state) ranked first, second, and last, respectively, among the forty-six developed and emerging-market economies on the IMD's world-competitiveness scoreboard in the last five years (1995–1999) offers intriguing empirical referents for rethinking the relative importance of size versus speed (in information technology, innovations, and state action).

Second, there is no discernible correlation between the extent of diplomatic globalization and ranking in economic competitiveness. Hong Kong (0) and Taiwan (9), the two least diplomatically connected "countries" in our sample, outscore Japan (185) and Korea (183), the two countries with the greatest diplomatic globalization.

Third, while East Asia has consistently outranked all other regions in real GDP growth and absolute poverty reduction over the years, most East Asian countries rank low in the UNDP's Gender-related Development Index (GDI) and Gender Empowerment Measure (GEM). South Korea ranks thirtieth in the UNDP's global Human Development Index (HDI), for example, but drops to seventy-eighth place in GEM ranking. Although not addressed in depth in this volume, globalization is supposed to be revolutionizing and universalizing women's rights. There is no evidence that such a normative revolution is taking place in East Asia—at least not yet or not fast enough to make any significant contribution to women's rights.

Fourth, another area where East Asian countries score poorly is in the Transparency International's (TI's) Bribe Payers Index (BPI) and Corruption Perceptions Index (CPI) rankings. With the exception of Singapore (seventh in CPI and eleventh in BPI), none of the East Asian countries, not even Taiwan, has made it to the top ten among corruption-free countries.

Last but not least, environmental protection is another area of poor performance for most East Asian countries, with serious social and economic consequences. North Korea's famine in the 1990s was caused more by man-made ecocide than natural disasters. It is a mountainous country with less than 20 percent arable land and few trees. The state is still promoting unsustainable terrace farming and monoculture with a concentration on rice production. China stands out as a global polluter beyond compare, responsible for generating more than 14 percent of the global total of carbon dioxide emissions. A major study of China by the World Bank concludes that "as many as 289,000 deaths a year could be avoided if air pollution alone were reduced to comply with Chinese government standards" and that "the economic costs of China's air and water pollution have been estimated at 3–8 percent of GDP a year."[38] Consider as well China's 1998 Yangtze River floods, which reportedly cost China 2,100 lives and some $30 billion. In other words, China's GDP has been growing at about 0 percent a year, not 8 to 9 percent, if we factor in ecological deficit financing.

Surviving the Financial Crisis

Those East Asian countries, especially Taiwan and Singapore, that survived the Asian financial flu unharmed had several things in common: high foreign-exchange reserves, positive current-account balances, relatively low levels of debt, and small size that aided in speedy adaptability in state policy. As Dittmer explains in chapter 2, Taiwan and Singapore have had the highest levels of international reserves, positive current-account surpluses throughout the 1990s, and high ranking on global competitiveness scoreboards (see table 1.2). Despite the pigeonholing of South Korea, Taiwan, Hong Kong, and Singapore as the "four little dragons" in the global political economy, they differ not only in size but also in their approach to globalization. The Hong Kong and Taiwan economies, in contrast to Korea's, are driven largely by small and medium-size enterprises, accounting for the low-risk exposure to foreign loans. As White shows in chapter 7, Taiwan's economy has been more globalist than that of the other "dragons," certainly more than Korea's. Taiwan has underwritten the general price of labor less than Hong Kong or Singapore (whose housing policies for most workers are cryptosocialist), concentrating instead on providing state subsidies to research and development (R&D). While South Korean *chaebol* have often made export products that compete directly with the output of Japanese or American companies and with each other, notably in the auto industry, Taiwan emphasized the development of "technological complementarities" with other economies and often arranged for the production of exports or parts that sell under brand names from larger countries.

Moreover, the extent and scope of social and economic devastation in each East Asian country differs according to country-specific conditions and state strategies, the amount of short-term foreign debt, the amount of foreign-exchange reserves, the degree of transparency and accountability (or "moral hazard"), and the adequacy of state regulation and monitoring. Table 1.3 shows the extent of the economic shocks of 1997–1998 and the degree of the economic rebound or recovery during 1999–2000. There is a wide variation in the extent of the economic "shock" (defined at the bottom of the table): Taiwan and China are at one extreme, with virtually little or minimal shock, and Indonesia (–31.3 percent), Malaysia (–23.5 percent), and Korea (–23.1 percent) are at the other extreme of maximal shock.

What is even more revealing is that there is also a wide variation in the rate of economic recovery. The growth rates of real GDP for 1999 in table 1.3 are based on the IMF's updated projections of early October 1999 (in its biannual *World Economic Outlook*). Consider Korea's real GDP growth rate for 1999. The predictions of late 1998 that Korea's real GDP would grow at a rate of about 1 percent at best were followed by a series of revised estimates of approximately

Table 1.3   Impact of the "Asian Finacial Crisis," 1997-2000

	Real GDP (Annual percent change)					Current Account Positions (% of GDP)				Inflows of FDI (US$ million)		
	1997	1998	1999*	2000*	"Shock"	1997	1998	1999	2000	1997	1998	1999
China	8.8	7.8	6.6	6.0	-2.2	3.8	3.4	1.3	1.1	44236	45460	n.a.
Hong Kong	5.3	-5.1	1.2	3.6	-16.7	-3.2	0.7	1.5	2.4	6000	1600	n.a.
Indonesia	4.7	-13.7	-0.8	2.6	-31.3	-1.8	4.0	2.4	0.7	4677	-356	n.a.
Japan	1.4	-2.8	1.0	1.5	-8.0	2.2	3.2	3.4	3.1	3200	3192	n.a.
Korea	5.0	-5.8	6.5	5.5	-23.1	-1.7	12.5	5.9	3.4	2844	5143	n.a.
Malaysia	7.7	-6.7	2.4	6.5	-23.5	-5.1	12.9	11.7	5.1	5106	3727	n.a.
Taiwan	6.8	4.9	5.0	5.1	-2.0	2.7	1.3	2.6	3.0	2200	222	n.a.
Thailand	-1.3	-9.4	4.0	4.0	-21.5	-2.0	12.8	8.8	5.9	3745	6929	n.a.
Average	4.8	-4.4	3.2	4.4	-16.8	-0.6	6.4	4.7	3.1	9001	8240	n.a.

"Shock": the difference between the rates of real GDP growth in 1997 and 1998, plus the difference between such rates in 1998 and 1999.

*The 1999 and 2000 figures are the IMF's projections made as of October 1999.

Sources: Adapted from IMF, *World Economic Outlook* (Washington, DC: October 1999), pp. 5, 13, 23; UNTACD, *World Investment Report 1999* (New York and Geneva: UNCTAD 1999), pp. 477, 479-480, 485-486; and World Bank, *World Development Report 1999/2000* (New York: Oxford University Press, 1999), pp. 270-271.

4 percent in April, 6.5 percent in early October, and 10 percent in early December 1999, up from −5.8 percent in 1998. The official GDP growth rate for 1999 turned out to be a whopping 10.7 percent. In addition, the unemployment rate dropped from 7.5 percent at the end of 1998 to 4.6 percent in August 1999. Foreign-exchange reserves reached the $84.5 billion mark in April 2000 and was then projected to reach $100 billion by the end of 2000 (up from $5 billion in early December 1997). The Korean won soared to a two-year high against the dollar (at 1,113 won per dollar) in early 2000, up from nearly 2,000 won per dollar at the peak of the crisis in December 1997.

On the other hand, Taiwan managed to make itself immune to the Asian financial flu. There are several reasons, according to White. First, it was always first, second, or third in the world as a holder of foreign-exchange reserves, a financial fortress not only against China but also against international hedge-fund managers. Second, Taiwan's government in 1996, before the crisis, had specifically discouraged further investment in Southeast Asia. Third, Taiwan had consistent trade surpluses, with growth rates in 1997–1999 of about 6 percent annually. Fourth, because Taiwan's economy was dominated by thousands of small and medium-size firms, the risk of one giant conglomerate, such as South Korea's Daewoo, going belly up had already been dispersed and minimized.

Given that China is so deeply enmeshed in the Asian-Pacific economic matrix that it is burdened by enormous debt (some 100 percent of GDP by most estimates), why has it emerged relatively unscathed from the Asian financial crisis? A combination of factors, no single factor, explains China's relative immunity. These include the nonconvertibility of its currency, substantial foreign-exchange reserves (about $140 billion) to defend against speculative attacks on the yuan, and a large inflow of FDI, only a small percentage of which is portfolio investment, which is more vulnerable to quick withdrawal in a panic. Hong Kong also has been remarkably successful in responding to the challenges and opportunities of globalization. Important conditions for this success include its strategic location as the gateway between China and the world and its institutional strengths, such as its policy independence, adaptiveness, and robust legal system.

In short, not every East Asian country contracted the Asian financial flu, nor has every infected crisis-ridden country rebounded with the same speed. As Dittmer suggests, "Any attempt to use Asian values or an Asian model of developmental capitalism to account for Asia's susceptibility to the [financial crisis] must first define precisely what traits constitute that model, only to find that the model can then be applied only to the five Asian countries that were actually stricken."

WHITHER EAST ASIAN GLOBALIZATION?

The principal conclusion emerging from this volume is that globalization has had subtle but profound consequences for East Asia's political, economic, social, cultural, ecological, and security development. Contrary to the hyperglobalization and globaloney theses, the state is not obsolete, let alone disappearing, but neither is it as robust as it once was. Instead, globalization functions as a double-edged sword, posing at one and the same time dangers and opportunities and thus undermining the certainties associated with the state-centric self-help Realpolitik. Indeed, what it takes to be a competent and effective state is constantly being redefined in this rapidly globalizing world.

Successfully coping with today's challenges requires an effective strategy for choosing among various competing and constantly evolving options, in the correct sequence, even as the state, precariously balanced between domestic and international politics, is constrained simultaneously by what external globalization agents will accept and what domestic constituencies will ratify. The role of state adaptability is crucial in this respect. More than ever before in human history, the rise or fall of an effective state, even a "great power," is keyed to and determined by the speed with which it can establish congruence between domestic and foreign policies amid the changing trends and requirements of globalization.[39]

Globalization has effectively punctured beyond repair the notion of any sustainable Asian developmental model. The World Bank has come a long way from the classical laissez-faire model of development. The *World Development Report 1999/2000,* which focuses on the twin themes of globalization and localization, makes a decisive break away from any universal developmental paradigm: "Certain policies that helped Japan develop in the 1950s and 1960s, generated growth in East Asia in the 1970s and 1980s, and sparked China's economic boom in the 1980s and 1990s were specific to the time and place. They may not have worked well in other countries, nor are they likely to be appropriate in the opening decades of the 21st century."[40]

The AFC has put to rest cultural-relativist claims about "Asian values" or any single Asian developmental model. Country-specific circumstances plus the pressures of globalization and its principal agents, not any Asian values or Asian "situational uniqueness," explain why some East Asian countries were so severely hit, why others escaped the crisis unscathed, and what are their differing prospects for and pace of recovery. Institutional restructuring and changes in decision-making processes will not take a predictable or linear form. However, it is likely that most East Asian states will redefine their roles, pulling back from some forms of intervention while expanding it in others, especially (in the latter case) the state's role in prudent regulation and monitoring of corporations to promote greater transparency and accountability.

The impact of the financial crisis in the context of globalization is far-reaching, especially in its social impact and in the distribution of wealth. It has pushed 20 million Asians back into poverty, made 40 percent of the Russian people poorer than ever, forced 6.1 million Indonesian children to leave school, and produced growing unemployment in Korea and Brazil.[41] In fact, the Gini index of inequality is rising in most East Asian countries, especially in China, Hong

Kong, and South Korea, at the same time that the financial crisis has caused havoc for foreign migrant workers in Malaysia, South Korea, and Japan. These workers, as Grimes describes in the case of once-homogeneous Japan, have had profoundly unsettling social and cultural impacts, particularly in factories, warehouses, household service, and the sex/entertainment industry. Women more than ever before are the most oppressed and exploited group in most East Asian countries. Without deliberate and humane intervention by the global community, globalization will increase these inequities and inequalities. For China, Taiwan, and Hong Kong, globalization has profound and sometimes paradoxical meaning for national identity. Chinese leaders are taking a two-handed approach, using globalization to accelerate the march to great power status while simultaneously attacking Chinese "splittists" at home and nearby. At the same time, Hong Kong, China's new "special administrative region," has emerged as a cultural center in the transnational Chinese public space, infecting the mainland with a "Hong Kong cultural fever." In the cyberspace of cultural China, the periphery has become the center (see chapter 6). Taiwan's adaptability is also made manifest in a flexible situation-specific fusion of localizing and globalizing identities. Meanwhile, its leaders finesse the central but elusive issue of "national identity." Faced with a clear and continuing security and national identity threat from the mainland, Taipei wants to have its own Taiwanese–Chinese identity cake and eat it, too.

What does it mean to be or feel "secure" in an era of globalization? In the 1990s, both the agency and the scope of "threat" as well as the sources and effects of security globalization have become more complex and diverse than ever before. In addition, the traditional boundaries delimiting international and domestic ("intermestic") threats have been substantially blurred if not completely erased. Among several important results in the context of East Asian globalization is the emergence of new pressures from the United States for accelerated market opening and economic liberalization, and new, essentially nonmilitary threats to regime legitimacy and survival. Leadership changed in crisis-hit Thailand, South Korea, and Indonesia. The UNDP's promotion of the concept of "human security" in 1994 has been made more relevant and telling, thanks to relentless globalization pressures and the Asian financial crisis. To promote "globalization with a human face" is to further conflate globalization with threats to human security—economic insecurity, food insecurity, health insecurity, environmental insecurity, community and cultural insecurity, and personal insecurity.[42]

This is not to say that globalization has simply swept away the traditional conflicts over divided nations, territory, and nuclear proliferation. As Van Ness argues in chapter 11, globalization so far seems to have made no major difference either in ameliorating or exacerbating these conflicts, even as the traditional twin security dilemmas of being either overly dependent on or abandoned by allies have made a comeback in a new form. There is a double irony at work in the post–Cold War East Asian security situation: On the one hand, most East Asian countries, including Japan and China, are concerned about their autonomy and sovereignty in relation to the United States, while on the other they worry about the sustainability of the American hegemonic security regime in the Asia-Pacific region.

The prospect of a more humane and cooperative East Asian approach to globalization depends not only on *how* but also on *where* we look. The Asian financial crisis may well serve as a great teacher of the reality principle that in an era of globalization, local problems are global problems and global problems are local problems. Their solution requires nothing less than coordinated responses at all systemic levels—local, national, regional, and global.

NOTES

1. "Annual Report of the Secretary-General on the Work of the Organization," UN Document A/53/1 (September 3, 1998), para. 168.

2. Anthony Giddens, BBC Reith Lectures 1999: Lecture 1, "Globalization," available at <http: news.bbc.co.uk/hi/english/static/events/reith_99/week1/week1.htm>.

3. UN Development Program (UNDP), *Human Development Report 1999* (New York: Oxford University Press, 1999), 3, 5.

4. World Bank, *World Development Report 1999/2000* (New York: Oxford University Press, 1999), iii-iv.

5. David Held, Anthony McGrew, David Goldblatt, and Jonathan Perraton, *Global Transformations: Politics, Economics and Culture* (Stanford, Calif.: Stanford University Press, 1999), and Thomas L. Friedman, *The Lexus and the Olive Tree* (New York: Farrar, Straus & Giroux, 1999).

6. For a more extensive discussion of the globalization literature and debates, see Samuel S. Kim, "Korea and Globalization (*Segyehwa*): A Framework for Analysis," in Samuel S. Kim, ed., *Korea's Globalization* (New York: Cambridge University Press, 2000), 4–27; Held et al., *Global Transformations,* 2–28.

7. Kenichi Ohmae, *The Borderless World: Power and Strategy in the Interlinked Economy* (New York: HarperBusiness, 1990); Robert Reich, *The Work of Nations* (New York: Vintage, 1992); Susan Strange, "The Defective State," *Daedalus* 124, no. 2 (1995): 55–74, and *The Retreat of the State: The Diffusion of Power in the World Economy* (New York: Cambridge University Press, 1996).

8. Dani Rodrik, "Sense and Nonsense in the Globalization Debate," *Foreign Policy,* no. 107 (summer 1997), 19; Rodrik, *Has Globalization Gone Too Far?* (Washington, D.C.: Institute for International Economics, 1997), 2.

9. Walden Bello, "The Answer: De-Globalize," *Far Eastern Economic Review,* April 29, 1999, 61.

10. David Goldblatt et al., "Economic Globalization and the Nation-State: Shifting Balances of Power," *Alternatives* 22, no. 3 (1997): 269–85; Samuel Huntington, *The Clash of Civilizations and the Remaking of World Order* (New York: Simon & Schuster, 1996).

11. Peter Beinart, "An Illusion for Our Time: The False Promise of Globalization," *New Republic,* October 20, 1997, 20–24; Paul Hirst and Grahame Thompson, *Globalization in*

Question? (Cambridge: Polity Press, 1996); Stephen Krasner, "Compromising West-phalia," *International Security* 20, no. 3 (1995): 115–51.

12. World Bank, *World Development Report 1997: The State in a Changing World* (New York: World Bank, 1997), 12; Robert O. Keohane and Joseph S. Nye Jr., "Power and In-terdependence in the Information Age," *Foreign Affairs* 77, no. 5 (September–October 1998): 82.

13. Beinart, "An Illusion for Our Time"; Paul N. Doremus, William W. Keller, Louis W. Pauly, and Simon Reich, *The Myth of the Global Corporation* (Princeton, N.J.: Princeton University Press, 1998); Jonathan Perraton et al., "The Globalization of Economic Activ-ity," *New Political Economy* 2, no. 2 (1997): 257–77; Louis Uchitelle, "Globalization Has Not Severed Corporations' National Links," *New York Times,* April 30, 1998.

14. Held et al., *Global Transformations,* 149–88.

15. See Nicholas D. Kristof and Edward Wyatt, "Who Sank, or Swam, in Choppy Cur-rents of a World Cash Ocean," *New York Times,* February 15, 1999; Nicholas D. Kristof and David E. Sanger, "How U.S. Wooed Asia to Let Cash Flow In," *New York Times,* February 16, 1999; Nicholas D. Kristof and Sheryl WuDunn, "World Markets, None of Them an Island," *New York Times,* February 17, 1999; Nicholas D. Kristof and Sheryl WuDunn, "The World's Ills May Be Obvious, but Their Cure Is Not," *New York Times,* February 18, 1999.

16. Rodrik, "Sense and Nonsense," 21.

17. Keohane and Nye, "Power and Interdependence," 84.

18. Strobe Talbott, "Globalization and Diplomacy: A Practitioner's Perspective," *For-eign Policy,* no. 108 (fall 1997), 79.

19. Friedman, *The Lexus and the Olive Tree,* xvii.

20. See Andrew Kohut, "Globalization and the Wage Gap," *New York Times,* December 3, 1999.

21. Friedman, *The Lexus and the Olive Tree;* Held et al., *Global Transformations,* 424–35; Jeffrey Sachs, "International Economics: Unlocking the Mysteries of Globaliza-tion," *Foreign Policy,* no. 110 (spring 1998), 97–111; UNDP, *Human Development Report 1999* (New York: Oxford University Press, 1999).

22. UN Conference on Trade and Development (UNCTAD), *World Investment Report 1999* (New York: United Nations, 1999).

23. Sachs, "International Economics," 97–98.

24. *Business Week,* August 31, 1998, 116; Goldblatt et al., "Economic Globalization."

25. Perraton et al., "The Globalization of Economic Activity"; Goldblatt et al., "Eco-nomic Globalization"; UNDP, *Human Development Report 1999,* 30.

26. Benjamin Cohen, "Phoenix Risen: The Resurrection of Global Finance," *World Pol-itics* 48, no. 2 (1996): 268–96.

27. UNCTAD, *World Investment Report 1999,* 477, 483.

28. Beinart, "An Illusion for Our Time"; UNCTAD, *World Investment Report 1997* (New York: United Nations, 1997), and *World Investment Report 1998* (New York: United Nations, 1998).

29. James N. Rosenau, "The Dynamics of Globalization: Toward an Operational For-mulation," *Security Dialogue* 27, no. 3 (1996): 247–62.

30. Friedman, *The Lexus and the Olive Tree,* 7–8.

31. Held et al., *Global Transformations,* 74–77; Charles Oman, *Globalisation and Regionalisation: The Challenge for Developing Countries* (Paris: Organization for Economic Cooperation and Development, 1994).

32. International Monetary Fund, *World Economic Outlook* (Washington, D.C.: IMF, October 1999), 115.

33. See "Armed Conflicts and Fatalities 1945–1994," in *The Military Balance 1997/98* (London: International Institute for Strategic Studies, 1997).

34. Kim Dae Jung, "Era of 'Universal Globalism' Dawning," *Korea Times,* November 4, 1998.

35. Qiao Liang and Wang Xianghui, *Chaoxian Zhan* (Unlimited war) (Beijing: People's Liberation Army Cultural Press, 1999).

36. Wang Yizhou, "New Security Concept in Globalization," *Beijing Review,* no. 7 (February 11–15, 1999), 7. See also Wang Yizhou, *Dangdai guoji zhengzhi xilun* (Analysis of contemporary international politics) (Shanghai: Renmin chubanshe, 1995), esp. 19–46.

37. World Bank, *World Development Indicators 1998 CD-ROM* (Washington, D.C.: World Bank), table 1.5.

38. World Bank, *China 2020: Development Challenges in the New Century* (Washington, D.C.: World Bank, 1997), 71.

39. Barry Gills makes this argument in explaining the rise of South Korea and the fall of North Korea in the context of the two Koreas' politics of competitive legitimation and delegitimation. See Barry Gills, *Korea versus Korea: A Case of Contested Legitimacy* (London: Routledge, 1996), 257–77.

40. UNCTAD, *World Development Report 1999/2000,* 2.

41. Roger Cohen, "Redrawing the Free Market: Amid a Global Financial Crisis, Calls for Regulation Spread," *New York Times,* November 14, 1998.

42. UNDP, *Human Development Report 1999,* 36.

2

Globalization and the Asian Financial Crisis

Lowell Dittmer

ASIA AND GLOBALIZATION

"**G**lobalization," a hallmark of the zeitgeist whose implications are more fully explicated in Samuel Kim's introductory chapter, will be defined more concisely here in terms of the increasing frequency and scale of the exchange of people, commodities, capital, and ideas across international borders. Distance and other geographic barriers have diminished in cost and formidability, permitting international trade, transportation, and communication to flow more freely. Globalizing trends are far from new—belief systems such as Christianity or Marxism have had transnational appeal for centuries; commodities and personnel have long been mobile (e.g., there was greater demographic and capital mobility than today in the late nineteenth and early twentieth centuries)—but the revolution in telecommunication and computer technology has resulted in an unprecedented upsurge of global mobility.[1] This has resulted in the enhancement of markets as a way of coordinating transnational activity, with regional and international markets subsuming and integrating national markets.[2] International trade is greater in absolute scale and geographic reach than ever before; its share of world gross domestic product (GDP) has doubled since 1950 and continues to grow. Some $1.2 trillion currently changes hands daily in foreign-exchange markets, six times the amount of a decade ago and some 85 percent of total government foreign-exchange reserves.[3] Thus, globalization offers opportunities for generating both higher profits for multinational corporations (MNCs) and more rapid economic growth for host nations. Contrary to dependency theory, globally integrated national economies average higher GDP growth rates than "self-reliant" ones.[4]

As a social process, globalization is autonomous and self-sustaining, although it also fits into other causal chains, including "political" ones, as either a dependent or an independent variable. Its self-sustaining dynamic is in part a response to declining unit costs of communication and transportation in the international market. Since 1945, average ocean freight charges have fallen by 50 percent, air transportation costs by 80 percent, and transatlantic telephone calling charges by 99 percent. As a dependent variable, globalization is, however, affected not only by technical innovations that curtail transportation or communication costs but also by political decisions that tend either to enhance or reduce mobility constraints. The most recent trend, of course, has been toward constraint reduction: China's post-Mao policy of "opening to the outside world," the agreements reached in the North American Free Trade Agreement (NAFTA) and in the successive rounds of the General Agreement on Tariffs and Trade (GATT) and World Trade Organization (WTO) talks, and the liberalization of trade and opening of new markets unleashed by the end of the Cold War. Geopolitically, East Asia has been a conspicuous recent beneficiary/victim of globalization: The share of global trade for which Asia (excluding Japan) accounted rose from 9 to 15 percent between 1980 and 1991, while developed countries' trade share slipped from 72 to 63 percent.[5] Between 1994 and 1996, ASEAN (Association of Southeast Asian Nations) and East Asian nations recorded the world's highest rates of increase in merchandise trade, achieving some of the world's highest trade ratios.[6]

The purpose of this chapter is to analyze the relationship between globalization and the Asian financial crisis (AFC). The causal relationship is reciprocal: As an independent variable, globalization results in the diffusion of new value-added processes and consumption patterns. That diffusion precipitates an increase in the level of competition, which eventuates in an equalization of costs (albeit not of incomes[7]) and capabilities, leading toward institutional convergence as financial and monetary institutions adapt to the same functional requisites. In this sense, globalization has ostensibly contributed both to the Asian economic "miracle" in the 1980s and early 1990s and to its more recent collapse. We will need to test this hypothesis carefully, vis-à-vis competing theories that attribute the AFC not to globalization but to such factors as the "Asian" cultural heritage that has accompanied and shaped these countries' economic emergence. As an independent variable, in contrast, the AFC has hypothetically contributed to political economic changes in the region, both in the domestic arenas of affected countries and in these nations' relations with one another, either bilaterally or in international organizations.

THE CRISIS

Origins

The AFC, which according to conventional periodization began with the collapse of the Thai baht in July 1997, is noteworthy in a number of respects. As Radelet and Sachs put it, "It has prompted one of the largest financial bailouts in history. It is the sharpest financial crisis to hit the developing world since the

1982 debt crisis. It is the least anticipated financial crisis in years."[8] The AFC is the third-largest economic collapse in the twentieth century, after the 1929 crash and the 1973 first oil shock. As such, it is the latest in a series of financial crises, including the reverses of 1990–1993 (in Finland, Norway, and Sweden), 1992–1993 (Europe), 1994–1995 (Mexico), and May 1998 (Russia), that came in the wake of the financial liberalization that followed the collapse of the Bretton Woods Agreement in 1972. After Margaret Thatcher's "big bang" reforms of October 1986 in Great Britain, which were adopted in France, Germany, Belgium, and the Netherlands shortly thereafter, rapid liberalization of financial markets ensued, resulting in daily transactions at the ten main stock markets of the world of U.S.$900 million per day by 1992, rising to $1.3 billion per day in 1995. Much of this money is speculative, so that it can move quickly with sometimes unanticipated consequences.

The AFC struck by surprise, as tends to be characteristic of crises (indeed, that is part of what makes them crises); the early-warning macroeconomic indicators relevant to the 1994–1995 Mexican peso crisis—too much consumption (too low saving), persistent budget deficits, and a high rate of inflation—did not apply in the East Asian cases.[9] Right up to the eve of the crisis, traditional growth indicators remained sound as the region retained savings and investment levels reaching one-third of its GDP. East Asia, after all, had been heralded as a model of development in the World Bank's 1993 publication *The East Asian Miracle,* which told the story of how eight nations—Japan, Korea, Hong Kong, Singapore, Taiwan, Indonesia, Malaysia, and Thailand (China was excluded because its economic structure was not deemed "comparable")—had since 1960 grown faster than all other regions of the world.[10] Indeed, between 1980 and 1995, their pace of growth accelerated to a rate nearly three times that of the world economy, and all this had been achieved amid declining income inequality and poverty.[11]

In the immediate precrisis period, the five most severely stricken economies (Thailand, Malaysia, Indonesia, South Korea, and the Philippines) had low inflation rates (less than 10 percent), budgets generally in surplus, and declining government foreign debt (as a fraction of GDP). During the 1990s, these governments seemed to engage in responsible credit creation and monetary expansion, and unemployment rates remained low. For example, Indonesia boasted 10.4 percent export growth in 1996, its government budget was in surplus each of the previous four years, and its current account deficit was only 3 to 5 percent of GDP; or, consider the Republic of Korea: Its annual per capita industrial output was only U.S.$8 in the mid-1950s, but by the mid-1990s it was the world's fifth-largest manufacturer of automobiles, the largest producer of DRAM microchips, and home of the world's most efficient steel industry. Within thirty-five years, per capita income had increased from $200 per annum to nearly $10,000.[12] On the eve of the crisis, South Korea had a seasonally adjusted unemployment rate of 2.1 percent (the lowest in the country's history), while the current account deficit hovered at 3 percent of GDP (compared to 8 percent in Thailand).

In retrospect, however, there were also serious structural flaws in the crisis economies, including a high reliance on external private capital, a poorly developed banking system (with an opaque regulatory apparatus), cronyism between the financial sector and high-ranking government officials, and a lack of transparency in the workings of financial institutions. The region's export boom was first unleashed in the mid-1980s by the depreciation of the U.S. dollar (to which many of these currencies were pegged) relative to the yen in the Plaza Accord, making exports more competitive than Japanese exports internationally. Also helpful was the rapid influx of Japanese, Taiwanese, and Hong Kong investment to avoid rising domestic labor costs. The domestic policy response beginning in the late 1980s was to liberalize the financial sector to take advantage of the influx of foreign capital, resulting in many unsound investments (e.g., Tommy Suharto's "National Car" project in Indonesia) and in a tendency to overheat. Southeast Asia inherited Japan's "bubble economy syndrome" qua asset inflation, specifically stock and real estate booms, whereas in South Korea the large conglomerates, or *chaebol,* took advantage of massive subsidized "political" loans to engage in highly leveraged overinvestment in productive capacity. Inasmuch as these economies depended on export growth in the 20 to 40 percent range to service debt loads, the loss of global competitiveness when export growth declined in East and Southeast Asia between the summer of 1995 and the summer of 1996 adversely impacted their fiscal balances. Southeast Asian firms had saturated many of their traditional export sectors, such as clothing, footwear, and household electronics, and were facing increasing competition from other low-wage producers, such as China, which, following its 50 percent devaluation of the renminbi (RMB) in 1994, plus the introduction of a 17 percent value-added tax (VAT) export rebate, was able to underprice its competitors. Meanwhile, a global slowdown in demand for office automation equipment and consumer electronics hit South Korea, especially the market for 16-bit memory chip (which accounted for about 20 percent of Korean exports). Devaluation of the RMB helped revalue the U.S. dollar to appreciate against the yen (by 56 percent from 1995 to 1997), which in turn drove up the partially pegged ASEAN currencies, pricing their exports out of the market.[13] For all these reasons, East Asian exports grew by only 4.3 percent in 1996, after a growth of 20 percent in 1994 and 22 percent in 1995. At the same time, trade liberalization, strong currencies, and rising domestic demand spurred a growth in imports; combined with sagging export growth, this resulted in high current-account deficits and depleted foreign-exchange reserves (with Thailand registering the highest deficit at $13.5 billion at its peak in 1995). Whereas long-term sovereign debt was kept under control, the ratio of short-term private debt to foreign-exchange reserves in Thailand, Korea, and Indonesia exceeded 1.0 beginning in 1994. The current-account deficits were financed by inflows of foreign capital, which in turn exerted pressure to keep currency values high to maintain financial credibility. However, declining GDP growth and decreasing competitiveness of exports staunched the influx of foreign capital (in

1995–1996, the rate of export growth plunged from 26.3 to 8.4 percent for Korea, from 20.1 to 10.1 percent for Malaysia, and from 242 to 3.3 percent for Thailand), making it more difficult to finance dollar-denominated short-term loans and current-account deficits. Doubts about creditworthiness, fed by several bankruptcies in early 1997, then had an unexpectedly rapid and drastic demonstration effect on all foreign investors and lenders, creating a financial crisis.

Denouement

The first events leading to the AFC were the failures of certain large South Korean conglomerates, or *chaebols*. In January 1997, Hanbo Steel declared bankruptcy, the first bankruptcy of a leading Korean conglomerate in a decade. This was followed in March 1997 by the failure of Sammi Steel and by rumors of imminent collapse of Kia, Korea's third-largest automaker. Meanwhile, in Thailand, Samprasong Land, a finance company burdened by large, bad real estate loans, missed its February deadline for payment on its foreign debt. The Thai government was expected to step in with a rescue package, but after promising to do so on March 10, it reneged, leading to the collapse of Samprasong and thence to the bankruptcy of Thailand's largest finance company, Finance One, on May 23. When foreign investors began moving their money out of Thailand because of concern about the risk of default, the central bank responded by buying baht with its dollar reserves and raising interest rates. However, the increase in interest rates drove down prices for stocks and land, which excited suspicion about the value of loan collateral, at which point it became evident that the banking system was swamped with unpaid loans and foreign investors withdrew short-term capital. When the Thai central bank ran out of dollars to support the baht, it permitted a "controlled float," which quickly resulted in a plunge in currency value, precipitating a similar devaluation throughout the region.

The plunge in asset values ultimately had an adverse impact on the economies. South Korea entered a recession in early 1998 (with a record-high 1.2 million people unemployed), and the impact of the crisis in Indonesia was even worse, with a 7 to 8 percent GDP contraction, a 45 percent inflation rate (April 1997–April 1998), and an official estimate (unduly modest) of 10 percent unemployment. An averaging of all these economies suggests that an Asian asset worth $100 in June 1997 was worth $25 by September 1998. That loss of 75 percent compares in magnitude with the U.S. crash of 1929–1932, when Standard & Poor's index declined 87 percent. Beyond the immediate region, Australia and New Zealand incurred losses in export and tourist markets that had become increasingly dependent on East Asia. Even American and European banks and MNCs faced reduced export demand and bad debts, leading the International Monetary Fund (IMF) to conclude that world economic growth in 1998 would be 1 percent lower than predicted, and others to apprehend worldwide deflation.[14] Table 2.1, showing the stock markets and currency markets in the crisis-affected countries, indicates how the two markets interacted in a negative feedback loop in response to external shocks. From July 1, 1997, to February 18, 1998, the stock market in the worst-hit country, Indonesia, fell by over 80 percent, while the exchange rate fell against the U.S. dollar by almost 75 percent.

ANALYSIS

To simplify somewhat, the theories relating the AFC to globalization as a dependent variable may be categorized into two schools of thought. According to the "Downfall of Asian Exceptionalism" thesis, endorsed, for example, by the IMF, the crisis arose because of serious weaknesses in the Asian economies most adversely affected: overextended investment on relatively high risk ventures financed with short-term (often foreign) capital and investments poorly supervised by banks acting in collusion with political patrons. The crisis occurred in response to violations of economic fundamentals and should be corrected through further integration into the world market, henceforth in adherence to universal rules transparently applied. The second argument, the "Globalism Run Amok" thesis, espoused most vocally by Malaysian prime minister Mohamed Mahathir (but also credited by some Western economists),[15] is that the crisis arose because of indiscriminate lending by foreign direct investors and international financial institutions, followed by panicky withdrawal when rumors began to surface of the debtors' inability to repay. Thus, the crisis was first and foremost a consequence of "casino capitalism," hence a salubrious object lesson to the host nations and to the international financial community, which would be well advised to constrain the forces of globalization and reconfigure the regional financial architecture. Let us critically review each of these theses in turn.

Table 2.1 Southeast and East Asian Countries: Percentage Movements in Equity Markets and Exchange Rates (July 1, 1997-February 18, 1998)

Country	Equity Markets (against US$)	Exchange Rate
Indonesia	-81.2	-73.5
S. Korea	-32.3	-48.1
Thailand	-47.9	-43.2
Malaysia	-59.0	-33.3
Singapore	-45.0	-13.2
Hong Kong	-36.6	pegged to US$

The Fall of the Asian Model?

Most serious attempts to link the AFC to Chalmers Johnson's "capitalist developmental state" or to some other model of East Asian capitalism involve the notion of overinvestment, disregard of profits in hell-bent pursuit of market share, and the subordination of interfirm competition to collective interests. A national industrial policy inevitably entails "picking winners" by noneconomic criteria, resulting in "crony capitalism," including investment in economically unprofitable or marginal projects. Such excess is arguably not in the best long-term interests of the economy, but it also leads to two more immediate problems. First, the combination of government-business-finance interrelationships generates a "highly geared" corporate sector (i.e., characterized by a high debt-to-equity ratio), making the corporate sector financially fragile and vulnerable to interest rate shocks. Being underregulated and rife with political favoritism, the financial sector tends to overinvest in areas of high return at high risk, such as (during inflationary booms) property, with the tacit guarantee that the government will bail it out if serious problems develop.

Second, for many of the same reasons, the markets lack adequate information (transparency) about the true financial status of the corporations and the banks. If unpleasant economic information (e.g., the weaknesses of the central banks' international reserve positions) surfaces, it could lead to a collapse of confidence, conceivably manifested in a run on the banks. The lack of transparency and the implicit faith in sovereign loan guarantees give rise to "moral hazard," blindly inflating the asset bubble. In Korea, for example, opacity had become so systemic that corrective action came too late to prevent the collapse of market confidence; the IMF finally was authorized to intervene only days before potential bankruptcy.[16] This financial cronyism and lack of transparency also exacerbated capital flight once the bubble was punctured: Given that investors knew so little about the financial soundness of specific investments, they were apt to bail out at the slightest rumor of trouble.

Yet the neoliberal explanation blaming the AFC entirely on the Asian model of capitalism is not entirely satisfying. For one thing, there is some question about the adequacy of transparent banking rules in ensuring against currency crises. Both Germany and Japan have analogous restrictions on transparency, but neither has been frequently susceptible to bank panics (although Japan currently has problems with bad loans and other financial problems analogous to those faced by the AFC victims). India's corporate sector is also highly geared, second only to Korea's (and more than Malaysia's or Indonesia's), yet it was not hit by financial crisis. Currency crises are endemic to capitalism and can occur with or without transparency; thus, the financial sector in the Scandinavian countries is high in international transparency, yet in the early 1990s they had a banking crisis with serious effects on the real economy. Although not much can be said in defense of corruption, cronyism, and financial opacity, they are hardly unique to the Asian model, and if they were such crippling financial afflictions, how then were the Asian economies able to prosper for so many years nonetheless?[17] Even if these conditions foster a vulnerability or predisposition to crisis, they cannot qualify as "sufficient cause" for the collapse.

Although this is less a refutation than a qualification, to attribute the AFC to "Asian values," or a distinctively "Asian" model of economic development, involves considerable oversimplification in view of various differences among them. For example, the Southeast Asian economies such as Malaysia and Indonesia were considerably more open to foreign investment than the Republic of Korea, which was limited to loans; and whereas the Southeast Asians began in the 1990s to invest heavily in property, assets, and other nonproductive assets, the Korean *chaebol* did invest in expanded productive capacity. The degree and effectiveness of state intervention into precrisis economic development also varied, Korea being at the top and perhaps Thailand at the bottom. Southeast Asian countries, with a relative abundance of natural resources and relatively large domestic markets (except for Singapore), have more entrenched import-substitution trade policies than export-oriented South Korea or Taiwan.

Finally, the Asian model cannot absorb all the blame simply because not all Asian economies were equally afflicted by the AFC. Those countries that survived the crisis in best shape had three things in common: high foreign-exchange reserves, positive current-account balances, and relatively low levels of debt. Taiwan and Singapore have the highest level of international reserves, and both registered positive current-account surpluses for all the years in the 1990s (in contrast to the other Asian countries). The Hong Kong and Taiwan economies are driven largely by small and medium-size firms (in contrast to, say, Japan or Korea), accounting for the low exposure to foreign loans. In Singapore, the high level of foreign ownership, mainly in the form of branch offices of leading MNCs (which tightened oversight following the Baring's scandal a year earlier), limits exposure to debt; while the domestically owned sector, dominated by government-linked companies, has also closely monitored the accumulation of offshore debt. Singapore and Taiwan suffered only relatively minor currency devaluations of some 20 to 30 percent (versus 40 to 75 percent for their neighbors), while the Hong Kong dollar was insulated by its peg to the U.S. dollar (although Hong Kong equity markets were severely hit).

The People's Republic of China is a special case: Although its state-owned banking system is burdened by debt (around 100 percent of GDP by 1997) and specifically nonperforming loans, a state-owned enterprise sector with a debt-to-equity ratio of six to one (higher than South Korea's), and enormous excess capacity, it emerged from the AFC relatively unscathed. There are four reasons for this: its nonconvertible currency; a current-account surplus with substantial foreign exchange reserves (about $140 billion); a heavy influx of FDI, which afforded the authorities the luxury of strictly regulating capital movements; and a very slight proportion of foreign investment vulnerable to quick withdrawal. The only portion of foreign capital roughly equivalent to portfolio investment was funneled to a fringe of provincial quasi-banks, called international trust and investment corporations (ITICs), such as the Guangdong International Trust and Investment Corporations (GITICs); however, the amount invested was relatively small, and the 1998 closure of GITIC for financial irregularities (and its subsequent bankruptcy in the winter of 1999) precipitated widespread foreign capital flight from the ITICs. Whereas China thus seems to have saved itself from the worst ravages of the AFC, the economy has felt its impact, principally in the decline in exports and in the influx of foreign investment, aggravated by a slump in domestic demand (despite falling retail prices since 1998). The regime's immediate response to these difficulties seems to have been a more cautious attitude toward further reforms.[18]

In sum, any attempt to use Asian values or an Asian model of developmental capitalism to account for Asia's susceptibility to the AFC must first define precisely what traits constitute that model. It must also explain how such a model can account both for the Asian miracle and for its subsequent collapse. In the end, the model may be tautological, applicable only to specific conditions shared at the relevant time span by the five Asian countries actually stricken.

A Crisis of Globalism?

The second thesis, that the AFC is a demonstration of the dangers of financial globalization, also has considerable empirical support.[19] The proliferation of "emerging market" and other international funds in the United States in the 1990s resulted in the availability of increasing amounts of short-term investment capital. The American equity markets of the United States were awash in liquidity in the early 1990s for a variety of reasons: the tendency of investors to shift from low-velocity real estate to high-velocity stocks and bonds, Japan's need to recycle the proceeds from the trade surplus that it continued to collect from most trade partners, and an apparently massive capital flight from postcommunist Russia seeking remunerative Western investment opportunities. In addition, resolution of the debt crisis and the (approximately simultaneous) collapse of the iron curtain brought a liberalization of cross-border financial transactions. In 1990, the inflow of FDI into less developed countries was $44 billion, according to the World Bank; by 1996, it had reached $244 billion; from 1990 to 1997, cumulative inflows totaled no less than $938 billion.[20] In 1995, East Asia alone received two-thirds of total FDI outflows to developing countries. Net capital inflows to five affected Asian countries (South Korea, Indonesia, Malaysia, Thailand, and the Philippines) in 1994, 1995, and 1996 was $47 billion, $80 billion, and $91 billion, respectively, representing a rate of growth of 25 to 30 percent per annum (1992–1996).[21] Moreover, an increasing proportion of this investment came in the form of portfolio investment, highly liquid and hence sensitive to interest rate fluctuations. When the crash occurred, this money swiftly took flight: In 1997, there was a net outflow of $12 billion and an additional $4 billion in 1998, amounting to nearly 11 percent of the GDP of the countries involved. In terms of the value of listed companies' shares on the stock market, Southeast Asia's market capitalization was valued at $565 billion in January 1997; by mid-1998, that value had plummeted to $160 billion.[22]

The precipitate withdrawal of foreign funds made it impossible for governments to maintain their peg on the dollar. After repeated assurances that the baht would not be devalued, on July 2 the Bank of Thailand announced that it would allow the baht to float, at which point foreign investors withdrew their capital and speculators launched an attack on the currency: The baht promptly lost 20 percent of its value (losing an additional 20 percent by late September), after which the peso, ringgit, rupiah, and won tumbled in value like so many dominos. The Philippine peso came under attack almost immediately, followed a few days later by the Malaysian ringgit. The Indonesian rupiah did not come under severe pressure until mid-August; but by late January 1998, it had lost 83 percent of its value against the dollar. By November, the Korean won had lost 55 percent of its value. As the crisis reached its peak, foreign-exchange rates approached free fall, and by October, the crisis had spread to the stock markets as well: In 1997, five East Asian stock markets—in Indonesia, Malaysia, the Philippines, South Korea, and Thailand—lost more than three-fifths of their value in dollars. The result was not a cascade in which one default logically implied another but a "herd" response to subtle danger signals amid a dearth of hard financial information. This type of "rational contagion" realizes some of the implications of globalization as defined here.[23]

The fundamental issue in Asia was not large public sector deficits, as in Mexico, but private-sector liquidity. The problem was twofold: Debt was concentrated in short-term liabilities, and reserve assets were low.[24] In Korea, for example, foreign indebtedness was relatively moderate until 1995, but the proportion of short-term debt increased markedly; by the beginning of 1997, Korea's reserves were less than half of short-term liabilities (and much of the reserve was elsewhere committed).[25] Easy credit produced a breeding ground for excessive risk taking, unsound bank lending, and financial fraud. The economies hurt most by the crisis had long histories of problems with their banking systems and were in the midst of financial reform and liberalization as part of the move to full capital convertibility just before the crisis, resulting in a hiatus during which investment was relatively unregulated. According to one interpretation, it was in fact poorly administered liberalization, not the Asian model of capitalism or untrammeled globalization, that precipitated the crisis.[26] Because the emerging Asian economies, following Japan's lead, favored banks over equity markets for financial intermediation (and because many of the Southeast Asian economies began in the early 1990s to channel investment into nonproductive asset markets and service sectors), little public debt was tradable. In a credit crunch, lenders immediately invoked credit rationing, borrowers were denied new loans, and when new funds stopped flowing from international markets, a liquidity crisis could transform itself into insolvency.

In sum, it may be plausibly argued that although the affected economies were beset by weak economic fundamentals and certain structural problems endemic to the "Asian model," the imbalances were not sufficiently severe to warrant a financial meltdown of the magnitude that took place in the second half of 1997. Insofar as globalization facilitates the transmission of information, capital, and other resources across political boundaries, it may be said to have contributed to the AFC in at least two respects: First, it made it possible for foreign capital to be invested in these countries in greater mass and speed than would have otherwise been conceivable, thereby providing much of the "gas" with which the huge asset bubble was inflated. Second, when the bubble burst, the globalization of financial and information markets facilitated the swift, indeed precipitate, withdrawal of that capital. Yet globalization alone cannot explain the crisis: It begs the question of why market confidence suddenly nose-dived in the affected Asian economies—if financial panic could be touched off without more specific cause than the easy availability of mobile funds, financial crises would be far more frequent and ubiquitous than has been the case.

The present attempt at a syncretic explanation includes elements of both the Asian model and the globalization thesis plus extraneous factors. While there was a panic surrounding the influx and precipitate flight of short-term capital, that panic was not based solely on investor irrationality: Weak regulation, combined with implicit deposit guarantees, had left local bankers free to gamble with the money that global capital markets had poured into their coffers. Whereas corruption is universal, the Asian model of close coordination between state and private sectors perhaps exhibits a certain "immune deficiency" for rent-seeking behavior and "moral hazard." Inherent weaknesses in the financial sector were exacerbated by the timing of the crisis to coincide with financial reform and liberalization. The exposure to easy foreign credit in the context of liberalization and financial reform forged a link between the forces of globalization and collusive local political-economic interests. Asian neomercantilism, with its export-oriented obsession with market share conquest and positive trade balances, having spread from Japan to numerous competing NIC (newly industrialized country) imitators, gave rise to saturated markets, overinvestment, and global overcapacity; when productive investment opportunities could no longer be found for available pools of foreign capital, financial bubbles were produced. When the bubbles burst, currencies plunged and deflation ensued.[27]

THE SOLUTION

Although the AFC victims had previously ignored IMF warnings to implement financial reform, they now had little recourse but to turn to this international lender of last resort. When Thailand's appeals for Japanese assistance were rebuffed, it appealed to the IMF on July 28, 1997, providing the basis for a $17.2 billion emergency international rescue package; Japan's ExIm bank pledged to contribute U.S.$4 billion, and China offered $1 billion. In return, Thailand accepted an IMF austerity package that imposed a tight monetary policy (to stop authorities from printing money to rescue failing financial and property companies) and draconian fiscal cuts. The IMF imposed similar conditions on its emergency rescue packages of $43 billion for Indonesia and $58 billion for Korea, much to the dismay of the recipients. The impact of the IMF package has also stirred controversy among economists, with U.S. Treasury Undersecretary Lawrence Summers leading the applause and Harvard's Jeffrey Sachs taking exception. The critics argue essentially that tight money policy and fiscal austerity dried up the money supply and precipitated cash crunches and bankruptcies among companies with high debt exposure, some of which might have otherwise survived, thereby precipitating a "stampede mentality" among foreign creditors. After an IMF bailout package was announced, the country in question became an immediate target for currency speculators.

To some extent the issue is moot, as the IMF was the only lender prepared to step into the breach, and the affected countries were in any event able to recover with IMF help—although it can be argued that they would have been less sharply affected by the crisis or able to recover more swiftly under a different regimen of prescriptions.[28] Equity markets in Korea, Tokyo, Hong Kong, and Indonesia already made an impressive rebound in 1999. South Korea seems to have made the most spectacular economic recovery: After a contraction of 5.8 percent in 1998, it grew by 7 to 8 percent in 1999 and early 2000 despite falling consumer prices and very high government debt (about 19 percent of GDP in 1998 versus 11 percent in 1997, by low estimates).[29] According to early estimates, GDP should increase in Asia by 4.4 percent in 1999 and by 5.9 percent in 2000, with Beijing leading the growth sweepstakes.[30]

CONSEQUENCES

Although the two categories are causally intertwined and sometimes conceptually indistinguishable, let us divide the consequences of the AFC into socioeconomic and political and discuss each in turn.

Socioeconomic Consequences

Perhaps the single most important general consequence of the AFC has been to reconfigure the political economic role of the nation-state in East Asia, subtly but profoundly. Inasmuch as the AFC was almost from the beginning a regional and not a national crisis—in that it defied the best efforts of national governments to deal with on an individual basis—it demonstrated as never before the weakness (if not the impotence) of the nation-state per se. In a region in which nationalism is still quite vibrant, the crisis called for more than a nationalist or even national response. That is by no means to say that the nation-state or national political leadership is obsolescent, only that these now exist on a different plane. Henceforth, the rise or fall of a nation-state, even a "great power," will be more closely keyed to and determined by the speed with which states can establish a fruitful congruence between domestic and foreign policies amid the changing functional requirements of globalization.

If the AFC demonstrated the impotence of the state, its aftereffects further strained it, giving rise to waves of globalization qua negative externalities. One immediate instance has been an escalation in the level of labor protests and domestic unrest. Sometimes, as in Indonesia, unrest lead to lethal communal riots, once again threatening the economically pivotal overseas Chinese community (and a rare rebuke from Beijing) and eventually resulting in the secession of East Timor. Interstate tensions also irrupted over the flow of migrant workers. Malaysia, Singapore, and Thailand had previously ignored this; 20 percent of Malaysia's workforce is believed to be illegal immigrants from Indonesia. However, for Indonesians, the sharp drop in the value of their currency made the prospects of working abroad still more attractive, giving rise to an unbrookable escalation of migration. Singapore cracked down harshly on illegal immigrants, and both Thailand and Malaysia also began repatriating foreign labor. One proposed solution has been some form of international collaboration among labor unions, permitting labor to share in the advantages of globalization by equalizing wages and benefits (and thereby also removing the leverage hitherto enjoyed by MNCs). Yet, although border relations have become more tense over such issues, the quasi-arms races that materialized in the 1980s on the basis of bounteous defense budgets and bargain-basement communist-bloc weapons sales seem to have quietly dissipated along with the economic hypergrowth that afforded them (except in such flash points as the Taiwan Strait).[31]

It is difficult to generalize about state responses to the crisis, which tend to diverge into at least two patterns. On the one hand, states such as South Korea and Thailand have plunged into international capital markets as a way of subjecting domestic industrialists to international market discipline, while on the other Malaysia has joined North Korea and Vietnam in reintroducing tight capital controls and deferring further opening.[32] Korea's Kim Dae Jung regime, the first to be led by a democratic opposition party, fully opened financial markets to foreign investors (attracting a record U.S.$8.9 billion in 1998), inaugurated a new electronic stock market (KOSDAQ, an obvious analog to NASDAQ), and initiated extensive privatization, including selling stakes in state-run steel and electricity companies to foreign investors, making Seoul the poster child of the IMF—and, as noted, the Korean recovery has indeed been impressive. However, efforts to break up the internecine *chaebol* network (with the exception of

Daewoo, formerly the second largest) have met concerted resistance. China's initial response placed it in the more isolationist camp, with the reimposition of regulations limiting imports and raising import prices—yet, if the ongoing negotiation of barriers to entry into the WTO culminates in success, as intimated by successful completion of Sino–U.S. talks in 1999, compliance should reinvigorate globalizing reforms there as well.

The overall trend thus seems to be away from divergence toward a distinct Asian model of capitalism and toward greater conformity with Western models; that is, globalization implies institutional convergence. Thus, in immediate response to the financial meltdown in the summer of 1997, those countries that formerly had fixed or "pegged" exchange rates (namely, Thailand, Indonesia, Malaysia, Philippines, South Korea, Taiwan, and Vietnam—all but Hong Kong and the People's Republic of China) dropped them in favor of floating exchange rates. Bank regulatory systems have been substantially improved in all the stricken economies and mechanisms to resolve banking failures put in place. Central banks in many cases have been given greater independence. Those countries with notorious cases of cronyism or bureaucratic corruption (e.g., Japan, Korea, Indonesia, and China) have launched rectification drives and underscored the rule of law. The region still faces the challenge of managing excess capacity, and nonperforming loans remain a problem for several economies. Although I have argued that the problem of overcapacity transcends the wherewithal of individual nation-states, having to do with anarchic competition among a plurality of neomercantilist NICs, insofar as national policymakers can rationally adjust, they seem likely to rely more heavily on developing domestic markets as engines of growth, or at least moving to a more technology-intensive value-added level of export production.

Although there are thus still some remedial policies that can be adopted at the state level, so many of the causes of the crisis seemed to stem from international causes that there has also been a tendency, relatively unusual in the Asian context, to appeal to international or regional actors for a solution. This meant, in accord with hegemonic stability theory, turning to one of the two regional economic superpowers in search of guidance. Yet neither was willing or able to conform to the role requirements of this model. The United States unexpectedly declined to contribute to the bailout package, abandoning the role of hegemon that it had accepted when Mexico collapsed in December 1994. Thus, the IMF perforce became the lender of last resort. Yet the IMF solution was greeted with considerable ambivalence by host countries, partly because it was suspected of representing U.S. interests; and, in fact, it appears to be the case that U.S. economic interests were well served by the IMF bailout package: The debtor regimes imposed painful austerity measures on their economies in order to repay foreign (often American) creditors. In addition, IMF-prescribed financial sector reforms allowed international banks to make major inroads into the region's banking sectors (e.g., in Thailand, Citibank took a majority share in a major Thai bank; in

Korea, after December 1998, the way was likewise cleared for a major foreign stake in the Korean financial sector).[33] Liberalizing conditions paved the way for U.S. firms to achieve unprecedented market access to boot: In the first four months of 1998, there were 479 mergers and acquisitions in Asia amounting to U.S.$35 billion; these buyouts were dominated by U.S. and, to a lesser extent, European banks, MNCs, and financiers. Moreover, U.S. MNCs (such as GE Capital Company) have been major beneficiaries of the bargains to be had in East Asian "fire sales." Thus, the role of the IMF has been resented not only because its austerity regimen was painful but also because it seemed to be functioning as a Trojan horse of "neoimperialists" intent on realizing privileged gains from the Asian disaster without assuming any corollary responsibility. The IMF itself was criticized for demanding transparency while being all but transparent in its own decision making. It should be emphasized that this critique is not necessarily endorsed in this chapter—after all, the IMF did not cause the crisis, and a certain amount of self-righteousness is only to be expected when the disasters about which it had been warning came to pass—but having made more intrusive demands for political change in the host countries than ever before, the IMF came in for its share of abuse.

Widespread discontent with available international financial mechanisms revived interest in possible regional substitutes—after all, the AFC was primarily regional, although there were a few international side effects (led by the Russian devaluation in August 1998). In the spring of 1999, Japanese prime minister Keizo Obuchi, following a proposal by the Ministry of International Trade and Industry (MITI), called for a free-trade zone in Northeast Asia, taking the lead in a bilateral agreement with Korea, eventually to include Hong Kong and Japan; later the same year, the People's Republic of China was invited to participate as well, and Beijing indeed joined with Seoul and Tokyo in a tripartite meeting on the sidelines of the November summit meeting of the Asian Pacific Economic Cooperation (APEC) forum in Manila.[34] It was pointed out that two-thirds of the 134 WTO members simultaneously belonged to regional trade organizations such as the European Community or NAFTA, making East Asia one of the few regions bereft of such an arrangement. The Japanese Institute for International Monetary Affairs, with the Asian Development Bank Institute, has been studying the feasibility of a single-currency system for Asia. ASEAN also proposed in late 1997 to set up a regional equivalent to the IMF, an Asian Monetary Fund (AMF) consisting solely of Asian states, to provide emergency regional support and avoid what many leaders saw as the humiliation of relying on the IMF for financial salvation. Tokyo promptly promised to underwrite the fund (with support from Singapore and Hong Kong), to be initially capitalized at U.S.$100 billion, but both China and the United States immediately opposed the idea, and by November 1997 it was a dead letter. The Americans raised financial objections, defending the IMF's role and pointing out that with over $100 billion in nonperforming loans, Japan was hardly in position to underwrite such a venture (although it is also possible that political considerations, to be reviewed yet here, may have been behind the veto). For its part, Japan may have been seeking to compensate internationally for its even greater incapacity to play the desired role of regional economic locomotive. Having been in a state of economic stagnation since its own bubble burst in the early 1990s, Japan was in no position to accept the exports that the East Asian NICs will need to sell to revive their economies, even under the dubious assumption that this bastion of neomercantilism should agree to do so. As of 1999, Japan, which exports some 40 percent of its exports to Asia, consumed only 12 percent of the region's exports, compared to 15 percent for Europe and 21 percent for the United States. Southeast Asia was also the destination of the bulk of Japanese FDI, and its banks hold large proportions of Southeast Asian foreign debt (nearly 50 percent in Thailand and 40 percent in Indonesia).[35]

Political Consequences

Paradoxically, although the AFC illustrated the impotence of the nation-state to socioeconomic dislocation, one of the most striking reactions to the crisis has been a reassertion of nationalism throughout the region. This has been visible in the revival of threats and coercive diplomacy across the Taiwan Strait; North Korea's pointed test flight of a Taepodong I ballistic missile over Japan on August 31, 1998; and increasing signs of Sino–Japanese rivalry (such as the September 1998 Tokyo summit, in which Japan refused to provide another apology for war crimes). In the context of China's decade-long series of double-digit increases in defense spending, including purchases of high-profile Soviet weaponry, Japan too has become more nationalistic, symbolically represented by the readoption of the World War II "rising sun" battle flag and national anthem. This trend is both cause and effect of the decline of regional organizations, such as ASEAN, the Asian Regional Forum, and APEC, none of which demonstrated much efficacy in coping with the AFC; at one time, APEC had been animated by dreams of mutual elimination of trade barriers, but the role of footloose capital in the crisis has cooled enthusiasm for the further reduction of such barriers for the time being.

Amid this efflorescence of nationalism, some nations have become more assertive than others. The AFC significantly enhanced the relative importance of China and the United States while reducing the power and status of the adversely affected NICs and Japan. While the United States took a low public profile, it was widely assumed that its interests were represented by the IMF; while its exports to the Pacific Rim declined, U.S. investment benefited from Asian flight capital. The People's Republic of China pledged to contribute $1 billion to the Thai bailout and decided quite early not to devalue the RMB, as it had in 1992 and 1994, steadfastly adhering to this position thereafter. China was in a position to do so not only because it had large foreign-exchange reserves but also because its large internal market makes it less dependent on international cyclical dynamics.

Moreover, Beijing did not wish to jeopardize the peg of Hong Kong currency to the U.S. dollar so near the time of retrocession (July 1, 1997). Thus, China became what U.S. Treasury Secretary Robert Rubin called an "island of stability" in Asia. The result was that Washington worked for the first time in tandem with China rather than Japan (which devalued) in a major economic crisis, with conceivably important strategic implications for the triangular balance among the three countries. In June 1998, when the yen seemed to be falling below 150 to the dollar, Chinese officials expressed concern, hinting that they might have to devalue after all; this subtle hint was sufficient to prompt Washington to reverse course and support the yen.

Some have deemed China's "responsible" role in the AFC its first effective participation in global financial policymaking, and it has (perhaps not coincidentally) been followed by suggestions that Beijing be invited to participate in the Group of Eight. In contrast, Washington seemed to spurn the AMF and other Japanese remedial proposals as a threat to its regional leadership role analogous to the East Asian Economic Caucus (which excluded Caucasians), reinforcing the post–Plaza Accord trend of Japanese replacement of the United States as major source of FDI, major force for production, and principal aid donor in the region. As signaled through such diplomatic slights as President Bill Clinton's refusal (at Beijing's reported insistence) to include Tokyo in his June 1998 China summit trip, this shift has caused Japan evident concern. With the Japan–U.S. trade deficit at its historic high point, Washington was pressuring Japan to accelerate economic reform, banking reform, and financial liberalization and help bail out the Southeast Asian countries at a time when Tokyo was struggling to revive its economy via more traditional measures. These concerns may have contributed to anti–Liberal Democratic Party votes in the 1998 elections to the upper house of the Japanese Diet, leading to the fall of Prime Minister Ryutaro Hashimoto. Hashimoto's fall temporarily slowed Japanese reform efforts and led to a further decline of the yen, raising the unwelcome prospect of another round of competitive devaluations, which would have made U.S. exports less competitive and increased the U.S. balance-of-payments deficit still further. However temporary this may prove to be, the strategic impact of the AFC was thus to strengthen the Sino–U.S. "wing" in the triangular balance at Japan's expense while marginalizing the role of ASEAN (not to mention Russia).

CONCLUSION

The Asian financial crisis was probably the most serious jolt to have befallen the "Asian way" since the smaller East Asian "tigers" first achieved takeoff in the early 1960s. It is also a significant portent of the logic and potential impact of "globalization." However, the argument presented in this chapter is that the AFC has discredited neither the Asian model nor globalization. To be sure, if anyone assumed that developmental capitalism had through its synthesis with Asian values achieved some sort of definitive answer to the dilemmas of modernization, recent developments provide a bracing correction. Asian values must be sorted out from Asian cultural patterns and mores, which may or may not be more broadly applicable; certainly, the tight family structures characteristic of the Asian systems are Janus faced. Corporatist political-economic arrangements can be both an extremely efficient functional substitute for Weberian bureaucracy during boom times and self-protective cronyism during economic downturns. Nepotism is "one of the weaknesses of Confucianism," concedes Singapore's Senior Minister Lee Kuan Yew, a champion of Asian values, calling it "the bane of East Asian countries."[36] Thus, Singapore's reaction to the AFC has been to reemphasize transparent rules and to denounce the system of personal connections (*guanxi*) in favor of meritocratic personnel policies. Asian values, such as the emphasis on education and hard work, and the high personal savings rates (the world's highest, accounting for more than half of world savings) have by no means been discredited, or do Asian values consist merely of absolute trust in a personal leader, avoidance of conflict, tolerance of corruption, and a preference for hierarchically coordinated collectivism? These countries will no doubt need to sort out exactly what they mean by Asian values in terms of both traditional sentimental attachments and the functional requirements of industrial modernization.

Our tentative verdict on globalization is that while it can certainly exacerbate crises in the short term, it is also an important part of the reason that these economies became "miracles" in the first place. Globalization has also contributed to the speedy convalescence of the stricken NICs. By the spring of 1998, it seemed quite plausible, in the light of the dizzying falls experienced in the five countries most seriously affected by the crisis, to predict a decade of doldrums following in the wake of Japan; it also seemed likely that the crisis might drag the rest of the world into recession. Yet, although the negative after effects of the crisis may linger in the most badly affected economies, the region seems to be en route to recovery; and, as noted in this chapter, the most spectacular comebacks seem to have been made by those attempting to implement the globalist agenda endorsed by the IMF.

The impact of the AFC on the debate between democracy and more authoritarian management is more complex. It has been argued that the transition from authoritarianism to democracy is particularly vulnerable because of the opportunity for various forms of corruption to proliferate in the context of deregulation. It should be conceded at the outset that the roots of the crisis were really in the private sector; the governments concerned did too little, not too much. Whereas authoritarian regimes could impose higher interest and taxes on businesses almost at will, this became difficult with the increased political influence of businesses over elected legislatures. Thailand's series of coalition governments (five in six years), frequent general elections, and extensive vote buying ($1.1 billion in the

November 1996 election alone) made it particularly vulnerable to the opposition of vested interests to the fiscal and monetary contraction necessary to correct an external imbalance. Democracy also may have contributed to crony capitalism, as suggested by the close links between political parties and *chaebol* in South Korea. Under the financial deregulation launched by Kim Young Sam, the first directly elected civilian chief of state in more than thirty years, the leading *chaebol* were able to borrow huge sums of investment funds at government-subsidized interest rates and to pay off the politicians who serviced their interests, resulting inter alia in the amassing of enormous slush funds by former presidents Chun Doo Huan (1981–1987) and Roh Tae Woo (1988–1992). In Malaysia as well, there was a tendency to favor businesses with United Malays National Organization (UMNO) party connections in public-private infrastructure projects, resulting in several scandals that the Mahathir regime later blamed on liberal former vice president Ibrahim Anwar, using this as a pretext to indict Anwar on trumped-up criminal charges and to impose constraints on capital convertibility. To be sure, government involvement in industrial policy qua crony capitalism, resulting in overinvestment and overcapacity, is hardly unique to democracies, as the crash of both Malaysia and Indonesia make plain. Moreover, the case of Taiwan indicates that democratization need not entail loss of effective regulatory control over the financial sector.

If Asia's democracies were hardly immune to crisis, they seem to have adapted more promptly and effectively to reform than their more authoritarian counterparts.[37] Functioning electoral mechanisms enabled Thailand and South Korea to divest themselves of discredited leaderships with relative alacrity and without the debilitating riots that afflicted Indonesia, where the AFC spurred a transition to democracy after Suharto's military finally turned on him. The Thais could blame the coalition government of Prime Minister Chavalit Yongchaiyudh for failing to prevent and then worsening the crisis: Chavalit resigned in three months and was replaced by Chuan Leekpai, whose popularity enabled him to put competent technocrats in key ministerial positions for the implementation of necessary reforms. In December 1997, South Korea also changed leaders, blaming the crisis on the now unpopular President Kim Young Sam and giving his successor, Kim Dae Jung, a mandate for sweeping reform. The AFC's impact on authoritarian regimes in Malaysia and China has been more problematic, seemingly contributing to elite entrenchment.

I will conclude this discussion with a set of somewhat disquieting paradoxes. The first is that democracies may be both more vulnerable to financial crises such as the AFC and better equipped to adapt rationally to them; moreover, their reforms may make them even more vulnerable to such global crises in the future. Globalization can facilitate prosperity, but not, it seems, without risk. The second is that the AFC has resulted not only in weakened states but also in intensified nationalism and national assertiveness. This suggests a possibly dangerous compensatory propensity on the part of national governments. The third is that the international institutions that have moved into the power vacuum left by weakened states seem to have been both more effective and more intrusive than previously imagined in implementing rescue packages while at the same time being devoid of legitimacy. They exercise a new (and probably far more fragile) type of authority based sheerly on competence rather than sovereignty, tradition, or ethnic ties. Although criticized chiefly on ideological or moral grounds, even their competence has been contested by other experts. Thus, the IMF has come under attack from both the right (for creating "moral hazard" by functioning as lender of last resort) and the left (for imposing tight monetary and fiscal policies that exacerbate the crisis). This typifies the half-baked new order in the Pacific, rife with discontent with both power politics and international institutions.[38] For now, it would appear that the region will be only too willing to live with this contradiction on its way to economic recovery amid a reasonably stable new triangular balance of power.

NOTES

1. Actually, foreign direct investment (FDI) was about the same (as a proportion of world output) in 1913 as in the mid-1990s. The first wave of globalization was driven by the Industrial Revolution (ca. 1820–1914), while the second, beginning in the 1960s, was driven by the "hi-tech" revolution beginning in the 1960s. Both waves were driven by radical reductions of policy and technological barriers to international transactions, but communications seems to have played a relatively greater role in the current "wave" (Richard E. Baldwin and Philippe Martin, "Two Waves of Globalization: Superficial Similarities, Fundamental Differences" [National Bureau of Economic Research Working Paper 6904, January 1999]).

2. Steven Weber, introduction, in Weber, ed., *Globalization and European Political Economy* (New York: Columbia University Press, 2000) .

3. Byron C. Auguste, "What's So New about Globalization?" *New Perspectives Quarterly* 15, no. 1 (winter 1998): 16–21.

4. Stephen J. Frenkel and David Peetz, "Globalization and Industrial Relations in East Asia," *Industrial Relations* 37, no. 3 (July 1998): 282–310.

5. David McNally, "Globalization on Trial," *Monthly Review* 50, no. 4 (September 1998): 1–14.

6. For example, the ratio of combined imports and exports to GDP had, by 1996, reached 195 percent in Malaysia, 96 percent in Taiwan, 89 percent in Thailand, 80 percent in the Philippines, 67 percent in South Korea, and 54 percent in Indonesia (Masanori Okura, "The Asian Currency Crisis and Future Policy Problems," *Social Science Japan* 13 [August 1998]: 13–15).

7. The rise of several East Asian economies, notably the "four small dragons" (Hong Kong, Singapore, South Korea, and Taiwan), to developed-country income levels and the rapid growth rates in China are hopefully cited as examples. Such convergence in incomes may eventually occur, but the overall recent trend has been more toward polarization than convergence. Whereas in 1965, 52 of 108 developing countries had per capita incomes 20

percent or less that of the rich countries, in 1995 the corresponding proportion was 88 of 108 ("What's So New about Globalization?" 16–20).

8. Steven Radelet and Jeffrey Sachs, "The East Asian Financial Crisis: Diagnosis, Remedies, Prospects," *Brookings Papers on Economic Activity,* no. 1 (spring 1998), 1–91.

9. Neither the 1929 nor the 1987 stock market crash had an obvious precipitating event (in contrast to the sharp market declines in fall of 1973 and 1980, which were caused by OPEC's announcement of its oil embargo and the fall from power of the shah of Iran, respectively). Similarly, the 1992 crisis in the European exchange rate mechanism and the recent Mexican crisis did not have clear triggers.

10. In South Korea and Singapore, for example, real per capita income grew more than 700 percent between 1965 and 1995, while Taiwan and Hong Kong logged a more than 400 percent increase, and Malaysia, Thailand, and Indonesia averaged more than 300 percent (Shalendra Sharma, "Bitter Medicine for Sick Tigers: The IMF and Asia's Financial Crisis," *Pacific Rim Report,* no. 8 [June 1998]: 3; see also Ajit Singh and Bruce A. Weisse, "The Asian Model: A Crisis Foretold?" *International Social Science Journal* [June 1999]: 203ff).

11. Thus, in Thailand, poverty (measured in purchasing power parity, or PPP) was reduced from more than 57 percent in the late 1960s to about 13 percent in 1996; in Indonesia, the proportion living below the official poverty line declined from 64 percent to about 11 percent between 1970 and 1996 (Sharma, "Bitter Medicine for Sick Tigers," 4).

12. Singh and Weisse, "The Asian Model," 203ff.

13. At this point Thailand, Indonesia, Malaysia, the Philippines, South Korea, Taiwan, and Vietnam all had fixed exchange rates partially pegged to the value of the U.S. dollar.

14. *Financial Times* (London), January 13 and 15, 1998. In 1998, U.S. exports to the region fell by 11.6 percent.

15. For example, see Radelet and Sachs, "The East Asian Financial Crisis."

16. According to IMF reports, the Republic of Korea wasted U.S.$10 billion by not responding promptly when the economy showed signs of decline.

17. Singh and Weisse, "The Asian Model," 203ff.

18. Hence, China's export growth slowed from 21 percent in 1997 to 0.5 percent in 1998. Whereas FDI had increased by an average rate of 59.3 percent between 1991 and 1997, the rate dropped to 8.5 percent in 1997 and a mere 0.7 percent in 1998 (*Beijing Review,* April 12–18, 1999, 23). Because much of China's growth in the preceding decade could be attributed to FDI inflows and accelerated export growth, the fall in both of these categories had an impact on economic growth, exacerbated by a shrinkage in domestic demand.

19. For example, see Malaysian prime minister Mohamad Mahathir's jeremiad: "Asian countries will prosper again but not as Asian countries. Their economies would be dominated and run by the huge foreign corporations, practically all owned and managed by non-Asians. Southeast Asia will provide a base for the production of low-cost products to compete with those of certain large Asian economies which refused to be controlled. In the end these countries too will give in" (cited in *Straits Times* [Singapore], June 7, 1998).

20. See Ramesh Garg, Suk H. Kim, and Eugene Swinnerton, "The Asian Financial Crisis of 1997 and Its Consequences," *Multinational Business Review* 7, no. 2 (fall 1999): 32–36.

21. UN Conference on Trade and Development (UNCTAD), 1996; Sharma, "Bitter Medicine for Sick Tigers," 5.

22. *Straits Times,* August 16, 1998.

23. Guillermo A. Calvo and Enrique Mendoza, "Rational Contagion and the Globalization of Securities Markets" (National Bureau of Economic Research Working Paper W7153, June 1999).

24. According to the Bank for International Settlements 1998 estimates, the ratio of short-term external debt to foreign exchange reserves in mid-1997 was 1.82 percent for Indonesia, 2.14 for Korea, 0.62 for Malaysia, 0.88 for the Philippines, and 1.53 for Thailand, meaning that Indonesia, Thailand, and Korea had far from enough reserves to cover short-term external debt when a liquidity crisis occurred (Kon S. Lai, Dong-Woo Lee, Jean Loo, and Jong-Hwan Yi, "Asian Financial Crisis Shows Globalization Can Promote Risks as Well as Opportunities," *Business Forum* 23, nos. 1–2 [winter–spring 1998]: 5–14).

25. Until 1994, foreign debt in the Korean economy was stable at about 14 percent of GDP, but the ratio increased to 23.8 percent in 1995 and 28.4 percent in 1996. Moreover, the share of short-term debt increased from 25 percent in 1994 to 50 percent in 1995–1996 (i.e., of total indebtedness; its proportion of GDP was 15.3 percent in 1994 and 20.6 percent in 1996).

26. Singh and Weisse, "The Asian Model," 203 ff. Although Thailand is most frequently noted for lax supervision of banks and finance companies, this was also true elsewhere. In Korea, the financial market had been tightly regulated and insulated from the outside world until the early 1990s. South Korea's entry into the OECD, along with the campaign reforms accompanying democratization, created pressure to liberalize, leading inter alia to the formation of more loosely regulated new mercantile quasi-banks.

27. There was excess capacity in products from steel and auto production (e.g., Samsung's 1996 decision to become Korea's sixth major automobile manufacturer) to memory chips and glass turbines, particularly after 1996, when India and China became major producers. "Pricing pressures are dramatic across sector after sector," says GE Chair Jack Welch. "There is excess global capacity in almost every industry" (cited in William K. Tabb, "The East Asian Financial Crisis," *Monthly Review* 50, no. 2 [June 1998]: 24–39); see also the incisive article by Lance L. P. Gore, "State via Market, Market via State: When States Become Market Players and Market Consists of State Actors" (unpublished paper, Singapore National University, East Asian Institute, October 25, 1999).

28. Jessie P. H. Poon and Martin Perry, "'The Asian Economic Flu': A Geography of Crisis," *Professional Geographer* 51, no. 2 (May 1999): 184ff.

29. Survey in the *Financial Times,* October 20, 1999.

30. Asian Developmental Bank, "Outlook 1999" (Manila, April 1999). The estimates indicate a continuing slight decline for Hong Kong's GDP in 1999, no change from 1998 for Indonesia and Thailand, and increases for the rest of the region.

31. The devaluation of local currencies effectively doubled the price of many of their procurements on the international market, making defense procurement programs a budgetary albatross. Thus, Thailand had to negotiate with the United States to extricate itself from a planned purchase of F/A-18 fighters, South Korea's defense budget has been cut drastically, and the Philippines, Indonesia, and Malaysia have deferred planned purchases.

32. The new special functions minister, Diam Zainuddin, announced, "Malaysia's new currency controls are based on China's model" (Robert Wade and Frank Veneroso, "The Gathering Support for Capital Controls," *Challenge* 41, no. 6 [November–December 1998]: 14ff.).

33. Richard Higgot, "The Asian Economic Crisis: A Study in the Politics of Resentment," *New Political Economy* 3, no. 3 (November 1998): 333–56.

34. The meeting agreed to establish a joint research team from among the three countries' economic institutions to investigate ways of institutionalizing trilateral cooperation and to ease the problems of overcapacity and overinvestment.

35. Richard H. Pettway, "Asian Financial Crisis: The Role of China and Japan in the Post-Asian Crisis Era," *Multinational Business Review* 7, no. 2 (fall 1999): 13–21.

36. Cited in Donald K. Emmerson, "Americanizing Asia?" *Foreign Affairs* 77, no. 3 (May–June 1998): 46–57.

37. See Dani Rodrik, "The Asian Financial Crisis and the Virtues of Democracy," *Challenge* 42, no. 4 (July–August 1999): 44–59.

38. Although the IMF is widely scolded, what should replace it? Some have suggested combining the World Bank and the IMF into a new and more powerful instrument for global financial regulation. The new body would not only intervene once a crisis has occurred but would also provide timely advice and warnings to prevent crises. According to others, such as Japan, a regional response would be more geopolitically appropriate, especially if the dimensions of future crises are, like the AFC, containable within a discrete region.

3

Japan and Globalization: From Opportunity to Restraint

William W. Grimes

GLOBALIZATION FOR REAL?

The debate over "globalization" has been nearly unavoidable in many countries in the late 1990s, and Japan is no exception in this regard. Over the last century, Japan has been host to many debates on how external forces and technological change are forcing internal transformation. However, unlike "internationalization" (*kokusaika*), which was the buzzword of the late 1980s, Japanese commentators have tended to keep the concept of globalization (*gurobaruka*) at arm's length. For whatever reason, there seems to be an emerging consensus in contemporary Japan that globalization is changing Japan, and not necessarily in welcome ways.

While in theory globalization can affect any or all domestic institutions and processes, some of the most profound effects of 1990s-style globalization on Japan have been of an economic nature. It has long been the case that external pressures and competitive conditions have shaped Japan's economic policies.[1] However, the globalization of the 1990s appears to be having economic (and, by extension, political and legal) effects of a qualitatively different nature than international pressures in earlier years.

After decades of pronouncements to the effect that "this time the Japanese economy really is changing," Japanese and foreign observers are pointing out what they claim to be irreversible changes in the factors that made the Japanese economy unique, including lifetime employment, close business–government relations, and a tightly regulated financial sector whose primary role was to channel money to manufacturing industries.[2] As the process of globalization alters the costs and benefits of various sorts of regulations, the impact is inexorably extending into the policy world as well and perhaps even changing the calculus of power among politicians, bureaucrats, and interest groups.

Nowhere is the impact of economic globalization more clear than in the financial sector. There, advances in telecommunications and computing, the resulting development of worldwide operations, and ultraflexible labor markets (at least in some subsectors, such as derivatives trading), along with the loss of protection of domestic markets, have hit a sector that was already in the midst of its broadest-based and most serious postwar crisis. The effects have been startling to many, particularly those who had spent their entire careers insulated from competition and rapid innovation by a paternalistic Ministry of Finance. Since the 1980s, the meaning of globalization for Japanese finance, particularly banking, has changed considerably—from opportunity to constraint.

The Japanese government has taken the issue of globalization to heart and is welcoming it, at least at a formal level: "This trend is profoundly deepening world markets and leading the world toward the formation of a borderless single market. . . . It is axiomatic that the advance of globalization will, fundamentally, greatly benefit not only the Japanese economy but also the global economy." Nevertheless, even the 1998 Diplomatic White Paper, which enthusiastically promotes the cause of globalization, calls for far-reaching changes in Japan's domestic economic structure as well as major extensions of international rules on cross-border interactions of all kinds.[3] In other words, the Japanese government officially recognizes that globalization requires different types of competence than in the past.

Because of the rapidity of globalization-induced changes in the area of Japanese finance, this chapter focuses there, with emphasis on changes in both the business itself and Japanese-style regulation. It is not entirely clear that globalization-induced changes in the financial sector will be a template for changes elsewhere in the Japanese political economy, but they will probably define the limits and a sense of the direction of other, subsequent changes.

THE GLOBALIZATION DEBATE IN JAPAN

Globalization has been held to mean a variety of things.[4] It is, for example, difficult to imagine that environmentalists who protested against it at the World Trade Organization (WTO) meetings in Seattle in November 1999 were engaged in the same debate as financial regulators worried about accounting standards. In chapter 1, Samuel Kim offers a value-free baseline definition of globalization as "a series of complex, independent yet related processes of stretching, intensifying, and accelerating worldwide interconnectedness in all aspects of human relations and transactions—economic, social, cultural, environmental, political, diplomatic, and security—such that events, decisions, and activities in one part of the world have immediate consequences for individuals, groups, and states in other parts of the world." While analytically helpful, this begs several questions, including ones of measurement and whether globalization is a "good" thing.

Extent of Globalization

By most measures, Japan's global involvement has become considerable. On the economic side, its level of trade is close to 20 percent of gross domestic product (GDP), interest rates respond immediately to changes elsewhere in the world, and assets on the order of 70 percent of GDP are held overseas in the forms of loans and portfolio and direct investment.[5] Social indicators seem to tell the same story—nearly 17 million Japanese traveled abroad in 1997, of whom over half a million had extended stays (e.g., for study and business), while Internet connections have increased to about 17 million.[6]

Indeed, it can be argued that Japan is more permeated by global forces than at any time since the end of the U.S. occupation. This is perhaps most clear in the number of Japanese who have spent significant time overseas, living in one or more foreign countries for work or study. Perhaps even more strikingly, there has been a qualitative change in the type of involvement of foreigners in Japan. From a social perspective, the most evident is the role of foreign workers, particularly from other Asian countries—including around 300,000 undocumented workers.[7] They now permeate Japanese society to an unprecedented degree, particularly in household service and the sex/entertainment industry. In addition, many work in factories, warehouses, and other menial jobs. This has led not only to occasional bad feelings between Japanese and foreign workers but also to a recent movement to grant voting rights (at least in local elections) to legal foreign residents.[8] It is not yet clear what this level of mixing will mean, other than increases in foreign remittances, bicultural marriages, and transnational transmission of venereal diseases—areas in which the Japanese state has been slow to respond at all, let alone effectively. Meanwhile, publicized cases of victimization of foreigners (especially undocumented women in the entertainment industry) occasionally create a counterweight to the usual assumption that migrant workers are the sources rather than victims of criminal behavior in Japan. These issues are already raising some angst in a country that likes to think of itself as racially and culturally homogeneous, even if there is not yet a serious debate over the meaning of citizenship, such as Sassen has predicted.[9]

A similar dynamic appears to be on the rise in the corporate world. Over the last several years, there has been a drumbeat of foreign acquisitions of Japanese firms and financial institutions. Some of these, particularly in the financial sector, have been extremely well publicized, such as the acquisition by Merrill Lynch of a large chunk of Yamaichi Securities (formerly Japan's fourth-largest securities firm) following Yamaichi's spectacular failure in November 1997 and the acquisition of the failed Long-Term Credit Bank of Japan by an investor group led by Ripplewood, a U.S. firm. Less well publicized but also impressive has been the rapid expansion of GE Capital into Japan's nonbank financial sector. Outside of finance, there has been considerable movement as well, especially in the automobile industry, where in 1998 Ford upped its stake in Mazda to a controlling interest and Renault took a controlling interest in Nissan Motors in the spring of 1999. Both installed foreign managers, with the mission of turning the companies around. These foreign intrusions may be having an impact on the behavior and structure of Japanese-owned firms as well. Again, this is most evident in the financial sector, where a variety of mergers have been announced over the past year or so, but can be seen elsewhere as well. Examples include Toyota, which has taken full control of two affiliated automobile and truck companies (Hino and Daihatsu); Sony, which has ostentatiously announced a shift to performance-based pay; and Marubeni, which recently reorganized into a multidivisional corporate structure.[10]

There is some irony to the current process of economic globalization, especially in the financial sector. One irony is that Japan is the largest creditor nation in the world. Although its citizens' savings remain the world's largest pool of transnational capital, at least in a net sense, its own banks are withdrawing from international business at the same time that it is experiencing meaningful penetration throughout its domestic financial sector. Of course, a great deal of this has to do with changes in regulation, at least some of which was instigated by foreign governmental pressure. However, the weakness of Japanese financial institutions of all sorts is also driving the transformation of the sector, and, ironically, globalization processes are having their greatest effect on Japanese finance at the very point at which Japanese banks are becoming less globally active.

A more general irony of the perception of globalization within Japan is that commentators often ignore the ways in which Japanese culture has spread outward through the globalization process. Japanese popular culture, embedded in Pokémon, *anime, manga,* and even electronic pets, has widely penetrated youth culture throughout the world, while Japan's pop music, fashion, and corporate culture (through investments by Japanese multinational corporations [MNCs]) have penetrated deeply into other Asian countries. Nonetheless, satisfaction with the spread of Japanese cultural artifacts abroad seems almost nonexistent, especially in comparison with the vast amount of writing on how economic globalization affects Japan.

Debate

In the face of these facts, Japan is confronting the same issues as other advanced industrialized countries. One of these is distribution of gains and costs. As Dani Rodrik has shown, globalization tends to have differential effects on labor versus capital and to accentuate the growing disparity of income between highly skilled and unskilled labor.[11] Since capital can easily move abroad, workers' bargaining power—and thus their ability to receive a share of a given company's profits above their productivity gains—is reduced. The tendency toward disparity is reinforced by the related shift of tax burden away from capital and onto labor in the form of income and consumption taxes.[12] The citizenship of corporate entities is thus being increasingly called into question in this process that has been characterized as "McWorld."[13]

In Japan, the debate over globalization-induced disparities has been particularly sharp in the ways in which commentators and citizens have reacted to corporate restructurings. While the recent announcement of large-scale downsizing at Renault-controlled Nissan by its European chief operating officer has received particular attention, one can find in the pages of leading Japanese journals numerous debates and warnings about the dangers facing Japanese workers.[14] Even though the dangers are seen as more extreme at foreign-owned companies, employees of Japanese-owned firms have also been given cause to worry.[15] In any event, as one survey of the economic literature concludes, "All these studies indicate that globalization will likely have an impact on jobs" in Japan, although it also concludes that deregulation will reduce the effect.[16]

Ironically, these sorts of class issues were not even nascent in Japan until very recently. As a number of studies have shown, Japanese companies have been very active in promoting a regional or global division of labor since at least the late 1980s.[17] Nonetheless, an implicit social bargain maintained Japan's labor aristocracy to a striking degree. The combination of global competitive forces, domestic financial crisis, and economic stagnation that has held since the second quarter of 1997 has finally ignited the debate over globalization-induced restructuring.

The government's response has so far been schizophrenic. On the one hand, it has engaged in traditional attempts to cushion workers and small business from the pressures of greater competition. Specific policies include subsidies to companies that hire or retain unnecessary workers and a large-scale loan guarantee program for small enterprises.[18] We can also see recent statements of disapproval of Nissan's restructuring plan by top Japanese politicians and cabinet ministers as an example of that tendency.[19] On the other hand, the Japanese government is proceeding aggressively with economic liberalization in a number of areas, even in the face of opposition from potential losers in given industries. Overall, it is hard to see in Japan today the state that in past decades responded to severe external shocks by facilitating efficient redeployment of resources while cushioning the impacts on domestic society.[20] Instead, the Japanese government seems flummoxed by what Samuel Kim calls the "intermestic" issues of globalization in chapter 1.

In addition to distributional consequences, many Japanese opinion leaders fear that the postwar "Japanese system" is itself under attack by global forces and in danger of crumbling away. As one author puts it, "By politely acceding to international accounting standards in order to make it easy for American financial industry to invest in Japanese stocks, [Japan is] working hard for the destruction of its own system."[21] Resentment of "global standards" in particular runs high. Sakakibara Eisuke, former vice minister of finance for international affairs and one of the most vocal and prolific participants in the Japanese

discourse on globalization, warns of the danger to local systems of global ho-
mogenization of systems. He suggests that globalization is an attack from outside; this is true, he argues, for both Japan and other (especially Asian)
economies and cultures. Going a step further, some authors argue that global
standards are actually "American standards" and are nothing more nor less than
a manifestation of U.S. hegemony.[22] Although policy prescriptions vary considerably among such authors, the degree of hostility to the hegemony of international (or American) markets is a common thread.

The "Japanese system" that is held to be under attack by critics of globalization is portrayed as one in which long-term relationships between management
and labor, customers and suppliers, and lenders and creditors are maintained on
the basis of mutual trust and respect. The erosion of any of these elements is presented as a decaying of Japanese society.[23] Proponents of globalization not surprisingly see a different system: In their view, the Japanese economy and society
are riddled through with inefficiencies, protection, and disincentives to innovation.[24] Thus, they are not nearly as disturbed as the critics by indications that
Japanese society and corporate behavior might be changing fundamentally. To
date, the evidence is ambiguous, but it appears that Japanese firms might be more
wary of shedding workers and relationships than the most enthusiastic proponents
of restructuring have predicted.[25]

A third stream of writing concentrates on the increased volatility—and Japan's
susceptibility to that volatility—that seems to be associated with economic globalization. The issue is particularly germane to financial globalization because of
the ability of money to move rapidly from one economy or class of assets to another. Such rapid movements of money naturally lead to rapid movements of
prices for financial assets—not only stocks and bonds but also interest rates more
generally, as well as exchange rates. This is what Sakakibara has described in a
variety of venues as the "crisis of global capitalism."[26]

From the viewpoint of other Asian countries, which were much harder hit by
the financial crisis of 1997–1999, Japan's feelings of vulnerability might seem
odd. After all, despite a number of bank failures and the emergence of recession,
Japanese citizens' standard of living has not seemed to decline radically, and its
credit crunch was almost entirely self-imposed. While Japan's vulnerability is
certainly small compared to smaller Asian economies with poorly developed financial markets, it has surely increased relative to dangers from the global financial system in previous years. One example is the gyrations of the yen since
1994.[27] Moreover, in the 1997–1999 crisis, the level and speed of worldwide
"contagion" were unprecedented, and despite Japan's vast reserves of savings and
the provision of large amounts of official financing, the Japanese state was unable
to stop the spread of the crisis throughout some of its major trading partners. The
inability of even resolute state action to make much apparent difference has fundamentally colored Japanese perceptions of the costs of globalization, despite the
fact that Japan itself suffered relatively little from financial contagion. This is an-

other example in which the state's basic competence in the face of external shock has been thrown into question.

Thus, globalization is seen much less as a dialectical process between Japan and the rest of the world than as an assault (sometimes amorphous) on Japan from without. In this respect, the concept of globalization differs from two other key buzz-words—"internationalization" and "information society"—that the Japanese media have popularized as a way of summarizing the forces driving the major changes facing the Japanese economy over the past fifteen years or so. In a globalizing world, Japan is seen as victim rather than agent—a return of a very old worldview.

"Internationalization" as a concept was particularly popular in the 1980s, as Japan began asserting itself in the global political economy. Internationalization was not a state-centric concept but rather suggested an opening up to the outside world. It meant taking advantage of Japan's newfound strength but also required intimate knowledge of the outside (primarily Western) world, which in turn particularly meant mastering the English language. The label "internationalist," essentially meaning cosmopolitan, was a great compliment; it meant someone who could represent himself and his country and gain respect from the outside world.

The term "information society" also began to be popular in the 1980s. At the time, Japanese manufacturers were becoming dominant (or in some cases seemingly dominant) in industries in which the information revolution was beginning to have an impact, such as semiconductor, fax, and telecommunications manufacturing and international banking. Japanese commentators converted early to the idea that knowledge-based industry would soon be at the core of economic growth.[28] As it has turned out, the promise of the information society has been largely unfulfilled in Japan, even as it has borne fruit in the United States.

In the cases of both "internationalization" and the "information society," Japanese public opinion embraced change. Moreover, change appeared to move from the inside out as Japanese economic and social actors entered new realms from positions of strength. In contrast, however, "globalization" has more sinister overtones than the other two despite the enthusiastic response to some works that have trumpeted it.[29] As the domestic debate has developed, the whole concept carries distinct implications of being imposed from the outside in and being beyond Japanese control. Sakakibara epitomizes many of the fears that Japanese hold on the subject. In particular, he argues that financial globalization necessarily leads to extreme instability and thus to a "crisis of global capital," even while he waxes rhapsodic and nostalgic about locally produced food, wine, and culture.[30]

GLOBALIZATION OF FINANCE: OPPORTUNITIES AND CONSTRAINTS

Internationalization

The internationalization of Japanese finance dates back at least to the Yen-Dollar Agreement and accelerated rapidly after 1985 in tandem with the rapid rise in the yen after that year's Plaza Agreement.[31] Both sets of events were associated with a rapid rise in Japan's current-account surpluses that made Japan the world's premier creditor nation by 1986. Combined with rapid yen appreciation, major Japanese banks' ability to pool the savings of Japan's high savers on a national level meant that, soon after their arrival as players on the international scene, they were in fact among the largest players.[32] Securities companies such as Nomura, Daiwa, and Yamaichi similarly took leading positions in international finance.

By the late 1980s, virtually any major syndicated international loan had to include at least some Japanese financial institutions. While major Japanese commercial banks had long had limited branch networks overseas in order to service Japanese multinationals, economic forces and relaxation of regulations concerning capital movement led to a large-scale expansion. This was true both for major banks, which became true multinationals, and for smaller banks, which for the first time chose to venture overseas.

Meanwhile, the 1980s also began to see an increase—albeit a limited one—in foreign financial institutions' operations within Japan. At first, they operated under severe restrictions, but as U.S. and other negotiators pushed for equal access for their countries' financial institutions, those restrictions gradually subsided. Liberalization was earliest in the field of securities; only in the last few years have banking rules been similarly eased.

Globalization

Globalization in the financial sector has been driven by technological and market changes, even though its effects on corporate behavior and regulation have varied by country.[33] Improvements in computing and telecommunications technology, by lowering the time and costs of pricing and making trades, vastly increased both the density and scope of international financial transactions. Meanwhile, deregulation in a small number of financial centers (starting with the United States) was changing the economic calculus even for financial firms that did business elsewhere.[34] The existence of both parallel markets (such as Eurocurrency markets) and transnational capital (large institutional investors) inevitably affected more protected markets' interest rates and stock prices. In addition, what Frieden and Rogowski call the "costs of closure" expand as efficiency gains in the vanguard markets are not matched within protected home markets—in other words, the widening of opportunities for capital between home and international market leads to a buildup of economic and political pressures to equalize them.[35] The only way to do this efficiently is by altering regulations to meet world standards.

Thus, financial globalization compels states to react, although not necessarily in a uniform way. In Japan, the first several waves of responses to financial globalization (early 1980s to mid-1990s) sought to do three things: to minimize the impact on weaker Japanese financial institutions, to maximize the benefits to stronger Japanese financial institutions, and to maintain a balance between the interests of banks and securities firms.[36] In doing so, Japanese regulators maintained considerable protection over the domestic market.

Theoretically, we might expect to see competition among states toward greater liberalization if liberalization really offers competitive advantages. Indeed, regulators in the Hong Kong and Singapore financial markets followed such a route with the result that, despite being attached to relatively small economies, both of those markets have consistently had higher volumes of certain international transactions than has Tokyo. From another perspective, however, less permissive national systems of regulation might also be used to confer advantages on domestic firms.[37] One possibility would be to protect domestic markets for the benefit of providing a base for internationally competitive financial institutions. In addition, having less stringent rules than other major states on capital-adequacy requirements or providing explicit or implicit government subsidies or guarantees to financial institutions would tend to give them an advantage in expanding their market share, although at the same time potentially leading to serious moral hazard problems.

The last point reminds us of another facet of economic globalization: the danger of contagion. The core of globalization in any field—be it finance, communications, pollution, or disease—is interconnectedness and rapid transmission from one place to another. Globalization in finance inherently carries the risk of widespread crisis, as we have indeed seen in the recent Asian financial crisis. If a given state in the system is gaining advantage for its financial institutions by enforcing lower levels of prudential regulation than other states, then it is also exposing those other states' financial systems to increased levels of risk. If enough states choose to act in this way, the system runs into a classic public goods problem—incentives to free ride result in a suboptimal level of prudential regulation for the system as a whole, increasing the likelihood of severe crises in individual economies and contagion to other economies. Like any public goods problem, the theoretical solution is the establishment of an authority for the system as a whole—in other words, a global regulatory standard and enforcement system.

According to U.S. and British regulators, free riding through insufficient prudential regulation was exactly what Japan was doing in the late 1980s. In an effort to prevent systemic risk and to dull the competitive advantage that Japanese financial institutions held as a result of domestic protection and implicit government guarantees, they initiated the process that led to the Basle Accord on capital-adequacy requirements (also known as the "BIS standards") for internationally active banks.[38] This agreement sought to ensure that those banks that were most involved in global finance would have sufficient capital to handle large-scale losses on their lending portfolios while also reducing pressures on more cautious state regulatory agencies to lower standards below what they believed to be prudent.

The BIS standards were unpopular in Japan from the start. As Kapstein shows, Japanese negotiators accepted them only grudgingly and with provisions to make them easier for Japanese banks to meet.[39] Even as they were first coming into effect in 1993, Ministry of Finance officials were publicly calling for their temporary suspension. It is still relatively common to hear that BIS standards were a major contributor to Japan's credit crunch of the 1990s.[40] The BIS standards are perhaps the most widely resented of all "global standards" and the ones most seen as having been imposed on Japan by jealous competitors. (In fact, the BIS standards probably did contribute somewhat to credit contraction. However, regardless of their effect on the Japanese financial system, they did what they were supposed to do at the global level: They prevented irresponsible lending by Japanese banks from creating a global financial crisis.)

Finally, globalization raises the problem of capabilities. With rapid changes in technology and markets driving globalization in finance, it is not surprising that regulators have had a hard time keeping up. Not only has it been difficult to stay abreast of such innovations, but it is also analytically difficult to judge either the effects of new financial products and processes or the effects of policies meant to address those effects. These challenges may have been particularly severe for Japan, which was slow to adopt several key policy changes and whose financial regulators are often career officials with formal education in law. Financial globalization has thus eroded the competence of the Japanese state in several ways that the existing system of regulation is ill equipped to handle.

GLOBALIZATION OF JAPANESE FINANCE

From "Protectionism" to the "Big Bang"

The transformation of Japanese finance over much of the last twenty years has been characterized by incrementalism and often grudging acceptance of changes that had already happened.[41] While considerable advances were made in terms of relaxing rules on international activity—a near necessity, given the immense amounts of excess savings—and in blurring the lines between various types of financial institutions, there remained a strong local flavor due to protective intervention by Japanese regulators.[42]

Virtually all Japanese analyses of banking regulation in recent years have concentrated on the distortions created by the so-called convoy system—the implicit guarantee that more competitive banks would be constrained in their functioning in order to ensure the survival of less competitive banks.[43] This set of protectionist policies was a relic of the days when international trade meant trade in goods and when national financial sectors existed for the purpose of servicing manufacturers. As access to Euromarkets and higher retained profits reduced Japanese firms' demand for bank loans, however, Japanese financial institutions of all types were constrained in their abilities to lend to their traditional customers.[44]

At the same time, the slowness of changes at the retail level ensured that most Japanese citizens left their savings in low-yielding bank accounts or paid extremely high fees for the privilege of participating in the domestic stock market, thus ensuring plenty of funds and profits for banks, securities firms, and insurance companies to exercise as they saw fit.[45] In the late 1980s, with the additional spur of loose monetary policy and a rapidly appreciated yen, those financial institutions used their exclusive access to such low-cost funds to take world finance by storm, achieving seemingly dominant positions in project finance, syndicated loans, and especially the servicing of Japan's powerful multinationals.[46]

While Japanese financial institutions were internationalizing, however, a new round of globalization was already beginning. The development and profitability of derivatives, as well as the rapid development of information and telecommunications technology that has allowed for large-scale real-time trading on a global scale, have had immense impacts on world financial markets—even those of states (like Japan) that have sought to regulate their introduction and use. The most evident example is in international currency markets, where total market volume dwarfs the amounts needed just for trade and where activity in forwards and options outweighs spot transactions.[47] Similar effects have occurred in other areas as well. The crash of Russian securities values in the late summer and early fall of 1998, for example, was attributed partly to the overextended positions of hedge funds.

The impact of these developments on the Japanese markets has been threefold. First, they have shattered the ability of regulators to dictate differentiated interest rates to maintain the status quo among insurers, city banks, long-term credit banks, and regional banks. It is simply too easy for outside actors, even with relatively limited direct holdings of actual Japanese securities, to affect prices. Second, at the same time, regulations meant to protect weak institutions and to maintain stability in the financial sector had the additional effect of preventing even strong institutions from participating fully in the global financial revolution. Not only were they restricted from doing so, but protection made them less interested in forcing the issue. Finally, acquisition of the highly technical knowledge that is essential to the new game of global finance—which U.S. and European financial firms have been obtaining by hiring from outside their organizations and often even from outside the financial sector—has proven difficult for Japanese firms, with their emphasis on long-term employment and rank-based pay.[48]

In the face of this immense global wave of hyperefficient financial competition, Japanese financial firms have thus been at a major disadvantage. Banks and securities firms have been stuck dealing with an increasingly unprofitable retail business, while insurance companies have been less than adept at adapting to the new game of risk management. In combination with the severe financial position of Japanese financial institutions in the postbubble era and the increased access of foreign commercial and investment banks to the Japanese market (secured via years of contentious negotiations, particularly between Japan and the United States), efficiency-based competition has created terrible problems for traditional Japanese financial institutions. Already, top firms in the Tokyo market have been forced to move increasingly toward head-hunting and performance-based pay, reluctantly accepting "global standards" in their management practices and beginning to jettison what had become accepted convention in Japan's postwar economy.[49]

Financial regulation more broadly has also occasioned major changes not envisioned by many analysts. Steven Vogel's *Freer Markets, More Rules,* probably the best political analysis of Japanese financial liberalization in either Japanese or English, emphasizes bureaucrat-led reregulation of the financial sector as a key characteristic of liberalization.[50] However, Vogel's analysis only runs through the 1992–1994 reforms, a time when globalization was still just taking hold in the Japanese markets. By 1996, the reforming Prime Minister Hashimoto Ryutaro was championing a "Japanese Big Bang" in finance in a move meant to parallel London's eponymous grand financial deregulation of a few years earlier. A year later, the implementing legislation had been approved. The reforms contained in the Big Bang go far beyond any previous Japanese reforms and, if fully carried out, will provide a legal infrastructure comparable to those in the United States and Europe.[51]

Vogel is surely correct that Japanese bureaucrats have sought to maintain their authority and to protect domestic institutions, and his interpretation holds well for the lateness and the slow pace of the Japanese Big Bang (which, unlike the all-at-once English version, is being carried out from 1998 to 2001). However, the logic of liberalization has become a self-reinforcing cycle. In particular, since the "convoy system" was breached with the spectacular failure of the Hokkaido Takushoku Bank in November 1997, it has become clear that regulators are no longer able to keep the promise of preventing all bank failures, even for major institutions.[52] If any doubt remained, the 1998 bankruptcies of Nippon Credit Bank and the Long-Term Credit Bank of Japan, immediately following the revision of rules on bank bankruptcies, surely lifted them.

It has become clear that the constraints posed by financial globalization have been one important reason why "Japanese-style" regulation was unable to extricate Japanese banks from their postbubble bad loan messes: Without the discretionary power to adequately protect specific banks from competition, regulators cannot ensure profits, nor do they have the carrots and sticks necessary to force mergers. Once the final props of the convoy system were removed, banks were forced to contend for funds in global markets on the basis of their financial health, and as a result many have become very sick indeed.

The Debate over "Global Standards"

The debate within Japan over the imposition of "global standards" has also taken an interesting turn in recent years. "Global standards" in the area of finance refers specifically to common standards of accounting, legal treatment of financial activity, and functioning of settlement systems. These standards are largely derived from U.S. practice and have been adapted in the major markets of Europe as well as Hong Kong and Singapore. Global standards are meant to provide for both a maximal level of efficiency in transactions and a high level of disclosure of financial information.

After years of denying the need for (or sometimes even the existence of) global standards, financial discourse has finally been forced to confront the issue head on. Certainly, there has been and remains considerable resentment to the idea of acceding to standards imposed by the outside world, which often fly in the face of existing Japanese attitudes toward information management.[53] What is most interesting about this discourse is that—except for a small, angry fringe—it singles out not foreign *governments* as having created the major pressure for global standards but rather *global markets*. Japanese policymaking, which has long been bedeviled from the outside by foreign government pressure, is now being moved by markets that are not always closely tied to a specific foreign country.[54]

Speaking broadly, the global standards debate breaks down into three camps. At the fringe is a group that is deeply suspicious of global standards and argues that they are a new form of U.S. domination. As Tokyo Governor Ishihara Shintaro wrote recently, "The United States constantly tries to push on other countries frameworks convenient to itself, saying they are globally accepted standards, but there is certainly no need [for Japan] to sacrifice all the potential of the future merely for the sake of the United States even in case Japan has to accept the US demands for liberalization."[55]

A second camp contends that global standards are necessary to reinvigorate Japanese capitalism and clear away the anticompetitive practices that have weakened the Japanese economy.[56] In other words, it attacks the state's lack of competence in addressing challenges of development and globalization. As one author puts it, "In comparison to the development of manufacturing, Japan's financial industry and system are remarkably closed and separated from world competition, leading to distorted development" for Japan as a whole.[57] In order to create a modern and efficient financial sector, global standards are essential and desirable for the entire Japanese economy. Interestingly, this view can coexist with nationalist alarm about rapacious foreigners "eating up" Japanese financial institutions, as seen in a popular magazine article that accuses incompetent regulation of weakening the financial system and making it ripe for attack from outside.[58]

The third camp, while suspicious of global standards, is resigned to the fact that globalization has forced the issue, at least in finance. While authors such as Sakakibara argue that there is nothing inherently wrong with Japanese-style financial practice and regulation, they recognize that the globalization and "virtualization" of finance make it difficult for any one country to buck trends.[59] Thus, in order to participate in the world economy, Japan must adopt existing global standards, even while fighting to adapt the global system to allow for local heterogeneity of systems.

At least for the moment, acceptance of global standards has won the day, in both the Ministry of Finance and the Diet. International accounting standards have indeed been imposed, and BIS capital-adequacy standards for international banks are being enforced strictly. Indeed, since April 1997, thirteen banks forfeited their international operations because they were unable or unwilling to meet BIS standards combined with strengthened enforcement.[60]

Changing Corporate Behavior and Regulatory Style

These globalization-inspired trends have had several specific effects, and more are likely to arise. The most obvious point concerns regulatory style. Traditionally, Japanese authorities have operated on a preapproval basis both for new types of financial instruments and for specific issues.[61] Preapproval is no longer possible in either instance. For one thing, it is too easy to use international markets or to combine existing financial products in order to skirt prohibitions on specific instruments. More fundamentally, the longtime practice of gaining approval before issuing a new security is excessively time-consuming in an industry where prices change in milliseconds and where even short delays in execution constitute a hindrance to competitiveness with other markets. The result has been a wholesale shift away from preapproval to postnotification, a shift that is finally being completed in the Big Bang. Moreover, in order to have a postnotification system that works efficiently, regulators must have full access to clear and comprehensible financial accounts. This need has strengthened the demand for global standards of accounting, thus weakening one of the most striking idiosyncrasies of Japanese finance—the high degree of informal regulation despite the high level of economic development.

These shifts fundamentally change the role of regulators in Japanese finance. Where before they were often interventionist and could be seen almost as financial actors in their own right, now their function is moving toward a purely regulatory one. In combination with reforms that break down the walls among various types of financial institutions, these changes are likely to shift the overall relationship of firms, regulators, and lawmakers in finance. Where before advantage often could be found by persuading lawmakers to legislate protection or regulators to offer special treatment, in the future such assistance will be helpful only in extremis.

The movement to global standards of regulation has potentially profound implications for firm behavior and structure as well. Financial institutions are being forced to become more "competitive" in a Western sense by focusing on lower costs and more rapid innovation rather than long-term relationships. "Convergence" is often seen as a dirty word in the social sciences, but in high finance, convergence is almost certainly necessary for survival, at least in a few respects, such as labor mobility and corporate governance. Anecdotally, we are already seeing much greater labor mobility among specialists at the top Japanese investment banks and securities houses, and this is likely only to increase. That labor mobility is fueled by results-based pay systems that mimic those of foreign firms.

While there is less pressure for such changes at the retail level, there is at least a possibility that changes in the personnel structure at the elite level will filter down through organizations.[62]

Globalization-induced changes in regulatory style mean potentially far-reaching effects in Japanese politics as well. A great deal of Japanese politicians' time has been spent in trying to influence bureaucrats' enforcement of regulations for specific clients. As regulation becomes more arm's length and transparent, this sort of relationship becomes less beneficial for private sector clients, and thus the old clientelistic ties are likely to be reshaped. Instead of seeking intervention in implementation, firms will have to try to shape regulations themselves. However, insofar as Japan's law-drafting system presents relatively little room for shaping regulations to favor one or two firms, industry groupings should become a more important nexus of pluralistic influence. If such changes weaken the ties between individual politicians and individual firms, it will likely help to change the balance of power between politicians and their parties as well.

From the bureaucrats' point of view, transparency will have drastic effects. If they become primarily the technocratic implementers of clear-cut rules and regulations, their cachet will decline. With less courting by clients and politicians to provide favorable enforcement, their political power will also decline. They will still retain some clout as law drafters, but the more extreme microeconomic incentives that have contributed to bureaucratic power in Japan are under attack because of globalization. None of this is to say that the state will necessarily be less "effective," as the "hyperglobalization school" has suggested.[63] However, the political gains from trade for various types of administrative activities will surely be altered fundamentally.

Most devastating of all will be the effects on weak financial institutions. As the market logic of financial globalization sweeps through Japan, many of these will disappear, either through bankruptcy or through forced mergers. While the struggle to keep them afloat has been a major preoccupation of politicians for decades, the battle is essentially already lost. With their demise, the interests of more efficient financial institutions will take precedence in policymaking. This is, of course, a recipe for continued liberalization in finance, even if we cannot make that prediction nearly as easily for other economic sectors.

CONFRONTING GLOBALIZATION: INTERNATIONALIZATION OF THE YEN

Explaining the Asian Financial Crisis

At the same time that regulators and firms are trying to adjust to globalized financial markets, there is also an increasing recognition that globalization creates greater vulnerabilities at the macroeconomic level. Although policymakers have concluded that it is no longer possible to protect specific financial institutions or even the banking system as a whole from competitive changes, they still hope to be able to protect the overall economy from the increasingly violent swells and troughs of the globalized economy.

The potentially dangerous effects of globalization in finance were brought home to Japan and the world by the Thai currency crisis of July 1997 and the subsequent "contagion" to other markets in Asia and elsewhere.[64] The crisis understandably mobilized a great deal of examination into how such crises could have occurred despite seemingly strong economic fundamentals and whether Japan could have done anything to prevent them. While it is easy to dismiss as extremist or silly those published works that blamed a U.S. plot for Asia's distress,[65] there were also some more serious analyses that argued that the dollar-dominated international financial structure was a major culprit in the troubles.

Specifically, two arguments have been put forward. One is that overreliance on the U.S. dollar among Southeast and Northeast Asian economies (i.e., pegging local currencies to the dollar on a nominal basis) led to very severe consequences for those economies' balances of payments when the yen depreciated relative to the dollar starting in late 1995. The damage done to Asian economies' exports to Japan (and exports elsewhere that competed with Japanese goods and services) led to the inability to sustain currency values and thus to the 1997 crisis. Thus, a greater role of yen in the region would help to stabilize non-Japanese Asian economies at the same time that it would reduce currency risks for Japanese firms and financial institutions.[66]

The second argument is that excessive liberalization of developing economies' financial systems (a result both of globalization and U.S. pressure)[67] was a fundamental cause of the crisis. As developed by the indefatigable Sakakibara Eisuke, the argument goes that this is not simply a problem of excessive liberalization in the undersupervised markets of a few developing countries with thinly traded currencies but rather a "crisis of global capitalism."[68] This argument complements analyses that finger overreliance on the dollar, and it too calls for increased "internationalization" of the yen as a means of reducing the negative effects of financial globalization on the Japanese and regional economies.

Internationalization of the yen means primarily greater regional use of the yen—as a currency for invoicing trade and lending, as a settlement currency in foreign exchange transactions, and in the reserves of states and firms in East and Southeast Asia.[69] While regional use of the yen had increased considerably in the latter 1980s and early 1990s, it has been on a generally downward trend by virtually all measures since 1994.[70] Since regional currencies have not moved with the yen, less use of the yen means greater volatility in earnings and expenses for Japanese firms and financial institutions operating in the region.[71]

From a purely economic standpoint, the evidence is less than convincing that underweighting of the yen in regional currency baskets was a major cause of the recent crisis.[72] Nevertheless, it appears to make good sense for Asian economies not to tie their currencies strictly to the dollar since Japan is roughly equivalent to the United States as a trading partner for the region as a whole as well as for individual countries.[73] If a multicurrency system actually were to buffer the effects of rapid movements of global capital and thus make the region's economies more stable, that would clearly be of positive benefit for both the Japanese and the global economies.

However, there is also an element among some participants in the debate of building an alternative to the globalized, dollar-dominated system rather than just a means of reducing volatility. This is most clearly seen when we consider the concrete measures for which yen internationalization advocates call. Some measures—particularly those of the more economically minded advocates—fit neatly into the globalization/financial liberalization paradigm. For example, in order to make the yen more attractive as a reserve currency, advocates of yen internationalization succeeded in 1999 in carrying out large-scale changes in short-term Japanese government securities markets—in essence, bringing the government bill market in line with "global standards."[74] In addition, the Bank of Japan is studying ways to improve its currency settlement system, and prearranged "swap lines" with Asian central banks are being expanded. All these measures are meant to facilitate the global financial system.

In addition to this market-based, evolutionary approach to yen internationalization, however, other voices call for more activist measures. Emblematic of the activists' ideas is the concept of an "Asian Monetary Fund" (AMF). The idea was first broached by then–Vice Minister of Finance for International Affairs Sakakibara Eisuke in the fall of 1997 in the midst of the Asian financial crisis.[75] While not really fleshed out at the time, it essentially called for a large pool of funds ($100 billion was the number generally mentioned) that could be deployed rapidly to rescue Asian currencies from speculative attack. The justification was that the International Monetary Fund (IMF) was too slow, too stingy, and clearly ill equipped to deal with the kinds of extreme short-term movements of money that can and do occur in an era of globalized finance.[76] An Asian fund (funded mainly by Japan), advocates claim, would act more quickly and decisively.

Despite a lack of support from other states, calls for the establishment of an AMF have not disappeared and continue to have some resonance among some current and former Japanese officials.[77] Less ambitious plans to enhance the regional use of the yen are also popular. They grow from the analysis of many observers that Japanese financial liberalization alone will not be enough to guarantee widespread use of the yen and include a number of other interesting policies and policy proposals. For example, the "New Miyazawa Plan" of lending to East and Southeast Asian countries includes $15 billion in short-term money to help stabilize individual economies' currencies as well as $15 billion in medium- to long-term bilateral aid. While the primary purpose is to aid economies injured by the Asian financial crisis, New Miyazawa Plan funds are intentionally disbursed in yen in order to increase the weight of yen in reserves and in regional transactions.

Non–Miyazawa Plan lending to Asian countries from the Japan Bank for International Cooperation is also being denominated in yen as a matter of policy rather than according to the request of recipient countries or firms.[78]

It is not clear that these measures will achieve their goals, nor is it clear that Japan is prepared for the leadership role they will require. Nonetheless, they constitute a rather active agenda on the part of Japanese policymakers to insulate Japan from the "crisis of global capitalism." Thus, some advocates are trying to use regionalization as a hedge against globalization, in contrast to Samuel Kim's general point about the mutually reinforcing nature of regionalization and globalization in chapter 1. From whatever angle, the whole public debate on internationalization of the yen amounts to an intellectual struggle to find a way to insulate Japan in some way from the dangerous effects of financial globalization. This is true both for those analysts who feel besieged by globalization in general and for those who are just looking for a technocratic fix to a specific problem raised by a specific pattern of financial globalization. As one advocate of an Asian Monetary Fund put it recently, "Unless Asian countries have a strategic concept to defend themselves and the region from capital and financial 'globalism,' they will again be taken advantage of by international capital, and will again suffer from crisis and confusion."[79]

Globalization and the Quest
for a New International Financial Architecture

In addition to this active regional agenda, the Japanese government (in the persons of Finance Minister Miyazawa and his former international deputy, Sakakibara) has been uncharacteristically active in pushing better international regulation and governance of the global financial system. These efforts to move insulation to a supranational level constitute a recognition of the limited capability of states to regulate their own money in a world of globalized finance. The main foci of Japan's efforts have been on increasing the amount of international funds available to deal with future crises, stricter regulation of hedge funds, and, most controversially, international acceptance of capital controls for developing countries.

An analysis of published Japanese proposals and of speeches by Miyazawa and Sakakibara in 1998 and 1999 makes clear that Japan has been far more interested in carrying out these reforms than its G-7 partners.[80] While Japanese proposals for increasing international funds have been at least partly accepted in the form of the new IMF Contingent Credit Lines (CCL), the constraints on access remain more stringent than the Japanese side originally proposed. Indeed, the basic requirement for accessing the CCL is strict adherence to specific global standards of information disclosure, financial supervision, and macroeconomic management.[81] In terms of hedge-fund regulation and capital controls, Japanese proposals have met with less acceptance. The Cologne Economic Summit communiqué of June 1999 offers only further study for the former and is decidedly negative on the latter.[82]

The promotion of capital controls is particularly meaningful insofar as it represents an attempt to get global regulators to return some degree of control to states—a reversal of the process by which states have been losing control over their domestic economies in the face of global financial pressures. Broadly speaking, in all these efforts the Japanese government's objectives have stemmed from a comprehensive view of the dangers of financial globalization. This decidedly pessimistic view is most fully developed in Sakakibara's 1998 book on the subject, a book that paints a clear picture of globalization's harmful impacts on local and regional cultures and societies. Nonetheless, economically and socially harmful though globalization is, Japan's leaders have decided that it must be embraced in the realm of finance. Even Japan's advocacy of limited capital controls for developing economies is meant only to dampen some of globalization's effects rather than to turn the tide.

CONCLUSION

Japan's recent experience of globalization has been fundamentally different from that of 1980s-style internationalization. Internationalization then was at its core a process of moving from a position of domestic strength into a world of opportunities. In contrast, globalization forces its way inward. Japanese firms are now fundamentally incapable of controlling the pace of their own exposure to globalization, leading to the fin de siècle anxiety that is so evident in the domestic discourse. This is perhaps the first time since the end of the U.S. occupation that Japan's corporate leaders and policymakers have been unable to control or take advantage of rapid change in the global economy. Thus, globalization now represents constraint rather than opportunity and challenges the very effectiveness of the state.

This is particularly true in finance. For most of the postwar era, Japanese finance was a highly regulated industry, characterized by strict segregation of institutions by function. Although it supported Japan's most advanced industries, it was itself one of the most backward sectors. Thus, it has been particularly jarring for it to encounter the new world of finance—certainly the most globalized and technologically driven service industry of the new, global economy.

The Japanese state has mounted a three-pronged response to financial globalization: reluctant acceptance of global standards at home, attempts to insulate Japan from globalization-induced shocks at the regional level through internationalization of the yen, and attempts to improve international financial regulation and safeguards at the global level. All three grow out of a profound suspicion about globalization, which remains a foreign concept but which can no longer be evaded in the area of finance.

Financial globalization is combining with long-term economic stagnation to force other economic changes. More competitive, securities-based finance creates greater shareholder demand for profits, pressuring firms to cut long-term supplier, customer, and credit relationships that are no longer economically efficient and to shed their holdings of stock in related companies that are not performing well. These changes are likely to have a self-accelerating effect: The larger the percentage of firms' outstanding shares held by nonstable shareholders, the more important will become rates of return, thus forcing them to sell shares in affiliated firms and so on. Corporate management will also need to seek higher profits by lowering costs generally. In an economy that is heavily burdened by underutilized workers, this is likely to mean reductions in workforce.[83]

This is not all to say that Japan is converging toward an "Anglo-Saxon" economic model, but it does suggest an erosion of the public and private structures that have cushioned Japanese society from external shocks in the past. This is as true of social issues—especially labor adjustment and immigration—as it is of economic ones. In order to be effective in a globalizing world, the Japanese state will need to stop reacting to shocks by protecting established economic networks. Instead, the state should turn toward more arm's-length regulation based on outcome rather than procedure—as it already has in some areas of finance—while providing help in the direction of positive adjustment to globalizing society and markets.

NOTES

1. See Kent Calder, "Japanese Foreign Economic Policy Formation: Explaining the Reactive State," *World Politics* 40, no. 4 (July 1988): 517–41; Leonard Schoppa, *Bargaining with Japan: What American Pressure Can and Cannot Do* (New York: Columbia University Press, 1997).

2. Sahoko Kaji, "La fin du Japon que nous avons connu," *l'Economie Politique,* no. 6 (2e trimestre 2000): 83–93 (also available as "The End of Japan as We Have Known It," Keio Economic Society Discussion Paper 9912; available at <kes@econ.keio.ac.jp>). Sakakibara Eisuke, *Kokusai kin'yu no genba: Shihonshugi no kiki o koete* (The arena of international finance: Moving beyond the crisis of capitalism) (Tokyo: PHP Shinsho, 1998).

3. Japanese Ministry of Foreign Affairs, *1998 Diplomatic White Paper* (available at <www.mofa.go.jp/policy/other/bluebook/1998>). The quotations are from sections II.B.1(a)(i) and (ii).

4. In discussing the "debate," I am concentrating primarily on opinion-leading journals, such as *Bungei Shunju, Chuo Koron, and Sekai,* and on popular trade books. In general, these sources track newspaper reporting and elite public opinion rather closely. Even the scandal-mongering weeklies generally reflect the arguments that appear in the elite monthlies, although tending to be more reactionary and conspiracy oriented. My discussion of the debate is based on broad reading in the Japanese press; this chapter is not the place for a rigorous and full-scale content analysis.

5. International Monetary Fund, *International Financial Statistics*; *Japan Statistical Yearbook 1999*, table 12-14.

6. Management and Coordinating Agency, *Japan Statistical Yearbook 1999*, table 2-33; Ministry of Posts and Telecommunications, *Communications White Paper 1999* (available at <www.mpt.go.jp>).

7. For numbers and some relevant issues, see Jorge V. Tigno, "ASEAN Labor Migration: Strategic Implications for Japan in Southeast Asia," *Asian Migrant* 10, no. 3 (July–September 1997): 86–89; and Kenichi Furuya, "Labor Migration and Skill Development: Japan's Trainee Program," *Asian Migrant* 18, no. 1 (January–March 1995): 4–13.

8. "Diet Spotlight on Vote for Foreigners," *Asahi Evening News*, November 2, 1999, 1.

9. Saskia Sassen, *Losing Control? Sovereignty in an Age of Globalization* (New York: Columbia University Press, 1996), esp. 34–39.

10. For details on all the recent financial mergers, see the special issue of *Ekonomisuto* entitled "140 *cho en ginko tanjo e*" (Toward the birth of the ¥140 trillion bank), October 31, 1999. The others have been reported extensively in the U.S. and Japanese business presses, and details can be found easily through Lexis searches.

11. Dani Rodrik, *Has Globalization Gone Too Far?* (Washington, D.C.: Institute for International Economics, 1997).

12. Rodrik, *Has Globalization Gone Too Far?*, chap. 4.

13. Benjamin Barber, *Jihad vs. McWorld* (New York: Times Books, 1995); see also Sassen, *Losing Control?*

14. See, for example, Morinaga Takuro, "*Mazu keieijin mizukara chinsage o fukumu risutora o danko shi, genba no koyo o mamorubeshi*" (First boldly carry out restructuring that cuts executive pay, but protect employment), in *Nihon no Ronten 2000* (Tokyo: Bungei Shunju, 1999), 432–35.

15. "*Shitusgyoritu josho no genjo to taisaku o kento suru tame no kiso chishiki*" (Basic knowledge for discussing the rise in unemployment and policies to address it), in *Nihon no Ronten 2000*, 440–43.

16. Takenaka Heizo and Chida Ryokichi, "Japan," in Charles E. Morrison and Hadi Soesastro, eds., *Domestic Adjustments to Globalization* (Tokyo: Japan Center for International Exchange, 1998), 91.

17. Walter Hatch and Kozo Yamamura, *Asia in Japan's Embrace: Building a Regional Production Alliance* (Cambridge: Cambridge University Press, 1996); Dieter Ernst, "Mobilizing the Region's Capacities? The East Asian Production Networks of Japanese Electronics Firms," in Eileen Doherty, ed., *Japanese Investment in Asia: International Production Strategies in a Rapidly Changing World* (Berkeley, Calif.: BRIE, 1994).

18. See "*Shitusgyoritu josho no genjo to taisaku o kento suru tame no kiso chishiki*," 443; see also Cabinet Economic Policy Council, "*Keizai shinsei taisaku*" (Plan for economic rebirth) (mimeograph), 4–7.

19. "Nissan's Planned Cuts Arouse Ire and Offers of Help in Japan," *New York Times*, October 20, 1999, C4.

20. G. John Ikenberry, *Reasons of State: Oil Politics and the Capacities of American Government* (Ithaca, N.Y.: Cornell University Press, 1988); Nobuhiro Hiwatari, "The Domestic Sources of U.S.-Japan Economic Relations" (paper presented at the annual meeting of the American Political Science Association, August 1996).

21. Kaneko Masaru, "*Gurobarisumu to iu yojutsu*" (The sorcery of globalism), *Shokun!*, December 1999, 51.

22. Masaru, "*Gurobarisumu to iu yojutsu*," 51–54.

23. See Sakakibara, *Kokusai,* esp. chap. 5.

24. A good example is Takenaka Heizo, *Keiseisaimin* (Government for the good of the people) (Tokyo: Diamondsha, 1999), chap. 4. This book reflects Takenaka's work on the government-commissioned Higuchi Report.

25. See, for example, Andrew Gordon, "Scaring the Salaryman Isn't the Japanese Way," *New York Times,* October 30, 1999, A27.

26. See, among others, Sakakibara, *Kokusai,* and Sakakibara Eisuke, "*Rotei shi tsutsu aru gurobaru shihonshugi no kekkan—ima Nihon wa nani o subeki ka?*" (The defects of global capitalism exposed—What should Japan do now?), in *Nihon no Ronten 1999,* 58–66.

27. These have been considerable, with swings of up to 80 percent in dollar terms and over 40 percent in terms of real effective exchange rate (Bank of Japan data; available at <www. boj.or.jp/en/down>).

28. For one rather eccentric example, see Research Project Team for Japanese Systems, *Japanese Systems: An Alternative Civilization?* (Tokyo: Sekotac, 1992).

29. One such work is Ken'ichi Ohmae, *The Borderless World: Power and Strategy in the Interlinked Economy* (New York: HarperBusiness, 1990).

30. Sakakibara, *Kokusai,* and "*Rotei.*" The food reference is in *Kokusai,* 168–72.

31. On the Yen-Dollar Agreement, see Jeffrey A. Frankel, *The Yen/Dollar Agreement: Liberalizing Japanese Capital Markets* (Washington, D.C.: Institute for International Economics, 1984), and Frances McCall Rosenbluth, *Financial Politics in Contemporary Japan* (Ithaca, N.Y.: Cornell University Press, 1989), chap. 3. For the period of the yen's rapid rise, see Yoichi Funabashi, *Managing the Dollar: From the Plaza to the Louvre* (Washington, D.C.: Institute for International Economics, 1988).

32. This rapid ascendance led to real alarm among many Americans and Europeans, as evidenced by the publication of such books as Daniel Burstein's *Yen!: Japan's New Financial Empire and Its Threat to America* (New York: Simon & Schuster, 1988).

33. Steven K. Vogel, *Freer Markets, More Rules: Regulatory Reform in Advanced Industrial Countries* (Ithaca, N.Y.: Cornell University Press, 1996), chap. 1.

34. Vogel, *Freer Markets, More Rules,* chap. 1.

35. Jeffrey Frieden and Ronald Rogowski, "The Impact of the International Economy on National Policies: An Analytical Overview," in Robert Keohane and Helen Milner, eds., *Internationalization and Domestic Politics* (Cambridge: Cambridge University Press, 1996), 25–47.

36. For the specific cases, see James Horne, *Japan's Financial Markets: Conflict and Consensus in Policymaking* (London: George Allen & Unwin, 1985); Rosenbluth, *Financial Politics in Contemporary Japan;* and Vogel, *Freer Markets, More Rules.*

37. For an incisive discussion of "strategic reregulation," see Vogel, *Freer Markets, More Rules,* chap. 1.

38. Ethan Kapstein, *Supervising International Banks: Origins and Implications of the Basle Accord* (Princeton University Essays in International Finance 185, 1991).

39. Kapstein, *Supervising International Banks.*

40. Personal interviews.

41. For economic and political overviews of reforms prior to the 1998–2001 "Big Bang," see Frankel, *The Yen/Dollar Agreement;* Horne, *Japan's Financial Markets;* Rosenbluth, *Financial Politics in Contemporary Japan;* and Vogel, *Freer Markets, More*

Rules. See also S. Eijfinger and A. van Rixtel, "The Japanese Financial System and Monetary Policy: A Descriptive Review," *Japan and the World Economy* 4, no. 4 (December 1992): 291–309.

42. Nakakita Toru, *Nihon ginko: Shijoka jidai no sentaku* (The Bank of Japan: Choices in the era of marketization) (Tokyo: PHP Shinsho, 1999), makes an especially strong case that relaxations of the foreign exchange law prior to 1998 were only marginal, although other observers have been more impressed by earlier reforms.

43. See, for example, Nakakita, *Nihon ginko;* Elizabeth Norville, "The 'Illiberal' Roots of Japanese Financial Regulatory Reform," in Lonny E. Carlile and Mark C. Tilton, eds., *Is Japan Really Changing Its Ways? Regulatory Reform and the Japanese Economy* (Washington, D.C.: Brookings Institution, 1998), 111–31.

44. Dick Beason and Jason James, *The Political Economy of Japanese Financial Markets: Myth vs. Reality* (New York: St. Martin's, 1999), chap. 3.

45. Time and demand deposits account for 56 percent of households' financial assets, while insurance policies amounted to about 30 percent, according to the *Japan Statistical Yearbook 1999,* table 16-10.

46. For an alarmist contemporary view, see Burstein, *Yen!*

47. BIS statistics quoted in Koichi Ito, *A Proposal for Reform of the International Currency System* (Harvard University Program on U.S.-Japan Relations Occasional Paper, 1998).

48. It is difficult to get firm empirical evidence on this question, but the anecdotal evidence is very strong. From my own limited perspective, I can say that this statement is consistent with the experiences of at least a dozen personal friends in Tokyo and elsewhere.

49. Again, I am forced to rely on the experiences of friends and acquaintances in Tokyo.

50. Vogel, *Freer Markets, More Rules.*

51. For an overview of the Big Bang reforms, see Beason and James, *The Political Economy of Japanese Financial Markets,* chaps. 7, 8.

52. Hokkaido Takushoku was not the first bank to go under in the postwar era—that honor went to Hyogo Bank in 1996, and a number of other regional banks and credit cooperatives had also gone bust before November 1997. Nonetheless, Hokkaido Takushoku Bank was a city bank and one of the top twenty banks in the country in terms of assets.

53. Japanese businesses have often been loath to fully disclose their financial conditions or business activities, creating a considerable market for blackmail based on corporate dirty laundry. Recently, the combination of stricter law enforcement and technological development has created an ingenious idea: a Web page where paying members have access to secret information about companies that have chosen not to pay (see <www.rondan.co.jp> to sample some such information that has been made available to the public).

54. Of course, when a specific foreign government is mentioned, it is invariably the United States; see, for example, Kaneko, "*Gurobarisumu to iu yojutsu.*"

55. Ishihara Shintaro, "Writer Ishihara Blames US for Asian Crisis," *Bungei Shunju,* August 1998, 110–24 (FBIS online translation).

56. See, for example, Nakakita, *Nihon ginko,* 198–215.

57. Nakakita, *Nihon ginko,* 198.

58. "*Gaishi kin'yu kikan sekken no rekishi*" (The history of conquest by foreign financial institutions), *Kin'yu Bijinesu,* December 1999, 6–9. The revealing subtitle is "A Mirror Reflecting the Emptiness of Japanese Finance and Accounting."

59. Sakakibara, *Kokusai*.

60. Heather Montgomery, "The Effect of the Basle Accord on Bank Portfolios in Japan," (unpublished paper, revised November 1999).

61. See, for example, Eijfinger and van Rixtel, "The Japanese Financial System and Monetary Policy."

62. This does not mean that the retail level does not have far too many employees. See William W. Grimes, "Japan's Worrisome Workfare," *Japan Digest*, April 19, 1999, 24.

63. Samuel Kim, "Korea and Globalization (*Segyehwa*): A Framework for Analysis," in Samuel Kim, *Korea's Globalization* (Cambridge: Cambridge University Press, 2000).

64. For overviews and a preliminary view of contagion effects, see Morris Goldstein, *The Asian Financial Crisis: Causes, Cures, and Systemic Implications* (Washington, D.C.: Institute for International Economics, 1998), and Marcus Noland, Li-Gang Liu, Sherman Robinson, and Zhi Wang, *Global Economic Effects of the Asian Currency Devaluations* (Washington, D.C.: Institute for International Economics, 1998). For a Japanese perspective, see Masaru Yoshitomi and Kenichi Ohno, *Capital-Account Crisis and Credit Contraction* (Tokyo: Asian Development Bank Institute, May 1999).

65. See, for example, Ishihara, "Writer Ishihara Blames US for Asian Crisis."

66. This argument is the premise of the analyses in Foreign Exchange Council, "Internationalization of the Yen for the twenty-first Century: Japan's Response to Changes in Global Economic and Financial Environments," April 20, 1999; Institute for International Monetary Affairs, *Internationalization of the Yen: Implications for Stabilization of Financial Systems and Currencies in Asia* (Tokyo: Institute for International Monetary Affairs, March 1999), and *Stabilization of Currencies and Financial Systems in East Asia and International Financial Cooperation* (Tokyo: Institute for International Monetary Affairs, March 1999); and Sakakibara, *Kokusai*.

67. The point about U.S. pressure can also be found in the *New York Times* series of articles authored by Nicholas Kristof that ran from February 15 to 18, 1999.

68. Sakakibara, *Kokusai*.

69. Foreign Exchange Council, "Internationalization of the Yen for the Twenty-first Century," appendix, 4.

70. See the various graphs and tables in Foreign Exchange Council, "Internationalization of the Yen for the Twenty-first Century," appendix, 11–45.

71. Kenichi Ohno, *Exchange Rate Management in Developing Asia* (Tokyo: Asian Development Bank Institute, January 1999).

72. Kenichi Ohno, in *Exchange Rate Management in Developing Asia,* makes the econometric case. Put briefly, the effects of incorrect weighting were far outstripped by countries' adherence to a nominal rather than a real peg. Ohno does not address the decline in Japanese demand for imports independently of movements in exchange rates.

73. According to Foreign Exchange Council figures, Japan accounts for 16 percent of the trade of the nine major non-Japanese East Asian economies, the United States for 17 percent, and the fifteen economies of the European Union for 14 percent ("Internationalization of the Yen for the Twenty-first Century," appendix, table III-1).

74. These changes included a liberalization in pricing (public auction rather than fixed price), the elimination of tax withholding and taxation at the source for foreign purchasers, and the elimination of the Securities Transaction Tax; see Foreign Exchange Council, *Internationalization of the Yen for the Twenty-first Century;* Kimura Shigeki, "'En no kokusaika' ni tsuite kangaeru" (Thinking about "internationalization of the yen"), *Fainansu,*

January 1999, 37–43; Ministry of Finance, "En no kokusaika no suishinsaku ni tsuite" (Policies to promote internationalization of the yen) (mimeograph, December 22, 1998). Short-term government securities markets are particularly important for foreign-reserve holdings because they are extremely liquid and bear no default risk.

75. See, for example, James Kynge and Gillian Tett, "Asian Monetary Fund Debate Hots Up," *Financial Times,* November 14, 1997, 3.

76. For a balanced overview of this phenomenon, see Barry Eichengreen, "The Asian Financial Crisis: The IMF and Its Critics," in *Great Decisions 1999* (Washington, D.C.: Foreign Policy Institute, 1999), 19–29.

77. Personal interviews, August and November 1999.

78. Official publications on the New Miyazawa Plan can be found at <www.mof. go.jp/english/if/sien.htm>; see also Kishimoto Shuhei, "Shin Miyazawa koso no shimei to Ajia tsuka kikin" (The mission of the New Miyazawa Plan, and the Asian Monetary Fund), *Fainansu,* May 1999, 31–48.

79. Shinohara Hajime, "The End of Globalism," *Kokusai Kin'yu,* no. 1031 (September 1, 1999): 26.

80. A sampling of relevant speeches can be found in English on the Ministry of Finance home page at <www.mof.go.jp/english/if/system.htm>.

81. For details, see International Monetary Fund, "IMF Tightens Defenses against Financial Contagion by Establishing Contingent Credit Lines," Press Release 99/14, April 25, 1999 (available at <www.imf.org/external/np/sec/pr/1999/pr9914.htm>).

82. "Strengthening the International Financial Architecture: Report of G7 Finance Ministers to the Koln Economic Summit" (Cologne, June 18–20, 1999) (available at <www.mof.go.jp/english/if/system.htm>).

83. Grimes, "Japan's Worrisome Workfare."

4

South Korea and Globalization: The Rise to Globalism?

Barry K. Gills and Dong-Sook S. Gills

THE KOREAN CONCEPTION OF GLOBALIZATION

It is commonly accepted that South Korea is undergoing a dual transition: from authoritarianism to democracy and from a developmentalist model to a liberal free-market system. Assessment of the relationship between "globalization," democracy, and restructuring in South Korea requires analysis of the reconfiguration of state–capital–labor relations. There are two primary interpretations of globalization that have informed recent changes in South Korea in the 1990s. First, there is a broad notion of globalization as a fulfilment of mature development in all aspects, including an acceptance of international norms as practiced by the most developed societies and international rules established multilaterally.

This broad notion of globalization implies a national change in perceptions of the world, abandoning narrow parochialism and isolationist nationalism and embracing a more internationalist or even cosmopolitan sense of identity, rights, and obligations. Such an understanding applies to virtually every aspect of social life, from politics to economics to culture. Everything from women's rights to welfare and social security, computer literacy, knowledge of the English language, and attitude to foreigners is affected.

The second interpretation of globalization in South Korea focuses on the national economic system and specifically on the idea that competition should be the guiding principle both domestically and internationally. The thrust of this type of globalization is to bring about a "level playing field" between domestic and international finance and enterprises. Initially, large Korean companies sought to take advantage of this opportunity to further encourage their emergence as fully fledged multinational corporations operating on a global scale. However, the government, especially that of President Kim Dae Jung, has tended to interpret this idea as a means of exposing domestic firms to increasing foreign competition and thereby of breaking the oligopolistic position of the giant firms, the *chaebol*, in

the domestic economy. Therefore, in the South Korean case, corporate deconcentration emerges as the central issue of globalization.

Corporate deconcentration is directly related to important changes not only in
the relationship between the state and capital but also in the role of organized
labor in the political and economic system. Organized labor, long suppressed
under the previous developmentalist model, seeks to extend its rights within the
new context of democratization. Above all, labor desires to consolidate and legitimate a new social and political role, asserting its right to participate in corporate and government policymaking. However, there is inherent conflict among
labor, government, and business interests, as labor strongly resists the negative
impact of globalization and restructuring on employment and living standards.

The national division of Korea and the anticommunism of the South undermined the position of organized labor over the past several decades. Militance by
South Korean labor was often attributed to pro–North Korean sympathies and
therefore was treated as a serious threat to national security. Democratization,
particularly under President Kim Dae Jung, has begun to include a gradual soft-
ening of domestic anticommunism in respect to organized labor. This change is
in parallel with a more conciliatory approach to relations with North Korea. The
shift reflects broader changes in the regional situation, including the end of the
Cold War, the emergence of China, and the severe economic crisis in communist
North Korea.

GLOBALIZATION AS ADVANCED-NATION STATUS

South Korea's interpretation of globalization in the 1990s has involved formulating far-reaching programs of domestic change designed to enable it to take its
place among the most advanced countries. President Kim Young Sam's vision of
globalization embraced a wide range of reforms, including transparency of transactions, fair competition, financial deregulation, tax reform, industrial relations
reform, expansion of social security, and political and administrative reform.
Economic growth alone was insufficient and had to be "accompanied by an
equally substantial endeavour for balanced and equitable social development."[1]

The best example of this comprehensive approach was the Globalization Commission (*Segyehwa Ch'ujin Wiwonhoe*), which was established by Kim Young
Sam on January 21, 1995. Led by Prime Minister Lee Hong-koo, its membership
was composed of representatives from government ministries, research institutes,
academia, and "socially eminent persons." The range of the tasks that the commission undertook was indeed very extensive, including six major areas of reform: education, legal and economic, politics and mass media, national and local
administration, environment, and culture.

The sweeping rhetoric that characterized Kim Young Sam's *segyehwa* policy
set a broad agenda for change that remains important, at least as a set of goal

posts. Many elements of this agenda continue in the present administration of Kim Dae Jung, whose slogans include the "reconstruction of the nation," the "parallel development of democracy and market economy," and "opening a new era through structural reform."[2]

Implementation of this broad agenda has been quite limited, however. For example, Kim Young Sam's *segyehwa* was more sloganistic than substantive. Social insurance reform, for example, consisted of a very modest expansion of coverage for the indigent [3] and the computerization of the social security system. Overall, the reforms in welfare were insufficient in scope, depth, and speed. No consequential measures followed to support the announcement of the welfare state. Republic of Korea (ROK) social welfare spending remained the lowest in the OECD (Organization for Economic Cooperation and Development) countries except on education.[4] Government appealed to private business to become more involved in employee welfare, primarily on a workfare basis.

The failure sufficiently to expand the social safety net during the Kim Young Sam period left Korean workers badly exposed when the subsequent economic crisis in 1997–1998 brought high unemployment. President Kim Dae Jung was compelled to increase government spending on unemployment and related benefits in the context of the national economic crisis. Coverage of unemployment insurance was extended to companies hiring five or more employees, from ten or more, and the minimum payment period was extended from thirty to sixty days. Funds were also earmarked for retraining schemes. Reform of the "social safety net" has remained an important element of globalization under President Kim Dae Jung. However, the grandiose agenda of social transformation through globalization is translated at a practical level into structural reform, particularly corporate restructuring, to which we now turn.

GLOBALIZATION AS ECONOMIC RESTRUCTURING

Creating a New Development Model

The second interpretation of globalization, where economic restructuring is central, relies on a perception of external challenge and historical necessity. An external environment increasingly characterized by demands for market opening, technological innovation, and increased capital mobility requires national adjustments in order to sustain international competitiveness. The origins of South Korea's export-oriented industrialization and its developmental state model arose in a particular historical conjuncture in the 1960s, when the world economy was expanding and the New International Division of Labour was emerging.[5] This produced an economic structure very heavily dependent on international trade. Indeed, at 75 percent in 1998, South Korea's trade-to-GDP ratio is one of the highest in the world.

Globalization over the past decade has been stimulated by further reorganization of global production and finance systems, emphasizing greater openness and integration. Kim Young Sam described globalization as a "global trend" and an era of "a borderless global economy" in which "room for asserting national sovereignty in economic affairs is sharply diminishing."[6] This interpretation seems to encourage the transition from the developmental state to a liberal market economy. However, South Korea's "strategic choice" over globalization policy has never been about whether to "open" to the global economy but rather precisely how to organize the sequence of reforms, namely, external opening versus domestic corporate restructuring.[7]

In practice, rather than creating a new model, Kim Young Sam's policies maintained and perhaps even strengthened the status quo of endemic state–*chaebol* collusion. His government failed fully to implement domestic economic restructuring, particularly in the crucial area of corporate deconcentration. In a retrospective on the lessons of the global crisis of 1997–1998, the International Monetary Fund (IMF) has concluded that although capital market opening and financial liberalization remain desirable and beneficial for development, each government must carefully assess its own situation, make careful preparations, and ensure a proper sequence of reforms.[8]

Kim Dae Jung's government emphasizes the necessity of making "a decisive break with the previous state-led development model" since "in the age of globalization, mercantilist notions based on the idea of an independent national economy have no place."[9] This means that the present government "is determined to overhaul the government-big business-banking triad," which the government sees as the root cause of the recent financial crisis. In other words, Kim uses globalization partly as an exigency through which radically to alter the state–capital relationship. Once again, structural reform of the financial and corporate sectors becomes the central element of globalization under Kim's administration.

President Kim seeks to establish a competitive capitalist model aligned to current trends of globalization. His government wants to reconfigure the state–capital alliance by aggressively emphasizing deconcentration measures aimed at breaking the *chaebol*'s stranglehold on the national economic structure. Politically, this has taken the form of a national corporatist experiment, seeking not only to expand the social safety net and welfare system but also to incorporate organized labor into the state's decision-making process concerning economic restructuring.

The Kim Dae Jung government has used the strategic window of opportunity presented by the so-called IMF crisis to tighten constraints on the *chaebol* and revive the economy via drastic restructuring. This has proceeded first in the financial and banking sector of the economy, which proved rapidly successful in stabilizing the banking sector but presented new difficulties in relation to curbing the financial and economic power of *chaebol*.[10]

Corporate Deconcentration and the *Chaebol*

The *chaebol*, the growth of which was actively fostered under the regime of Park Jung Hee, had once been considered an asset for the disciplining of industrial investment and pursuit of international export advantages. Developmentalist principles of state regulation of the economy, such as price stabilization, prevention of "excessive competition," and "reinforcement of competitiveness," had worked to protect the monopolistic status of enterprises and legitimize business combinations. All this facilitated concentration and thereby hampered "market competition," technological innovation, and productivity gains.[11]

Having attained a dominant position in the national economy by the 1970s, the tail began to wag the dog. The power of the *chaebol* began to challenge the power of the state. Over the past twenty years since the assassination of Park Jung Hee in 1979, the struggle for power between the *chaebol* and the state has been a fundamental underlying feature of the political economy of South Korea. The autonomy of the developmental state and its capacity to constrain the *chaebol* in their relentless pursuit of expansion have been seriously curtailed by "money politics," that is, the financial dependence of politicians on the *chaebol*. As the state weakened, it was in danger of becoming a mere instrument of big capital.

By the mid-1990s, the *chaebol* were increasingly recognized as a liability by both economists and the public. The traditional government–*chaebol* alliance, which involved government financial collusion with business, was plagued by increasing corruption and corporate debt. This created fundamental weaknesses in the national financial system. The role of the *chaebol* in promoting national industrial health and economic growth came into question as capital fled from productive industrial investment into *Jai-tech* ("financialization") and speculation. The litany of *chaebol* sins included their ambitious but reckless investment strategies, antiquated management structures, confrontational industrial relations, private family financial control, dangerous financial practices (e.g., the mutual guarantee system), hidden debt structure, and rent-seeking behavior.

Moreover, the threat of increased unemployment and deindustrialization loomed as Korean companies relocated production abroad. In October 1995, the government imposed more stringent financial requirements for Korean firms investing overseas, although with little real impact. The problem of capital flight was addressed partly by a decision to accelerate liberalization of foreign investment into Korea in hopes of attracting new technologies and thereby sustaining international competitiveness.

South Korean liberal economists long argued that constraints on the *chaebol* and active promotion of small and medium-size enterprises (SMEs) were indispensable to achieving a pluralistic competitive national economic structure. Giving a greater role to SMEs depends on effective measures to limit the powers of the *chaebol*. Thus, the precondition to achieve vigorous domestic competition and fair trade is the implementation of effective regulation to prohibit monopolistic or oligopolistic business practices. Despite the existence of formal rules governing the establishment of cartels, many loopholes in the regulatory system have allowed the *chaebol* to circumvent restrictions, especially in the finance and insurance sectors.

In contrast, some argued that the policy of accelerated economic liberalization and external opening could in itself be an effective means of bringing about needed reform in the domestic economic structure. For example, in anticipation of membership in the World Trade Organization (WTO), the Economic Planning Board took the view that the goal was an "open and fair competition system," which required "ceasing its practice of market intervention and removing regulations which had become entrenched in the past when concerns regarding market failure were much greater."[12] The guidelines included the further liberalization of finance, foreign direct investment, agriculture, and fisheries. If forced to choose, the *chaebol* preferred a policy of external economic opening, first to one of vigorous corporate deconcentration.

However, the sequence of reform in which external opening occurred before deconcentration ran the risk of further entrenching the *chaebol*. This, in turn, reduced the scope for domestic restructuring. Moreover, it entailed increased risks of macroeconomic destabilization from external shocks, particularly in or via the financial sector of the economy. The debts incurred by the *chaebol* to finance their continued breakneck pace of expansion in the mid-1990s mounted to dangerously unsustainable levels. South Korea's total external liabilities increased from $43.8 billion in 1993 to $154 billion by late 1997, when the financial crisis erupted with full ferocity. As Korea's debt-to-equity ratios among the leading *chaebol* skyrocketed, so did its competitiveness ratings plummet, from sixth place in 1993 to a dismal thirty-fifth by 1998.[13]

President Kim Young Sam's initial deconcentration policy pursued the real-name financial disclosure system, a reform that his predecessor, Roh Tae Woo, had abandoned. The policy also included a battery of measures, such as the "core company system" or specialization policy, credit control restrictions on borrowing and *chaebol* financial holdings in private commercial banks, limitations on the expansion of *chaebol* subsidiaries, limitations on equity holdings by *chaebol* family members, efforts to separate ownership and management of large firms, and restrictions on cross-payment guarantees. The chaebol were pressured to produce greater efficiency gains and to commit increased resources to research and development.

These deconcentration measures and attempts to root out corrupt practices met considerable resistance. They made part of the middle classes uneasy, reviving a conservative backlash against reform. Most significant, the deconcentration program was met by a "strike by capital," with overall economic growth falling to 3.4 percent in 1993, the lowest since the severe recession of 1980–1981. This prompted a reverse course by the president. To restore business confidence, Kim Young Sam implored *chaebol* leaders to resume investment in manufacturing and solicited their involvement in national infrastructural projects. Nevertheless, the 1996 Globalization Commission report still recommended measures for deconcentration and acknowledged the need to prepare a legal foundation to prevent monopoly behavior.

The IMF Crisis and Kim Dae Jung's Response

In the autumn of 1997, there was an abrupt change in the national economic situation, turning sharply from growth to crisis. After a series of major corporate bankruptcies in South Korea (e.g., Kia Automobiles and Hanbo Steel) and currency crises in Thailand and Indonesia, South Korea's foreign-exchange reserves dropped precipitously, prompting a full-scale financial crisis and the necessity of massive IMF assistance. This financial debacle, which resulted partly from government inaction until it was too late to prevent, revealed all the deep structural problems in the banking and corporate sectors. The crisis was suddenly exacerbated by an acute short-term credit crunch, as mobile capital (especially short term) fled from Korea, and by speculative attacks on the value of the national currency, the won.

In response, the government of South Korea struck an agreement with the IMF on December 3, 1997, on a rescue package of nearly $60 billion, the largest in history. The agreement stipulated far-reaching reforms in the financial sector, accelerated liberalization of trade and investment, and called for radical corporate restructuring measures. The IMF rescue package initially entailed sharp budget cuts, higher interest rates and taxation, and reduced growth. These deflationary austerity measures set off a national unemployment crisis and a deepened recession.

Immediate legislative action was taken in response to the financial crisis. The National Assembly passed a package of financial reform bills on December 29, 1997, that established the independent Financial Supervisory Commission (FSC), liberalized foreign ownership in the Korean stock market, and enforced the independence of the central bank. The aim was "the end of government-controlled financial resource allocation" and the restoration of foreign-investor confidence in the Korean economy.

The dawning of the "IMF crisis" coincided with a historic political transition. Kim Dae Jung was the first opposition party candidate to be elected president since the founding of the ROK in 1948. He explicitly identified the source of the economic crisis as the corrupt relationships of traditional government–business collusion (*jungkyong yuchaek*) and the failure of the old state-led development model. Therefore, he set about to impose a new state interventionism, aimed specifically at the *chaebol,* to force restructuring in both the industrial and the financial sectors. The flagships in this campaign are the Financial Supervisory Commission and the Fair Trade Commission, both of which have been deliberately strengthened with presidential support. At the same time, Kim further opened the doors to foreign investment and accepted the need for Korea to adopt international/IMF norms on transparency of corporate governance. His administration took the view that the IMF prescriptions for Korea were basically sound but that there was a need to negotiate on certain parameters, such as the interest rate and the fiscal deficit.

The free-market philosophy and vision of a competitive economy embraced by the government of Kim Dae Jung is not really different in principle from that of the previous government. Market forces, including foreign capital, were not sufficiently in operation to ensure competitiveness and reduce structural distortions in the economy. However, whereas Kim Young Sam was unable to implement corporate deconcentration measures effectively, the Kim Dae Jung government appears to have both the opportunity and the will to pursue this goal with vigor. As previously, however, economic liberalization is the easier of the two to achieve, and corporate restructuring remains fraught with difficulty because of *chaebol* resistance.

In the area of financial liberalization, the Kim Dae Jung administration regards foreign investment as necessary for long-term financial stabilization. In theory, by shifting from heavy reliance on foreign debt to more foreign direct investment, South Korea should reduce its vulnerability to external shocks, ease the pressures of debt servicing, lower the domestic interest rate and the exchange rate, stimulate new corporate governance norms, and attract new technology.

In early 1998, Korea opened its capital and real estate markets to foreign investment and allowed mergers and even hostile takeovers by foreign firms, including in the financial sector. The successful renegotiation of short-term domestic banking debts of $21.8 billion into long-term government-guaranteed loans in April 1998, alongside significant improvement in the current-account balance and substantial increase in foreign reserves, contributed to a stabilization of the financial crisis by the end of May 1998. The exchange rate, which also stabilized, was now fully determined by the market. Thus, the new government used the acute short-term financial crisis to bring about a radical deepening of economic liberalization.

On December 7, 1998, the top five *chaebol* magnates met with Kim Dae Jung and formally agreed to a sweeping corporate restructuring program. This landmark corporate restructuring agreement (with Hyundai, Samsung, Daewoo, SK, and LG) requires the *chaebol* to stop their reckless expansion juggernaut and sell off marginal and unprofitable businesses and subsidiaries. The "five great reforms" at the center of this plan are greater transparency in corporate management, ending mutual debt guarantees among *chaebol* subsidiaries, establishing a healthy financial structure, emphasizing core business lines among *chaebol* and encouragement of SMEs, and increasing managerial and majority shareholder accountability."[14]

Part of the plan involves the so-called big deals. These entail "swaps" among the empires in order to rationalize seven main industrial sectors, including petrochemicals, aircraft, rolling stock, power generation, ship engines, semiconductors, and oil refining.[15] The Fair Trade Commission is charged with monitoring the swaps to prevent delays in restructuring. The commission, further enabled by revision of the Fair Trade Act, will seek to monitor and prevent abuses of *chaebol* intragroup transactions, which continue to allow the empires to shift resources from core companies to weak subsidiaries.

At the same time, a new Foreign Investment Promotion Act, passed on November 17, 1998, provided unprecedented incentives to foreign investors. These were designed to encourage foreign participation in the government's ambitious ongoing privatization program as well as in private corporate restructuring. In addition, the Regulatory Reform Commission aimed to slash the number of economic regulations on the statute books by as much as half. On the other hand, new regulatory strictures were being promoted to improve the corporate governance system in Korea in order to lessen the influence of majority shareholders, bring in outside directors to corporate boards, and increase transparency in accounting methods.

The Daewoo Case

As many as ten of the top thirty *chaebol* have gone bankrupt since 1997, including Kia, Halla, Newcore, Jinro, Hanbo, and Daenong and, most spectacularly, the near bankruptcy of Daewoo, thus shattering the "too big to fail" myth.[16] However, this does not mean the total elimination of the *chaebol* clan. As in the past, the leading *chaebol* continuously resist government attempts "to force them to prune their sprawling industrial empires and concentrate on core businesses." They still retain the ability to exploit the liberalization of the domestic financial sector to raise capital "to keep even their weakest operations in business."[17]

Although reduction in debt levels and the elimination of cross-subsidiary debt payment guarantees has been mandated by the government, the *chaebol* have reacted by attempting to strengthen cross-share holdings among subsidiaries. This process has been facilitated by the recent recovery of the stock market and issue of new shares. The *chaebol* have opportunistically exploited a previous easing of the rules on cross-share holding in 1998 that was actually intended to make mergers easier in the context of restructuring and the "big deals." Instead, money from healthy units was used to shore up weaker ones and thus to defend the empires.[18]

The challenge of globalization for Kim Dae Jung, however, is that in order for the state to enforce a transition to a market economy via deconcentration and other reforms, it must first regain for the state sufficient autonomy and capacity to impose these changes on business and labor. In other words, in the short term, Kim Dae Jung seeks to wield the powers of a strong and interventionist state in order to bring about a liberal order in the long term. The best recent example of this assertion of state interventionism is the case of the Daewoo restructuring process and "workout plan." Daewoo, among the top five *chaebol,* recently succumbed to a radical restructuring package. Under impending threat of bankruptcy due to colossal debts incurred in its expansion efforts, the government utilized the financial vulnerability of Daewoo to force it to negotiate with its domestic creditors under the direct arbitration of the FSC. The outcome of this unprecedented negotiation process effectively dismembers the Daewoo empire, while attempting to resuscitate its most vital companies.[19] The Daewoo case clearly illustrates how the restructuring and deconcentration of the major *chaebol* requires strong government intervention. Reliance on market forces alone or on *chaebol* voluntarism have not proved sufficient to accomplish the reforms. Moreover, it illustrates how the balance of forces between the state and capital may shift, depending on circumstances.

The dismantling of Daewoo illustrates a dilemma for the national economy of South Korea, led traditionally by great "national champions" such as Daewoo. The *chaebol* can certainly fail and be undone, but by doing so they invite a brave new world of foreign ownership and leaner competitive firms. Not only among the corporate elite, but many Korean workers and those still adhering to economic nationalism are highly skeptical about the ongoing transition. No textbook can predict the ultimate outcome of this open experiment in economic restructuring. The government must tread a precarious path between not doing enough to restructure the *chaebol* and doing too much and thereby damaging national development and prosperity.

The financial crisis presented South Korea and the Kim Dae Jung government with both a challenge and an opportunity. The public exposure of colossal corporate debts and mismanagement, combined with the negative attitude of the IMF and many other external actors toward the prevailing practices of South Korea's major corporations and banks, contributed to a weakening of the *chaebol*'s sociopolitical position. The *chaebol* were almost universally blamed for having brought the crisis on Korea, aided by the collusion of the Kim Young Sam administration and its slide into "crony capitalism."[20] The government of Kim Dae Jung has skillfully exploited the IMF crisis environment to establish a new interventionary policy for deconcentration while appealing to labor and the public to lend their political support to this endeavor. Winning the allegiance of organized labor, however, has been far from easy, given the negative impact of restructuring on employment and living standards for the working majority.

ECONOMIC RESTRUCTURING AND LABOR

The Rocky Path toward a "Social Compromise"

From the onset of democratization in 1987 until the present, the issue of labor reform has been a central one in South Korea. The politics of globalization has involved addressing long-standing union grievances against restrictive elements of the law, including the prohibition on plural unionism, third-party intervention, public sector unions, and union participation in party politics. While organized labor has tried to gain social and political acceptance as a legitimate social partner of government and business, the *chaebol* have demanded new powers to discipline labor and make it more flexible.

From the outset, invoking globalization as a guiding principle of reform has implied significant change in industrial relations. On his inauguration in February 1993, Kim Young Sam outlined a new policy of government nonintervention in labor–management disputes. From the government's point of view, there were two goals of labor reform: to reduce the rigidity of the labor market and to bring Korea's labor practices up to international norms and International Labor Organization (ILO) standards in preparation for OECD membership. In principle, this was an important departure from the interventionist and corporatist tradition of the previous authoritarian governments. On the other hand, the preparations for South Korea's entry into the OECD increased the urgency of making headway in industrial relations and labor reform. The ILO was dissatisfied with South Korea's record of compliance with international labor standards.

However, the emphases in Kim Young Sam's *segyehwa* policy on growth first, "flexibilization" of labor, and reconfiguration of the government–*chaebol* alliance elicited a defensive response from organized labor. The labor movement called for plural unionism, legalization of union political activity, third-party intervention, and public sector unions. In contrast, big business, represented by the Korean Confederation of Employers (KCE), insisted on maintaining the prohibition of plural unions and union political activity and called for the right to replace striking workers and abolish severance payments on redundancy. A new phase of industrial relations conflict ensued.

Kim Young Sam established the Presidential Commission on Industrial Relations Reform (PCIR) on May 9, 1996, including representatives from the major national trade union federations: the FKTU [21] and the KCTU.[22] The mediation process was not entirely successful. The KCTU withdrew from the PCIR, claiming that it was biased in favor of the interests of business. A new government committee prepared draft legislation for the flexibilization of labor that included relaxed rules for dismissal of workers and substitution for striking workers. Third-party intervention was to be allowed for registered organizations, and the teachers' union was to be recognized from 1999 but banned from striking. Multiple unions were to be permitted at industry level, delaying their introduction at the enterprise level. At the last minute, however, the ruling party introduced a controversial change: a decision to delay implementation of multiple unions by three years.

In the absence of opposition members in the National Assembly, in the early hours of the morning of December 26, 1996, the bill was passed along with ten others, in seven minutes flat. The ruling party's abrupt reversion to improper methods in the National Assembly raised public fears of a new authoritarianism. Moreover, the attempt to legislate labor flexibility threatened the job security of a wide section of the working population, even the white-collar and professional sectors.

The KCTU responded by declaring a national strike. Recognition of the full right of freedom of association for unions was a key goal of the action. The extraordinary two-month period of the national strike was possible because of the public sympathy that it gathered. When the FKTU joined the strike action, the government agreed to reopen debate on the labor law. A special session of the National Assembly was convened in February, and the new labor law was approved on March 10, 1997.

The law made concessions to business demands by increasing the flexibility of the labor market, allowing redundancy dismissals and replacement of striking workers. However, labor won a crucial two-year moratorium on the use of redundancy dismissals, approval for union financial support to full-time union officers, and the removal of the prohibition on political activities by unions (except in cases in which the main purpose was to promote a political movement). The government hoped that this compromise would lay the basis for a participatory and cooperative industrial relations system.

However, this compromise did not survive the national economic crisis in late 1997. The crisis further exacerbated the underlying tensions in labor's relations with both business and government. Unemployment rose to over 8 percent at the peak of the crisis, and per capita gross national product (GNP) dropped sharply from $10,543 in 1996 to $6,750 in 1998. Kim Dae Jung's new government had little option other than to make relieving distress from unemployment a high priority alongside restoring financial stability.

One of the key points of reform under Kim Dae Jung was "to recognize labor as a key factor in production, and bring labor into the policy making process."[23] The government could not realistically hope to overcome the national crisis without the cooperation of labor. Although the PCIR and the Labor Relations Commission (LRC) could be seen as precedents, the newly established Tripartite Commission (*No-Sa-Jong Wiwonhoe*) represents a fresh attempt to bring labor into formal policy consultations. It is based on the idea of equal trilateral representation among government, business, and organized labor and reflects corporatist ideas under democratic conditions. However, the operation of the tripartite system, initiated on January 15, 1998, was contingent on certain expectations by all three parties to the agreement.

The problems in stabilizing the tripartite formula have centered on three main issues: redundancy dismissals, "fair burden sharing," and recognition of union rights. Labor insisted that the national crisis be resolved on the principle of "fair burden sharing"; that is, the *chaebol* would be held responsible for the economic crisis and duly punished. The cost of adjustments would be borne by business as well as by labor in order to avoid victimization of workers.

In the first round of tripartite talks, the FKTU and the KCTU agreed to accept new labor legalization, passed in February 1998, permitting redundancy dismissal on the condition that such dismissals would be for reasons of economic re-structuring only. Relinquishing the moratorium achieved after the national strike in 1997 was a step backward for labor, made acceptable only by the promise of substantial economic and social reform, which became known as the "Social Compromise."[24] The unique success of the first round depended greatly on the urgency of the financial crisis and the expectation by labor of further economic and social reform under the new government.

Resumption of Labor–Management Strife

By the time of the second round of talks in June 1998, however, the situation had changed. The sense of common feeling had dissipated as the immediacy of the foreign-exchange crisis subsided. In addition, there was already a growing frustration on the part of labor that the agreement on fair burden sharing was not being carried out by either government or business. Unions, and especially the KCTU, became more militant in opposing growing unemployment, while the companies demanded autonomy in dealing with internal industrial disputes and punishment of illegal strikes. The government maintained that its role was limited to mediation and not enforcement of a solution.[25] Nevertheless, the government threatened to deal severely with illegal strike action as well as with "unfair business practices" by corporate managers.

Initially, the unemployment problem particularly hit unorganized workers in small and medium-size industries and female workers in most industries. However, the threat of large job cuts spread to previously well-protected organized workers in the major companies, including the financial sector and even the public sector, which were targeted by the government for drastic restructuring involving downsizing. As unemployment spread and affected both the private and the public sectors, conflict intensified among labor, business, and government.

In this context, it is little wonder that the Tripartite Commission confronted serious obstacles in regard to implementation of the agreed principles. Unions accused government of maintaining the traditional government–*chaebol* alliance against organized labor.[26] Business claimed that fair burden sharing was already taking place, via loss of assets, dismissals of managerial staff, and multiple reform measures aimed at *chaebol* restructuring.[27] Both business and labor threatened to abandon the Tripartite Commission as a mediation forum.

By mid-1998, labor returned to vigorous protest action. The KCTU organized a national demonstration on May Day, followed by a brief general strike in July. The FKTU joined forces with the KCTU to stage large protest rallies in Seoul, presenting labor's joint demands for a halt to mass dismissals and for fulfilment of government promises. Although these joint actions never reached the intensity of the national strike of 1996–1997, they were indicative of the growing tension. The dispute at Hyundai Motors in 1998 over the issue of redundancies was particularly bitter and widely regarded as a key test case. Although worker militancy reached new levels of intensity and unions explicitly demanded a moratorium on mass dismissals, the company prevailed in the end. Government sympathies indicated that workers should accept the reality of the need for redundancies in the course of restructuring. The unfortunate result was a serious deterioration of confidence in the tripartite process.

Austerity measures by the IMF had exacerbated recessionary tendencies in an economy undergoing structural adjustment. However, labor looked to government to take effective action to reverse the process and protect the interests of ordinary workers. In order to counter the spiral of contraction and growing unemployment, the government somewhat belatedly began to use stimulus spending by September 1998. Nevertheless, economic restructuring has remained the key policy of the Kim Dae Jung administration, and this inevitably entails short-term costs of adjustment, including increased redundancies. The government insists that these reforms will create more employment in the long term by strengthening competitiveness. The unemployment rate for the first quarter of 1999 (January–March) was approximately 8.5 percent, up from a mere 2 percent prior to the crisis. Real wages had dropped by as much as 10 percent by the end of 1998 compared to the previous year. Labor costs were reduced during the restructuring process, while in some cases profits were up.[28] The issue of spiraling redundancies in the course of implementing economic restructuring remains at the center of the turbulence in industrial relations and undermines the stability of the tripartite formula.

A new crisis emerged in February 1999, when organized labor withdrew from the Tripartite Commission. The KCTU, under the leadership of Lee Kap Yong, withdrew on February 24 and presented the government with a list of demands. These included stopping the industrial restructuring and redundancies and calling for shortening working hours and establishing the social safety net. The FKTU, under the leadership of Park In Sang, also threatened to withdraw from the Tripartite Commission if certain conditions were not met. These included prior consultation with unions on industrial restructuring decisions and stronger measures to eliminate illegal labor practices.

In mid-March 1999, the Ministry of Labor responded by agreeing to meet directly with the FKTU, excluding business, to discuss normalization of the Tripartite Commission. To resolve the situation, the government moved to establish a formal legislative basis defining the independent role of the Tripartite Commission, which had been established initially as an informal consultative body. The KCTU, however, took the view that the Tripartite Commission had lost its function as a tool of social negotiation and had returned to militant tactics outside the corporatist framework. In the spring of 1999, the KCTU initiated major strike and protest actions aimed at opposing the government's restructuring policies and entrenchment of *chaebol* self-interest. In late October, both the FKTU and the KCTU separately warned the government that they would actively resist the drive to restructure public enterprises and the Daewoo group. In the spring of 2000, the Korean automobile sector was crippled by renewed strikes.

This shift to militancy by the KCTU and its members should be understood alongside a parallel shift to formal participation by labor in party politics. In September 1999, former KCTU presidents Kwon Young Kihl and Lee Kap Yong presided over the founding of a new political party, the Democratic Labor Party (*Minju Nodong Dang*), backed by KCTU unions and allied social movements.[29] The initial aim was to win several working-class seats in the upcoming National Assembly elections in the spring of 2000. The new party was narrowly defeated in several such constituencies but won no seats in the Sixteenth National Assembly. Although short-term prospects for electoral success are meager, in the long term this development may be extremely significant. It could represent the beginning of much-needed political reform, including the formation of national political parties based on class or sectoral interests rather than on the prevailing regionalism and leader-centered party factionalism.

The continuing conflict and tension between organized labor, the government, and big business in South Korea speaks volumes about the real conditions of the transition to democracy and a liberal free-market economic system. Liberal theory tells us that more marketization promises more democracy. However, in South Korea, the reality is far more complex. There is a profound conflict of interests between labor and capital at the heart of the economic restructuring process. The outcome of this conflict is contingent on how the state positions itself in relation to the antagonists. Can Kim Dae Jung really deliver meaningful participatory democracy while aggressively pursuing Korea's neoliberal globalization?

FOREIGN POLICY: TOWARD A NEW REGIONALISM AND GLOBALISM

The Impact of Domestic and International Forces

The interpretation of globalization as the means to enhance Korea's international standing has been a key element of ROK foreign policy in the 1990s. The new emphasis on international competitiveness was concomitant with aspirations to join the WTO and the OECD. Foreign Minister Han Sung Joo, under the Kim Young Sam government, viewed internationalization (*kukjehwa*) as "an inevitable process which every nation-state must undergo to ensure sustained stability and prosperity." The best means of meeting the challenge of globalization in the "post Uruguay Round order" was to "enhance competitiveness."[30] The essential goal was to elevate South Korea's international status and consolidate its "graduation" into the top rank of world powers.[31] The "New Diplomacy" (*shin oekyo*) was initiated by Han Sung Joo, consisting of five fundamental elements: globalism, diversification, multidimensionalism, regional cooperation, and future orientation.

South Korea's New Diplomacy built on the success of its "economic diplomacy" and "Nordpolitik" of the 1980s, which had resulted in a widening of diplomatic relations, including with communist states such as the Soviet Union and China, entry into the United Nations, and numerous international organizations.[32] Foreign policy was now more directly linked to the pursuit of economic and trade goals. To further elevate economic diplomacy, President Kim Young Sam redesignated the Ministry of Foreign Affairs as the Ministry of Foreign Affairs and Trade.

The impetus for change was not merely internal but involved significant external influences. Since its reconstruction after World War II, the regional political economy of East Asia has had a distinctive position in the global system. Strategic interests defined American geopolitical doctrine in East Asia and produced a tolerance for East Asian nonconformance to liberal economic norms. In the past decade, the structure of the regional East Asian economy has been profoundly influenced by several factors. These include the decline of Russia, the liberalization and increasing regional economic integration of China, the incipient democratization of several East Asian states, the increasing criticism of authoritarian developmentalism, and the continuing impact of the U.S.-led agenda of neoliberal economic globalization.[33] In the eyes of the United States, the end of the Cold War and the demise of the Soviet Union largely removed the strategic justification for neomercantilist practices and developmental state institutions in East Asia. The shift in U.S. priorities to its economic interests opened the possibility of combining expansion of regional economic integration with a relaxation of ideological and strategic tensions.

Bilateral pressure from the United States was a significant factor in the decision to emphasize economic liberalization and globalization in both domestic and foreign policy. By the mid-1990s, South Korean economic officials routinely cited U.S. demands as a key impetus for the acceleration of economic liberalization. This pressure extended to the industrial, service, and agricultural sectors, including financial liberalization and eventual full capital market opening. The post–Cold War era in East Asia has been characterized by continuous pressure from the United States for accelerated market opening and economic liberalization.[34] President Bill Clinton, in his budget message to the U.S. Congress in 1994, put it succinctly: "We have put our economic competitiveness at the heart of our foreign policy."[35]

Accompanying his aspirations for economic modernization, Kim Dae Jung takes a rationalist, cosmopolitan view of domestic and international politics and advocates universal values of freedom, human rights, justice, peace, and efficiency in an era of "universal globalism."[36] He has demonstrated these values through, for example, continued ROK financial support to the United Nations despite the national economic crisis and to collective security action, such as in East Timor and several UN peacekeeping operations. Seoul advocates a Northeast Asia security dialogue, but its renewed interest in regionalism goes beyond security issues. For example, at the summit of East Asian governments in Manila in November 1999, attended by the ASEAN (Association of Southeast Asian Nations) countries plus China, Japan, and South Korea, Kim Dae Jung voiced his aspiration for further regional integration. He endorsed the vision of the formation of a giant free-trade zone among East Asian countries in order to engage members of the European Union and the North American Free Trade Agreement in cooperation as well as competition.

Perhaps more than in any other area of foreign policy, however, Kim Dae Jung's approach to North Korea has attracted much international attention and support. Whereas Kim Young Sam had spoken of moving beyond traditional North–South confrontation, in practice he pursued a unification policy that perpetuated hostility and blocked progress toward normalization of diplomatic relations with North Korea by the United States and Japan. Until very recently, relations between the United States and North Korea had made very little progress since the promising signing of the Agreed Framework in 1994. By this agreement, Pyongyang promised to end its nuclear weapons development program in exchange for energy assistance from the United States and the KEDO (Korean Peninsula Energy Development Organization) consortium.[37]

Kim Dae Jung's "Sunshine" or "Engagement" policy begins with the idea of reassuring North Korea that there is no threat from the South or any plan to absorb the North. The success of his policy reorientation is illustrated in President Clinton's alignment with Sunshine policy and the content of the Perry Mission report and subsequent U.S. actions. In September 1999, the Perry report, commissioned by President Clinton to review U.S. policy on North Korea, advised a significant change in policy. Following Perry's recommendations, the U.S. government has removed economic sanctions imposed on North Korea and accelerated the high-level talks with North Korea carried out by Charles Kartman of the State Department. The hope is to move ahead to establish direct diplomatic representation between Washington and Pyongyang.[38] Japan has followed the trend by easing sanctions imposed on North Korea after the Taepodong missile incident in August 1998.

The new measures are designed to help North Korea achieve a "soft landing" after years of severe economic crisis and to maintain the arrangements of the Agreed Framework concerning nuclear weapons, which now also includes missile development. Moreover, the new approach explicitly endorses continued policy coordination among the United States, Japan, and South Korea (a product of the Sunshine policy) and one that enhances prospects for multilateral diplomacy in the region. Seoul now supports parallel four-party talks among the ROK, the DPRK, the United States, and China. At the same time, it supports Japan's proposal for a six-party dialogue on inter-Korean relations, which includes Japan and Russia. The ROK favors the United States and Japan establishing diplomatic relations with North Korea "at any time" and is open to replacing the Korean War armistice with a formal peace agreement.[39] The emphasis now is on providing

North Korea with sufficient and effective incentives to open up its economy and undertake domestic reforms.

What remains to be accomplished is not only the rapid normalization of North Korea's relations with the United States and Japan but eventually mutual diplomatic recognition between North and South Korea themselves. A historic North–South summit was held between President Kim Dae Jung of the ROK and Chairman Kim Jong-il of North Korea from June 13 to June 15, 2000. The agreement reached included a new commitment by both sides to promote reunification via a federal or confederal formula, to act speedily to reunite families separated by the national division, to expand economic and other forms of cooperation, and to continue the North–South dialogue with greater vigor. This breakthrough augurs very well for the future of the Korean peninsula.

CONCLUSION

Globalization is an uncharted sea that requires great skill to navigate successfully. *Segyehwa* policy was originally intended to bring about a new economic structure, conforming to liberal international norms and capable of sustaining international competitiveness and growth. This implied liberalization not only of trade but also of finance and foreign investment. The developmental state was to give way to a liberal model. The *chaebol* were to be downsized and prepared for competition on a level playing field, both domestic and international. Society was to be reformed and democratized, allowing more scope for citizen participation and inclusion. Welfare and social spending were to expand, broadening the social safety net and enhancing human development.

Kim Young Sam's government failed to break the traditional government–*chaebol* alliance. The failure to tackle these structural problems in good time revealed the underlying vulnerability of the economy, exposing it to increased risk. The failure sufficiently to prepare the social safety net left workers in an exposed position when the economic crisis came in 1997–1998. The failure of the *segyehwa* policy to tame the power of the *chaebol,* and in particular to reform their financial practices, led directly to the onset of the IMF crisis.

The intervention of the IMF set a new agenda that has resulted in rapid rather than gradual adjustment. Domestic reform and external opening have now been compressed into a single and time-shortened framework that demands drastic change. The IMF crisis was a watershed in several ways. With the change of government, it provided an opportunity to redeploy state power toward the goals of corporate deconcentration, financial reform, and liberalization. The national economic crisis and the perceived threat to national interests created a mood of urgency and solidarity between all sectors of society. This climate provided organized labor with the ground on which to assert a new national political role, which was facilitated by the government's initiatives for a new "tripartite" corporatism.

However, as the full effects of unemployment deepened, first as a result of the financial crisis and IMF austerity measures and subsequently as a by-product of further economic restructuring advanced by the government, the situation has deteriorated from social cooperation to conflict. The economic results, however, appear to be positive from the point of view of a restoration of growth.

Economic recovery apparently began during the first half of 1999, with a series of monthly increases in manufacturing output and an increase in investment to meet expected demand.[40] South Korea is now growing at one of the fastest rates in the world, the trade surplus is widening ($2.17 billion for October 1999), and foreign direct investment in the first ten months of 1999 rose 83 percent to a record $10.25 billion from a year earlier. The four largest remaining *chaebol* were on track to meet the government's end-of-year targets for debt reduction, having pared debts and sold assets. On the other hand, they are also strengthening their centrality by buying up new assets on a large scale.[41]

On balance, this recovery is still tentative, and many observers remain skeptical of its long-term viability. Fears of a new financial crisis remain palpably real. The Daewoo situation prompted the government to announce in late October 1999 that it would take "every imaginable" measure to stabilize financial markets to prevent such a recurrence of national financial meltdown. While government remains adamant on tightening its grip, the *chaebol* that survived the crisis may yet manage to manipulate the new environment to resist deconcentration.

Kim Dae Jung has deployed a hybridized mixture of social democratic, neoliberal, and corporatist ideological elements. There is no precedent, no model, for this open experiment that he has embarked on. He must tread a tightrope between going too far (undermining national capital to the benefit of foreign interests) and not going far enough (allowing the *chaebol* to continue to dominate the economy). In either case, he would lose public support. The restructuring program undertaken by Kim Dae Jung is not really supported by either big business or organized labor, although it has the backing of powerful foreign interests. For labor, restructuring of the private and public sectors is a threat to its security and livelihood. To date, although the voice of labor has become louder and its participation in the political process is increasing, no real gains have yet resulted.

There should be a healthy caution against the naive belief in the benign effects of globalization. The art of the politics of globalization is precisely to navigate between the extremes of nationalism on the one hand and of international liberalism on the other. The public instinct to fear a wave of foreign acquisitions in what was once "Korea Inc." is not entirely misjudgment. While the *chaebol* certainly should not continue as they have in the past, nor should there be an unwarranted confidence that foreign firms will necessarily defend the national interest of the Korean economy. The overall record of heavy reliance on foreign participation as experienced in other developing countries does not lead to such confidence.

There remains the vexing question of the nature of globalization's impact on democratization in South Korea. This depends on the prospects for enhancing meaningful participation by civil society in a democratic framework of decision making. The relationship between government authority and civil society in South Korea is evolving but still remains ambiguous. Despite the growth of civil society since democratization began in 1987—which includes not only the labor movement but also emergent nongovernmental organizations (NGOs), such as the Citizen's Coalition for Economic Justice, the Korean Federation of Environmental Movements, and People's Solidarity for Participatory Democracy—the government's relationship with such new social movements is not entirely clear, and there is fear among the grassroots of centralization and mobilization from above in government–NGO relations. Kim Dae Jung's government has been criticized for its penchant to wield authority heavy-handedly.

The rise to globalism in South Korea implies breaking with its authoritarian power structures, both corporate and political. Democratization is therefore a central aspect of economic change in South Korea. A commitment to democratization in the South Korean context implies that the traditional "growth first" model should be abandoned, probably accepting lower rates of growth in order to achieve other social goals. These social goals should include a new democratic industrial relations system accompanied by broadened social inclusion, increased welfare spending, a redistribution of income from capital to labor, and the strengthening of civil society's role in the political system. These goals are certainly not incompatible with corporate deconcentration. However, they imply more than the obsession with the achievement of a competitive capitalism. The breaking of government–*chaebol* collusion, which flourished under Kim Young Sam, provides a political space for a new social alliance in pursuit of broad reform. In some respects, Kim Dae Jung has made a promising start, but much remains to be done to overcome the inherent conflict between economic globalization and democratic consolidation. In particular, it requires providing social justice as well as establishing new rules for capital. This is the great challenge of globalization.

NOTES

1. Korean Overseas Information Service, *The Segyehwa Policy of Korea under President Kim Young Sam* (Seoul: Korean Overseas Information Service, 1995), 19.

2. Ministry of Finance and Economy, Overall Economic Policy Division, *Challenge and Chance: Korea's Response to the New Economic Reality* (Seoul: Ministry of Finance and Economy, June 1998), 7, 9.

3. Globalization Commission, *The Globalization Commission Report* (Seoul: Globalization Commission, 1996), 536, provides figures on extension of coverage for minimum income support to the indigent from 70 to 80 percent by 1996, to 90 percent by 1997, and to 100 percent by 1998.

4. Kwon Soon Won, "Economic Justice and Social Welfare: New Principles of Economic Policy" (paper presented at the International Conference on Democratization and Globalization in Korea, Seoul, August 18–19, 1997).

5. Barry K. Gills, "The International Origins of South Korea's Export Orientation," in R. Palan and B. K. Gills, eds., *Transcending the State/Global Divide: A Neo-Structuralist Agenda in International Relations* (Boulder, Colo.: Lynne Rienner, 1994), 203–22.

6. Korean Overseas Information Service, *The Segyehwa Policy of Korea under President Kim Young Sam,* 7.

7. For further discussion of the issue of strategic choice over the sequentialization of reforms, see B. K. Gills and D. S. Gills, "Globalization and Strategic Choice in South Korea: Economic Reform and Labor," in Samuel S. Kim, ed., *Korea's Globalization* (Cambridge: Cambridge University Press, 2000).

8. "Camdessus Plea for Change to Statutes," *Financial Times* (London), September 29, 1999, 6.

9. Ministry of Finance and Economy, *Challenge and Chance,* 5–6.

10. For a recent analysis of continuing problems with financial reform, see "Financial Times Survey: South Korea," *Financial Times,* October 20, 1999 (available online at <http://www.ft.com/ftsurveys/>).

11. Globalization Commission, *Kyongjaeng chokjin ul wihan Kongjong korae jedo kaeson bang-an* (Improvement plan for the fair trade system for promotion of competition) (Seoul: Globalization Commission, 1996), and *Segyehwa chujin chonghap bogoso* (Globalization Commission Comprehensive Report) (Seoul: Globalization Commission, 1997), 345.

12. Economic Planning Board, "The Economic Globalization Plan for Remaking the Korean Economy," *Republic of Korea Economic Bulletin* (Seoul: Economic Planning Board/Korea Development Institute, July 1994).

13. Total external liabilities as of October 1998 were still $153.5 billion, a decrease of only $4.5 billion from the end of 1997 (Samuel S. Kim, "Korea's Segyehwa Drive: Promise versus Performance," in Kim, ed., *Korea's Globalization*).

14. Kim, ed., *Korea's Globalization.*

15. Information Office, *Korea News Views* (London: Embassy of the Republic of Korea, December 1998), 1–2.

16. *International Herald Tribune,* October 25, 1999.

17. *Financial Times,* October 20, 1999, I.

18. John Burton, "The Empires Strike Back," *Financial Times,* October 20, 1999, III.

19. A final rescheduling agreement was reached on November 25, 1999, ninety minutes before the deadline of the "standstill" agreement reached in August that had postponed payment on Daewoo's debts for three months. A massive debt-for-equity swap was agreed, converting $20.6 billion of debts of the parent company Daewoo Corporation and Daewoo Motors into equity, and another $2.3 billion of fresh funds were injected into the firms to sustain them. Other companies in the group (the twelve main firms in the group have total liabilities of $74 billion, $21 billion greater than total assets) also negotiated for new terms, including deferred repayments and debt-for-equity swaps. More than seventy foreign creditors (holding $6.8 billion in Daewoo debts) must also reach agreement on Daewoo debts. Daewoo founder and chairman Kim Woo Chung and the twelve presidents of the group's main companies all offered their resignations to the government's Corporate Restructuring Agency. The threat by the FSC to place the Daewoo Corporation under court

receivership proved an effective tool to force through restructuring, which entails effective dismantling of the Daewoo empire.

20. It was under the Kim Young Sam administration and its almost complete retreat from both traditional economic planning and industrial policy that the state–capital relationship was altered in such a way as to foster corruption on a new "particularistic" basis. The result was gross overinvestment and distortion of the manufacturing base; see Ha-Joon Chang, Hong-Jae Park, and Chul Gyue Yoo, "Interpreting the Korean Crisis: Financial Liberalization, Industrial Policy, and Corporate Governance," *Cambridge Journal of Economics* 22, no. 6 (November 1998): 735–46.

21. The Federation of Korean Trade Unions is the officially recognized peak organization. It has a reputation for moderation and "bread and butter" unionism.

22. The Korean Confederation of Trade Unions was formed in November 1995 as an illegal rival national confederation composed of "democratic" trade unions espousing a broad social agenda. The KCTU was given legal status in November 1999.

23. Choi Jang Jip, "Korea's Political Economy: Search for a Solution," *Korea Focus* 6, no. 2 (March–April 1998): 15.

24. Korea International Labour Foundation, *Handbook of the Social Agreement and New Labour Laws of Korea* (Seoul: Korea International Labour Foundation, 1998), i–iii.

25. *"Wigi ui No-Sa-Jong"* (*No-Sa-Jong* in crisis), *KBS Report,* July 31, 1998 (statement by You Jong Keun, economic adviser to Kim Dae Jung).

26. *"Wigi ui No-Sa-Jong"* (statement by Cho Hui Yon, policy director of Ch'amyo-yondae).

27. *"Wigi ui No-Sa-Jong"* (statement by Kong Byong Ho, director of the Free Enterprise Centre).

28. *International Herald Tribune,* March 5, 1999, 17. In the case of Korea Telecom (71 percent government owned), the workforce was cut by 11 percent in 1998 while operating profits jumped by 43 percent.

29. <http://www.kdlp.org/main.htm>.

30. An address delivered by Foreign Minister Han Sung Joo to the Korean Council on Foreign Relations, May 1993.

31. Barry K. Gills, "Economic Liberalization and Reform in South Korea in the 1990s: A 'Coming of Age' or a Case of 'Graduation Blues'?" *Third World Quarterly* 17, no. 4 (1996): 667–88.

32. For more discussion of the reasons for the success of "economic diplomacy," see Barry K. Gills, *Korea versus Korea: A Case of Contested Legitimacy* (London: Routledge, 1996).

33. Barry K. Gills, "The Crisis of Postwar East Asian Capitalism: American Power, Democracy, and the Vicissitudes of Globalization," *Review of International Studies* 26 (2000): 381–403.

34. Barry K. Gills, "The Crisis of Postwar East Asian Capitalism"; Walden Bello and Shea Cunningham, "Trade Warfare and Regional Integration in the Pacific: The USA, Japan, and the Asian NICs," *Third World Quarterly* 15, no. 3 (1994).

35. Michael Cox, *US Foreign Policy after the Cold War: Superpower without a Mission* (London: Royal Institute of International Affairs, 1995).

36. President Kim Dae Jung's inaugural address, *Korea Herald* (Seoul), February 26, 1998.

37. Barry K. Gills, *Prospects for Peace and Stability in Northeast Asia: The Korean Conflict* (London: Research Institute for the Study of Conflict and Terrorism, 1995).

38. *International Herald Tribune,* September 16, 1999.

39. Park Sang-Seek, "Sunshine Policy (Engagement Policy) toward North Korea" (talk presented at the Royal Institute of International Affairs, London, September 29, 1999).

40. *International Herald Tribune,* September 30, 1999.

41. *International Herald Tribune,* July 3–4, 1999, 9, and July 8, 1999, 1.

5

China and Globalization

Thomas G. Moore

Opening to the outside world is a long-term basic state policy. Confronted with the globalization trend in economic, scientific, and technological development, we should take an even more active stance in the world by improving the pattern of opening up in all directions, at all levels and in a wide range, developing an open economy, enhancing our international competitiveness, optimizing our economic structure and improving the quality of our national economy.[1]

—Chinese president Jiang Zemin

Globalization (*quanqiuhua*) is a fairly new term in the lexicon of China's leaders, bureaucrats, and strategic analysts. While there have been occasional references to *quanqiuhua* over the years, especially in academic writings, until recently it received much less attention than terms such as economic integration (*jingji yitihua*) or world economic interdependence (various phrases such as *shijie jingji de xianghu yicun*). Indeed, the first major reference to *quanqiuhua* in official documents was President Jiang Zemin's statement (in this chapter's opening epigraph) in his political report to the Fifteenth National Congress of the Communist Party of China (hereafter, Fifteenth Party Congress) in September 1997.

Since *quanqiuhua* is a relatively new term, definitional and conceptual debate about globalization is still in a formative stage among Chinese observers. With few exceptions, in fact, globalization is synonymous with *economic* globalization. While some Chinese scholars have acknowledged the social, cultural, political, diplomatic, and security dimensions of globalization, economic globalization is widely regarded in China's academic and policymaking communities as the most advanced realm of the larger "globalization" phenomenon. Moreover, it is the economic dimension that is seen as driving globalization in the other dimensions. (For their part, Chinese leaders have publicly acknowledged only economic globalization, broadly understood to include science and technology.)

Since the story of China's integration into the world economy and its growing participation in world affairs more generally has been told elsewhere and need not be recounted in detail here, this chapter instead focuses on how globalization has become an increasingly important context for understanding major policy directions in China. At the risk of understating the actual impact that deepening ties with the world economy (as defined by flows of capital, goods, and technology) have had on Chinese institutions, policies, and economic structures, I argue that the greatest importance of globalization is as a lens through which China's leaders have come to view the economic tasks facing the country. While the *impact* of globalization is obviously difficult to disentangle analytically from the *perception* of globalization processes held by China's leaders, my point is simply that globalization may be more important as an idea (and, perhaps, future reality) than as a contemporary reality. For all of China's increased participation in world markets, the degree of integration between the Chinese economy and the world economy is still limited in critical respects. That said, globalization does appear to be serving increasingly as the geoeconomic (and, by extension, geopolitical) context within which leaders, such as Jiang and Prime Minister Zhu Rongji, formulate long-term strategies for making China rich and strong.

I adopt this approach in part because China's leaders have themselves suggested in their public statements that the challenge posed by current and future globalization has been a profound influence on their reform priorities, development strategies, and foreign policy positions. Unlike South Korea's *segyehwa,* however, China does not have an official policy for globalization; indeed, there is not even an undeclared drive to "globalize" the Chinese economy fully in the near future. (Despite its impressive evolution over the last two decades, China's Open Policy still falls somewhat short of advocating this goal.) Beijing has instead concentrated primarily on taking steps toward the creation of a modern economy that can benefit from, and compete effectively in, a world economy that China's leaders clearly expect to be even more interconnected in the future. In unprecedented fashion, Jiang has used many of his major speeches since 1997 to define China's national economic identity in terms of its participation in a fierce global race for comprehensive national strength (*zonghe guoli*), a race that intensifies day by day.

For all its importance, globalization remains surprisingly underconceptualized by Chinese leaders, bureaucrats, and strategic analysts alike. As it turns out, this may be no accident. For China's leaders, in particular, it may well reflect the conceptual flexibility necessary for using "globalization" as a shorthand reference for the wide-ranging set of economic tasks the country must address. By some measures, China's response to globalization has thus far been long on rhetoric and short on actual policy implementation. For example, if one considers the disappointing progress made in areas such as bank restructuring and the reform of state-owned enterprises (SOEs), the gap between words and deeds is quite apparent. Although Beijing's actions have often failed to keep pace with its globalization rhetoric, the November 1999 Sino-American agreement on China's accession to the World Trade Organization (WTO) raises the prospect that this gap may narrow in the future. Assuming the additional steps necessary for China to become a full member of the WTO can be accomplished and that local officials and companies in China will abide by its terms (either voluntarily or otherwise), membership in the WTO will lead the country closer to the specific goals identified by its leaders as necessary for national success in the age of economic globalization.

The rest of the chapter proceeds as follows. The next section examines China's performance under economic globalization. After reviewing its growing participation in international markets for goods and capital, I briefly discuss the implications of China's declining position in the leading international "competitiveness" rankings. Adopting an analytical framework from the larger literature on globalization, this section also provides a conceptual overview of the various "impacts" associated with globalization in the Chinese case. In the second section, I examine evolving Chinese conceptualizations of globalization. Here, my main finding is that globalization is still conceived for the most part as an "objective condition" in the world economy rather than as a manifestation of U.S. hegemony. Furthermore, globalization retains a positive association for most Chinese observers since it is seen as reinforcing multipolarity internationally. I also argue that Chinese thinking, while still primarily state-centric in focus, more closely resembles a network-based rather than a market-based conceptualization of globalization. According to this view, network-based corporate hierarchies intersect with, but are not equivalent to, state-based hierarchies in the world political economy. The third section surveys three issue areas—the creation of a knowledge economy, Internet promotion, and SOE reform—where Chinese leaders have explicitly invoked globalization as a motivating force in shaping their policies. The fourth and final section builds on these examples to analyze how economic nationalism is increasingly expressed, especially by China's leaders, in terms of meeting the challenge of globalization through broad participation in international economic competition.

CHINA IN A GLOBALIZING WORLD ECONOMY

Enter the Dragon: China's Performance in the World Economy

By now, many of the basic facts about China's growing participation in the world economy have become quite familiar. Measured by foreign trade and investment flows, China's integration into the world economy has increased substantially since the Open Policy was launched two decades ago. Based on nominal figures for gross domestic product (GDP), Chinese trade has consistently averaged about 40 percent of GDP each year since the mid-1990s, more than

triple the 13 percent figure for 1980.[2] By this yardstick, China's economy is
today both significantly more open than in the past and relatively open by international standards. As a result of growth rates in foreign trade that have averaged
16 percent annually over the last two decades, China has risen from thirtieth
place among world traders in 1977 to a rank of eleventh in 1998, this despite the
ill effects of the Asian financial crisis (AFC). As an exporter, in fact, China has
been firmly ensconced in the world's top ten since the mid-1990s. This success
in exports has also helped Beijing maintain foreign-exchange reserves among
the highest in the world in recent years.

As spectacular as China's rise as a trading power has been, its success in attracting foreign capital has been equally or more impressive. It is well known that
China in recent years has been the world's second-leading recipient of foreign direct investment (FDI), trailing only the United States; in the process, China has
accounted for roughly 40 percent of the total FDI flow to developing countries.
By the mid-1990s, FDI accounted for sizable (and growing) percentages of domestic investment, industrial output, exports, tax revenues, and jobs in China.
(Every year since 1996, for example, foreign-invested enterprises have accounted
for more than 40 percent of China's total exports. Similarly, these firms are estimated to produce between 15 and 20 percent of total industrial output.) All told,
China received $269 billion in utilized FDI between 1979 and 1998, more than
$200 billion of which was recorded from 1990 onward. Long a leading recipient
of loans from the World Bank and other sources of public finance, China has also
emerged in recent years as a major borrower from private banks, taking in about
10 percent of the world's commercial debt flows. While its success in tapping into
expanding cross-border flows of portfolio investment has been less signal, some
progress has been made in this area as well. Overall, China's participation in
world capital markets is now quite substantial. That said, current levels of external indebtedness do not appear to pose a major problem, as evidenced by the fact
that China's debt-to-service ratio remains well within international norms and
compares quite favorably to most of its neighbors (see chapter 1, table 1.2).

For all its successes as a growing participant in the world economy, China's
position in the most widely cited international "competitiveness" rankings has
actually slipped marginally in recent years.[3] While some of this decline may reflect the effects of the AFC, it also suggests that China will need to deepen reform and opening in the future in order to participate more effectively in the increasingly competitive global marketplace. Whatever the cause, foreign
investment and exports have been sluggish and show little sign of returning to
their robust growth of the mid-1990s. Judging from the reform-oriented terms of
Beijing's agreement with Washington on WTO accession, China's leaders seem
committed in principle to a comprehensive overhaul of the Chinese economy.
While concern remains that Chinese firms will be battered by their foreign rivals, at least initially, the Sino-American WTO deal suggests that the Chinese
leadership genuinely believes that the country's companies—and the Chinese

economy more generally—will become stronger only through greater exposure to international competition.

Prior to Zhu's April 1999 visit to Washington, China watchers were highly skeptical about both the willingness and the ability of China's leaders to meet the terms of U.S. negotiators. The fact that the Chinese leadership delivered not just once but twice during 1999, this despite serious tensions in the bilateral relationship, speaks volumes about how WTO membership figures centrally in Beijing's long-range plans for achieving domestic stability and managing its participation in globalization. The fact that the Chinese economy was even more sluggish in November 1999 than in April 1999 only adds an exclamation point to Beijing's decision to move forward with an agreement. By some accounts, however, China's leaders may actually have proceeded with the WTO bid because of, rather than in spite of, the condition of China's economy, such was their concern over weak growth in foreign investment and exports. Either way, the decision to push ahead was a bold political move both domestically and internationally.

The Impact of Globalization on Contemporary China

In their magisterial work *Global Transformations,*[4] David Held and his collaborators identify four distinct types of impacts associated with globalization—decisional, institutional, distributive, and structural—each of which can be applied to China in very illuminating fashion. Decisional impacts, for example, refer to the ways in which globalization processes influence outcomes by increasing or decreasing the costs of certain policy choices. One recent example of this type would be how globalization shaped China's preferences in formulating its currency policy in response to the AFC. Although insulated from the worst of the financial storm, Beijing still found its policy options constrained (against devaluation) as a result of its deepening economic interconnectedness with the East Asian region. While this was just one of several considerations that led to China's "no devaluation" policy, the costs of a possible devaluation in the wake of the AFC were by most accounts affected significantly by forces associated with globalization.[5]

The notion of *institutional* impacts goes beyond effects of globalization on policy preferences, as they pertain to a particular decision, to consider the ways in which globalization reconfigures "the agenda of decision-making itself and, consequently, the available choices which agents may or may not realistically make."[6] According to this conceptualization, globalization processes actually structure (or, perhaps more accurately, restructure) the range of policy options available, often widening as well as narrowing the agenda. Applied to the Chinese case, this notion of institutional impacts is consistent with an idea I have developed elsewhere about the "global logic" of China's reform and opening.[7]

One of the most important *distributive* impacts associated with globalization in the Chinese case is the widening of economic disparities between both the coastal and interior areas and the urban and rural areas. Despite annual growth rates for the national economy that have averaged 9.5 percent since 1978, with per capita income doubling not once but twice between 1978 and 1996, socioeconomic cleavages have by most accounts only deepened over the last two decades. According to the international standard for poverty used by the World Bank and the United Nations ($1 a day), there are an estimated 270 million Chinese currently living in poverty, with untold tens of millions living above this level, but only perilously so. While few would identify globalization itself as being responsible for the current situation in China, it should be noted that the benefits of the country's growing participation in the world economy have certainly not been shared equally. Indeed, the question of who wins and who loses in China as the result of globalization is growing in relevance with each passing year. Especially in the wake of China's likely WTO accession, urban unemployment is destined to grow as inefficient firms fail. Workers in bankrupt SOEs are thus prime candidates to become losers in the globalization game.

By some reckonings, of course, globalization processes also represent an opportunity to cope with the employment needs of the vast "floating population" that is already conservatively estimated to exceed 100 million if both rural migrants and laid-off urban workers are included. Specifically, many economists believe the expanded opportunities for export manufacturing that will accompany further globalization—mainly for nonstate firms—can absorb a sizable portion of the surplus labor created by China's ongoing economic transformation.

The final type of impact identified by Held and his collaborators concerns the influence that globalization processes can have on domestic *structure*, broadly understood to include economic, social, and political structure. In the Chinese case, there is already a growing body of literature that examines patterns of domestic adjustment to the evolution of the Open Policy.[8] While few studies have focused on China's response to changing global conditions, as opposed to the impact of the Open Policy (and other reforms) within China itself, it is not difficult to identify some possible structural consequences of globalization. For example, a number of recent institutional changes within the Chinese state can be explained, at least in part, as responses to forces associated with globalization. By some accounts, the major institutional restructuring undertaken within the State Council following the Ninth National People's Congress (NPC) in March 1998 represented an effort to create a state apparatus better able to serve Chinese interests in the heightened international economic competition that defines the age of globalization.[9] The creation of the Ministry of Information Industry (MII) less than a month after the conclusion of the NPC stands out as an especially timely and important institutional response to globalization processes.[10] Other recent examples of organizational adaptation that arguably reflect the impact of globalization include the restructuring of the People's Bank of China in 1998 (which was modeled after the U.S. Federal Reserve

Bank) and the establishment of asset management companies for each of China's big four state-owned commercial banks in 1999 (which were modeled after the U.S. Resolution Trust Corporation).

CHINESE THINKING ABOUT GLOBALIZATION

Basic Conceptualizations

For most Chinese observers, globalization is understood to be an "objective condition" in the world economy characterized by increased flows of capital, goods, and technology. With the end of the Cold War, in particular, the focus of human activity is said to have shifted primarily to economic development. As a result, economic integration—a long-standing trend in world affairs—has recently reached a point where the world is now experiencing a phenomenon better understood as "globalization" than mere "internationalization." In this sense, the term is used by Chinese observers to convey not only the cumulative scale of change but also the increasing speed of change, especially in the 1990s.

Unlike internationalization, interdependence has not been replaced by globalization as a subject of study. While globalization has clearly become the more popular buzzword recently, especially in the wake of the AFC, interdependence retains its own conceptual identity in debates about contemporary international relations. Unlike works on interdependence, in which there are easily identifiable liberal and realist perspectives among Chinese observers, studies of globalization have not yet focused to the same degree on the power relationships that flow from deepening economic interaction between countries. As defined by one analyst writing in the authoritative journal *Xiandai guoji guanxi,* economic interdependence is "an order in which actions between countries are characterized by mutual influence."[11] By contrast, the director of the Institute of World Economics and Politics at the Chinese Academy of Social Sciences (CASS) defines globalization in the following terms:

> the free circulation and rational allocation of the key elements in production on a global scale and the gradual elimination of various kinds of barriers and obstructions, with a resulting continual strengthening of economic ties and interdependence between states. It is the inevitable result of development toward high levels in productive forces and international division of work.[12]

As this quotation suggests, globalization is understood to involve mainly economic rather than political dynamics; interdependence remains a related but distinct concept. Even in the aftermath of the AFC, not to mention developments such as the U.S.-led NATO intervention in Kosovo and the subsequent bombing of the Chinese embassy in Belgrade, globalization is still seen quite narrowly in terms of *economic* processes. Specifically, it is conceived mainly, at least officially, as an "objective condition" in the world economy rather than as a manifestation of U.S. hegemony. In Jiang's speeches, for example, "hegemonism and power politics" are ritualistically identified as the main threat to world peace, but even after Washington's "aggressive" actions and declarations in 1999 (e.g., Kosovo, Iraq, theater missile defense in East Asia), his comments have never sought to establish a connection between U.S. hegemony and globalization per se. The closest example was a speech during Jiang's September 1999 visit to Thailand, in which he referred to "the new 'Gunboat Policy' and economic neo-colonialism pursued by some big powers."[13] For the most part, however, concerns about value transmission and external challenges to national sovereignty have been directed narrowly at the United States rather than at globalization. In a joint statement issued at the conclusion of Russian president Boris Yeltsin's December 1999 visit to China, for example, Moscow and Beijing implicitly criticized Washington for trying to force "the international community to accept a unipolar world pattern and a single model of culture, value concepts, and ideology" while "using the concepts of 'human rights are superior to sovereignty' and 'humanitarian intervention'" as instruments to impose its will.[14]

While globalization is recognized to pose challenges to China, these are almost exclusively economic in nature. By contrast, it is U.S. hegemony that is seen as the primary source of political, cultural, ideological, and security threats. Except perhaps for Chinese hard-liners, globalization is not equivalent to Americanization. Globalization does create pressures for openness, to be sure, but the future shape of globalization is not regarded by most Chinese observers as predetermined. From this perspective, China's increasing participation in globalization processes, including the WTO, is designed to allow Beijing to exert greater influence over the course of globalization. Here, China's words and deeds indicate an interest in what might be called "managed" globalization. As regards both the pace and the scope of globalization (e.g., the inclusion of labor and environmental standards into the WTO agenda), Beijing still greatly prefers a "controlled" opening to the outside world.

While the Chinese media have certainly acknowledged that globalization "provides an opportunity for the United States to pursue its hegemonic strategy," as the official news agency *Xinhua* observed in August 1999, the very same analyses also typically argue that "as an objective trend, globalization is actually a 'double edged-sword' which also brings about major constraining factors for the United States' pursuit of its hegemonic strategy."[15] Indeed, globalization is regarded by most Chinese observers as reinforcing the multipolarization (*duojihua*) of world politics, a position reflected in the conclusion of the *Xinhua* analysis cited previously:

> To maintain its hegemonic position, the United States must try hard to prevent the appearance of other superpowers. However, globalization will make it hard for the United States to achieve this intention.[16]

On the whole, the dominant perception seems to be that globalization processes are in fact beyond the direct control of the United States and will, over time, only strengthen the trend toward multipolarity. This would be consistent with Jiang's statements during his October 1999 trip to France, in which he emphasized that globalization and multipolarity are objective trends "conducive to the establishment of a new, just and fair, international political and economic order."[17] At the same time, many Chinese observers, including the country's leaders, undoubtedly do see a greater connection between U.S. power and contemporary globalization than scholarly articles and official statements would suggest. (Interviews with Chinese analysts confirmed this assessment, even before the embassy bombing and other recent actions that have increased concerns about U.S. behavior.) These reservations notwithstanding, leaders such as Jiang and Zhu have apparently recognized the necessity of maintaining reasonably positive ties with the United States in order to pursue their economic goals and raise the country's international stature more generally. For this reason as well, therefore, globalization continues to be characterized officially as an "objective trend."

The Continued Primacy of the State

Chinese thinking about globalization is marked by an apparent paradox: While the concept is often defined quite narrowly in terms of increasing cross-border flows of goods, capital, and technology, the consensus is that globalization has actually increased the importance of state activism. Contrary to the views of some Western observers, Chinese leaders and strategic analysts categorically reject the notion that state sovereignty, not to mention the viability of the nation-state itself, is significantly imperiled by globalization. To be sure, state sovereignty may be constrained (or even reduced in some respects), but globalization has not resulted in any fundamental change in the basic (interstate) nature of world politics. The instruments of state power are changing to some degree, and the basis of national power certainly depends more on economic factors than it did previously, but states still wield significant influence to shape events. While not blind to the raw power of the "globalization currents" through which they must navigate, China's leaders appear to be banking on the fact that globalization can empower states and that state control can be exercised effectively even in the context of globalization. True to their reputation for Realpolitik thinking, therefore, Chinese leaders and strategic analysts view globalization processes from the perspective of a competitive interstate system in which the national economy remains the main unit of analysis. In this sense, globalization has not—contrary to the claims of some Western globalists—created a new world order. That said, nation-states are seen as operating in a fast-changing, increasingly unforgiving world economy, especially after the AFC. In his speech at the five-nation summit of Central Asian countries held in Kyrgyzstan in August 1999, Jiang observed that the "accelerated development of economic globalization has triggered . . . unprecedentedly fierce competition and increased financial and economic risks."[18] Similarly, Wang Mengkui, director of the State Council's Development Research Center, has argued that "economic globalization does not at all mean that countries will make no distinction between one another and will be as intimate as a family. Rather, it means that they will compete with one another by the same rules of the game on the playing field."[19] Finally, in a more extreme example, Liu Ji, a CASS researcher, predicted that

> state-to-state competition will become unprecedentedly fierce. Unprecedented wars—economic wars, commodity wars, technology wars, and wars over talented people—will erupt among developed nations, between developed nations and developing nations, and among developing nations. In the process, not only inferior enterprises, but also inferior states and nations, will be eliminated.[20]

Even prior to the AFC, however, globalization was already understood to be leading to increased international economic competition. Like their counterparts abroad, Chinese researchers have long argued that the transportation, telecommunications, and computer revolutions are reducing the effective economic distance among nations, thereby intensifying competition in the world economy and raising the stakes of having a competent state that can harness international forces for the benefit of the national economy. For countries with effective states, globalization brings with it considerable upside potential for economic development, one that in theory allows latecomers to catch up with, and perhaps even leapfrog, earlier developers. At the same time, globalization also carries with it the downside risk that countries with ineffective states may find themselves even further behind as new synergies of economic dynamism catapult the winners into new frontiers of human development.

Based on an extensive review of China's foreign relations literature, including speeches by Chinese leaders, policy analysis published in the Chinese media, and scholarly articles written for academic and policy discussion in China, the mainstream Chinese view of globalization can be defined as follows: an increasingly competitive struggle among national economies over the means to create wealth within their territories. While globalization has not changed the basic state-centric nature of world affairs, it has significantly changed the strategic context within which states function, especially economically. State-to-state relations are certainly still dominant, but state–firm relations have increasing salience since governments at both the national and the local levels find that they must bargain with firms—"foreign" and "domestic" alike—over the terms of a firm's willingness to locate economic activity in their territory. In this sense, the role of the state as an economic manager has changed substantially. States continue to carry out "traditional" economic tasks, of course, but increasing effort is devoted by governments across the world to promoting their country's integration into increasingly decisive *transnational* production and financial structures.

Network-Based Conceptualizations of Globalization

Unlike many of their Western counterparts, Chinese observers do not think about globalization primarily in denationalized, market-based terms. Where those outside China often see deterritorialized flows of capital, goods, and technology, most Chinese observers see a network-based globalization in which the reach of multinational corporations (MNCs) extends both farther around the world and deeper into individual national economies with each passing year. While economic activity is global, in the sense that economic structures and processes are now increasingly transnational (rather than narrowly national) in character, globalization reflects not so much the invisible hand of global markets as the visible hand of global corporate hierarchies. Specifically, in the view of most Chinese observers the global production structure is dominated not so much by an expansion of free-market activity as by the proliferation of transnational manufacturing networks (TMNs). While the national economy remains the basic unit of analysis for state decision makers, MNCs have become increasingly influential actors through their organization of these TMNs (also known as commodity chains or production networks). Indeed, Chinese reports on world affairs are replete with references to the growing importance of MNCs in the world economy:

> Multinationals . . . have formed a colossal network of production and sales covering all parts of the world. They account for one-third of production, two-thirds of trade, 70 percent of total direct investment, and over 70 percent of patent rights and transfer of technology across the world.[21]

Chinese observers may not use the language of "network power" popularized recently among Western scholars, but their emphasis on MNC-led globalization shares much in common with this analytic framework.[22] Except perhaps for financial capital, one area where market-based globalization is regarded by many Chinese observers as a fairly accurate characterization, a network-based conceptualization of globalization represents the dominant approach. On the basis of this understanding, China's emphasis in recent years on developing large conglomerates modeled after South Korea's *chaebol* is far from surprising. While the results of the AFC have raised serious questions about the wisdom of China's quest for gargantuan MNCs, questions that have yet to be fully resolved in Beijing, it seems that China's leaders still believe that the imperatives of global competition require enterprise groups of a certain size. Moreover, most indications are that China's leaders believe the problems experienced by South Korean (and, for that matter, Japanese) conglomerates had more to do with management hubris and unsustainable financial arrangements than problems with size per se. Consequently,

many observers ultimately expect a modification rather than a wholesale refutation of China's existing policy on conglomerates. (Evidence here includes the recent provision of government financial support for six companies—including
well-known giants such as Haier and Baoshan Iron and Steel—with the explicit
goal of helping them attain Fortune 500 status by 2010.) That said, the AFC still
represents a major challenge to the consensus that had been building in China
since the early 1990s in favor of a *chaebol*-style strategy for developing enterprise groups that could thrive in a globalizing world economy.

Between Internationalism and Transnationalism: The Globalization of Production

Even if globalization has not changed the state-centric character of world politics,
what it has done is change the economic and technological context within which
the creation of wealth and pursuit of national power takes place. As described by
Long Yongtu, China's deputy foreign trade minister and chief negotiator for international economic affairs (including WTO accession), "The main characteristic of economic globalization is production globalization."[23] Specifically, his
analysis shows an understanding of how product cycle analysis, which focuses on
the transfer of entire industries across national economies and is a popular
framework for understanding the development success of South Korea and Taiwan, needs modification in light of contemporary changes in the world economy:

> Economic globalization is a worldwide industrial restructuring in which the devel-
> oped countries dominate and the multinational companies are the main motive force.
> This industrial restructuring not only reacts to the extent of moving . . . entire indus-
> tries, but, and still more important, to [the extent] of moving . . . production links in
> the same industry.[24]

As a result, globalization has produced a fundamentally different international division of labor, one that many Chinese observers believe provides a substantial
opportunity for China to accelerate its own industrial transformation. According
to Long's analysis, which is generally consistent with comments made by Jiang
and Zhu over the last few years, China should integrate itself into the world economy on the basis of "labor-intensive production links in capital and technology-
intensive industries," recognizing that globalization has fundamentally changed
the context in which contemporary development strategies are formulated. Here,
his views are worth quoting at length:

> In the past, when the speed of enhancing production technology and upgrading prod-
> ucts was comparatively slow, the developing countries, especially countries with rel-
> atively large domestic markets, could carry out nationalization under the protection
> of state policies, establish their own industrial systems, and catch up with the ad-
> vanced world levels by importing advanced technology. In an era when new things

in science and technology are appearing every day, however . . . we must develop these industries in an environment of opening up to the world, and the short cut is to use foreign investment and to cooperate with multinational companies that have ample capital and technology, to become the foreign production bases of these companies and a link in their entire global production line and a part of their international sales network. . . . This is an opportunity that was not available to Japan and Korea in the 1960s and 1970s.[25]

According to this understanding, therefore, outward-oriented industrialization is to be favored over any variant of import-substituting industrialization. Consider, for example, Long's explanation for Beijing's decision to take part in the much-ballyhooed Agreement on Information Technology, a multilateral pact on tariff reduction in telecommunications, semiconductors, and computer products. According to Long, "The main purpose of this is to enable China to become part of the multinational companies' global base for IT (information technology) products and thus simultaneously enter the world sales network."[26] In this way, China seeks to adjust its development strategy to what Long called a "new pattern" of international trade:

A country no longer blindly seeks to completely occupy one industry, but instead . . . exerts itself to seize the high-tech and high value-added production links in an industry; at the same time it leaves labor-intensive and low value-added production links to other countries, thus forming a new division of work system in international trade.[27]

Based on the premise that the ability to generate wealth is the primary determinant of long-term national power, an increasing number of Chinese observers seem convinced, as an official at the Central Party School put it, that "taking part in the international division of labor and economic globalization is imperative for all countries."[28] Despite "a certain amount of embarrassment about being just a link in the production chain of a multinational corporation, and . . . ranking [only] at the third level of the 'flying goose' V formation," China must, this official argued, intensify efforts to pursue positions within the TMNs that now define the international division of labor.[29] There are advantages and disadvantages, to be sure, but failure to adjust now to the contemporary world economy will only leave China further behind later. As explained by Long, "If one does not participate in the global production and market networks of the multinational companies . . . then it is very difficult to join in the main world current of the development. . . . Hence, we must adapt to the tide of globalization and establish a strategic partnership of long-term cooperation with multinational companies."[30]

This type of analysis, while increasingly in the mainstream, also remains somewhat controversial since one clear implication is that the primary role of the state as an economic manager is now to make China an attractive location for foreign firms to locate production. For some observers, this strategy is at cross-purposes with Beijing's stated desire to develop its own MNCs. To others, such as Long, the two strategies can be complementary, especially over time, as foreign partnerships strengthen the competitiveness of Chinese firms.

CHINESE POLICIES FOR A GLOBAL AGE

Staying the Course: Economic (but Not Political) Reform and Opening

As discussed in greater depth later, globalization is generally associated in China with arguments for greater reform and opening, even after the AFC. As described by Jiang in a speech during his trip to Japan in November 1998, when the AFC was still uppermost on the minds of regional leaders, the key to success in the age of globalization is further reform and opening:

> We must continue to work hard and exert ourselves to catch up with the global economic, scientific, and technological development trend. We must continue to widen the scope of opening up and actively absorb all progressive achievements of human civilization to speed up our modernization drive.[31]

Not surprisingly, perhaps, Beijing's increasingly sophisticated understanding of the economic prerequisites for successful participation in globalization processes does not yet extend to the political domain. Specifically, the need for substantive political reform to increase the effectiveness of the Chinese state in an increasingly competitive world economy remains wholly unrecognized at an official level. In fact, China's leaders have been absolutely unyielding on this issue, as evidenced by their crackdowns on the short-lived "Beijing Spring" in 1998 and the Falun Gong movement in 1999.[32] For his part, Jiang appears alternately as a modern economic leader and an unreconstructed political conservative. However important clean government, political accountability, and the rule of law are for national success in the era of globalization, official thinking about globalization in China still focuses almost exclusively on economic issues. While a comprehensive review of China's economic policies is beyond the scope of this chapter, especially in the wake of Beijing's complex and multilevel response to the AFC (see chapter 2 for an overview of China's role within the larger regional context), the following sections examine several areas where China's leaders have explicitly invoked globalization as a motivating force in their decisions.[33]

The Knowledge Economy

Recognizing that the role of the state as an economic manager has changed as a result of globalization, China's leaders have promoted a number of initiatives aimed at increasing the long-term competitiveness of the Chinese economy. One example is the importance that Jiang and Zhu have attached to the creation of a "knowledge economy" (*zhishi jingji*) as part of the country's bid to achieve sustained, robust economic growth during its ongoing economic transition. Indeed, the advent of a knowledge economy is hailed as one potential solution for coping with the long-term reemployment problem created by SOE restructuring. Zhu, in particular, has been a staunch advocate, publicly declaring that "developing the country by relying on science and education is one of the government's most important tasks."[34] For his part, Jiang has also been a strong proponent, touting the idea of a knowledge economy by observing that "a nation will not be able to stand in the family of the world's advanced nations if it lacks the ability to innovate."[35] One example of Beijing's commitment to a knowledge economy was the previously mentioned creation of MII, a high-profile "superministry" designed to better serve Chinese interests in a globalizing world economy. In the wake of Minister Wu Jichuan's obstructionist behavior during China's WTO accession talks with the United States and his efforts to place greater restrictions on foreign investment in China's telecommunications industry more generally, MII has many detractors, both inside and outside China, who argue that the ministry is likely to inhibit rather than enhance the development of the country's information industry. For better or for worse, however, MII will undoubtedly play a central role in shaping China's bid to develop a knowledge economy.

Catching the Globalization Wave: Internet Promotion and Electronic Commerce

While interest in the knowledge economy is a relatively recent phenomenon, it is of course fully consistent with the long-standing focus that top leaders such as Jiang and Zhu have placed on high technology as a centerpiece of the country's development. Indeed, few public statements by Jiang or Zhu on economic issues in recent years have failed to highlight the importance of science and technology for national strength, international competitiveness, and domestic living standards. One area where these sentiments have become manifest recently is Beijing's promotion of the Internet. As widely reported, the government is investing heavily in telecommunications infrastructure with a goal of making China one of the world's biggest Internet users (in absolute numbers) over the next few years. (Private estimates predict about 35 to 40 million users by 2003, with as many as 80 million possible by 2005. Even this last figure, it should be noted, would still represent only about 6 percent of China's population.[36]) Recent state policies to promote Internet use have included cutting access fees by half and offering free installation of a second residential phone line. The result was a tripling of users in 1999 to nearly nine million at year's end, this after the number of users doubled every year from 1996 to 1998.

For technocrats such as Jiang and Zhu, both trained as engineers, the Internet is reportedly seen as a tool to accelerate development of a knowledge economy. Indeed, there is evidence that the Internet is seen in China as a "great equalizer" among developed and developing countries. One prominent example here is electronic commerce (e-commerce), an innovation Jiang has described as "the future of business."[37] To this end, he used the 1998 APEC (Asian Pacific Economic Cooperation forum) summit in Kuala Lumpur to call for greater development of e-commerce among the forum's member economies. As early as January 1997, in fact, an international e-commerce center was established in Beijing. Indeed, Chinese leaders have approved plans to have 80 percent of local governments and Chinese companies linked to the Internet by 2000 and 2001, respectively. (Most ministries already have Web sites.) By reducing the effective economic distance both within China's far-flung borders and between China and the outside world—especially in terms of redressing the chronic information deficit that has long plagued market development—the Internet is seen as a tool not only for "catching the globalization wave" but also for creating jobs and rationalizing the economic structure at home. In sum, Beijing has high hopes for e-commerce and Internet usage more generally as a mechanism for stimulating further domestic reform and improving the competitiveness of Chinese goods abroad.

As made clear by the new Internet regulations issued in January 2000—the full impact of which will not be clear for quite some time—Beijing is certainly not blind to the dangers of the Internet for Party rule, especially as a means to disseminate information and organize political activities.[38] That said, China's leaders seem determined to promote the Internet all the same. To this point, at least, they apparently believe either that the risks to the Party's political control can be managed or that the risks to the country of not being wired outweigh the risks of being wired. Here, perceptions of globalization are undoubtedly important given Jiang and Zhu's conviction that the Internet is an indispensable tool for developing the knowledge economy they regard as so vital for China to become rich and strong.

For now, Beijing's strategy is clearly to promote use of the Internet for economic purposes while vigorously censoring its use for political activity. Certain Web sites continue to be blocked, especially foreign Web sites, and strong examples have been made of transgressors such as Lin Hai, the Shanghai computer technician sentenced to two years in prison in 1999 for selling 30,000 Chinese e-mail addresses to dissident and human rights groups in the United States. Similarly, Internet companies were ordered to suspend Web-based e-mail following reports of its use by followers of the Falun Gong movement in organizing the April 1999 protest in which 10,000 demonstrators surrounded the leadership compound in Beijing. As this last episode underscores, the balancing act between promotion and control of the Internet is going to be a difficult trick for China's leaders. Success is by no means guaranteed; they may well find it impossible to have their cyber-cake and eat it, too.

Whatever the outcome, top leaders such as Jiang and Zhu have identified information technology as a critical component of the country's drive for national strength, both as a tool for economic modernization and for its military applications. From all indications, globalization is understood to mean that countries face little choice but to join the technological revolution. While it would be a huge exaggeration to say that Beijing has accepted the idea of technology without borders, for it most certainly has not, China's leaders have indicated—both by their words and by their deeds—their belief that China cannot afford to opt out of the Internet revolution. Indeed, what is most notable about the current wiring of China is that the government is actually promoting Internet usage rather than simply presiding over its growth.

SOE Reform

In the last few years, China's leaders have apparently come to realize, however grudgingly, that SOE reform is an absolute prerequisite for the country's continued economic development. Indeed, this issue has enjoyed a high profile on the reform agenda since the Fifteenth Party Congress in September 1997. It was at that landmark event, the first since Deng Xiaoping's death, that Jiang originally announced the decision to move 10,000 of China's 13,000 large and medium-size SOEs to a shareholding system in which the state would no longer be the primary owner of industrial assets. While there were undoubtedly several reasons why this new initiative to corporatize China's SOEs was launched, including Jiang's need to demonstrate bold leadership only six months after Deng's death and the fact that the financial burden of carrying so many loss-making SOEs was increasingly unsustainable for Beijing, globalization was unquestionably an important backdrop. As Jiang explained the move at the time, "We must be soberly aware that international competition is becoming increasingly acute, that the economic, scientific, and technological gap between China and the developed countries has brought great pressure to bear on us, and that we ourselves still have many difficulties."[39] During an August 1999 inspection tour of SOEs, he acknowledged explicitly the external imperative China faces in addressing the deficiencies of its SOEs:

> The core of international economic competition today is knowledge and technological renovation and the industrialization of high technology. . . . [In the absence of reform], it will be difficult for state-owned enterprises to have momentum for development and it will be difficult for us to maintain the sustained, rapid, and healthy development of the national economy.[40]

Elsewhere in this same speech, Jiang in fact suggested that SOE restructuring was one of the most difficult hurdles facing China in meeting the challenge of globalization:

> We are at an important historical moment at the turn of the century. Peace and development is the main theme of the current era. . . . Modern technology is advancing rapidly and industrial and economic restructuring on a global scale is speeding up.

Competition based on overall national strength will increasingly become the leading
factor deciding a country's future and destiny. We are facing rare development opportunities as well as grim challenges. Only by constantly improving our economic
strength, national defense strength, and national cohesiveness, can we remain invin-
cible amidst increasingly intensive international competition and truly safeguard our
national sovereignty and national pride. . . . To build a socialist market economic system . . . we must closely attend to reforming state-owned enterprises—the central
link of reform of the economic system.[41]

As these comments suggest, Jiang regards SOE reform as a top (albeit fairly long-
term) priority. Based on Zhu's relatively low-profile position during the second
half of 1999, as well as the fact that Jiang chose to make industrial restructuring
the subject of his first major policy address (the previously quoted speech) after
the annual Beidaihe leadership meeting held in August 1999, it is widely believed
that Jiang has in fact taken greater personal command of efforts to advance the
cause of SOE reform, albeit at a much slower pace than Zhu's original three-year
plan set forth in 1998. (By some accounts, Jiang's time frame for SOE reform is
closer to a decade.) Recent developments that point toward the slower privatization of SOEs, such as the August 1999 announcement that China would begin a
program of debt-for-equity swaps (rather than auctions) for SOEs and the relatively weak communiqué on SOE reform that emerged from the Fourth Plenum of
the Fifteenth Party Congress in September 1999, seem to confirm this analysis.

Even if the pace of SOE reform has fallen short of the expectations set two or
three years ago, China's leaders do seem to understand that difficult reforms such
as SOE restructuring cannot be postponed indefinitely without serious consequences for China's long-term economic success. As Jiang himself suggested
during a September 1999 inspection tour of Shanghai just prior to taking part in
celebrations marking the fiftieth anniversary of the People's Republic of China,
Beijing has decided that the nature of ownership must change for the restructuring of Chinese industry not to fall further behind the industrial transformation occurring worldwide. For his part, Zhu used an anniversary reception at the Great
Hall of the People to emphasize the centrality of SOE reform to the long-term development of the national economy. From their statements, it seems that the top
leaders—not to mention influential bureaucrats such as Long—increasingly view
China's own economic challenges within the larger context of global industrial
restructuring. (Gills and Gills make a similar argument about South Korea in
chapter 4.) For this reason, the China described by Jiang himself—a leader not
formerly known for looking at the world through an economic lens—has increasingly been a China at an economic crossroads. In this sense, the issue of
SOE restructuring has, to adopt another metaphor, come to represent Jiang's—
and, for that matter, Zhu's—Rubicon. Will they cross it? If their deeds finally
catch up to their words, and the ownership system for SOEs is in fact fundamentally changed, a major breakthrough will have occurred in the reform experiment
begun two decades ago.

CHINA'S EVOLVING NATIONAL ECONOMIC IDENTITY

Toward a "Global Nationalism"?

For all the concern in the West about reform backsliding in the wake of the AFC, not to mention worry that the AFC has rekindled jingoistic debate in China over the concept of economic security (and in so doing provided fodder for those who regard globalization as a threat to China's economic well-being), China's leaders seem relatively undeterred in their commitment to reform and opening. There has been a gap between rhetoric and action, to be sure, but a comparison of statements by top leaders before and after the AFC reveals surprising consistency in their views on China's proper strategy (reform and opening) for national economic revitalization. Talk about "economic nationalism" has enjoyed a resurgence among Chinese observers recently, but it has not generally been used by China's leaders to advocate strategies associated with mercantilism. (By contrast, some commentators—including the authors of the controversial best-selling book *China's Road: Under the Shadow of Globalization*—do favor greater attention to "strategic" economic policies that favor genuine "national" industries [*minzu gongye*] rather than merely "domestic" industries [*guonei gongye*], even if they do not explicitly oppose China joining the WTO or participating in globalization processes more generally.[42])

As mentioned previously, Jiang's major speeches since 1997 have increasingly defined China's national economic identity in terms of meeting the challenge of globalization through greater domestic reform and deeper participation in the world economy, even if this results in higher levels of interdependence.[43] To be sure, references to self-reliance and an independent foreign policy are invoked as well, albeit somewhat ritualistically, but the dominant image is one of China facing the imperatives of global economic life forthrightly, especially as regards international economic competition. Care must be taken not to overstate this point, and one must always retain a healthy degree of skepticism in interpreting the meaning of public pronouncements for which there are multiple audiences (at home and abroad), but the "reality" of globalization can now be said to assume an unprecedented place in the formation of China's national economic identity. Consider the following statement by Jiang at Deng Xiaoping's eulogy in February 1997:

> Opening up to the outside world is an essential condition for China to achieve its socialist modernization. Comrade Deng Xiaoping emphasized repeatedly that the current world is an open one, that China's development is inseparable from the world, and that it is imperative to pursue the policy of opening up to the outside world on the basis of persisting in self-reliance.[44]

Jiang's obeisance to Deng aside, he has actually recast China's national economic identity far beyond anything articulated by Deng, emphasizing not just economic prosperity and advanced technological capability but also broad participation in global economic life. In this sense, Jiang is continuing the reshaping of China's post–Mao Zedong national identity begun by Deng and Zhao Ziyang. Building on Deng's depiction of Mao's China as backward economically and weak internationally and therefore in need of national rejuvenation to restore China to its historic greatness, Jiang has placed China's reform in a much more explicitly global context. Whereas Deng (and even Zhao) focused more narrowly on economic modernization, Jiang has increasingly expressed China's national economic identity (and, indeed, its national identity more generally) in terms of global economic competition and China's aspirations to achieve its rightful place in "the family of the world's advanced nations."[45] (This conception, it should be noted, bears a strong resemblance to the South Korean interpretation of globalization described in chapter 4, although the Chinese version focuses much more narrowly on economic achievement.)

On numerous occasions, Jiang has noted China's current "underdevelopment" as a way of emphasizing the imperative of pursuing economic modernization. In his speech at the Fifteenth Party Congress in September 1997, for example, he explicitly contrasted China's "underdevelopment" with the "advanced world standard" that serves as the target of its ambitions. As George T. Crane has pointed out, the Chinese economic nation is now quite literally defined by the global context.[46] Referring to the primary stage of socialism, Jiang described it as "a stage in which we will gradually narrow the gap between our level and the advanced world standard and bring about a great rejuvenation of the Chinese nation on the basis of socialism."[47] Two months earlier, in his speech celebrating the return of Hong Kong, Jiang had invoked images of China's past indignities, such as the Opium War, implicitly warning his countrymen about what could happen if China fails to continue its contemporary opening to the outside world:

> A major cause for the backwardness that China suffered . . . was the unwise closed-door policy . . . [that] forfeited China of its ability to advance with the times and to resist the imperialist aggression, leaving it many records of national betrayal and humiliation.[48]

In this way, China's long period of suffering and victimization since the Opium War is used as an argument for, rather than against, integration into the world economy. To safeguard against a repeat of past indignities, China must continue its policy of reform and opening, albeit at its own pace, even when this entails sacrifices (e.g., the unemployment associated with SOE reform and market access concessions required for WTO accession). These sacrifices, however painful, are necessary to achieve the "advanced world standard" identified by Jiang as the measuring stick for national achievement. In this sense, national greatness is increasingly defined not in terms of socialist virtue or revolutionary spirit but in terms of China's ability to compete globally. While China's leaders are undoubtedly committed to creating a modern economy with "Chinese characteristics," this goal is (at least partly) at cross-purposes with an evolving national economic identity that might be called "global nationalism" given its focus on China's position within the international community.

Here, it is important to note that the challenge of globalization need not be met, in Beijing's opinion, through the immediate adoption of neoliberal economic policy or openness to social, cultural, and political forces outside China. As discussed earlier, globalization is not considered to be synonymous with the deterritorialization of world economic activity. In fact, globalization is depicted as a distinctly *national* challenge in which economic competition determines which countries will be rich and strong. As such, the goal remains a strategic opening rather than the kind of indiscriminate opening consistent with ideal-typic neoliberal economic precepts. Especially in the wake of the AFC, China's leaders are well aware of the country's economic vulnerabilities and, therefore, of the need to protect the country's economic security. In this sense, there may be two main lessons from the AFC: first, the need for greater long-term reform and opening in order to make China competitive internationally and, second, the need for greater vigilance in the sequencing and timing of short-term initiatives as China opens to the outside world, all in an effort to minimize its vulnerability to adverse forces.

Taken as a whole, however, statements by Chinese leaders have been remarkably consistent in their acceptance of globalization as a fact of economic life, a reality that China can ignore only at its own peril. While it is true that China has neither fully embraced interdependence as a worldview nor substantially changed its strategic focus on national power in response to globalization processes, there is some evidence that reform and opening are now seen not simply as means for pursuing national economic revitalization but also as *limited* ends in themselves. Jiang's speeches, in particular, suggest that China's national greatness must be defined in part by its participation in world affairs, especially as regards its long-term openness to the world economy. From this perspective, reform and opening are not simply tools for becoming modern but also expressions of China's evolving nationhood. To reestablish itself as a great nation, the argument would go, China must meet the challenge of globalization by succeeding through openness. Notably, this sentiment has continued even in the wake of the AFC, as revealed in Jiang's comments at the depth of the regional economic turmoil in August 1998:

> Economic globalization, being an objective tendency of the development of the world's economy, is independent of man's will and cannot be avoided by any country. The world today is an open world and no country can develop its own economy if isolated from the outside world. We must firmly implement the policy of opening up, keep in line with economic globalization, energetically take part in international economic cooperation and competition, and make full use of various favorable conditions and opportunities brought by economic globalization.[49]

This theme, which Jiang also trumpeted during his visits to Britain and France in October 1999, could also be detected in Beijing's renewed bid for WTO accession in 1999, an effort that was apparently part of a broader decision by China's leaders to pursue specific domestic and international changes identified as critical for China's long-term economic security. According to this view, the AFC only reinforced the belief among China's leaders that globalization is a high-stakes game, one in which China must be ready to play or risk being marginalized. If "the world today is an open world," as Jiang claimed in the previous quote, then the benefits of WTO membership can be seen as necessary for China to achieve a level playing field vis-à-vis other developing countries in the competitive economic struggle that defines the age of globalization. Indeed, in an interview published in *Renmin ribao,* the official Party newspaper, Long defended Beijing's November 1999 WTO agreement with Washington as necessary for China to join the trend of economic globalization.[50]

Following Zhu's visit to Washington in April 1999, during which U.S. president Bill Clinton rejected an offer very similar to the one he eventually accepted seven months later, a commentary in *Jingji ribao,* the State Council's official newspaper for economic affairs, had argued that given "the overall inevitable trend of economic globalization, joining the WTO is in keeping with this trend, a necessary option for blending in with the world economic tide."[51] Even more directly, a commentary in *Renmin ribao* had rejected the notion that the changes China would have to make as part of its WTO accession should even be considered "concessions," referring to them instead as "a necessity for reform and opening up to enter a new stage. . . . Moreover, it is the only way to become an organic part of the world economy."[52] This same strategy was heavily employed by Long and other Chinese officials who were charged with defending the terms of the final Sino-American agreement in the Chinese media.[53]

Even in the wake of the AFC, therefore, China's pursuit of economic security is still predicated on the basic policy of reform and opening that began more than two decades ago. To be sure, "stability" is again the prevalent watchword, and opening is now pursued with heightened vigilance—lest China leave itself unnecessarily vulnerable to future financial storms and other sources of instability in the world economy. Similarly, economic reforms have been pursued with extreme caution everywhere since the AFC and in some areas not at all. All of this said, there is every indication that the main lesson drawn by China's leaders from the region's tumultuous episode is the need for more extensive economic reform and opening in the future. This belief, in turn, owes much to the emergence of a more comprehensive view of national security in the aftermath of the AFC. As described by Wang Yizhou, noted scholar of international relations theory and deputy director of the Institute of World Economics and Politics at CASS, "Security should be realized in a changing, opening, and progressive process, which is closely related to a country's capability [for] . . . self-reform, creation, and openness."[54] This, of course, is the very essence of China's evolving "global nationalism."

China Today: Realists in a Globalizing World Economy

As Samuel Kim notes in chapter 1, China is especially difficult to classify in terms of the major contending schools of thought in the globalization debate. The vast majority of Chinese observers, including its top leaders, are neither hyper-globalists nor true skeptics. Most are skeptics to the extent that the state in their view remains a robust actor in globalization processes, but at the same time there is a growing sense among Chinese observers that the contemporary period of globalization marks more than just a return to earlier forms of globalization. As discussed previously, contemporary "globalization" is often distinguished in China from the mere "internationalization" of the past. In this sense, globalization processes are certainly taken seriously in China, especially since the AFC. Much as Hamilton-Hart describes the Thai view in chapter 8, globalization is seen as both real and consequential in China. Specifically, it is viewed as fundamentally changing the geoeconomic context within which countries compete for comprehensive national strength (*zonghe guoli*). In this sense, most Chinese observers believe the message for leaders across the world is, "Defy globalization at your own peril." Especially through their words, but also increasingly through their deeds, China's leaders have indeed acknowledged the need for all countries—advanced industrial and developing countries alike—to adapt to a globalizing world economy.

In sum, there is simply too much recognition of change in the world economy for most Chinese observers to be properly regarded as skeptics per se. Instead, most Chinese observers, including its top leaders, are better characterized as "realists in a globalizing world economy." Because of the specific challenges (as well as opportunities) that globalization presents, national success is now thought to depend, more than ever before, on having a competent state that can manage the country's participation in the world economy effectively. In this sense, the state retains its critical role because of, rather than in spite of, globalization.

While dangers are present, globalization is not generally regarded in China as the kind of predatory force described by Welsh in chapter 10 on Malaysia. In part, this undoubtedly reflects the fact that China did not suffer as deeply from the AFC as did many of its neighbors. More broadly, it may also reflect the fact that China's deepening participation in the world economy over the last two decades is widely perceived as having contributed substantially to the country's rising living standards, not to mention the perceived growth in its international stature. In this sense, China's cautious embrace of globalization depends in no small measure on the relatively good economic times the country experienced during the 1990s. While globalization certainly represents a threat to the livelihood of some Chinese (e.g., employees of SOEs), for many others it is associated with improved livelihood. This differs not only from countries in Southeast Asia hit hardest by the AFC, but also, more unexpectedly, from an advanced industrial country such as Japan, which William Grimes tells us in chapter 3 associates globalization fairly strongly with long-term economic vulnerability.

For now, globalization is not regarded as a major threat to state power in China, at least not an unavoidable or unmanageable one. Indeed, the official line is that globalization can be restricted primarily to the economic dimension. Realistic or not, the belief is that globalization can be used to empower the country (and, for that matter, the state itself) without becoming a transmission belt for ideological, political, or security globalization. As "realists in a globalizing world economy," China's leaders are actively trying to foster the emergence of a "global nationalism" that will not only confer short-term legitimacy on the regime but also allow the country to face the imperatives of global economic life successfully and thereby achieve great power status in the long run. As such, globalization is one of the primary lenses through which Chinese domestic and foreign policy should be viewed today.

NOTES

1. Jiang Zemin, "Hold High the Great Banner of Deng Xiaoping Theory: Carrying the Cause of Building Socialism with Chinese Characteristics to the Twenty-first Century," *Xinhua,* September 21, 1997, in FBIS-CHI-97-266. Throughout this chapter, the abbreviation "FBIS-CHI" stands for Foreign Broadcast Information Service, *China Daily Report* (Internet version).

2. Estimates using purchasing power parity as the basis for estimating GDP result in a much lower figure. Using either method, however, the main utility of these estimates is simply to document the upward trend in China's integration into the world economy.

3. For 1999 data, see chapter 1, table 1.2. For data on earlier years, see the Web sites for the World Economic Forum and the International Institute of Management Development listed as source information for table 1.2.

4. David Held, Anthony McGrew, David Goldblatt, and Jonathan Perraton, *Global Transformations* (Stanford, Calif.: Stanford University Press, 1999).

5. For more detail on this case, see Thomas G. Moore and Dixia Yang, "Empowered and Restrained: Chinese Foreign Policy in the Age of Economic Interdependence," in David M. Lampton, ed., *The Making of Chinese Foreign and Security Policy in the Era of Reform, 1978–2000* (Stanford, Calif.: Stanford University Press, in press).

6. Held et al., *Global Transformations,* 18.

7. For a recent overview of this idea, see Moore and Yang, "Empowered and Restrained." The notion of a "global logic" was first examined in Thomas G. Moore, "China as a Latecomer: Toward a Global Logic of the Open Policy," *Journal of Contemporary China* 5, no. 12 (summer 1996): 187–208. For a lengthier discussion on how external forces have restructured policy options as China's participation in the world economy has grown, especially in the context of specific industries, see Thomas G. Moore, *China in the World Market* (New York: Cambridge University Press, in press).

8. Notable contributions here include recent work by Susan Shirk and David Zweig. For Shirk's view, see especially her "Internationalization and China's Economic Reforms," in Robert O. Keohane and Helen V. Milner, eds., *Internationalization and Domestic Politics*

(New York: Cambridge University Press, 1996), 186–206. For an important argument by Zweig, see his "Developmental Communities on China's Coast," *Comparative Politics* 27, no. 3 (April 1995): 253–74. A lengthier examination of these issues is found in his unpublished book manuscript "Linking China with the World."

9. This rationale was even suggested, albeit implicitly, in the explanation given by Luo Gan, state councillor and secretary-general of the State Council. For the apparent text of his speech at the NPC, see *Ta Kung Pao*, March 7, 1998, in FBIS-CHI-98-068.

10. Established amidst the elimination (or merger) of fifteen ministries, MII combined the administrative assets of three former ministries: the Ministry of Posts and Telecommunications, the Ministry of Electronics, and the Ministry of Radio, Film, and Television. In addition, MII assumed government functions over the ministerial-level state corporations for the aerospace and aviation industries.

11. Zhang Yiping, "A New View of Post-Cold War World Security," *Xiandai guoji guanxi,* February 1997, in FBIS-CHI-97-091.

12. Gu Yuanyang, "Economic Globalization and the 'Rules of the Game,'" *Renmin ribao,* June 10, 1998, in FBIS-CHI-98-167.

13. *Xinhua,* September 3, 1999, in FBIS-CHI-1999-0903.

14. *Xinhua,* December 10, 1999, in FBIS-CHI-1999-1210.

15. Both quotes from *Xinhua,* August 10, 1999, in FBIS-CHI-1999-0822.

16. *Xinhua,* August 10, 1999, in FBIS-CHI-1999-0822.

17. This quotation, which is representative of the comments Jiang made throughout his six-nation trip, is from a written interview Jiang conducted with the French newspaper *Le Figaro*. For the text, see *Xinhua,* October 25, 1999, in FBIS-CHI-1999-1026.

18. *Xinhua,* August 25, 1999, in FBIS-CHI-1999-0825.

19. Wang Mengkui, "Asian Financial Crisis and China," *Qiushi,* November 1, 1998, in FBIS-CHI-98-341.

20. *Ta Kung Pao,* January 25, 1999, in FBIS-CHI-99-025.

21. *Xinhua,* December 22, 1998, translated in FBIS-CHI-98-356.

22. One prominent example in this literature is Peter Katzenstein and Takashi Shiraishi, eds., *Network Power: Japan and Asia* (Ithaca, N.Y.: Cornell University Press, 1997).

23. Long Yongtu, "On Economic Globalization," *Guangming ribao,* October 30, 1998, in FBIS-CHI-98-313.

24. Long, "On Economic Globalization."

25. Long, "On Economic Globalization."

26. Long, "On Economic Globalization."

27. Long, "On Economic Globalization."

28. Zhang Boli, "A Number of Matters Involved in Economic Globalization," *Guoji shangbao,* July 7, 1998, in FBIS-CHI-98-220.

29. Zhang, "A Number of Matters Involved in Economic Globalization."

30. Long, "On Economic Globalization."

31. Jiang Zemin, "Take Warning from History and Usher in the Future," *Xinhua,* November 28, 1998, in FBIS-CHI-98-333.

32. For an argument about how China's continued development depends on political as well as economic reform, see Minxin Pei, "Will China Become Another Indonesia?" *Foreign Policy,* no. 116 (fall 1999): 94–109.

33. China's domestic policy responses to the AFC have already received considerable scholarly attention. See, for example, Alvin Y. So, "China under the Shadow of Asian

Financial Crisis: Retreat from Economic and Political Liberalization?" *Asian Perspective* 23, no. 2 (1999): 83–109, and Charles Wolf Jr., "Three Systems Surrounded by Crisis," *Orbis* 43, no. 2 (spring 1999): 193–202. For an overview of China's foreign economic policy in response to the AFC, see Moore and Yang, "Empowered and Restrained."

34. Quoted in "Roundup on Knowledge Economy," *Xinhua*, January 11, 1999, in FBIS-CHI-1999-020.

35. Quoted in "Knowledge Economy and Learning Society," *Renmin ribao*, July 7, 1998, in FBIS-CHI-98-201.

36. James Kynge, "China's Online Date with Destiny," *Financial Times*, December 18, 1999, 8.

37. Jiang was quoted in *Xinhua*, June 16, 1999, in FBIS-CHI-1999-0616. This same *Xinhua* commentary identified e-commerce as a special area where China could catch up to the developed countries.

38. The new regulations set policy in four basic ways. First, they make Internet providers responsible for the content of the information they post. Specifically, the new regulations make formal the heretofore implicit understanding that China's "state secrets" laws do in fact apply to Internet activity. Second, companies that use encryption software are required under the new regulations to register with the government and disclose detailed information about that software. Third, Internet companies are required to receive new forms of bureaucratic approval before issuing stock. Finally, Internet companies are prohibited from having more than 50 percent foreign ownership. While these new regulations surely constitute a serious warning, their direct impact is less clear at present. For one thing, enforcement is likely to prove difficult. Moreover, strict enforcement—especially of the high-profile variety—risks scaring off foreign investors who have already pledged hundreds of millions of U.S. dollars to a sector that China's leaders themselves regard as critical to the country's long-term economic success.

39. Jiang, "Hold High the Great Banner of Deng Xiaoping Theory."

40. Jiang Zemin, "Strengthen Confidence, Deepen Reform, Create a New Situation in Development of State-Owned Enterprises," *Xinhua*, August 12, 1999, in FBIS-CHI-1999-0817.

41. Jiang, "Strengthen Confidence, Deepen Reform, Create a New Situation in Development of State-Owned Enterprises."

42. Fang Ning, Wang Xiaodong, and Song Qiang, *Quanqiuhua yinying xia de Zhongguo zhilu* (China's road: Under the shadow of globalization) (Beijing: Zhongguo shehui kexue chubanshe, 1999).

43. My arguments throughout this section of the chapter have been strongly influenced by the recent work of George T. Crane, especially his "Imagining the Economic Nation: Globalization in China," *New Political Economy* 4, no. 2 (July 1999): 215–32.

44. *Xinhua*, February 25, 1997, in FBIS-CHI-97-037.

45. Quoted in "Knowledge Economy and Learning Society," *Renmin ribao*, July 7, 1998, in FBIS-CHI-98-201.

46. Crane, "Imagining the Economic Nation."

47. Jiang, "Hold High the Great Banner of Deng Xiaoping Theory."

48. "Jiang Zemin's Speech at Public Gathering to Celebrate Hong Kong's Return," *Xinhua*, July 1, 1997, in FBIS-CHI-97-182.

49. "Jiang Zemin, Zhang Wannian Meet Diplomats," *Xinhua*, August 28, 1998, in FBIS-CHI-98-242.

50. *Renmin ribao,* November 17, 1999, in FBIS-CHI-1999-1117.

51. *Jingji ribao,* May 6, 1999, in FBIS-CHI-1999-0523.

52. *Renmin ribao,* May 7, 1999, translated in FBIS-CHI-1999-0523.

53. See, for example, *Renmin ribao,* November 17, 1999, translated in FBIS-CHI-1999-1117.

54. Wang Yizhou, "New Security Concept in Globalization," *Beijing Review,* February 15–21, 1999, 7.

6

Hong Kong and Globalization

Hongying Wang

Hong Kong is a rather unique entity. It has been variably labeled as a colony, an administrative region, and a world city. While all these descriptions fit in some sense, none accurately and fully describes the qualities of Hong Kong. Hong Kong was officially a colony of Britain from the mid-nineteenth century to 1997, but the reality of Hong Kong was at odds with the typical image of a poor and dependent territory. Toward the last few decades of British rule, Hong Kong became the only industrialized colony and achieved a remarkable degree of prosperity and autonomy.[1] In 1997, Hong Kong reverted to Chinese sovereignty and became a special administrative region (SAR) of the People's Republic of China. However, it enjoys a high degree of autonomy, one that other administrative units in China can only dream of. It has its own constitution (the Basic Law) and currency (the Hong Kong dollar). It maintains a socioeconomic system that is significantly different from the rest of China. Hong Kong has also been labeled as a "world city." However, unlike most other world cities, such as New York, London, and Tokyo, Hong Kong has not been an integrated part of a country. Instead, its relative autonomy makes it a special case of a world city that in many ways resembles a city-state.

This chapter explores the impact of globalization on Hong Kong. To anticipate the major findings, globalization—along economic, social, and political dimensions—has had powerful consequences for Hong Kong. Compared to most other areas in the world, Hong Kong has been remarkably successful in responding to the challenges and opportunities of globalization. Hong Kong's success lies in its strategic location as the gateway between China and the world and in its institutional strengths, including its policy independence, adaptive flexibility, and robust legal system.

ANALYTICAL FRAMEWORK

Globalization is a complex phenomenon. As Samuel Kim defines it in chapter 1 of this volume, it refers to "a series of complex, independent yet interrelated processes of stretching, intensifying and accelerating worldwide interconnectedness in all aspects of human relations and transactions . . . such that events, decisions, and activities in one part of the world have immediate consequences for individuals, groups, and states in other parts of the world."[2] Although one could certainly trace the beginning to the end of World War II, it was not really until the 1960s that the globalizing process started to gain momentum. Since then, the quantum leaps in technologies, especially those in the areas of transportation and communication, have dramatically increased and intensified the economic, social, and political connectivity among different parts of the world.

In a recent comprehensive study of globalization, David Held and his associates suggest four analytically distinct types of impacts of globalization: decisional, institutional, distributive, and structural. First, globalization has a decisional impact in that it changes decision makers' calculations of the costs and benefits of the policy choices they confront. Globalization makes some policy options more costly and others less so than they were before. A high impact fundamentally alters policymakers' preferences. Second, the institutional impact of globalization refers to the way in which globalization transforms organizational and collective agendas. For example, globalization can change the range of policy options for organizations and collectives by effectively excluding certain choices. Third, globalization also has distributional consequences. It benefits some groups and individuals more than others. The distributional impact of globalization is reflected in the changing allocation of power and wealth within and across societies. Finally, the structural impact of globalization refers to its consequences for the patterns of organization and behavior. Globalization forces societies, to various degrees, to restructure their economic and sociopolitical systems.[3]

The ensuing analysis adopts a modified version of this framework. I will classify the impacts of globalization on Hong Kong into three categories in the following order: structural, policy, and distributional. The policy impact subsumes both the decisional and the institutional impacts mentioned previously since their difference is a matter of degree. Decisional impact involves recalculations of costs and benefits that result in the choice and rejection of specific policies, while institutional impact involves more dramatic recalculations that result in reconfiguring the agenda. The main findings are summarized in table 6.1.

GLOBALIZATION: THE ECONOMIC DIMENSION

Contemporary economic globalization involves an explosion of global trade, investment, and financial flows across state and regional boundaries in the last

Table 6.1   Impacts of Globalization on Hong Kong

	Economic Dimension	Social Dimension	Political Dimension
Structural Impact	De-industrialization; Organizational changes of firms and banks	People movement; New localism	Politicization and democratization
Policy Impact	Enhanced competition policy; Increasing government intervention in market	*Not salient.*	*Not salient.*
Distributional Impact	Relative gains for Hong Kong city region; Polarization in Hong Kong	Hong Kong becomes center of transnational Chinese public	Relative gains for Hong Kong vis-à-vis Beijing

thirty years.[4] In addition to technological advances, this has resulted from the policies of economic liberalization first on the part of the advanced industrialized countries and then on the part of the developing and transitional countries. The globalization of trade, investment, and finance has had significant impacts on Hong Kong.

Structural Impact

Hong Kong began to industrialize after World War II. Because of its small territory and population, it was never in a position to adopt an inward-looking development strategy. The only viable way to achieve development was to fully participate in the world economy on the basis of its comparative advantage. Given a vast pool of cheap labor and small family enterprises uniquely adaptive to change, Hong Kong found a niche for itself in labor-intensive light consumer industries. At first, Hong Kong manufacturers exported plastic flowers, wigs, cheap garments, and toys. Later, their exports shifted to higher-end products, such as garments, electronic watches, and games. Like a number of other East Asian economies, Hong Kong achieved industrialization by riding the tide of growing international trade, investment, and finance. In other words, economic globalization provided valuable opportunities for Hong Kong's economic growth.

By the late 1970s, the very sources of opportunities became sources of challenges for Hong Kong. With the intensification of international trade, investment, and finance, more countries and regions entered the competition for market and capital. The rising price of labor and land made Hong Kong less competitive against some of the newer developing economies. Coincidentally and fortunately, just as Hong Kong was facing increasing difficulties in sustaining its competitiveness in manufacturing, the People's Republic of China came out of decades of isolation and opened its borders to international trade and investment. This opened up a golden opportunity for Hong Kong. In the last twenty years, most of Hong Kong's manufacturing facilities have moved to China, where the prices of labor and land are among the most competitive in the world. From 1979 to 1997, the percentage of manufacturing in Hong Kong's gross domestic product (GDP) dropped from 23.7 to 6.5 percent.[5] Employment provided by manufacturing fell from around 880,000 in 1979 to 257,000 in 1998.[6]

The exodus of manufacturing facilities to southern China led to a restructuring of Hong Kong's economy. The decline of manufacturing has been made up by the growth of service industries. Service industries—commerce, finance, real estate, community and personal services, and so on—rose from 67.5 percent of the GDP in 1980 to 85.2 percent in 1997.[7] By the late 1990s, services provide employment for close to 1.5 million people, or nearly half the labor force.[8] Thanks to the rapid growth of service industries, Hong Kong has maintained a remarkable record of economic growth. From 1992 to 1997, Hong Kong's GDP increased by an average 6.8 percent a year.[9]

In response to the global economic changes, Hong Kong has transformed itself from a newly industrialized economy to a world city. World cities are hub points of the global economy. They are basing points in the spatial organization and articulation of production and markets and are major sites for the concentration and accumulation of international capital. Typically, they are characterized by a concentration of corporate headquarters, banks, and firms specializing in producer services, such as accounting, advertising, and consulting, and have excellent transportation and communication connections with the rest of the world.[10] Although Hong Kong is not on par with London and New York in its centrality to the global economy, it has all the prominent features of a world city. As Tung Chee-hwa prepared to become the first chief executive of Hong Kong SAR in 1997, he expressed his vision of Hong Kong in the following way: "Hong Kong is indeed an international metropolis. . . . It will become the most important financial, trade, transportation, information, education and entertainment center. It is at the same time a command center of nearby industrial regions."[11] In his most recent annual Policy Address, Tung reaffirmed this vision: "Hong Kong should not only be a major Chinese city, but could become the most cosmopolitan city in Asia, enjoying a status comparable to that of New York in North America and London in Europe."[12] In late 1999, the Hong Kong government signed an agreement with the Walt Disney Company to build a multi-billion-dollar Disney theme park in Hong Kong, hoping that this will further strengthen the international credentials of the city.[13]

In addition to the restructuring of Hong Kong economy, economic globalization has also led to structural changes at the firm level. As noted previously, the pressure of competition from newer industrializers has forced Hong Kong manufacturing companies to move much of their operations away. In this process, these manufacturing companies have gone "multinational," keeping their design, marketing, and accounting functions in Hong Kong while setting up production facilities elsewhere. As a result, the management and coordination capabilities of Hong Kong companies have been greatly enhanced.[14] Similarly, Hong Kong's trading companies have also gone through significant reorganization in response to global economic forces. In the past, trading companies made profits by matching buyers and sellers. The rapid improvement of transportation and communication technologies in recent decades has reduced the needs for traditional middlemen. To survive and grow, Hong Kong trading companies have shifted to more complex services. Instead of simply matching buyers and sellers of a single product, they have become organizers of entire supply systems, managing dispersed manufacturing and maintaining cooperative relationships with suppliers around the world.[15] Finally, banks and other financial institutions in Hong Kong are going through structural changes as a result of globalization. Hong Kong has dozens of small banks, many of which are owned and managed by families. However, the pressure of competition from megabanks that operate on a global scale is pushing them to consolidate. More of the small financial institutions in Hong Kong are looking to merge with large overseas banks since the economy of scale is essential for their survival.[16]

Policy Impact

Hong Kong has long been exposed to the forces of economic globalization. In recent years, the government has explicitly called attention to the implications of globalization for Hong Kong. In his 1999 Policy Address, Tung Chee-Hwa pointed out that "the world's economy is becoming more globalized as a result of free trade and advances in information technology." He sees that as a momentous change that combines challenges with opportunities.[17] In response, the Hong Kong government has moved toward deeper involvement in the economy, even as its capacity to use policy instruments to shape the economy is declining.

Traditionally, the colonial government in Hong Kong adopted a policy that came closer to the laissez-faire ideal than almost any other government in the world. Aside from using its control of land to subsidize public housing and industrial establishments and granting monopoly rights in certain kinds of businesses, such as telecommunications and public utilities, government intervention in Hong Kong was minimal. However, recent years have seen a trend toward more government involvement in the economy. The pressure of international competition and the resulting deindustrialization has prompted the Hong Kong government to develop a set of competition policies. Since the mid-1980s, it has made numerous plans and investments to improve Hong Kong's infrastructure.[18] In the 1990s, the government established new agencies or strengthened old agencies to promote Hong Kong's economy. For example, the Hong Kong Trade and Development Council has stepped up efforts to assist small to medium-size companies to seek international market access.[19] The year 1996 saw the establishment of the Business and Service Promotion Unit under the Office of the Financial Secretary "to maintain Hong Kong as the best place in the world for business, the premier service center in the region."[20] In Tung Chee-Hwa's words, "The Government is acutely aware of the competitiveness issue, and everything it does in the economic sphere is intended to improve our competitiveness."[21] In late 1999, government involvement in the economy broke new grounds as it became a majority joint venture partner in the Disney theme park project.[22]

Increased government intervention has also taken place in macroeconomic policies. Since 1983, Hong Kong has adopted a linked exchange rate system, pegging the Hong Kong dollar to the U.S. dollar at the rate of U.S.\$1 = HK\$7.8. The monetary policy of Hong Kong has one clear goal: to maintain a stable exchange rate. This system has served Hong Kong well, making it one of the most credible and attractive trading partners and financial hubs in the world. On the other hand, it also means that the Hong Kong government is not in a position to use monetary instruments to achieve economic or political objectives. However, the increasing volatility of the global financial market has prompted the government into heavy-handed interventions in the market on occasion. In response to the Asian financial crisis, the Hong Kong government took unprecedented actions to stabilize Hong Kong's currency and economy. For example, in August 1998, the government injected \$15 billion into the stock market to defend the stock market and the Hong Kong dollar from attacks by international hedge funds. Government intervention prevented shocks to Hong Kong's economy in the short run. However, in other ways it tarnished the laissez-faire reputation of the Hong Kong government and the credibility of its monetary system.[23]

Distributional Impact

Economic globalization has created both losers and winners, if not always in absolute terms then certainly in relative terms. On balance, Hong Kong has clearly been a winner so far. As a member of the world's most dynamic region, its fortune has risen along with the rest of East and Southeast Asia. Furthermore, as economies become geographically dispersed and yet functionally integrated, they demand command and coordination centers. Cities in general are given new opportunities to grow.[24] Hong Kong, adapting successfully to the new global economy, has done especially well in taking advantage of this trend. From 1989 to 1997, Hong Kong's share of the total GDP of the four newly industrialized economies rose from 14.1 to 17.3 percent.[25]

The favorable distributional effect of globalization is true not only of Hong Kong itself but also of the city region around Hong Kong, including the Pearl River Delta.[26] In the last two decades, with the intensification of trade and investment linkages between Hong Kong and Guangdong, they have practically become one economic entity.[27] The development of Hong Kong into a world city and the spillover effect to its hinterland has enabled this city region to develop much faster than the rest of China. As a result, the region has gained increased economic leverage vis-à-vis other regions as well as the central government of China.[28]

Finally, within Hong Kong itself, economic globalization has benefited some groups and individuals more than others. The result has been a growing gap between the very rich and the very poor. The income disparity of Hong Kong was never small, but it has become even greater in the last two decades. A Gini coefficient above 0.4 or 0.5 indicates extremely unfair distribution. In the 1980s, the Gini coefficient for Hong Kong was 0.45. In 1996, it reached 0.52.[29] Growing income disparity is typical of many world cities. As industries give way to services, employment in these cities tends to expand at both the high and the low end and to shrink in the middle. Lawyers, bankers, accountants, and public relations specialists get paid extremely well, while restaurant and laundry workers, many of whom are new immigrants, barely get by.[30] Hong Kong is no exception. Furthermore, disparity in Hong Kong has been worsened by the formation of oligopolistic markets and skyrocketing real estate and stocks.[31]

GLOBALIZATION: THE SOCIAL DIMENSION

It is common to perceive globalization as a purely economic phenomenon, but it is in fact a multifaceted process. The social and political aspects of globalization are no less consequential than the economic aspect. Two salient manifestations of social globalization are the massive movement of people across state borders and the fusion of cultures on a global scale. Migration has existed as long as human history. However, in the last thirty years, the rapid improvement of transportation and communication technologies has made immigration and emigration more convenient and less costly than ever before. As a result, migration has taken on unprecedented scale and intensity. More people are migrating farther away and more frequently than at any time in history. The escalation of immigration in the last thirty years has prompted most states to tighten border controls. However, migrants are finding ways to adapt to or circumvent those controls with great effectiveness.[32]

Another, perhaps more visible manifestation of social globalization is fusion of cultures in a global space. On the one hand, symbols of Western consumerism—Coca-Cola, blue jeans, and MTV—are prevalent in far-off corners of the world. On the other hand, ethnic cuisine, fashion, and music from different parts of the world are now popular fixations of Western metropolises. Furthermore, the simultaneous and around-the-clock media coverage of major developments around the world brings common experiences to people of different places every day. If globalization ultimately means "one world," its has probably gone the farthest in the cultural arena.[33]

Structural Impact

People movement is not new to Hong Kong. Traditionally, Hong Kong was a major departure point for Chinese emigrants going to other parts of the world. During World War II and the Chinese civil war of the late 1940s, Hong Kong experienced large inward and outward flows of people. The aftermath of the Great Leap Forward in the late 1950s saw more Chinese refugees flowing into Hong Kong. In the late 1970s, tens of thousands of Vietnamese boat people arrived in Hong Kong, as did 400,000 mainland Chinese. Most of these earlier population flows were prompted by particular local developments. In contrast, more recent changes in Hong Kong's population structure are a result of the increasing ease of global movement of people as well as local dynamics. Large numbers of expatriates have chosen to come to Hong Kong to work at business and service jobs, making the city a cultural and ethnic mosaic. By 1996, the foreign population size in Hong Kong was roughly 1.5 million (out of a total population of about six million). The largest groups are Filipinos, Americans, Canadians, British, Indonesians, and Thai.[34]

In addition to an influx of foreigners, Hong Kong has undergone population movement in the opposite direction in the last fifteen years. In the mid-1980s, China and Britain negotiated and agreed on the ultimate transfer to Hong Kong back to China in 1997. The uncertainties of the future caused much anxiety in Hong Kong. The Tiananmen Square incident of 1989 further increased people's fears of major political and economic changes after the transfer. Large numbers of Hong Kong residents emigrated to North America, the South Pacific, and Europe.[35] The massive immigration has been assisted by the extensive international networks of Hong Kong residents.[36] In turn, it has further expanded those international networks. More Hong Kong families today have relatives overseas, and more Hong Kong residents have access to residency in another country, than ever before.

In addition to migration, the globalization of culture has also had a structural impact on Hong Kong society. Historically, Hong Kong was seen as a place where East met West. Its culture was bifurcated between the local and native on the one hand and the international and cosmopolitan on the other. The former appeals to the non-Anglophone sectors of the community, while the latter appeals to the expatriates and their local associates. In the age of globalization, however, this has changed. The fusion of colonialism with globalism since the 1980s has produced what one analyst calls "new localism."[37] Unlike the old localism, this new local culture is "nonprovincial" and exciting. It has many elements, just like the language of Hong Kong, which combines Cantonese, English, Mandarin, and so on. The prospect of Hong Kong's reunification with China introduced a sense of urgency to this distinctive Hong Kong culture. More people than ever before are now interested in Hong Kong culture because they see a distinctive cultural identity as a "first-line defense against total political absorption."[38]

Distributional Impact

Overall, both the increasing ease of global migration and the fusion of culture have enhanced the strength and status of Hong Kong. The movement of people in and out of Hong Kong has strengthened Hong Kong's position in multiple ways. First, the numerous expatriates in Hong Kong are a major source of strength of Hong Kong as a world city. The skilled foreign workers bring expertise to Hong Kong and help Hong Kong maintain close connections with the international financial and technological community. These human resources are crucial to maintaining Hong Kong's competitive edge.[39] Unskilled immigrants also contribute to Hong Kong's vitality in important ways. For example, Hong Kong's birth rate has fallen steadily in the last two decades. Without an increase in fertility, immigration is likely to be the core element of population change.[40] Furthermore, aside from their specific functions, immigrants in the city are vital for Hong Kong's cosmopolitan characteristics, which make it attractive to international businesses and talents.

Even emigration has positive consequences for Hong Kong. It is important to note that many who left Hong Kong have returned after gaining a permanent residence status in another country because for them Hong Kong provides economic and business opportunities unmatched by other locations.[41] For as long as they work and live in Hong Kong, their newly developed or enhanced international ties serve to make and keep Hong Kong connected, competitive, and cosmopolitan.

Cultural globalization has also worked to Hong Kong's benefit. It has widened and deepened Hong Kong's internationalization. In the meantime, Hong Kong has not only been a passive consumer and conduit of international cultural products but also become a producer and exporter. Hong Kong cultural products, be they indigenized international products or purely local creations, have become more influential in other places, especially other ethnic Chinese communities.[42] For example, direct satellite television brings Hong Kong kung fu movies, soap operas, and pop singers to ethnic Chinese homes from North America to South Africa and from western Europe to Southeast Asia. Furthermore, the ideologies and values embedded in these products become part of the shared consciousness of Chinese all over the world. As a result, Hong Kong has emerged as a cultural center in the transnational Chinese public.[43] The most remarkable and ironic consequence of Hong Kong's rise in the transnational Chinese cultural space lies in its influence over China. Ever since China opened its door to the world in the late 1970s, the Hong Kong way of life has been revered by the government and the public alike. While Deng Xiaoping called for the creation of several Hong Kongs in China, ordinary Chinese have enthusiastically embraced just about everything out of Hong Kong, from fashions to popular entertainment programs and from Hong Kong–style cooking to the Cantonese dialect.[44] In terms of cultural China, the periphery has become the center.[45]

GLOBALIZATION: THE POLITICAL DIMENSION

Political globalization refers to the tendency for political decisions and actions in one part of the world to generate widespread reactions and consequences elsewhere. The global movement of people, news, and images, along with the global flow of goods and capital, has turned many a local event into international concerns. Labor policies in one place can affect the wage levels of another. Environmental standards of one country can have ramifications for the quality of air in another. As a result, the distinction between internal and external politics is fast receding.[46]

In addition, political globalization involves the worldwide diffusion of norms. Once a set of norms gains prima facie legitimacy, it has important consequences for government and individual behaviors. In recent decades, human rights, democracy, and environmental protection have become prevailing norms around the world. They create opportunities for some actors and impose constraints on others, as violations of these norms are likely to bring strong international reactions and incur heavy costs.

Structural Impact

Political globalization has had various structural impacts on Hong Kong. The most important of these is the politicization of Hong Kong's population and the democratization of Hong Kong's political structure. Traditionally, Hong Kong was largely an "apolitical" territory. Living "on borrowed time in a borrowed place," many devoted themselves to business activities while showing little interest in politics.[47] The globalization of politics renders Hong Kong more sensitive to political development elsewhere in the world and vice versa. In the meantime, the diffusion of democratic norms has encouraged political participation in Hong Kong.[48] This interactive process has played out especially prominently during Hong Kong's transition to Chinese sovereignty.

In 1984, China and Britain signed their joint declaration regarding Hong Kong's return to Chinese sovereignty. The Chinese government agreed in the declaration that after Hong Kong's return to Chinese sovereignty, it was to enjoy a high degree of autonomy under self-rule and that the political and economic system of Hong Kong was to remain unchanged for fifty years. However, political development in China, particularly the events of the spring of 1989, caused widespread skepticism about China's promise. When students took to the street in Beijing demanding "democracy" and "freedom," people in Hong Kong held public gatherings and raised funds to support the students. When the Chinese government resorted to violence to crack down on the movement, Hong Kong people reacted with massive demonstrations. The images of tanks in Beijing and of candle lights in Hong Kong carried live by international televisions attracted worldwide attention, leading to heightened concern by the international community over Hong Kong's political future. For example, in 1992 the U.S. Senate passed the U.S.–Hong Kong Policy Act, obliging the U.S. government to monitor and report the situation in Hong Kong, especially regarding judicial independence and civil liberties.[49]

In the new international spotlight, Hong Kong political activists—lawyers, social workers, journalists, teachers, and professors—redoubled their efforts to push for political change. Their fight for democracy, which had been marginalized during earlier negotiations between China and Britain in the mid-1980s, gained wide support and visibility. Under pressure from the Hong Kong people and mindful of its international reputation, the British government took steps that it deemed necessary to ensure Hong Kong's stability, including the speeding up of democratization. In 1992, London appointed Chris Patten to be the last governor of Hong Kong. Patten took advantage of the loopholes in the Basic Law and introduced electoral proposals to expand popular participation, subjecting all members of the Legislative Council (LegCo) to direct or indirect election. The globalization of politics brought to Hong Kong a more democratic political structure.[50]

Distributional Impact

In an age when it is increasingly difficult to control cross-border flows of information and ideas, the traditional territorial power of states is giving way to the soft power of world cities. Political globalization has not only changed the political structure of Hong Kong but also imposed serious constraints on China's policy toward Hong Kong.

As expected, the Chinese government reacted negatively to the democratic changes in Hong Kong's political structure before its return to China. Beijing accused the British government of violating the Joint Declaration of 1984 and the Basic Law of 1990. Chinese officials also pointed out the hypocrisy on the part of Britain in trying to democratize Hong Kong toward the end of its 150-year rule. As promised, the Chinese government dismissed the elected LegCo after the transfer of Hong Kong back to China and replaced it with a Provisional LegCo. Until today, Beijing has been consistently and explicitly opposed to the politicization and internationalization of Hong Kong.[51]

However, overall the Chinese government has been quite tolerant of political and civil liberties in Hong Kong. In May 1998, Hong Kong voters participated in the first election of the LegCo after the transfer to China. The new democratically elected LegCo replaced the Provisional LegCo without intervention from Beijing. In the last two years, the Chinese government has allowed commemorations of the anniversary of June 4 in Hong Kong. Hong Kong artists have found their freedom of expression expanding rather than shrinking.[52] Beijing probably wishes to impose stricter political control over Hong Kong, as it does elsewhere in China, but its capacity to do so is seriously constrained by the political attention that Hong Kong commands on the global political agenda. Beijing's efforts to restrict

Hong Kong's autonomy cannot but cause international alarm and criticism, which would be costly to China economically and politically.[53]

CONCLUSION

On balance, Hong Kong so far has been a beneficiary of globalization. It has responded to the challenges and opportunities of globalization with considerable success. What are the conditions of Hong Kong's success? Several factors stand out from the foregoing analysis.

First and most obvious, Hong Kong has benefited a great deal from its strategic position: its proximity to China. In the last two decades, as Hong Kong quickly shifts its manufacturing facilities to southern China, it has emerged as the most important trade, investment, and financial center connecting China and other parts of the world.[54] The Hong Kong government is keenly aware of the importance to its China connection. Its chief executive admits, "Our economic link with the Mainland is our greatest advantage in developing Hong Kong into a world-class city."[55]

In addition, a set of institutional factors has been crucial to Hong Kong's ability to ride the tide of globalization. The first of these conditions is policy independence. Hong Kong has maintained a level of autonomy that is unusual for a colony and an administrative region. In that sense it has been practically a city-state. While being outside a larger political and economic entity has its costs— there is no cushioning of external shocks or safety net for bad times—a city-state has obvious advantages. It is free from the burden of policies and transactions typical of and necessary for larger political and economic entities, such as prolonged and unremitting military production, prolonged and unremitting subsidies to poor regions, and heavy promotion of trade between advanced and backward economies.[56] Since Hong Kong reverted to Chinese sovereignty, policy independence has become more crucial, even as it gets more difficult because of the nature of China's political and economic system.

Second, Hong Kong owes its success to its adaptive tradition and capabilities. Hong Kong economy and politics have gone through many ups and downs in the last 150 years. Hong Kong people have long been masters of uncertainties.[57] Their mentality, skills, and organizational structure make them extraordinarily flexible in adapting to ever changing circumstances.[58] Hong Kong business people are keenly aware of this advantage and make the best out of it.[59]

Third, a system of rule of law has been priceless to Hong Kong. Under British colonialism, Hong Kong adopted a system of common law. By providing reliable protection of private property and contracts and credible mechanisms for solving business disputes, such a system promoted both domestic and international business development in Hong Kong, making Hong Kong a magnet of talent and capital. In the early 1970s, the establishment of the Independent Commission Against

Corruption (ICAC) further strengthened the integrity of the legal system. Hong Kong's reputation for the rule of law has been a major source of its "global credentials."

None of the conditions underlying Hong Kong's success in its response to global economic, social, and political forces can be taken for granted. If they become eroded, Hong Kong may well be surpassed and even replaced by potential competitors in the region. For example, in the last decade, Shanghai has developed rapidly. The Chinese government does not hide its ambition to make Shanghai a leading financial center for China and the Asia-Pacific region. So far, Hong Kong has the advantage of having a system of rule of law and a great deal of policy independence. If these advantages erode, Hong Kong is likely to lose the competition to Shanghai. On the other hand, Singapore is another formidable competitor. Hong Kong's advantage over Singapore lies in its proximity to China and its entrepreneurship.[60] If the Chinese economy slows down relative to Southeast Asia and/or if Hong Kong loses its entrepreneurial talent, it is likely to be overshadowed by Singapore.[61]

To conclude, globalization has had significant impacts on Hong Kong. So far, Hong Kong has been very successful in dealing with the challenges and opportunities of globalization. However, the conditions of its success cannot be taken for granted. If these conditions erode, Hong Kong may lose its status as a vital world city in the Asia-Pacific region.

NOTES

1. According to UN statistics, in 1997 Hong Kong's GDP per capita was $26,567, compared to $21,921 of Britain (<http://www.un.org/Depts/unsd/social/inc-eco.htm>, December 1999). Since the mid-1980s, Hong Kong had become an autonomous and equal partner in many international organizations, including the General Agreement on Tariffs and Trade (GATT) and the Asian Pacific Economic Council (APEC). The *Yearbook of International Organizations* shows that as of 1995 Hong Kong was a member of fifty-three intergovernmental organizations (Jane C. Y. Lee and Gerald Chan, "Hong Kong's Changing International Relations Strategy," in Beatrice Leung and Joseph Cheng, eds., *Hong Kong SAR: In Pursuit of Domestic and International Order* (Hong Kong: Chinese University of Hong Kong Press, 1997), 177–91.

2. See Samuel Kim, chapter 1 in this volume, 10.

3. David Held and Anthony McGrew, David Goldblatt, and Jonathan Perraton, *Global Transformations: Politics, Economics, and Culture* (Cambridge: Polity Press, 1999), 18–19.

4. For details, see Kim, chapter 1 in this volume, 11–13.

5. *Hong Kong Yearbook 1980* (Hong Kong: Hua Chiao Jih Pao, 1980); <http://www.info.gov.hk/censtatd/hkstat/hkinf/gdp.htm>, December 1999.

6. *Hong Kong Yearbook 1980;* <http://www.info.gov.hk/censtatd/hkstat/hkinf/labor.htm>, December 1999.

7. It is important to point out that official statistics exaggerate the degree of "deindustrialization" of Hong Kong. Many of the services are producer services closely linked to production. Furthermore, the same activities, such as product design, customization, and delivery, were once counted under the manufacturing sector but are now counted under services. A discussion of this statistical pitfall can be found in Suzanne Berger and Richard K. Lester, eds., *Made by Hong Kong* (Hong Kong: Oxford University Press, 1997), 27–33.

8. Calculated from statistics in *China Hong Kong Yearbook 1998* (Hong Kong: Hsian Hsiang-Kang Nien Chien She, 1998).

9. Growth rate calculated from expenditure-based GDP at constant (1990) prices; see <http://www.info.gov.hk/censtatd/hkstat/fas/tgdp1.htm>, December 1999.

10. A similar label is "global city." For an excellent survey of this burgeoning literature, see John Rennie Short and Yeong-Hyun Kim, *Globalization and the City* (New York: Longman, 1999). An influential book on this subject is Saskia Sassen, *The Global City: New York, London, Tokyo* (Princeton, N.J.: Princeton University Press, 1991).

11. Tung Chee-hwa, "Gongtong Jianshe Ershiyi Shiji de Xianggang," in *China Hong Kong Yearbook 1997* (Hong Kong: Hsian Hsiang-Kang Nien Chien She, 1998), 186.

12. Tung Chee-Hwa, "The 1999 Policy Address: Quality People, Quality Home, Positioning Hong Kong for the Twenty-first Century" (<http://www.info.gov.hk/pa99/index.htm>, December 1999).

13. Tung Chee-Hwa declared that "Disney's choice of Hong Kong . . . is a vote of confidence in our city and in our future. [It will] enhance our international image as a 'world city' where things do happen" (quoted in Yulanda Chung, "Making a Magic Kingdom," *Asiaweek,* November 12, 1999, 52).

14. This is discussed extensively in Berger and Lester, *Made by Hong Kong.*

15. For a good illustration of these changes, see Joan Magretta, "First, Global, and Entrepreneurial: Supply Chain Management, Hong Kong Style: An Interview with Victor Fung," *Harvard Business Review* (September/October 1998), 102–14.

16. Laetitia Puyfaucher, "Bulking Up," *Far Eastern Economic Review,* October 1, 1998, 78.

17. Tung, "1999 Policy Address."

18. For details, see Yue-man Yeung, "Planning for Pearl City: Hong Kong's Future, 1997 and Beyond," *Cities* 14, no. 5 (1997): 249–56.

19. For details, see <http://www.tdc.org.hk>, December 1999. The Hong Kong government recognizes that Hong Kong has been transformed from an industrial center to a financial center, but it is seeking to provide assistance to "industries that can still compete in the international market" (Tung, "Gongtong Jianshe Ershiyi Shiji de Xianggang," 188).

20. See statement of mission at <http:///www.info.gov.hk/bpsu/mission/index.htm>, December 1999.

21. Tung, "1999 Policy Address." To be sure, these policies are not the same as winner-picking industrial policies typical of East Asian developmental states.

22. Yulanda Chung, "Making a Magic Kingdom."

23. In fact, *Global Finance's* 1998 report card gave Joseph Yam, head of Hong Kong Monetary Authority, an "F" for abandoning the discipline of a currency board; see E. Guthrie McTigue, "Global Finance's Central Banker Report Cards," *Global Finance,* October 1998, 101–3. For a defense of the action of the Hong Kong government, see Paul Krugman, "Hong Kong's Hard Lesson," *Fortune,* September 28, 1998, 36–38.

24. On this point, see Sassen, *Global Cities.*

25. Calculated from APEC statistics at <http://www1.apecsec.org.sg/member/gdp. htm>, December 1999.

26. For a discussion of the meaning and significance of city regions, see Jane Jacobs, *Cities and the Wealth of Nations: Principles of Economic Life* (New York: Random House, 1984), chap. 3.

27. For a detailed discussion of this city region, see David K. Y. Chu, "The Hong Kong-Zhujiang Delta and the World City System," in Fu-Chen Lo and Yue-man Yeung, eds., *Emerging World Cities in Pacific Asia* (Tokyo: United Nations University Press, 1996), 465–97.

28. On the increased leverage of southern China, especially Guangdong, see Sarah Munn, "Breaking the Shackles: The Political Economy of Guangdong's Quest for Autonomy," *Hong Kong Public Administration* 4, no. 2 (September 1995): 181–203.

29. Toyojiro Maruya, "Tasks for Hong Kong's Economy in the New Era—Shift to Service-Oriented Economy and Introduction of a Comprehensive Competition Policy," in Wong Siu-lun and Toyojiro Maruya, eds., *Hong Kong Economy and Society: Challenges in the New Era* (Hong Kong: Centre of Asian Studies, University of Hong Kong, 1998), 8.

30. This thesis is made in Sassen, *Global Cities*.

31. Maruya, "Tasks for Hong Kong's Economy in the New Era," 9.

32. For details, see Held et al., *Global Transformations,* chap. 6.

33. Some scholars emphasize that while people all over the world have become familiar with other cultures, they are holding on to their indigenous cultures. Even as they accept foreign cultural products, they transform these products through reinterpretation and reinvention; see, for example, Arjun Appadurai, *Modernity at Large: Cultural Dimensions of Globalization* (Minneapolis: University of Minnesota Press, 1996).

34. *The China Hong Kong Yearbook 1998.* On patterns of migration to Hong Kong, see F. L. N. Li, A. M. Findlay, and H. Jones, "A Cultural Economy Perspective on Service Sector Migration in the Global City: The Case of Hong Kong," *International Migration* 36, no. 2 (1998): 131–57.

35. From 1984 to 1992, Australia, Canada, and the United States took 362,371 immigrants from Hong Kong, or 6 percent of the Hong Kong population (calculated from Kim Richard Nossal, "Playing the International Card? The View from Australia, Canada, and the United States," in Gerard A. Postiglione and James T. H. Tang, eds., *Hong Kong's Reunion with China: The Global Dimensions* (Armonk, N.Y.: M. E. Sharpe, 1997), 85, table 3.1.

36. For a study of the role of kin networks in Hong Kong's recent immigration, see Wong Siu-lun, "Network Capital: Emigration from Hong Kong," *British Journal of Sociology* 49, no. 3 (September 1998): 358–74.

37. This is the phrase used by Ackbar Abbas in his interesting study of Hong Kong's culture, *Hong Kong: Culture and the Politics of Disappearance* (Minneapolis: University of Minnesota Press, 1997).

38. Abbas, *Hong Kong,* 142.

39. For an empirical study of the practice and importance of hiring expatriates in Hong Kong, see A. M. Findlay, F. L. N. Li, A. J. Jowett, and Ronald Skeldon, "Skilled International Migration and the Global City: A Study of Expatriates in Hong Kong," *Transactions—Institute of British Geographers* 21 (1996): 49–61.

40. Some scholars have suggested importing young immigrants from mainland China to solve Hong Kong's aging problem (Gren Manuel, "Waking up to the Baby Blues," *South China Morning Post,* November 1, 1999, 23).

41. Ronald Skeldon, "Migration from Hong Kong: Current Trends and Future Agendas," in Ronald Skeldon, ed., *Reluctant Exiles? Migration from Hong Kong and the New Overseas Chinese* (Armonk, N.Y.: M. E. Sharpe and Hong Kong: Hong Kong University Press, 1994); Anita S. Ma, "Skilled Hong Kong Immigrants' Intention to Repatriate," *Asian and Pacific Migration Journal* 6, no. 2 (1997): 169–84.

42. For an interesting analysis of Hong Kong's cultural internationalization along these dimensions, see Hoiman Chan, "Labyrinth of Hybridization: The Cultural Internationalization of Hong Kong," in Postiglione and Tang, eds., *Hong Kong's Reunion with China*, 169–99.

43. On the transnational Chinese publics, including one that is based on mass media, see Aihwa Ong, "'A Better Tomorrow'? The Struggle for Global Visibility," *Sojourn* 12, no. 2 (1997): 192–225.

44. Interestingly, Hoiman Chan sees a decline of this trend because of the cultural revitalization of mainland China and the failure of nerve and imagination on the part of Hong Kong (Chan, "Labyrinth of Hybridization").

45. The periphery of cultural China includes more than Hong Kong; see Tu Wei-ming, "Cultural China: The Periphery as the Center," *Daedalus* 120, no. 2 (spring 1991): 1–32.

46. For detailed discussion of this aspect of globalization, see James N. Rosenau, *Along the Domestic-Foreign Frontier: Global Governance in a Turbulent World* (Cambridge: Cambridge University Press, 1997).

47. This phrase was originally used by Han Suyin; see Abbas, *Hong Kong*, 142.

48. On the recent wave of democratization, see Samuel P. Huntington, *The Third Wave: Democratization in the Late Twentieth Century* (Norman: Oklahoma University Press, 1991). On the human rights regime, see Thomas Risse, Stephen Ropp, and Kathryn Sikkink, eds., *Power of Human Rights: International Norms and Domestic Change* (Cambridge: Cambridge University Press, 1999).

49. For a detailed discussion of the U.S.–Hong Kong Act, see Nancy Bernkopf Tucker, "Hong Kong as a Problem in Chinese-American Relations," in Warren I. Cohen and Li Zhao, eds., *Hong Kong under Chinese Rule* (Cambridge: Cambridge University Press, 1997), 213–28. For discussions of American as well as other Western countries' concern over Hong Kong, see Kim Richard Nossal, "Playing the International Card?," in Postiglione and Tang, eds., *Hong Kong's Reunion with China*, 79–101.

50. For details, see Alvin Y. So, "The Tiananmen Incident, Patten's Electoral Reforms, and the Roots of Contested Democracy in Hong Kong," in Ming K. Chan, ed., *The Challenge of Hong Kong's Reintegration with China* (Hong Kong: Hong Kong University Press, 1997) 49–83.

51. In 1993, the director of the Hong Kong and Macao Affairs Office, Lu Ping, warned, "Hong Kong in any case should not become a political center, let alone an international political center. If Hong Kong becomes a field where international political forces confront and enter into rivalry, it will bring disaster to the six million people living there" (quoted in Gerard A. Postiglione and James Tang, with Ting Wai, introduction, in Postiglione and Tang, eds., *Hong Kong's Reunion with China*, 10. This is still the position of the Chinese government today.

52. See Scarlet Cheng, "Questions of Identity," *Far Eastern Economic Review*, March 18, 1999, 42–43. On the other hand, there are indications of self-censorship on the part of the press in Hong Kong; see L. M. Stein, "Specter of Censorship," *Editor and Publisher*, October 25, 1997, 48–49.

53. Instances of this nature in 1999 include the overrule by Beijing of a decision made by the Hong Kong Court of Final Appeal, the firing of the editor of the *South China Morning Post*, and a proposal to establish a press council to regulate the press in Hong Kong.

54. Hong Kong has been one of the largest trading partners for mainland China. Hong Kong also accounts for roughly 60 percent of the total foreign direct investment in China. In addition, more mainland Chinese enterprises are listed on the Hong Kong stock exchange, raising large sums of funds from Hong Kong and around the world.

55. Tung, "1999 Policy Address." The same view has been expressed by Senior Minister Lee Kuan Yew of Singapore. Lee emphasizes that Hong Kong's future lies with China and that people should stop talking about turning Hong Kong into Singapore; see Frank Ching, "Lee Kuan Yew on Hong Kong," *Far Eastern Economic Review*, November 11, 1999, 34.

56. These are the very policies that lead to the decline of cities of imperial powers; see Jacobs, *Cities and the Wealth of Nations*, chap. 12.

57. This point is highlighted in D. R. Meyer, "Expert Managers of Uncertainty: Intermediaries of Capital in Hong Kong," *Cities* 14, no. 5 (1997): 257–63.

58. There is a large literature on why ethnic Chinese (including that of Hong Kong) business organization and culture is especially adaptive to change; see, for example, S. Gordon Redding, *The Spirit of Chinese Capitalism* (Berlin: Walter de Gruyter, 1993), and Gary Hamilton, "Competition and Organization: A Reexamination of Chinese Business Practices," *Journal of Asian Business* 12, no. 1 (1996): 7–20.

59. An indication of this is the fact that a very large number of Hong Kong companies are engaged in OEM (original equipment manufacturer) production, and they prefer it to production under their own labels (Berger and Lester, *Made by Hong Kong*, 38–39).

60. For a recent comparison of Hong Kong and Singapore as financial markets, see Paul Handley, "Hong Kong's Counterchallenge," *Institutional Investor* 32, no. 9 (1998): 142–43. According to Handley, in two key areas—foreign exchange and financial futures—Singapore has demonstrated its ability to beat Hong Kong.

61. For a discussion of the potential competition with Shanghai and Singapore, see Joseph C. K. Yam, "Hong Kong as an International Financial Center after 1997," in Wang Gungwu and Wong Siu-lun, eds., *Hong Kong in the Asia-Pacific Region: Rising to the New Challenges* (Hong Kong: Center for Asian Studies, University of Hong Kong, 1997), 64–68. Taipei may be another competitor in terms of transportation, media, communication, and commerce; see Tung, "Gongtong Jianshe Ershiyi Shiji de Xianggang," 187.

7

Taiwan and Globalization

Lynn T. White III

DIMENSIONS OF GLOBALIZATION

Globalization might seem too broad a topic if it were not so pervasive at the turn of the new millennium. As Samuel Kim writes in chapter 1, it is "a series of complex, independent yet related processes of stretching, intensifying, and accelerating worldwide interconnectedness in all aspects of human relations and transactions—economic, social, cultural, environmental, political, diplomatic, and security." Globalization refers to the "whole ball" of the world, as the Chinese word for it (*quanqiuhua*) makes especially clear.

International open free markets are by all accounts an important part of globalization, and these grow in a complex process of bargaining among many actors that no one of them can control. Thus, to deal with globalization mainly in terms of "epistemic communities" is to neglect that the phenomenon is created mostly by inadvertent "society," by *Gesellschaft* at least as much as *Gemeinschaft,* by unintended rather than specifically intended habits, above all by global markets. Price, which makes a market, is the aboriginal unexpected consequence. The seller wants it higher, and the buyer wants it lower. The relationship is created because of complementary differences that no one originally planned. To deal with globalization only in terms of leaders' pronouncements and assays of their performance is to miss that most established elites would, from the start, have preferred to retain their positions without having to deal with new challenges to their local power.[1]

Taiwan's leaders are ambivalent about their global environment because it contains two parts: mainland China, which threatens them intensely, and the rest of the world, whose trade and potentially protective functions are welcome. Thus, this chapter deals with Taiwan's globalization in a four-part matrix as generated by two dimensions. The first is a difference between unintended situations and "epistemically" intended norms. The second is the spectrum from the whole island as a unit to local groups (or individuals). If drawn to make a quadrant, these two dimensions generate four topic fields that may loosely be called the economy (which is mostly individual and situational), beliefs (individual-normative), group identity (collective-normative), and security (collective-situational). These four aspects of Taiwan's globalization form the chapter's main parts. It concludes by showing that Taiwan, as an isolated system, thus far has been successful in dealing with most aspects of its global environment; however, major security problems loom in the future.

The island's leaders see most of the world as tending to be unfair to Taiwan because of China. Taipei writer Bernard T. K. Joei titled a recent book *In Search of Justice: The Taiwan Story*.[2] President Lee Teng-hui sees Taiwan "amid the tectonic shifts" of global politics and openly calls for "a trilateral effort" by the United States, Japan, and Taiwan to contain China militarily.[3] Lee calls for a "New Taiwanese" identity that "puts Taiwan foremost" and is localist. It is globalist only for harnessing international powers to the island's cause.

Localization is thus a fellow traveler of globalization. Scholars who follow Karl Polanyi show that modern change involves not just market expansion but also political opposition to the treatment of human beings and groups as mere market commodities.[4] Globalization raises moral and identity questions.[5] The hopes of individuals and groups for human progress, not just surrender to an irresistible market juggernaut with uncontrollable effects, are included in globalist ideologies. Efficient markets bring wealth and, perhaps, happiness of a kind to all six billion of us, but too much global rationalization threatens to homogenize people.[6] Polanyi wrote about a "double movement": both market growth and regulation of the market for the sake of people. As we will see in the case of Taiwan, globalism spurs reactions.

Many think that globalization is, in particular, a political project of the U.S. government. "Globalization = Americanization" is an equation believed by people who range from McDonald's franchisees to Chinese Communist hard-liners. Peter Beinart writes, "Consider the way globalization looks from Beijing. . . . The United States has promoted growth and economic integration in East Asia, but as part of a broader American strategy to prevent any Asian power from gaining regional hegemony."[7] Beijing patriots see global "bourgeois liberalization" or "peaceful evolution" as a Washington plot to undermine their political order. By the same token, some in Taiwan are equanimous about the American aspect of this process; they hope that it will encourage the United States to help protect their island. *Quanqiuhua* is, according to Taiwanese interviewees, necessary for the island's "survival."

How do we know globalization when we see it? It involves objectively measurable change in the structure of a "situation" (as Parsons used that word). The situation of a system—such as the political system of an island—includes unintended factors affecting individuals and groups there. When new technologies are discovered, for example, entrepreneurs use them; when unwanted external armies threaten, governments oppose them. Other aspects of globalization, however, involve intentional "norms." Individuals who value symbols or groups that are socialized by them may be able to change them, for example, by adopting new ideas. The direction of such movement is easier to document than are exact identities or cultural habits, to which people often refuse to be pinned down.[8]

Thus, globalization involves both intended and unintended causes. A separate point is that it involves both large groups (nations, whole islands of people), and small groups, families, and individuals. Confusions about whether globalization is a matter of structure or process, conditioning situations or controlling choices, arise because it is a matter of both—and for collectives both large and small. A loose version of functionalism offers a natural approach to such a topic.

ECONOMIC EFFICIENCY IN GLOBAL MARKETS

Taiwan has no natural resources to speak of; a telling exception is marble, which is trivial on world markets. The island has scant coal or natural gas and practically no oil. This geology does not, without imports and exports, provide a resource base for an industrial economy. However, Taiwan has thrived by processing imports and organizing trade.

Taiwan's polity was founded by traders. The Minnan (i.e., South Fujian) pirate and shipper Koxinga (Cheng Chenggong, 1624–1662) was the first Taiwanese politician—and he was a globalist of his time. His mother was Japanese. His father, Zheng Zhilong, was baptized a Catholic and had worked for the Portuguese in Macau, the Spanish in Manila, in Taiwan, perhaps for the Dutch as well.[9] Koxinga's trading networks extended to Japan and Southeast Asia as well as to many South and East China ports. An international connection with Japan remained very important for Taiwan after that country annexed the island in 1895 at the end of the Sino–Japanese War. After 1949, Westerners paid attention to the island as Chiang Kai-shek's redoubt. Quick Taiwanese growth by the 1950s was fueled largely by industrial exports, and the advent of the information economy extended the island's need for global economic outreach. Taiwan's main resources are its enterprising people, with a frontier work ethic and a Confucian cult of education. These main factors of production are not physical. Thus, foreign markets have been required for the trade-, industry-, and information-based stages of Taiwan's growth.

World trade affects domestic political structures, not just international relations. Places such as Taiwan, with a scarcity of land but an abundance of labor and capital, tend to have free-trading, globalist domestic alliances of workers and entrepreneurs.[10] Government concessions to foreign merchants have often caused patriotic local entrepreneurs to demand equal treatment in their domestic operations as well.[11] Market politics tends to be interlocal and horizontal rather than centralized and hierarchical. It may not look like expressive politics, seeming to be just businesslike, but it leads to political globalization.

Niches for Worldwide Sales

Taiwan industry some years ago had many "fab companies" that made specific parts for specific foreign firms only. This pattern was especially obvious in early semiconductors. A famous example was Acer Computers, making random access memory (RAM) chips for Texas Instruments. Hsinchu's Winbond Company and Powerchip Semiconductor Corporation made circuits for Toshiba and Mitsubishi, respectively. In their early years, these Taiwan firms sold only small amounts to foreign clients other than their main ones, but they later developed more finished products to sell under their own brand names.[12]

Taiwan's economy is globalized, not regionalized, even though almost half the trade of the East Asian economies as a group (and most of the foreign investment in each of them) occurs within the region. Sales outside Asia, especially in the United States and the European Union, provide the crucial high profits for these transnational production networks. Links between companies in the largest East Asian economies are now less hierarchical than heretofore. Large companies in Japan, for example, once used Taiwan firms mainly as subsidiary suppliers; however, Canon, Fujitsu, Matsushita, and Sony now have all established equal compeer links to many Taiwan companies, and Oki Electric has a nonhierarchical arrangement with Nan Ya Plastics. New technologies and opportunities in global markets cause few entrepreneurs to found truly multinational corporations. Few have boards of directors of mixed citizenship. Many, instead, form alliances overseas.[13] This reduces transaction costs, but it is the opposite of international patronism.

Particular Taiwan businesses have focused not just on broad categories of commodities (e.g., shoes) but also on export niches for specific subtypes of these categories. Before the 1990s, Taiwan specialized in vinyl and plastic shoes, while China made canvas and rubber shoes, South Korea made sports shoes, Brazil made women's leather shoes, and Italy offered shoes with famous designers' names. For the computer chip market, Taiwanese firms specialized in made-to-order functional chips for appliances, toys, and video games, leaving South Koreans to make general memory chips and Singaporeans and Malaysians to make disk drives.[14] In the early 1990s, Taiwan supplied more than half the world's demand for computer monitors. For these changing markets, much of the low-end production now comes from mainland China or Southeast Asia. It is often organized by Taiwanese firms that once did the manufacturing on their island. However, technical and market knowledge crosses borders blithely. By the mid-1990s, Taiwan's Acer Corporation was making two-thirds of its monitors in Malaysia. By 1999, the island's companies had become the world's largest source of monitors, modems, motherboards, keyboards, power supplies, and scanners.[15]

Usually, however, semifinished parts for them were fabricated in Taiwan-owned factories in lower-wage Asian countries.

As wage structures changed, so did specialties. In the period of its fastest economic growth, Taiwan made a great deal of money exporting suits, shirts, and other apparel to the United States. However, by the 1980s and 1990s, Taiwan's high costs of labor for sewing meant that poorer countries (including China, Indonesia, and Thailand) displaced Taiwan as direct exporters of finished clothing. Companies from Taiwan continued to organize these trades as long as they could. They also still made synthetic textile fibers, yarn, and bolts of cloth on their island, shipping these to factories in low-labor-cost countries to be made into finished clothes, shipped mostly to First World markets (including Taiwan) for retail sale.[16] In many cases, Taiwanese wholly or partly owned the factories in the poorer countries. In some fields, Taiwan gave visas to an increasing number of foreign workers, largely Filipinos, who worked in island factories. The number of foreign workers in Taiwan was 152,000 in 1994, but it rose steadily to 279,000 by mid-1999.[17] So the island became involved in many transnational labor exchanges as well as production networks.

U.S. Markets, Mainland Production, and Island Management

President Enterprises, the island's largest food processing company, raises fowl in China for cooking at Kentucky Fried Chicken outlets in Taiwan. In 1990, President bought Wyndham Foods of Atlanta, Georgia. This company is owned through a subsidiary, President International Trade and Investment Corporation, registered in the tax haven of the British Virgin Islands. On Taiwan, President runs 530 7-Eleven stores as well as joint ventures with Japanese, German, and other food companies.[18]

It is difficult to gather exact statistics on such complex transnational operations, which involved shipments of goods from and through many different territories. However, Taiwan's own trade shows that the accessible U.S. market was roughly twice as large as the European one. Both low- and high-tech products were sent there. Taiwan's exports soared from $20 billion to $85 billion between 1985 and 1993. In both years, over nine-tenths of the exports were manufactures; but the real news is that industrial exports remained important even as the island achieved "First World" economic status. As a percentage of Taiwan's total gross domestic product (GDP), commodity exports fell in this period from 48 to 39 percent. However, this is still very high for such an advanced economy; in comparison, U.S. commodity exports in 1993 were only 7 percent of GDP and Japan's only 9 percent. In poorer countries, the 1993 commodity export/GDP ratios were somewhat higher (e.g., China, 22 percent; Thailand, 29 percent), but these numbers are still much lower than Taiwan's 39 percent, even though the island's people were then already much wealthier.[19]

The situation becomes more complex if service export values are included in the calculation. About 5 percent of the island's exports were in labor services, not commodities—and this service portion was rising.[20] Taiwan's economy remained very globalized, especially for exports, at a higher income level than in any other sizable and sectorally diversified country.

Taiwan's global target markets were also diversifying geographically. In 1984, almost half of Taiwan's exports went to the United States; a decade later, the proportion was about one-quarter.[21] The American portion of Taiwan's exports was 23 percent in 1996, but the Asian crisis in other countries made exports to the United States rise again, to 27 percent in 1998. Japan bought only a modest portion of Taiwan's exports. Hong Kong and the People's Republic of China (PRC) apparently absorbed almost one-quarter of Taiwan's exports, but the United States took the largest share.[22] Taiwan's own market was important for selected U.S. firms. Without this, American politicians might have been more concerned about importing so many manufactures from the island. For Chrysler, Taiwan in the mid-1990s was the single-largest market outside North America. Citibank made more money from its credit cards on the island than it did in all of Europe.[23]

Taiwan's economic links to Japan are quite different from those with the United States or the European Union in two ways: First, Japan has been more reluctant to export technology or to import manufactures, so few Taiwanese–Japanese joint ventures exist at the Hsinchu Industrial Park, while many firms there are joint ventures with American or European companies. Second, over 90 percent of Taiwan's exports to the United States have been manufactures, but to Japan the portion has been less than 60 percent.[24] Japan imports less and especially less that involves jobs.

Taiwan's World Trade Organization Application

Because the trade of the Republic of China (ROC) on Taiwan is global, many on the island have wanted Taiwan to join all global economic organizations. Already by 1992, Taiwan had successfully negotiated with Western governments the conditions of its GATT (later World Trade Organization [WTO]) membership under the label "Chinese Taipei" (Zhonghua Taibei). Accession was expected within two years. A reporter in 1992 thought that "China is still insisting that it should be admitted before Taiwan. However, Beijing has been willing to go along with Taipei's application, apparently because it hopes that the eagerness of Western governments to admit Taiwan's huge economy will prompt them to accept China first as part of the package."[25] In connection with its application, Taiwan acceded to the WTO Agreement on Technical Barriers to Trade as well as to WTO sanitary standards for trade in foods, for practice on the island by foreign lawyers and brokers, and for many other kinds of exchange. American farm exporters, in particular, look forward to selling more rice, pork, and chickens to Taiwan after WTO accession.[26] Taiwan politicians had scant reason to offend their farmers further, opening their food markets more fully to U.S. exporters, as long as the WTO door remained barred for diplomatic reasons.

For years, Taipei has been in a position to qualify easily for WTO membership as a developed economy. However, Beijing has insisted on PRC entry first; and other members, in deference to the future size of the China market, have agreed to this demand. Beijing's concern with more than a name, its own delay and internal debates about becoming "GATTable," and its informal veto have long prevented Taiwan's accession from occurring. By 1999, Taiwan was the world's fourteenth-largest trader. Within the decade, it had already halved average ROC nominal tariffs to 8 percent. Even lacking WTO membership, this globalization had made Taiwan's economy more efficient. However, as an official admitted, "Without this foreign pressure, it would be very difficult for our government to liberalize markets and overcome vested interests."[27] By the fall of 1999, even before the U.S.–China agreement on Beijing's entry, many analysts expected that both the mainland and the island would join soon.[28]

Manual Labor, Clerical Labor, and Management

The market has created much of the ROC's regime legitimacy. Trade unionism is remarkably weak on the island. The economy has prospered quickly under a regime led by capital, and unionization has been slow. Nonetheless, a few Taiwan workers' groups have joined international labor organizations or, for diplomatic reasons, have been spurred by the ROC government to found them. The most prominent is in the most global field. The Chinese Telecommunication Workers' Union (*Zhonghua Dianxin Gonghui*) is a member of the Asia-Pacific Region Communications Industry Affiliates, which also includes unions from Japan, Hong Kong, South Korea, Singapore, New Zealand, and the Philippines.[29] The proletarian dictatorship across the water, where unionism is not a forte, is missing. Apparently, the Taiwan government supports this union. The communications workers in Taiwan are mostly state employees—and other prominent unions have also risen in public industries, notably in oil refining (*Taiwan Shiyou Gonghui*).

A still-unexplained political mystery about Taiwan is the strong and widespread sympathy for labor activism, as shown in attitude surveys among middle-class respondents.[30] Despite this, the number of union members on Taiwan declined steadily between 1994 and early 1999, from 3.3 to 2.9 million.[31] Solidarity and labor militancy seem to be popular images on Taiwan, but markets guided by capital are strongly legitimate as well.

Prospective unionists in Taiwan know that their companies often put capital overseas, where labor is cheaper. As a Taiwan shoe manufacturer said, "For the price of a factory worker in Taiwan, we can afford to employ 10 workers in China or 12 workers in Indonesia to do exactly the same job."[32] Taiwan's people are now unable to compete for unskilled jobs. By 1999, "little remains of the footwear industry besides some design shops and company headquarters; Taiwan-owned factories crank out Nikes, Reeboks, and Adidas in places like China's Pearl River delta."[33] Taiwanese are forced to excel in jobs that require higher levels of education, especially commercial, clerical, and management work.

Polling about "competitiveness" has become a global service industry. Some econometric agencies omit Taiwan from their studies.[34] However, the *Global Competitiveness Report*, compiled for the World Economic Forum (WEF) by a group including Harvard economist Jeffrey Sachs, uses an index of "the ability of a country to achieve sustained high rates of growth in GDP per capita . . . over the next five to ten years, on the basis of each country's current economic conditions and institutions." In 1999, Taiwan ranked fourth among the world's fifty-nine largest economies by that assessment.[35] This was a very good showing indeed, behind only the two Chinese city-states and the United States and well ahead of most OECD (Organization for Economic Co-operation and Development) countries and China (which is number thirty-two in that sweepstakes). The WEF report is designed as a briefing for business-people; it attempts to collate surveys of executives but also relies on standard economic data.

In 1999, the International Institute for Management Development (IMD) of Lausanne, Switzerland, gave Taiwan disparate rankings on different criteria. Taiwan's "science and technology" for business was rated tenth among forty-seven countries—a good rating, especially because several other countries in the top ten were small nations in Europe. In 1993–1994 alone, an estimated 23,000 people with doctoral or master's degrees (mostly from American universities) returned to Taiwan.[36] The IMD also attempts to assess the extent to which businesses are helped by the government. Taiwan was eleventh in a field of forty-seven. This list was apparently compiled according to executives' views of: "the ability of a state [government] to provide an environment that sustains and enhances the competitiveness of its business enterprises."

However, the IMD surveyors rated Taiwan notably lower (twenty-seventh) for "internationalization." The ROC government restrains foreign managers (whose opinions were polled to generate part of this rating) for the sake of defense against the PRC, and it lacks diplomatic relations with many countries. Apparently, executives say that these factors cause them problems despite all of Taiwan's trade offices.[37] Differences between the WEF and IMD results show how chancy such measures are as predictors of their subjects. Perhaps Taiwan's less good showing on this IMD criterion related to inflated business hopes about the medium-term effectiveness of any government to boost international efficiency.

Nonstate companies globalized Taiwan—whether or not they "internationalized" it. Matthew Miau, head of Taiwan's second-largest computer maker, Mitac, opined that "Taiwan has manufacturing capability, technology, good business sense, and channels for doing business worldwide. As long as the decision-making and engineering stays in Taiwan, it doesn't matter where you put your factory, be it China, the UK or the US."[38]

Cryptosocialism As a Flu Vaccine

Government regulation of transnational enterprise can have good or bad effects under different conditions. Many means are plausible for a government that wants to guide its economy. A state can control international trade by tariffs and quotas, it can guide investment by issuing business licenses preferentially for some sectors, or it can pass laws that favor stock purchases by specified categories of investors. The upside of mercantilist (antiglobalist) policies is that they protect local integrity. The downside is that they allow bureaucrats to seek "rents" for favors and to make miscalculations about efficiency, that is, to guide entrepreneurs into fields that are less than maximally productive.[39] The Asian financial crisis of the late 1990s demonstrated, for Taiwan, some virtues of illiberal regulation.

Taiwan is a market economy, but its state sector makes 10 percent of the GDP. The government has long monopolized telecommunications, oil, power generation, arms production, and alcohol and tobacco.[40] Despite plans to privatize some of these, a considerable socialist sector in Taiwan did not create an inefficient economy. The ROC government advertises its market freedoms but offers a great deal of economic guidance as well. This habit was first established by the Japanese colonial government. Since the middle of the twentieth century, Taiwan, like many other "free" economies, has never been as unregulated as its cadres suggest.[41] In the 1950s, U.S. advisers on the island, "although versed in Anglo-American economics, [chose] to jettison free market nostrums from the start and cooperate with Chinese officials to develop a state-centered strategy."[42] American propagandists advertised "Taiwan as a private enterprise success story," but this was just a half-truth, especially as regards ROC government support for research.

Taiwan's approach nonetheless has been more globalist than that of other Asian "dragons." The ROC has underwritten the general price of labor less than Hong Kong or Singapore (whose housing policies for most workers are cryptosocialist). Taiwan has given more subsidies to research and development. South Korean firms have often made export products that compete directly with the output of Japanese or American companies, notably in the auto industry. However, Taiwan's approach has been more globalist, emphasizing the development of "technological complementarities" with other economies and often arranging for the production of exports or parts that sell under brand names from larger countries. Taipei offers generous depreciation allowances, investment tax credits, deferral of income tax payments, and duty-free import of selected machinery and equipment to companies that the Science and Technology Advisory Group of the Executive Yuan favors.[43] The Hsinchu Science and Industry Park began in 1979. In the 1990s, about half the money for industrial research in Taiwan came from government (while in Korea the portion was approximately one-fifth and less than that in Hong Kong). Some of the officially funded laboratories at Hsinchu, notably the Electronics Research Service Organization, have been crucial in refining technologies that allow mutually profitable ROC cooperation with foreign firms. Such labs often employed young intellectuals who, after a stint in government, resign to make more money by founding private enterprises of their own.

Protected import markets can raise an exporting economy's "efficiency"— rather than decreasing it as liberal theory would predict—because foreign quotas force enterprising exporters to make higher value-added and better products.[44] Thus, mercantilism in some cases enhances economic performance. In addition, a concerted proglobalization drive can reduce Schumpeterian dynamic efficiency (as Kim Young Sam's "*segyehwa*" globalization campaign did) by legitimating unproductive loans to huge industrial combines (in Korea, the *chaebol*) rather than to leaner-and-meaner enterprises. This kind of globalism bodes economic crisis.[45] Hirschman has suggested the reasons in general: A situational threat to resource supplies may improve organizational performance, but only when normative communities will not supply other resources to replace them. A normative impulse may improve organizational performance, but only when the campaigners' own energies are themselves major situational resources.[46]

Neither the market, nor the plan, nor local interest alone adequately explains what happens.[47] Circumspect openness to international market forces has evidently helped Taiwan's growth since the 1950s, but the interests of national and local institutions—notably the originally mainlander's and then the multi-subethnic ruling party's (*Kuomintang* [KMT]) need to neutralize or mobilize Taiwanese talent—has also been extremely important. This domestic factor has meant that many ambitious Taiwanese made their careers in business rather than in the army or government. The island inherited an efficient market economy because of the early KMT's encouragement for leaders of the majority subethnic community to make money rather than go into politics.[48] In addition, Taiwan inherited ideals for regulating that market from intellectuals since Mencius and Sun Yat-sen.

Taiwan was immune to the Asian financial flu for several reasons. Throughout the 1990s, Taiwan was always first, second, or third (usually just after Japan, which has a larger economy and population) in the world as a holder of foreign-exchange reserves.[49] These enormous reserves guaranteed sure losses to any speculator who might mount a raid on the Taiwan dollar. Government funds in most "newly industrializing countries" have been much smaller than the pool of international investment money that accumulated by the mid-1990s. However, Taiwan, with huge financial reserves built up over many years as a financial defense against China, was less vulnerable to the tidal waves of capital that sloshed about the world. Thus, in 1997, Taiwan was among the few Asian economies not devastated by the retreat of this modern tsunami.

The ROC government in 1996, before the crash, had specifically discouraged further Taiwan investment in Southeast Asia,[50] so in 1997 the island's contagion was less. Taiwan had consistent trade surpluses, rising again after an earlier dip, and growth rates in 1997–1999 were about 6 percent annually.[51] The consumer price index rose in the late 1990s only at about 1 percent per year; Taiwan has had high growth with low inflation for a long time. Its government international debt in 1998 was tiny, just $100 million, while private-sector international debt was about $20 billion in a very large economy. Real estate and asset prices were high, as they had been in Bangkok and Jakarta before the crash, but a lesser speculative bubble in Taiwan had popped already in the early 1990s.[52] Forty-five foreign banks were registered in Taiwan by 1999, but none had very large operations. Bank regulators, enforcing ROC laws to head off bad loans, had prevented any huge accumulation of unpayable domestic debt. The island's economy had been dominated by the combined weight of thousands of small companies, not by a few huge combines as in the other "dragons." Thus, risk had been dispersed; the problems of any one Daewoo, Lippo, Hopewell, or Bangkok Bank could not damage the whole economy. Taiwan, unlike Russia or Brazil, did not catch the Asian flu.

Investment Out and In

Globally, Taiwan in 1998 was the world's seventh-largest foreign investor.[53] It was the third-largest investor in the ASEAN (Association of Southeast Asian Nations)-10 countries and second only to Hong Kong in the PRC. In 1997 and 1998 combined, the ROC's approved new investment into the PRC was approximately equal to that into the United States, Hong Kong, Singapore, and Thailand combined (roughly $6 billion). However, this underreports Taiwan's actual new investment in China during these years. The extent of Taiwan's links to other countries is also underreported by the ROC government. In the Philippines, whose Chinese community is overwhelmingly from South Fujian and thus speaks the same Minnan language as on Taiwan, an expert estimated that Taiwan's actual investment "may be two or three times the published amount, since much of it comes in through undisclosed channels into real estate, into the Manila stock market, and—with Taiwanese as silent partners—into joint ventures with Filipinos."[54] The ROC Ministry of Economic Affairs publishes on the World Wide Web the amounts of investment from Taiwan that have been approved by the government into various other countries.[55]

Low wages elsewhere are by no means the only reasons why the island's firms move their operations abroad. Formosa Plastics has invested in the mainland partly because Taiwan's environmental laws lower its profits from producing on the island, and Taiwan firms also invest in high-wage countries because this helps to expand their global markets. Giant Manufacturing, a Taichung firm that makes bicycles, opened a plant in the Netherlands. When its chief executive officer was asked why he would start in a plant with wages half again as high as on Taiwan, he cited shipping costs, hopes of building a brand name in Europe, hopes of avoiding EU antidumping rules, and hopes to "react quickly to customer demands such as color and size changes."[56] However, Giant also had two plants in China to make parts that involved much labor.

Taiwan's global investors have gone where others feared to tread: to Hanoi and even to Pyongyang. In Vietnam, especially in the north, the bureaucratic red tape facing foreign companies has been legendary among businesspeople. However, Taiwan's special interest in diversifying its investments away from China led a state-run ROC agency to finance a 100-acre "industrial park" near the Hanoi airport that helped firms from the island become acclimatized before they established operations further afield in Vietnam.[57] This pattern has allowed Vietnamese officials, who truly need capital but also love paperwork, to establish links to flexible Taiwan companies, including many small firms. Their owners were in many cases also the operational managers on site.[58] The corporations that globalized Vietnam's economy were often binational only, succeeding in part for that reason. Together, however, these small companies gave Taiwan the largest total foreign investment in Vietnam.

Another very communist country where the noncommunist Taiwanese state has explored economic links is North Korea. This began as a matter of trade, not investment. Fernando Chen, a Taiwan-based broker, led three business delegations to Pyongyang in the early 1990s. He indicated that some of the exchange took the form of "countertrade" (i.e., barter) and in 1994 noted that "textiles have been indirectly exported to North Korea for over 10 years through Hong Kong. We ourselves often buy raw materials from mainland China and sell them to North Korea. . . . North Korea is eager for Taiwan companies to invest, but their regulations are still quite backward and similar to those adopted by mainland China around 1985."[59]

The North Koreans' desire for capital remained as acute as their desire not to raise it in Seoul. A pyramid-shaped hotel in downtown Pyongyang had been designed as the world's largest, with 1,000 rooms, until that government's socialist planners ran out of money to finish constructing this grandiose monument. In 1997, it was offered to Yu Tai Corporation, one of the KMT party's own investment companies, as payment for shipments of rice, fuel, and fertilizer.[60] Taiwan also pays North Korea to accept its nuclear waste. The hermit regime runs a trade and visa office in Taipei. Few expected the Taipei–Pyongyang connection to flourish. That it was established at all, across political lines that craven people might have assumed impermeable, shows the ancient globe-searching economic prowess of Minnan entrepreneurs for making money as well as the globe-searching political prowess of the Taipei government for all available means to pique Peking.

In Taiwan, as on the mainland of China, most incoming foreign capital has taken the form of direct investment, not portfolio investment. However, selling parts of Taiwan companies to foreign buyers has been a means of spreading greater interest in the island's future around the world. In 1997, Taiwan's main international carrier, China Airlines (CAL), entered negotiation with British Airlines, aiming to sell 16 percent of the stock to the foreign company. CAL wanted to add London to its airports of call—and an investment company in

Taipei still held more than half of the stock. Thus, control of the airline did not leave Taiwan.[61]

In Taiwan's modern industries, as a reporter wrote, "any single firm, no matter how powerful, must work closely with many others. Often this is to obtain access to technology or manufacturing expertise. A web of a thousand joint ventures, cross-equity holdings, and marketing pacts now entangles every firm."[62] Investment, both onto the island and away from it, has been a means of confirming Taiwan's profitable global networks.

LOCAL BELIEFS AND GLOBAL NORMS

Studies of globalization can make clear not only that transnational units are important in the world today but also that smaller-than-national but larger-than-individual groups working in parallel over long periods have powerful effects on political structure. International trends spread not just because actors face parallel unintended modern situations but also because of empathetic echoing: One group can understand the ideas of another and can copy them. In 1949, Taiwan had a similar per capita income to mainland China. Already by 1992, this statistic for the island was above $10,000 per year (more than ten times the PRC average by any of the varying estimates).[63] By 1999, it was over $15,000. However, globalization brings normative costs as well, and it brings localization as a reaction.

Localist Resentment of Globalist Modernization

A reporter said that Taiwan's road-vehicle density in mid-1995 (including motorbikes) was twenty times that of the United States:

> Taiwan's air is worse than that of Los Angeles. Less than 3% of its sewage is treated; its urban waterways are malodorous cesspools. Rates of disease, including asthma and cancer, have exploded, as have alcoholism and drug abuse. The divorce rate has doubled since 1980, becoming the highest in Asia. Increasing numbers of Taiwanese are seeking psychiatric counseling for such maladies as panic attacks. As fewer and fewer Taiwanese are willing to settle for the cheap wages and sweatshop conditions that produced the island's economic miracle, manufacturers are turning elsewhere for labor—Southeast Asia and even mainland China.[64]

Quick modernization brings benefits—and hardships. Globalization intensifies both effects.

Environmental politics springs partly from tensions between Taiwanese (86 percent of the people) and mainlanders. Nativism implies care for the local land. This constrains the usual market orientation of officials. Environmental concerns led the ROC to cancel all limestone mining rights on the populated western side of Taiwan in the 1990s, even though cement had long been the island's main building material. Taiwan Cement increased its mining near Hualien, on the east side, while Asia Cement and Chia Hsin Cement financed plants in Shanghai and Jiangxi, where antipollution rule enforcement is less strict.[65] The United States is a leader in environmental protection equipment, and in 1990 Taiwan's Environmental Protection Agency laid down regulations to reduce industrial wastewater pollution by 75 percent, farming wastewater by 70 percent, and household wastewater by 30 percent.[66] American companies had the best technologies in this area. Thus, local groups' environmental politics led to imports.

Localism is also fanned by other threats to the current habits of small groups and individuals — not just to the island as a whole — and the most obvious of these hazards is strategic. Fears of invasion across the strait affect many on Taiwan personally. A best-selling novel during 1995, when China launched missiles near the island, had the English title *T-Day,* about an attack from the PRC.[67] Many other scary books, such as one called *Taiwan Blockade,* have been published in the 1990s.[68] The year 2010 appears in popular literature as a probable time of crisis in island–mainland relations. A nonfiction book, also sold widely in Taiwan, predicts that China will be a major sea power by that year.[69] This does not calm Taiwanese nerves. It is not just a matter of state strategy; it affects individuals' mentalities as well. One of the reasons for the reluctance of Taiwan's elected leaders to negotiate overseas, even though they might now have from Beijing credibly enforceable terms for autonomy and could thereby raise the objective security of their people, no doubt lies in a general sense on the island that the outside world is dangerous. The big dragon across the strait is, of course so, but other countries too have ambivalent links with the island. Not only is globalization strong on Taiwan; localization is very strong as well.

In the small Taipei suburb of Chiu-chuang, the primary school in 1999 still boasted a prominent statue of Chiang Kai-shek and a bust of Sun Yat-sen in front. Above the main entrance, however, in the horizontal space for an inspirational placard that had obviously once been Nationalist, a new red board had been hung with a less grandiose, not even islandwide message, simply saying, "I love Chiu-chuang."[70] Sometimes Taiwanese want to be left alone.

Religion serves as a retreat from quick modern globalization, which helps finance new churches and temples. These have sprouted like mushrooms all over Taiwan. The number of Taoist–Buddhist temples large enough to appear on government registers as of mid-1999 was nearly 10,000, and the number of churches and mosques was over 3,000.[71] A relatively new Buddhist sect, led by a nun, is based in Hualien and called *Ciji.* Her organization runs a university and a hospital with its own medical school (using mostly Western medicine). Many Buddhist and Christian sects are major providers of eldercare. The *Ciji* television station carries programs on which monks or nuns can be seen sitting behind lotuses, preaching calm sermons. Another television station is called "Buddhist Satellite" (*Fojiao Weixing*). At the end of August 1999, President Lee announced that the Buddha's birthday would be celebrated as a national holiday.[72]

Global Enthusiasms: Sportive, Feminist, Educational, and Cultural

Local and transnational interests were sometimes married happily, without need of an official license. Sports provide examples. In baseball, Taiwan teams could win international games. As early as 1968, a baseball club from a then-poor town in southern Taiwan upset the visiting Little League world champions, who were Japanese. The next annual championships were held in Pennsylvania, and Taiwanese teams won there—and in thirteen of the next twenty years. After that, "some of their best players moved to professional teams in Japan, seriously threatening the island's ability to remain a major competitor." The solution was to set up a professional league in Taiwan, but only global connections allowed this to happen without an excessive drain of local talent from the amateurs. "Organizers hope to increase spectator interest by inviting 16 foreign ballplayers to join the [Taiwan pro] league." According to a Taiwanese man who had recruited players from the United States and Latin America, "If you can get good foreign ballplayers who can throw well and hit hard, it will generate a lot of publicity and get people back into the stadiums."[73]

Sometimes the government was heavily involved in promoting transnational connections on the basis of interests that are inherently nongovernmental. Women's groups provided a basis for nonstate diplomacy. Nancy Zi Chiang, president of both Taiwan's YWCA and its Chinese Women's Association, attended a General Federation of Women's Clubs meeting in New Orleans and gave speeches for Louisiana audiences. She had interesting topics to discuss because the ROC Constitution guaranteed female quotas in legislative bodies and included a 1994 rights amendment promising "to further substantive equality between the sexes."[74] The Women's Federation for World Peace held its 1996 meeting in Taipei, promising "a global vision for peace from the standpoint of women."[75] Feminism allowed a people-to-people diplomacy that was not mainly economic, although no doubt the state was behind it.

Education is a famous Confucian value, as is the participation of intellectuals in government. However, obtaining an education is mostly the task of individuals and families. Surprisingly large numbers of people on Taiwan, including practically all in the economic and government elite, have received educations abroad, mostly in the United States. The doctoral degrees of the top hundred ROC leaders would surely number more than in any other government. Most cabinet members have Ph.D.s, as do most members of the standing committee of the ruling party and many in the various oppositions.[76] The high point of President Lee's difficulties with the PRC came from a return to his alma mater, Cornell University, to receive an honorary doctorate—where he had earlier earned a real one.

Support for education, including research at foreign institutions, was a natural interest in Taiwan. The Chiang Ching-kuo Foundation for International Scholarly Exchange has been generous to many academic projects whose conclusions it did not know in advance. When the University of California was involved in negotiations for funds from Taiwan, the matter became politically sensitive. Scholars who have worked with these institutions can doubt that problems would arise because of the care of people at each.[77] However, just as the norms of Taiwanese were sometimes challenged by global influences from outside the island, Taiwan sometimes challenged them elsewhere as well.

Foreign Fads

Japanese chic is evident on Taiwan, which is surely the least anti-Japanese place (except Japan) in the world. Asahi TV and an NHK channel, both broadcasting in Japanese, are widely viewed in Taiwan through satellite and cable connections. Of Taiwan's seventy-two channels available by cable or satellite in 1999, at least four are mainly in Japanese, five are American, several are from the mainland, and many of the others carry overseas programs.[78] Sushi and sashimi, like Japanese soap operas, are popular on the island (as they are in mainland China and Hong Kong despite very strong expressions of historical and possible future resentment against Japan among intellectuals).[79] According to a Western reporter,

> Throughout this island, Taiwanese youth are lapping up just about everything to do with pop culture from Japan. Young adults spend their pocket money on Japanese designer labels. Teenagers swoon over Japanese pop singers. Students neglect their homework to watch Japanese cartoons or read Japanese comic books. Children of all ages clamor for Japanese toys. . . . Japanese programs on cable television [are] carried by 75% of Taiwanese households. Within a short period, teenage girls deserted the American sitcom "Mad About You" for Japanese "matinee idol dramas." Boys forsook reruns of "The Simpsons" for Japanese animation, with its humor and depictions of clownish violence. Japanese singers such as willowy Namie Amuro, whose "Sweet 19 Blues" album is in Taiwan's Top 10, also fuel the made-in-Tokyo craze, although Madonna remains popular.[80]

Commercial fads for both Japan and the United States are strong. European-style brand names for items such as shoes also carry cachet. A Chinese couple named Hau founded "Sofia Boutique" to sell classy shoes. "Nowadays, fashion-conscious Taiwanese housewives do not blink at spending NT$3,000 (about U.S.$100) or more on a pair of shoes. . . . The Haus have introduced a medium-priced range of Italian imports that they have designed and made for the Taiwan market at contracted factories in Italy."[81] Publicity abets such globalization.

Cultural imperialism reached an acme when Green Giant, a branch of Pillsbury Foods and a seller of canned corn (grown in the United States), wanted to increase its Taiwan market by advertising. This took the form of a cooking contest on the model of Pillsbury "Bake-Offs," which had attracted mass attention in the United States. Green Giant strategists noted that corn soup "is a staple on the Taiwan table [but] few young Taiwanese cooks have time to prepare the soup. . . . We're looking for a simple recipe, the equivalent of the Rice Krispie bar, for vegetables. We need to find it ourselves—or have a consumer find it." The latter plan was surer, so the company held a contest and offered NT$1 million in prizes for the best recipes. It whittled down the number of entrants by holding a preliminary "coloring contest," in which Taiwanese amateur artists competed to paint the best pictures of "the Jolly Green Giant and his diminutive companion Sprout."[82] All of this evinced globalist norms, albeit they were pure corn.

This Jolly Green Giant campaign was sober in comparison with the "Hello, Kitty" fad that seems first to have broken out in Japan. A logo of a white kitten with a small colored hat attracted Japanese teenagers in numbers that even the most sanguine corporate strategists had not dared to imagine. Through links to an American company, McDonald's, "Hello, Kitty" (*Qidi Mao,* sometimes called *Zhaocai Mao*) spread to Hong Kong, especially in the form of dolls. A Taipei sociologist in the Academia Sinica recalled his astonishment at reading of their early popularity among middle-class Hong Kong youth. He admitted that he thought that Taiwan youngsters were more sensible. Thus, he was dismayed when, in the summer of 1999, this global contagion reached his island. Newspapers reported long, early-morning lines at the doors of McDonald's outlets that sold (along with Big Macs) "Hello, Kitty" dolls while the supplies lasted—which was not long. They were soon pirated, however, appearing in street stalls and night markets. Trademark laws and police were helpless against such a compelling symbol. At least one specialized "Hello, Kitty" store, dedicated to selling cloth dolls and ceramics of the icon (with various colored hats), opened on Taipei's Chung-hsiao East Road.[83]

NATIONAL UNITY AND GLOBAL IDEALS

Norms that are collective become involved with the state, and so with its claims to legitimate violence. For many years under Chiang Kai-shek, Taiwanese were taught that their relevant nation was China, the world's most populous and oldest continuous polity. Most were then proud to be Chinese, never doubting that they could be Taiwanese at the same time. Perhaps that is still the case—but concurrently or exclusively, they are now taught by most of their leaders that they are Taiwanese first. President Lee, for example, in his 1999 book subtitled *Taiwan's Pursuit of Identity,* is the most obvious cheerleader for this norm.[84]

Nationalities do not appear overnight, and the candidate Taiwanese nationality can be related to many historical events: from Zheng Chenggong's landing through the pioneer years and the Japanese experience, the 1947 killings by KMT soldiers, Chiang Kai-shek's rule, and the populist outreach of this son Chiang Ching-kuo. The December 1978 shock of U.S. derecognition did not create the Taiwanese political identity, which had long subsisted among some intellectuals and members of old landowning families. However, the American jolt was an external, unintended factor that made the Taiwanese identity norm politically more potent. At the end of 1978, Taiwanese were surprised by the American switch. President Chiang Ching-kuo said that "the United States government cannot be expected to have the confidence of any free nation in the future." A newspaper reporter protested that "Carter's human rights campaign is hypocrisy."[85] Few on Taiwan saw that the U.S. change was also inspired by the potential of liberalism in China, whose revolution was ending, and of an eventual truce across the strait.

Occasional commentators on the island had earlier mooted notions such as the development of a Taiwanese nuclear bomb, an alliance with Russia, or declaring an independent Republic of Taiwan. Before the U.S. derecognition, these ideas had always been marginalized as very dangerous; in fact, they still are so. However, by 1979 they were also raised more often and in more respectable circles. President Jimmy Carter, surely though accidentally, invoked Taiwanese political identity as a live option. On Chiang Ching-kuo's death in January 1988, the Taiwanese *hakka,* Lee Teng-hui, succeeded to the presidency and, after an internal power struggle, also to the chairmanship of the KMT.[86] Only 5 percent of Taiwan's 1987 population had been born on the mainland before 1950, and the grim reaper soon reduced this figure to practically zero. Thus, personal contacts with the mainland were mainly a matter of visits, whose numbers by 1992 swelled to an annual rate of 1.5 million (many of which were repeat visits by entrepreneurs).[87] Taiwanese increasingly nationalized themselves as such, even as their island was globalized and connected by various kinds of external links with the mainland. There is no need here to repeat all the well-known facts about President Lee's encouragement of this process.[88]

A minority of Taiwan leaders have long favored finding an identity for Taiwan people that moderates rather than exacerbates cross-straits relations. The head of Formosa Plastics, Wang Yung-ching, wrote an open letter at the height of the ROC drive for a UN seat asking, "Due to changes and progress, Taiwan has started to co-operate with the mainland to seek mutual interests after some forty years of separation. At this moment, isn't it an irony that Taiwan people are still disputing over the split?"[89] The dispute has arisen because Taiwan's long experience as a de facto state has encouraged many local leaders to reject their own previous Chinese nationalism as stale. They mobilize electoral support largely on the basis of Taiwanese nationalism.

Stately Identity?

In 1991, President Lee's government set forth "National Unification Guidelines," which posited that a united China might be achieved only after the mainland had reached a level of economic and political development similar to Taiwan's; then negotiations would have to occur between "two equal political entities." A 1995 white paper by the ROC's Mainland Affairs Council described Taipei and Beijing as heading two "equivalent political entities." Choosing words carefully, the council pointed out that "China, as it is traditionally defined, is now divided into two political entities: a free and democratic Republic of China on Taiwan, and the People's Republic of China on the mainland, which practices a socialist system."[90] At the end of 1996, Lee Teng-hui called a multiparty National Development Conference, which resolved that all political parties would have to consent before the government could reach any political agreement with Beijing. This was similar to the Democratic Progressive Party's call for a referendum; it assured that there would be no island–mainland truce. The ROC and PRC governments have committed themselves to support rival nationalities that are likely to result in a war.

In mid-1999, Lee Teng-hui opined to an interviewer from Germany (a once-divided country) that Taiwan and China had a "special state-to-state relationship," not an "internal" one, and that to call Taiwan part of China confused the issue. If this was a trial balloon, it popped predictably. Official Beijing was furious, threatening to cancel a visit to Taipei of chief PRC negotiator Wang Daohan. Many American friends of Taiwan were also disconcerted; the commentator Thomas L. Friedman, a signal proponent of globalism, wrote in the *New York Times* that Lee's effort to force clarity about sovereignty issues was "reckless and stupid" because of its effects on Beijing politics.[91] President Lee's insouciance about dangers across the strait was apparently inspired by his calculation that a "tough" Taiwanese stance would play well among voters in Pingtung (if not in Peking or Peoria). Under the ROC Constitution, Lee could not succeed himself as president, but he could have remained KMT chairman for two years after leaving the presidency, thus retaining great power based on the wealth of the world's richest political party.

Exclusive Identities?

Surveys on Taiwan in 1992, 1993, and 1996 asked two questions that separated the normative bases of political identity from the situational bases: (1) Some people think that *if* Taiwan after independence could maintain a peaceful relationship with the Chinese Communist government, then Taiwan should become an independent country. Do you agree? (2) Some people favor the idea that *if* Taiwan and China were to become comparably developed economically, socially, and politically, then the two sides of the strait should be united into one country. Do you agree? When the responses from individuals were cross tabulated, an increasingly large plurality (27 percent in 1992, 39 percent in 1996) claimed an entirely nonexistentialist national identity, favoring Chinese reunification after cross-strait disparities were lessened—but also favoring Taiwan independence if this could be safe.[92]

Independence sentiment has risen in the 1990s: An increasing minority of the respondents (one-tenth in 1992, one-fifth by 1996, perhaps more later) both opposed unification even after future PRC democratization and favored Taiwan independence if the island could then avoid war with the mainland. A sharply decreasing portion (41 percent in 1992 but 17 percent in 1996) both favored unification after PRC's political change and opposed Taiwan independence even if the island could then remain safe. Most islanders clearly preferred practice to symbols.

DIPLOMACY AND SECURITY IN A GLOBAL CONTEXT

In 1969, the ROC was recognized by sixty-seven governments, but by 1992 this number had dropped to twenty-nine. After South Africa switched its diplomats to Beijing (following a friendly farewell trip by Nelson Mandela to Taipei in 1993), the number of large nations recognizing the ROC became zero. Some new small states did so, but only after their entry in the United Nations, where China holds a veto on admission and mainly when they received unpublicized but large grants-in-aid from the ROC. Taiwan diplomats court prospective recognizers, such as leaders of the Kosovo Liberation Army or East Timor, on the understanding that an embassy at the United Nations would, for any new state, have priority over one in Taipei. Beijing follows a "Hallstein doctrine," breaking relations with any government or organization of states (as distinct from "economies" or "territories") that recognizes Taipei. Thus, Taiwan was in thirty-nine international state organizations in 1966 but in only seven by 1992.[93] In *non*governmental international organizations, the trend was opposite: Taipei participated in 182 during 1966, 695 in 1992, and 917 in 1997.[94]

Meetings that are partially UN-sponsored excluded Taiwan representatives lest China condemn them. A 1997 Geneva conference discussed foreign aid to the world's poorest countries, and it was called jointly by the WTO, the UN Conference on Trade and Development, and the International Trade Center. The PRC, like Taiwan, is not a member of some of these organizations, but Beijing objected to a suggestion that Taipei representatives be invited.[95] The ROC Ministry of Foreign Affairs publishes lists of international organizations in which it is a member, has observer status, has applied but not yet been admitted, or has had citizens invited as individuals.[96]

The number of Taiwan embassies has dropped over time, but the number of Taiwan trade and cultural missions has risen. Hungary, Brazil, Poland, and El Salvador are among the countries not recognizing Taiwan whose officials have spoken frankly about their hope to attract Taiwan investment capital. As a Brazilian said, "We think China represents a huge market, but Taiwan has the investment dollars." Nondiplomatic Taiwan offices opened during 1993 in ten countries without ROC embassies, including South Korea and the Czech Republic, and by 1995, more were planned in Mexico, Sweden, Venezuela, and elsewhere. "Some governments say they have come under pressure to upgrade diplomatic ties in exchange for loans and investment. Taiwanese officials argue that this is necessary to protect the interests of their investors."[97] However, few foreign regimes apparently buy that argument. Most want to have profitable relations with both the island and the mainland.

Taiwan traders can go where Taiwan diplomats cannot. An example is the ROC's main negotiator with Beijing, Koo Chen-fu, head of the Straits Exchange Foundation (SEF, or "*Haijihui*"). Koo is on the KMT Standing Committee but is also patriarch of the family that owns and runs ChinaTrust Bank (whose formal chief executive officer is his nephew Jeffrey Koo). The ROC Foreign Ministry allocates funds for the elder Koo's cross-strait activities in the "nonstate" foundation. However, the ministry also pays expenses for the head of a private bank, Jeffrey Koo, to engage in global "quasi-diplomatic endeavors, which include meetings with heads of state and other political figures whom Taiwan's leaders are unable to see because of China's objections."[98]

Financial Defense

On Taiwan, as on the mainland, the security aspects of globalization are seen as primarily economic.[99] For a while in the early 1990s, Taiwan had the largest foreign reserves (excluding gold) of any country in the world.[100] In mid-1998, Taiwan's reserves were $89 billion. Such funds can have various economic uses, but in the ROC's case, their intended function was mainly political: defense against the PRC, whose surest possible attack (military or otherwise) would at least begin with an assault on the economy. Taiwan's trade surplus made the accumulation possible, but the state's willingness to bank it (not spend it) was political rather than economic.

Localization of finance in Taiwan is also obvious in ROC policies of low borrowing from other countries and strict government regulation of bankers and brokers. As a former premier and economics minister, Sun Yun-suan, once said, "Our basic policy is somewhat different from our competitors. . . . Our way is somewhat conservative. We don't want to sacrifice stability for the sake of rapid growth. In the last fifteen years we always managed a budget surplus. We kept foreign borrowing down. . . . South Korea has a trade deficit, and to develop heavy industry they have to borrow. I always advocate that we generate investment capital from internal sources."[101] These policies were localist. They were also clearly linked to a global (or at least external) concern: the need for financial defense against expected PRC predations.

Another way to achieve this safety was to diversify the countries on which Taiwan depends for foreign banking. In the period of U.S. derecognition, Taipei branches were approved for the Banque Nationale de Paris, Banque de l'Indochine et de Suez, Société Générale de Paris, Banque de Paris et des Pays Bas, Grindlays Bank and Lloyds Bank of Britain, the European Asian Bank of West Germany, and the Hollandsche Bank Unie. None of the home countries of these banks had embassies in Taiwan—and by then, neither did Japan or the United States, whose large banks also have Taipei branches.[102]

The 1995 PRC missile tests hurt Taiwan's economy measurably. The Taipei stock market took a temporary plunge, and private capital fled from the island—by one estimate, at least $1 billion to southern California alone. As the *Los Angeles Times* reported, "Bankers in downtown's Chinatown, Monterey Park, and other predominantly Chinese communities watched their deposits multiply several fold over a matter of days."[103] The island had suffered previous capital flights (in 1949, then with the 1971 walkout from the United Nations, and with the 1978–1979 U.S. derecognition). Taiwan government officials in 1995 called such capital movements normal, but American bankers said that they had seldom seen such a massive reaction of cash to political news. Taiwan's globalized economy is definitely vulnerable to military threats.

Capital that could easily be withdrawn from the island in an emergency is officially discouraged from coming there. Overseas portfolio investment into Taiwan is kept low by government policy. It was only 2 percent of equity turnover in 1998. In 1997 and 1998, more indirect investment left the island than came to it.[104] "Onerous restrictions," designed by the ROC government to prevent PRC manipulations of the Taipei stock market, meant that most of Taiwan's indirect capital came from the island—which was enough because the amount available locally was large. Although Taiwan's WTO application provoked plans to lower barriers to incoming capital and foreign brokers such as Nomura established offices in Taipei,[105] stock market rules still had to take account of the island's financial defense.

Equities are not, because of these regulations, always the best way for entrepreneurs to finance their ventures. Some large Taiwan companies, such as Acer Computers, first listed their stock only in 1999.[106] Before that year, the Ministry of Finance restricted foreign ownership of equities on the Taiwan stock market to 30 percent. This was raised to 50 percent in April 1999. Looking toward WTO membership in 2000, there were plans to raise the allowance to 100 percent then.[107]

Software firms such as Ulead Systems quickly expanded their market capitalization, but the government stock market regulators insisted on such stringent standards for listing that the island's most successful software maker, Trend Micro, decided first to sell its stock in Japan instead. Trend's chief executive officer claimed, "Listing here is no good, because we can't offer stock options. [The regulators] are worried about the bad guys but they're killing the good guys."[108] Perhaps because of such regulation, Taiwan's stock market was "the region's healthiest."[109] One-quarter of Taiwan's households had investments in it.

ASEAN and the PRC: Cheap Bargains or Sovereign Friendships?

This chapter has discussed the economic bases of Taiwan involvement in the mainland, but both local and government politics affected investors as well. Taiwan's new approved investment into mainland China, as reported by ROC sources, rose in successive years from 1991 to 1998 as follows in billions of U.S. dollars: .17 in 1991, .24 in 1992, quickly up to 3.17 in 1993, down to .96 in 1994, then, in successive years, 1.09, 1.23, 4.33, then 2.03 in 1998, and at a slower pace in the first months of 1999.[110] The actual figures are almost surely higher, but the volatility of the rate is the main datum. Taipei authorities were under great local pressure to approve such investments, and they were very wary of doing so.

For years, Taiwan has been the largest external investor in Fujian, although during the PRC's early reforms most of this capital was registered for Hong Kong. By 1988–1989, 400 Taiwanese firms were in Fujian, with official approvals and investments of $680 million. During the next two years, 700 more of the island's companies had signed to invest $870 million more. By 1993, such firms numbered over 1,000, with capital of over $1.5 billion; by 1995, over 4,400 Taiwan firms were in Fujian, with approved investments of almost $7 billion. By 1997, the number of companies was over 5,000, with realized reported investments of $5 billion. A modicum of political influence inevitably flowed with capital in such large amounts. On the other hand, a large number of Taiwan investors had a great deal to lose if cross-strait relations broke down.[111]

Political risk was an obvious problem for these ventures. One strategy to reduce it was for Taiwan investors to link up with another nonmainland partner, often from Hong Kong. The Singapore and Taiwan chambers of commerce arranged joint investments in Singapore's "Suzhou project" in Jiangsu. The two chambers also agreed to set up a "World Chinese Business Network" of computers to "allow all Chinese entrepreneurs in the world to be linked up through Internet." As the head of the Taiwan chamber frankly said, "Cooperation with Singapore for investments in China also gives us added protection."[112]

On the other hand, local PRC cadres often offered attractive business deals to Taiwanese, whether Beijing's criteria for incoming capital were observed or not. Compatriots from the "precious island" could often arrange, especially during the early reforms or in rural areas, very sweet bargains, especially if reports or taxes to provincial or Beijing collectors could be minimized. Local "Greater China" sentiments helped bottom lines. If Beijing monitors complained, local PRC cadres could continue to collect their fees and say that they were just helping to reunify the motherland.

Taiwan investment flowed for security and other reasons to Southeast Asia, where 25 million ethnic Chinese live. In ASEAN, the ROC government involved itself by subsidizing Taiwan investors in hopes of diplomatic payoffs.[113] A "Go South" (rather than to the mainland) campaign among Taiwan investors aimed to restore old KMT ties with overseas Chinese, to provide Taiwan capitalists with alternatives to PRC cheap labor, and, if possible, to make the economic outreach diplomatic.

Subsidy Diplomacy

In the 1990s, Taiwan became one of the world's ten largest donors of foreign aid.[114] As with aid programs in other countries, donor governments usually expect benefits for themselves or their taxpaying corporations. Deputy Foreign Minister John H. Chang once said, "Some countries have realized that their ties with mainland China are empty. They have had relations for ten years and have not seen much benefit. They are disappointed. . . . We think it's the right thing to help countries in need, and what's wrong with getting some political benefit?"[115] The PRC, although it has much larger external and internal debts, also tries to woo countries with money. On a trip to Africa, Politburo member Li Tieying gave an interest-free loan to the Central African Republic and spoke about aid projects with leaders in Cameroon, Chad, and the Republic of Congo.[116] Stately progresses are linked to state handouts around the world.

The ROC government has announced long-term plans to finance as many as 100 industrial zones offshore, largely in countries that recognize Taiwan (Guatemala, Nicaragua, Costa Rica, El Salvador, and Honduras), but also in India, Indonesia, the Philippines, and Vietnam.[117] By 1997, Taiwan was not only the largest foreign investor in Vietnam, as mentioned, but also the second largest in Cambodia and Thailand.[118] The ROC in 1998 established a South East Asian Investment Company that aimed, over Beijing's sharp objections, to raise $1 billion and strengthen Taiwan–ASEAN links in the wake of the financial crash, even though no Southeast Asian nation recognizes the ROC. As a Taipei official said of the crisis, "Taiwan is one of the few Asian economies willing and able to do something."[119]

However, a liberal state cannot easily tell its companies what to do. One analyst in 1998 guessed that "while there will be interest by Taiwan's banks and securities companies in expanding their Asian networks, most manufacturers currently consider Southeast Asia to be too great a risk."[120] Insofar as Taiwanese companies had spare money and Southeast Asia was offering "the sale of the century" during the financial crisis, some purchases were made—for economic (or subsidized) reasons.

As Premier Vincent Siew toured Jakarta and Manila in 1998, a number of Taipei banks (including ChinaTrust, United World Bank, Chung Shing, and others) were in discussions about buying parts of Thai, Malaysian, and Indonesian banks. The KMT-owned Central Development Corporation planned to set up an international bank that was expected to open subsidiaries in Vietnam, Malaysia, and Indonesia. The ROC's "Fed," the Central Bank of China, earmarked money from its reserves war chest to provide a $20 million "fighting fund to encourage investment in Southeast Asia."[121]

"What does Taipei see in Southeast Asia that the rest of the world is missing? Enormous political opportunity," a reporter noted.[122] However, a Beijing spokesman said, "We oppose Taiwan's attempts to create two Chinas by providing so-called financial assistance." Just as predictably, a Taipei official claimed that the investment was all just "an act of neighborliness" toward Southeast Asian nations in distress.[123] The less political view, either way, is that it was also a matter of Taiwan firms "bottom fishing," buying when prices were low.

Diplomatic-Economic Existentialism

President Lee Teng-hui, in a 1999 speech on a visit to Honduras, said,

> To assert the fact that it exists, the island must establish ties with other countries. Of course, an official diplomatic relationship is the most ideal, but if this proves difficult, then a chiefly economic, *de facto* relationship will also do. . . . By keeping up non-governmental exchanges with other countries and maintaining good connections with key personages, we can gradually exert an influence on their policies. Such a pragmatic approach can bring about many breakthroughs in Taiwan's diplomatic efforts. Convention prescribes that operations such as the issuing of visas are impossible without official diplomatic relations. Yet we have overcome such obstacles by setting up offices in countries that have no diplomatic ties with Taiwan. . . . So long as we continue to develop Taiwan while striving to ensure its stability, the island will enjoy still greater growth at home and substantive ties with still more countries as well. At the same time, we can better assert in the international community the fact that Taiwan exists.[124]

Lee's explicit aim was to "shield Taiwan from forced unification by China as well as prevent the island from lapsing into isolation in the international community." He foresaw that the latter result could come from an overemphasis on independence, either in pragmatic diplomacy or in defiant isolationism. Lee drew the conclusion that the best policy was "promotion of cross-Strait ties" along with "pushing for pragmatic diplomacy."

President Lee practically ignored the security aspects of cross-strait ties and the nonsymbolic part of his diplomacy. As regards security, President Jiang Zemin has claimed that Beijing "prefers" peaceful reunification and that, in a "one China," Taiwan would retain its own army and would have no civilian administrators from the mainland. However, President Lee has not challenged Beijing to say that to a Taiwan official or unofficial representative in public or to address whatever other demands Taiwanese would consider necessary in a truce. No list of them has been heard from Taipei, apparently because Taiwan politicians think that they cannot even suggest to voters that they are in any serious negotiations with the mainland. The result is likely to be cross-strait war, not cross-strait security.

"Pragmatic diplomacy" contains a tension because it aims at state sovereignty through nonstate transactions. Formal diplomatic recognition by itself has seldom protected states from wars (in Kuwait, the United States was defending an oil patch, not a sheikdom). Even to the limited extent that money may buy embassies for Taiwan, they are unlikely to prove useful for security. There are many federal formulas for distributing sovereign pride so that it does ordinary people some good. Thus far, the ROC has never publicly challenged the PRC to see which scheme, presumably a loose confederation with both sides continuing their present global ties, could bring maximum pragmatic benefit for the people on Taiwan.

Beijing has blamed Taiwan's drive for global diplomatic recognition personally on President Lee Teng-hui. The Taiwan leader has certainly tried to use

Taiwan nationalism for his own party advantage, just as the leaders of the Chinese Communist Party try to use Chinese nationalism for theirs. Politicians do such things. Both Taipei and Beijing go global with propaganda for their own existential viewpoints. Perhaps the nonintellectual and nongovernmentalist majorities on both sides of the strait would be content to call off the dispute for some decades while Taiwan promises not to declare itself non-Chinese and China promises not to use military coercion for "unification" (whatever that word would exactly mean). However, elites who benefit from tensions and defense spending lead their people to war. Global comparisons suggest that China may be democratic after a few decades and that a war would not be fought after that time if more were done to prevent one in the next twenty years or so.

Official support from the United States for globalization is ideological. It is based on two historical correlations: that wealthy industrialized countries become democratic and that democratic countries do not attack each other. Specific U.S. administrations' support of globalist liberal and market politics has also derived from the special interests of partisan supporters. For example, as a presidential candidate, Governor Bill Clinton made an early impression on Wall Street magnates such as Roger Altman and Robert Rubin, who became big contributors to his campaign. They were profit-making globalists. "Our financial service industry wanted into [emerging Asian] markets," as his first top economic adviser, Laura Tyson, frankly said.[125] Support from the United States for liberal globalization is both long term and short term, based in both ideological and material interests. Liberal globalization is now a major tenet of U.S. foreign policy, and this threatens Taiwan when applied to China although not when applied to the island. Most Taiwanese realize that they are at least potentially part of the world's most populous country—and they are still searching for a secure way to square their free identity with a national one so that they can be citizens of the world on the same basis as people in other modern countries.

CONCLUSION

There are really no islands left. Localization is a sometime trend on Taiwan—and it is usually overwhelmed by links to the outside world that make most aspects of Taiwanese society not just global in fact but also globalist in ideals. As Samuel Kim has noted, "Economically, virtually every state today has a shared or compromised sovereignty."[126] This trend helps the interests of a diplomatically challenged state on an island that needs to export.

Globalization is less problematic for Taiwan than for poorer countries or for those less dependent on the "democratic peace." The reasons are several: The island now has fairly high wages, it needs to enforce regulatory laws and protect its currency value, and it tries to use global links to lessen the real peril in its security situation. Many postliberal critiques of liberalization do not yet apply cogently to this particular island.

Globalization has spurred academic debate about three other questions in particular,[127] and to each of these Taiwan provides fairly clear answers. First, do international or domestic forces mainly propel globalization? For Taiwan, the answer is, both do, together, strongly and inseparably.

Second, is the process fast because of the economic and political benefits it brings, or, instead, are factors of "relational contracting," patriotic path dependence, and bureaucratic monopolies of foreign transactions likely to slow the process? Does globalization enhance or decrease the power of the state? Some scholars argue that as international linkages appear, bureaucrats can collect economic "rents" as they lubricate transnational exchanges, but these change economic structures, raise competition, and eventually normalize transactions so that the costs of a transition to a more efficient structure tend to disappear quickly. Other scholars argue that bureaucratic "rent seeking" becomes a long-term pattern and that specific bureaucracies use patronist/corporatist authority structures to maintain their monopolies for a long time. This question for China, Taiwan, or anyplace else can be decided more convincingly by research than by any of the plausible theories (really ideologies in disguise) that are proposed to frame it. For Taiwan, there is a great deal of evidence that bureaucrats' concerns tend to be short term and centered on specific exchanges rather than long term and structural and that a fragmentation of authority rather soon reduces rents. In Taiwan, this process has been very fast. Clientelist speech is still common, but widespread behavior belies it.

Third, are the political decisions for or against globalization taken mainly by government power networks or instead by "social" power networks within countries or internationally? Again the Taiwanese answer is, both. Any state toots its horn about its effectiveness, and nonstate networks are more powerful than most reports suggest.

Any sentence about globalization has a subject that is a system smaller than a larger whole. That system's links to surrounding ideas and incentives can be looked at, but any choice of a topic always remains just analytic. Taiwan, as an island, makes a natural system, as might any local settlement or group there, or all of the Pacific region, or all the democracies, or all of China. None of these choices could permanently restrict the ways in which people will think. The best lesson of globalization is that situations and sympathies come in all sizes.

NOTES

I thank Samuel S. Kim for inspiring this project, Hsiao Hsin-Huang and Wu Naiteh of the Academia Sinica's Sociology Institute for providing crucial help, and Nevena Batchvarova and Wu Hsin-yi for research assistance. All remaining global and local mistakes are my own. The author is not a government official and uses the terms Republic of China (ROC) and People's Republic of China (PRC) only because people in those places do so. Pinyin romanization is used here, except for place names that usually have other spellings and personal names when the figure is known to prefer another form.

1. See Vilfredo Pareto, *The Rise and Fall of Elites* (New York: Arno Press, 1979), and Talcott Parsons, *The Structure of Social Action* (New York: McGraw-Hill, 1937).

2. *China Post Press,* 1997.

3. Lee Teng-hui, *The Road to Democracy: Taiwan's Pursuit of Identity* (Tokyo: PHP Institute, 1999), 74 and chap. 6.

4. See Karl Polanyi, *The Great Transformation: The Social and Economic Origins of Our Time* (New York: Rinehart, 1944).

5. Postmodern and other critiques are found in Fredric Jameson and Masao Miyoshi, eds., *The Cultures of Globalization* (Durham, N.C.: Duke University Press, 1998), and in J. H. Mittelman, ed., *Globalization: Critical Reflections* (Boulder, Colo.: Lynne Rienner, 1997).

6. These fears were expressed early by the great social scientist Max Weber, who thought that the bureaucratic future would hold "a polar night of icy darkness and hardness"; see "Politics as a Vocation," in H. H. Gerth and C. W. Mills, trans., *From Max Weber: Essays in Sociology* (New York: Oxford University Press, 1958), 128, which may be too pessimistic.

7. Peter Beinart, "An Illusion for Our Time," *The New Republic,* October 20, 1997, 23. Duan Ruofei, expressing a communist view, agrees; see "Persist in People's Democratic Dictatorship, Prevent 'Peaceful Evolution,'" *Renmin ribao (People's Daily* [Beijing]), June 6, 1991, 5, in *Foreign Broadcast Information Service,* June 10, 1991, 24. However, the "globalization = Americanization" view, which is often taken to imply that Americans always think in terms of individual interests and never in terms of social collectives, is based on a politically charged and partial reading of U.S. history. Correcting it would be beyond the scope of this chapter.

8. For example, the directions of three past normative identity changes (in Taiwan, Guangdong, and Hong Kong) can be related to three specific historical events; see Lynn White and Li Cheng, "China Coast Identities: Region, Nation, and World," in Lowell Dittmer and Samuel S. Kim, eds., *China's Quest for National Identity* (Ithaca, N.Y.: Cornell University Press, 1993), 154–93.

9. Hugh B. O'Neill, *Companion to Chinese History* (New York: Facts on File, 1987), 36.

10. See Ronald Rogowski, *Commerce and Coalitions: How Trade Affects Domestic Political Alignments* (Princeton, N.J.: Princeton University Press, 1989), e.g., 97.

11. John Waterbury, "The 'Soft State' and the Open Door: Egypt's Experience with Economic Liberalization, 1974–1984," *Comparative Politics* 18, no. 1 (October 1985): 65–83.

12. <http://web.lexis-nexis.com/universe/document?_ansset=geHauKO-MsSduaruruuzrva-dwwu-w-ccrwwerebwzebayeruraru&docnum=66&fmtstr=fuu&session=aOee5eb4-409d-ud3-9825...>, copying Mark Lapedus, "Taiwan Charts a DRAM Course," *Electronic Buyers News,* October 13, 1997.

13. Denis Fred Simon, "Charting Taiwan's Technological Future: The Impact of Globalization and Regionalization," *China Quarterly,* December 1996, 1196ff.

14. Gary Gereffi, "The Elusive Last Lap in the Quest for Developed-Country Status," in Mittelman, ed., *Globalization,* 59–61.

15. Andrew Tanzer, "Silicon Valley East," *Forbes,* June 1, 1998, 122–27.

16. For details and statistics, see Gary Gereffi and Pan Mei-Lin, "The Globalization of Taiwan's Garment Industry," in Edna Bonacich et al., eds., *Global Production: The Apparel Industry in the Pacific Rim* (Philadelphia: Temple University Press, 1994), 126–46.

17. <http://www.192.192.46.130/acdept/h20901.htm> (in Chinese). These "workers with foreign citizenship" (*waiji laogong*) sometimes conflicted with each other on Taiwan; rock-throwing incidents between Filipinos, Thai, and Indonesians there have involved ROC police (e.g., *China Post,* September 7, 1999, 1 [on an eight-hour riot]). The English-language press in Taipei has reporters to cover the Filipinos especially because they read those papers. On any Sunday, in the large mall across from the Taipei Railroad Station, the going language is Tagalog.

18. "Food for Thought—President Has Global Ambitions," *Financial Times* (London), October 10, 1990, 38.

19. Gereffi, "The Elusive Last Lap in the Quest for Developed-Country Status," 58.

20. ROC Ministry of Economic Affairs statistics (<http://www.moea.govt.tw> [in Chinese]).

21. The percentages were 49 percent, then down to 26 percent (P. T. Bangsberg, "Taiwan's Export Focus Shifting Away from U.S.," *Journal of Commerce,* April 4, 1995, 5A).

22. ROC Ministry of Economic Affairs data; see its Web site at <http://www/moea.govt.tw> (in Chinese).

23. Edward A. Gargan, "Long-Term Forecast for Taiwan Remains Upbeat," *New York Times,* March 23, 1996, 35.

24. See Simon, "Charting Taiwan's Technological Future," 1196ff., using 1994 figures here.

25. Jim Mann relied on Bush administration sources and diplomats in Washington for "Western Nations Open Way for Taiwan to Join GATT," *Los Angeles Times,* September 19, 1992, 6.

26. "Taiwan's Tiger Is a Regional Leader," *Business America,* September 1998, 12.

27. Julian Baum, "Ready and Waiting," *Far Eastern Economic Review,* April 22, 1999, 66.

28. Editorial, *China Post,* September 7, 1999, 4.

29. *Zhonghua dianxin gonghui* (title of both union and journal), no.16 (August 5, 1999), an eighty-page issue containing tables on the sizes of strike funds, memberships, and other information. This telecommunications union has, appropriately enough, a Web address: <http://www.ctwu.org.tw>.

30. For something really surprising, see Wu Nai-teh, "Social Attitudes of the Middle Classes in Taiwan," in Hsin-Huang Michael Hsiao, ed., *East Asian Middle Classes in Comparative Perspective* (Taipei: Institute of Ethnology, Academia Sinica, 1999), 291–318. Wu displays his results to a tee—and then admits with admirably scientific candor that he cannot explain them.

31. <http://www.192.192.46.130/acdept/h20202.htm> (in Chinese).

32. Luisetta Mudie, "Survey on Taiwan," *Financial Times,* October 9, 1992, 63.

33. Andrew Sherry, "What's Next?," *Far Eastern Economic Review,* February 11, 1999, 14.

34. China has induced several prominent measuring offices to omit Taiwan, which has the much largest population (and economy) not included in the United Nations. The UN

Development Program does this for the best general index of modernization, its annual "Table 1" in the *Human Development Report*, where Taiwan would rank about number twenty-five. The World Bank also does this for its more narrowly conceived *World Development Report*.

35. <http://www.weforum.org/publications/gcr/99rankings.asp>. Criteria are discussed at <http://www.weforum.org/publications/gcr/backgrounder.asp>.

36. See Simon, "Charting Taiwan's Technological Future," 1196ff.

37. See <http://www.imd.ch/wcy/factors/f3data.html> and <www.imd.ch/wcy/factors/f2data.html>.

38. Laura Tyson, "Plastic Toymaker Turns Big Investor," *Financial Times*, July 7, 1995, 19.

39. On the latter effects, see Anne Krueger, "The Political Economy of the Rent-Seeking Society," *American Economic Review* (June 1974): 291–303.

40. "U.S. Firms Can Benefit from Privatization of Taiwan's State Firms," *Business America*, September 1998, 9.

41. See Robert Wade, *Governing the Market* (Princeton, N.J.: Princeton University Press, 1990).

42. See Noam Chomsky, "Free Trade and Free Market," in Fredric Jameson and Masao Miyoshi, eds., *The Cultures of Globalization* (Durham, N.C.: Duke University Press, 1998), 360–61. Concerning another continuance of these colonial policies, see Atul Kohli, "Where Do High Growth Political Economies Come From? The Japanese Lineage of Korea's 'Developmental State,'" *World Development* 22, no. 9 (1994): 1269–93.

43. See Simon, "Charting Taiwan's Technological Future," 1196ff.

44. This refers to Joseph Schumpeter's "dynamic efficiency," which he contrasted to "static efficiency" that is the goal and raison d'être of the dominant neoclassical economic theory. For cogent applications to the PRC, see Thomas G. Moore, *China in the World Market: International Sources of Reform and Restructuring in the Deng Xiaoping Era* (New York: Cambridge University Press, in press). See also Cui Zhiyuan, "Epilogue: A Schumpeterian Perspective and Beyond," at <http://www.web.mit.edu/polisci..>, 1–15, and Gereffi, "The Elusive Last Lap," 53–82.

45. The startling failures of President Kim Young Sam's policies to meet advertised economic goals are detailed in Samuel S. Kim, *Korea's Segyehwa Drive: Promise versus Performance* (Cambridge: Cambridge University Press, 2000).

46. This is an adaptation of ideas from Albert Hirschman, *Exit, Voice, and Loyalty* (Cambridge, Mass.: Harvard University Press, 1970) in terms of the contrast between norms and situations from Talcott Parsons, *The Structure of Social Action* (New York: McGraw-Hill, 1937).

47. For the same story in another place, see David Zweig, *Linking China to the World: The Political Economy of Transnational Institutions* (in press).

48. For more, see Lynn White, "The Political Effects of Resource Allocations in Taiwan and Mainland China," *Journal of the Developing Areas*, no.15 (October 1980): 43–66.

49. See Samuel S. Kim, "Taiwan and the International System: The Challenge of Legitimation," in Robert Sutter and William Johnson, eds., *Taiwan in World Affairs* (Boulder, Colo.: Westview, 1994), 146. See also "Taiwan's Tiger Is a Regional Leader," 12.

50. Bruce Cheesman, "Taipei Ban on Overseas Investments Hits ASEAN," *Business Times*, October 31, 1996, 1. In 1992, an ROC official had discouraged investment in Malaysia, saying that Taiwan businessmen had become "targets of extortion" there; see

Walton Morais, "Taiwanese Firms Urged Not to Invest in Malaysia," *Business Times,* May 28, 1992, 1.

51. <http://www.moea.gov.tw/~meco/stat/four/z0-h.htm> (in Chinese) offers a Ministry of Economic Affairs table of indicators showing that the trade surplus was decreasing in 1997–1998 but began to rise again in 1999. Economic growth in 1997 and 1998 was 6.54 and 6.03 percent, respectively, and the 1999 rate through August was 5.74 percent — stronger on a sustained basis than is achieved in most economies at such a high per capita income. Another source, <http://www.140.129.146.192/dgbas03/bs8/test/select-3.htm>, from the ROC Statistics Office, gives a growth rate of only 4.65 percent for 1998; it is unclear which estimate is correct.

52. <http://www.boma.gov.tw/8803-4.htm> (in Chinese) lists them, with the net worth, assets, deposits, and loans of each as of March 1999.

53. "Taiwan's Tiger Is a Regional Leader," 12.

54. Keith B. Richburg, "Taiwan Overcoming Isolation by Investing," *Washington Post,* July 5, 1990, D1.

55. See <http://www.moea.gov.tw/~meco/stat/four/e-5-1h.htm> (in Chinese) for a table that, however, omits investment into the PRC. The same site (at <http://www.moea.gov.tw/~meco/stat/four/e-6-1h.htm>) offers a table of Taiwan capital outflows disaggregated by economic sector.

56. Weld Royal, "Made in Taiwan," *Industry Week,* February 15, 1999, 56.

57. P. T. Bangsberg, "Capital Flight Making Taiwan a Victim of Its Own Success," *Journal of Commerce,* October 7, 1994, 6A.

58. "Vietnam: Taiwan, the Most Effective Investor," *Saigon Times Magazine,* November 7, 1998 (available at <http://www.web.lexis-nexis.com>).

59. Dennis Engbarth, "Taiwan's Businesses Seeking More Trade with N. Korea," *Journal of Commerce,* June 21, 1994, 5A.

60. The KMT held off investing in the Pyongyang hotel pending a North Korean decision on whether enough visas would be issued to make it profitable (Jonathan Moore, Joyce Barnathan, and Sheri Prasso, "How to Make Friends and Irritate Beijing," *Business Week,* June 30, 1997, 30).

61. Nick Tabakoff, Dennis Engbarth, and Sheel Kohli, "BA in Line for CAL Stake," *South China Morning Post* (Hong Kong), January 1, 1997, 1.

62. "Who's NICst?" *Economist,* August 13, 1994, 31.

63. See Kim, "Taiwan and the International System," 145.

64. Donald Smith, "Taiwan's New Prosperity Is Exacting a Heavy Toll," *Los Angeles Times,* May 14, 1995, 18.

65. Laura Tyson, "Taiwan Cement Makers Look Overseas," *Financial Times,* July 31, 1997, 6.

66. "There Are Solid Export Opportunities in Taiwan's Major Projects and Environmental Sector," *Business America,* September 1998, 10.

67. James Pringle, "Chinese Missile Test Warning to Taiwan Fuels Invasion Fears," *The Times*, July 20, 1995 (available at <http:///www.web.lexis-nexis.com>).

68. *Fengsuo Taiwan* (Taipei: Dah-Jaan, 1997), a Chinese translation by Lin Ya-ch'ing of volume 3 of Ei Mori, *Shin Nihon Chugoku Senso* (The new Sino-Japanese war), *Taiwan fusa* (Tokyo: Gakken, 1996).

69. Ch'u Ming, *2010 nian liangan tongyi: Zhonggong maixiang haiquan shidai* (Unification of the two shores in 2010: The era when Chinese communism leaps to sea

power) (Taipei: Jiuyi, 1995). Earlier speculations are in Taiwan Research Foundation National Defense Research Small Group, ed., _Guofang baipishu_ (National defense white paper) (Taipei: Taiwan Yanjiu Jijinhui, 1992). A nice overview is provided in Chong-pin Lin, "The Military Balance in the Taiwan Straits," _China Quarterly_ 146 (June 1996): 577–95.

70. _Wo ai Jiuzhuang,_ observed in September 1999.

71. <http://www.moi.gov.tw/w3/stat/week/week29.htm> did not offer a time series on temple constructions. It did note 588,339 Christian, Moslem, and Ba'hai believers—and as modern global number mongers, we are not to doubt the strength of belief in those last 339 who were counted. The number of Buddhist–Daoists was put at 997,565. On a free Chinese island of more than 20 million, this is a mammoth underreport.

72. The government proposed to celebrate Buddha's birthday on the next Sunday, each year, after his actual lunar-calendar birthday (which in 2000 happens also to be Mother's Day, a more commercial festival). Thus, workers get no more time off. Taiwan has business norms as well ("Lee: Buddha's Birthday to Be National Holiday," _China Post,_ September 1, 1999, 1).

73. Paul Mooney, "Taiwan Baseball Starting to Think Big," _San Francisco Chronicle,_ October 6, 1989, D28.

74. Tina Soong, "Visiting Official Talks of Women in Taiwan," _Times-Picayune,_ November 8, 1998, 11F1.

75. Muharyani Othman, "Women to Meet in Taipeh on World Peace," _New Straits Times,_ August 22, 1996, 7.

76. For earlier information on this, see Li Cheng and Lynn White, "Elite Transformation and Modern Change in Mainland China and Taiwan," _China Quarterly,_ no. 121 (March 1990): 1–35.

77. See Michael Clough, "The University of California: The Perils of Foreign Entanglement and Money," _Los Angeles Times,_ December 8, 1996, 1.

78. Information courtesy of Wu Hsin-yi and another interviewee. In September 1999, Professor Michael Curtin of Indiana University was beginning a year-long research on the globalization of Taiwan's media.

79. Thomas Christensen has informally reported relevant information from his interviews of foreign policy makers in Beijing. If a survey of U.S. sushi/sashimi restaurants were made, it would almost surely find that most are owned and run by people whose family origins are in Taiwan, not in Japan.

80. Henry Chu, "Taiwan's Youth Casts Trendy Eye on Japan," _Los Angeles Times,_ May 2, 1997, 1.

81. Bob King, "In Step with Fashion," _Financial Times,_ November 12, 1987, 4.

82. Lee Svitak Dean, "Green Giant Goes after Burgeoning Market in Taiwan," _Star Tribune,_ March 4, 1992, 2T.

83. Data from interviews and observation. _Zhaocai Mao_ is a Ganesha-like avatar of the cat, a bringer of prosperity, apparently developed as such by an entrepreneur who saw the fad, wanted to cash in, and feared intellectual property problems (as modern lawyers would term them). The door of the _Qidi Mao_ store was directly opposite a grocery, not much larger in floor space, of the Wellcome chain, which came from an originally British firm in Hong Kong. Chung-hsiao East Road also has several McDonald's and Burger King franchises, 7-Elevens, Watson's drugstores, large Printemps and Sogo buildings, the

United Colors of Benneton, Starbuck's coffeehouses, at least a dozen clothing and shoe shops with Italian names, Pizza Huts, Sizzlers, and many other global gifts.

84. See note 3. This book was originally written in Japanese.

85. Jay Mathews, "Sudden Shift Stuns Taiwan," *Washington Post,* December 16, 1978, A1.

86. See Steven J. Hood, *The Kuomintang and the Democratization of Taiwan* (Boulder, Colo.: Westview, 1997).

87. Evan Feigenbaum, *Change in Taiwan and Potential Adversity in the Strait* (Santa Monica, Calif.: Rand Corporation, 1995), 9.

88. The author is currently writing another essay for the *China Quarterly* about Taiwan–mainland relations.

89. "Taipei Set to Consider Broader Diplomatic Ties," *South China Morning Post,* February 22, 1993, 8.

90. Dennis Engbarth, "Taiwan Hopeful of Entering GATT by End of Year," *Journal of Commerce,* October 7, 1994, 7A.

91. Thomas L. Friedman, "Buy Time, Not Guns," *New York Times,* July 27, 1999. In a formal sense, Lee's "state-to-state" position is realistic (the Vienna and Montevideo conventions defining a "state" clearly qualify Taiwan). As Max Weber pointed out, the peculiarity of a state is a claim about legitimate violence. In these terms, Lee's position is formally similar to Bejing's riposte about options of force against Taiwan. Politicians frequently hide the fact that violence, for good or ill, is the means of everything that governments do. Statesmen tend to ascribe an overly broad moral use to violence. (Among Chinese, Confucius and Mencius spoke cogently against that mistake.) Lee's specific statement was not factually wrong; it was politically localist to a fault, taking no account of the eventual or global context. State-to-state relations, whenever taken with such ultimate seriousness, are relations of war. Friedman's book on globalization is *Lexus and Olive Tree* (New York: Norton, 1999).

92. Wu Nai-teh, "Forming a New Nation: Ethnic Identity and Liberalism in Taiwanese Nationalism" (paper for the XVII Congress of the International Political Science Association, August 1997. The fourth logical possibility (a don't-think-about-the-problem-at-all stance) received scant support, 3 percent in 1996. Dr. Wu Nai-teh has conducted these surveys with large samples and low rates of nonresponse from the Institute of Sociology, Academia Sinica, Taipei.

93. Beijing suspended diplomatic relations with Riga when Latvia established "official but not diplomatic" links to Taipei. However, the PRC sometimes distinguishes small states from large ones, and visits of midlevel officials from large states cause Beijing to protest; see Kim, "Taiwan and the International System," 155–60.

94. Kim, "Taiwan and the International System" (updated at <http://www.mofa.gov.tw/almanac/3-2.html> [in Chinese]).

95. John Zarocostas, "Fear of an Uppity Taiwan Spurs Stall on Global Aid Plan," *Journal of Commerce,* July 17, 1997, 4A.

96. <http://www.mofa.gov.tw/almanac/3-2.html>.

97. Christopher Hines, "Trading Places Once a Source of Cheap, Skilled Labor," *San Francisco Chronicle,* January 8, 1994, 5.

98. Laura Tyson, "Bank Goes to Bat for Taiwan," *Financial Times,* November 11, 1994, 4.

99. The PRC view that "globalization is, first of all, an economic process. . . . The new security concept has, first of all, an economic connotation" is in Wang Yizhou, "New Security Concept in Globalization," *Beijing Review*, no. 42 (February 15–21, 1999): 7.

100. Feigenbaum, *Change in Taiwan and Potential Adversity in the Strait*, 35.

101. Henry Scott Stokes, "Europe Recognizes Taiwan in Trade," *New York Times*, February 17, 1981, 1.

102. Stokes, "Europe Recognizes Taiwan in Trade," 1.

103. Evelyn Iritani, "Waves of Capital," *Los Angeles Times*, November 5, 1995, 1.

104. See <http://www.moea.gov.tw/~meco/stat/four/g-4t.htm> (in Chinese), which offers a table on direct and indirect investment to Taiwan from 1985 through the first half of 1999.

105. Mure Dickie, "Nomura Securities Expands into Taiwan," *Financial Times*, June 1, 1999, 30.

106. Julian Baum, "Taipei: Star Performance," *Far Eastern Economic Review*, April 8, 1999, 64.

107. Julian Baum, "Ready and Waiting," *Far Eastern Economic Review*, April 22, 1999, 66.

108. Charles Bickers, "Soft Launch," *Far Eastern Economic Review*, November 26, 1998, 88.

109. Weld Royal, "Made in Taiwan," *Industry Week*, February 15, 1999, 56.

110. See <http://www.moea.gov.tw/~meco/stat/four/e-7-1.htm> (in Chinese).

111. Hsin-Huang Michael Hsiao, *Social Transformation, Nascent Civil Society, and the Taiwanese Capital in Fujian* (Hong Kong: Institute of Asia-Pacific Studies, 1998), 7–8.

112. Teh Hooi Ling, "S'pore and Taiwan Chambers Agree on Joint Ventures," *Business Times*, March 1, 1995, 6.

113. "Taipei Reaping Fruits of Southward Policy," *Business Times*, May 9, 1995, 2.

114. See Kim, "Taiwan and the International System," 146.

115. Nicholas D. Kristof, "Taiwan Is Seeking New Ties Abroad," *New York Times*, January 19, 1989, 13.

116. James L. Tyson, "Taiwan Eyes E. European Market," *Christian Science Monitor*, December 20, 1989, 6.

117. Laura Tyson, "Taipei Eyes Offshore Zones: Asia-Pacific News Digest," *Financial Times*, May 13, 1996, 5.

118. Bruce Cheesman, "Taiwan Targets Cambodia in South-Bound Investment Policy," *Business Times*, February 14, 1997, 4. The Thai claim comes from Woranuj Maneerungsee, "Investment Thailand Still Attractive to Taiwanese Companies: Willing to Endure 'Transitional Period,'" *Bangkok Post*, July 24, 1997, 12.

119. Vivien Pik-Kwan Chan, "Taiwan Offers Asian Aid to Broaden Links," *South China Morning Post*, November 18, 1998, 9.

120. Bruce Cheesman, "Taiwan Roadshow: Just Hot Air?" *Business Times*, January 19, 1998, 8.

121. Bruce Cheesman, "Taiwanese Banks Looking to Expand in Asia," *Business Times*, January 23, 1998, 4.

122. Jonathan Moore, "Pocketbook Diplomacy," *Business Week*, January 19, 1998, 23.

123. Lee San Chouy, "Taiwan Shops for Bargains in Battered S-E Asia," *Straits Times*, January 22, 1998, 58.

124. "Ask for the Advice of the People," *Straits Times,* May 23, 1999, 35.

125. Nicholas D. Kristof with David E. Sanger, "How U.S. Wooed Asia to Let Cash Flow In," *New York Times,* February 16, 1999 (reference courtesy of Samuel Kim).

126. Kim, "Taiwan and the International System," 178.

127. This list is rearranged and greatly changed from the conclusion of the forthcoming book *Linking China to the World* by David Zweig, who bears no responsibility for mistakes the present author may have introduced.

8

Thailand and Globalization

Natasha Hamilton-Hart

For over a decade, globalization has been the subject of lively political contestation in Thailand. The debate between "globalizers" and "localists" (as the Thai press has identified the two camps) involves figures from government, academia, research institutes, politics, private business, and nongovernmental organizations (NGOs). Thailand's monarch, King Bhumipon Adulyadet, entered this discursive arena at the end of 1997, giving new legitimacy to the localist side of the debate. The proglobalization forces, however, continued to dominate Thailand's public policy. While there is fierce disagreement about the costs and benefits of globalization, neither globalizers nor localists question the idea that globalization is real and consequential, constituting a powerful constraint on national policies. The Thai debate thus stands in curious juxtaposition to academic studies of economic openness, which, as described by Samuel Kim in chapter 1 of this volume, reveal a great deal of contestation over propositions taken as axiomatic by both critics and advocates of globalization in Thailand.

This chapter explores the politics of globalization as it has been interpreted in Thai public discourses and the political economy of globalization as a contested causal factor behind changes in national policy and political authority. Because of its long-standing integration into the world economy, the Thai case can add perspective to debates about globalization that are often focused exclusively on late twentieth-century manifestations of the dynamic between external forces and domestic change. How appropriate it is to base conclusions about globalization on the Thai case depends on one's position in the academic debate over it. The most trenchant rejection of many globalization theories tends to be based on studies of the developed countries of the North, which in general are less economically open and more politically able to define the terms of their openness than small developing countries.[1] Thailand is a developing country with fairly unexceptional political and institutional attributes. Given its high level of structural integration in both global and regional economies, Thailand should be an easy case for "hyper-globalists" and "transformationalists," who see globalization as having a signifi-cant impact on policy and political structure, but a difficult case for "skeptics."[2]

This chapter begins by identifying some of the competing claims about glob-alization that have surfaced in academic work over the last decade. Globalization is considered here, as it is in Thailand, primarily in terms of economic openness and capital mobility. The following sections illustrate the dynamic interaction be-tween global forces and Thai responses in different time periods, focusing first on the years leading up to Thailand's currency crisis in 1997 and then on the after-math of the crisis. The principal conclusion drawn from this study is that global forces have been deeply consequential for Thailand's political, economic, and in-stitutional development but have not been consistent or determinative. Domestic actors and institutions have always had pivotal roles in interpreting and mediat-ing external pressures and have at times influenced the degree to which Thailand has been structurally vulnerable to such pressures.

GLOBALIZATION: COMPETING CLAIMS

Globalization is considered here mostly in terms of its economic manifestations and political underpinnings. While globalization is indeed multidimensional, this focus is suggested by the need to distinguish different trends if one is interested in assessing their consequences for state policy and political authority. As Michael Mann has argued, trends such as ecological interdependence, cultural globalization, and economic internationalization may all be global, but on the issue of how they affect government, some plausibly weaken government au-thority and state structures and others plausibly strengthen them.[3] A focus on eco-nomic globalization and its domestic implications is also in line with the domi-nant usage of the term in Thailand.

There is virtually no scholarly consensus as to the implications of economic globalization. Opinion ranges from extreme formulations about the redundancy of states as political actors to theories about how globalization reconstitutes state authority to the view that globalization does not have significant effects on tradi-tional state powers. All these approaches assess globalization in terms of its degree and effects and have been categorized as "hyperglobalist," "transforma-tionalist," and "skeptical," respectively.[4] In Thailand, globalization has entered the national lexicon as a leitmotiv in debates over equity, political reform, and economic policy. The word stands as code for hugely powerful external forces that either cannot be resisted or, because they are so powerful, must be resisted. In the years before the 1997 crisis, the Thai debate was almost exclusively fo-cused on competing views within the "hyperglobalist" school—those who were critical, in normative terms, about the implications of globalization for stability and equity and those who were optimistic. Since the crisis, a perceived need to rebuild government institutions resonates with some "transformationalist" claims, but to a very limited extent: the kind of reform that is projected is congruent with maintaining territorial, national government as the primary source of political authority.

As to why globalization should have particular effects, two lines of reasoning are apparent. First, globalization may alter the costs and benefits of particular policies in a structural sense. The constraints that capital mobility imposes on monetary policy exemplify this potential. If capital is mobile, governments face a trade-off between monetary policy autonomy and exchange rate stability. As Thailand's recent experience attests, refusal to concede this trade-off will be costly and ultimately infeasible.[5] Less determinate but no less commonly cited are the incentives globalization creates for conforming to "market forces," which may "systematically constrain" government policy by rewarding some types of policy and punishing others.[6] However, predictions as to which policy mix is rewarded, or sanctioned, by the world economy depend on the analyst's beliefs about the inherent dynamics (and failures) of markets, governments, and politics.[7]

Second, globalization may affect policy, politics, and even political institutions in a more proximate way, that is, through the changes it brings about in the power and preferences of domestic actors. For example, economic integration may mean that industries that formerly agitated for protection now lobby for free trade, or the internationalization of finance may change preferences on financial regulation and macroeconomic policy. The power of different sectors or groups may also change with globalization as their weight in the economy shifts and as changing mobility affects their political voice.[8] While well theorized, there remains significant indeterminacy when such models are tested empirically or when assumptions about what motivates political actors are relaxed.

THAILAND AND GLOBALIZATION UNTIL 1997

A Nineteenth-Century Prelude?

A Thai intellectual argued in 1993 that "there has never been a time when Thai society was not globalizing."[9] Not only have conventional measures of economic openness been high, but adjustment to external forces has been a recurrent theme of the polity's history. Thus, the recent pronouncement by the World Bank's chief economist that open economies are inherently vulnerable, "like small rowboats on a wild and open sea," captures something of a Thai reality that predates the 1990s.[10] Even before the colonial powers began to press their demands in the middle of the nineteenth century, the Bangkok state founded in 1782 was ethnically plural, possibly predisposing modern Thailand toward cosmopolitanism.[11] More overtly significant in the post–financial crisis Thailand of the late 1990s is the memory of Siam's forced opening to foreign commerce, symbolized by the

Bowring Treaty imposed on Bangkok by the British in 1855. With the treaty came foreign commercial access to Siam's resources, an end to royal levies on external trade, and the establishment of European banks and trading houses in Bangkok. It also ceded extraterritorial judicial rights to foreign powers and, by no means coincidentally, ushered in a new wave of immigration from China. By the end of the nineteenth century, the marketization of the Thai economy was virtually complete, and its sensitivity to world market prices affected—albeit in very different ways—the lives of peasantry, laborers, aristocrats, and foreign expatriates.[12]

This nineteenth-century "globalization" was accompanied by efforts at state building in Siam—the centralization of political authority, the demarcation of territorial boundaries, and the development of bureaucratic structures—as in the colonized parts of Southeast Asia. The need to develop alternative revenue sources to replace the previous reliance on royal trade levies was a factor prompting the Bangkok monarchs to create a modern ministry of finance. The need to provide infrastructural support for commercial activity was another reason for the development of bureaucratic state structures. Meeting the demands of foreign traders and consuls in an effort to stave off outright colonization thus involved considerable state development as well as concessions, in the form of territory and privileges, to foreigners. Siam's internal reforms not only were prompted by outside pressures but also were carried out with the direct involvement of foreigners: The ubiquitous foreign consultant in today's Bangkok has his counterparts in the hundreds of foreign advisers, technicians, and administrators employed by King Chulalongkorn in the late nineteenth and early twentieth centuries.[13]

Boom Years

Postwar Thailand experienced two distinct periods of high growth, both intimately connected with the country's place in international political and economic structures. The first postwar boom came as a result of the global Cold War coming to Asia and America's war in Indochina, from which Thailand profited as a result of military spending, direct aid, and access to the U.S. market. As in the late nineteenth century, this period of growth, foreign involvement, and openness was associated with large-scale state-led development of physical infrastructure and the development of state structures themselves.[14] The second boom occurred from the late 1980s until the financial crash of 1997. The high growth of this period was fueled by massive inflows of foreign capital as first Japanese and then other Asian firms restructured their export and production strategies in response to the yen's revaluation in the mid-1980s, rising costs at home, and pressure from the United States.

It was in this era that globalization discourses gained prominence in Thailand, taking the place of the modernization mantras that had characterized the early postwar decades. The Thai term for globalization, *lokanuwat,* became a buzzword, a neologism coined at the end of the 1980s with the meaning of "turning with the world." The word, Pasuk and Baker write, "quickly became a catch-phrase, a fad. It became a routine part of everything, from the titles of seminars to the patter of television comedians." The word itself generated a certain amount of controversy, as the Royal Institute of Thailand argued that the term *lokanuwat* be replaced with *lokapiwat,* or "extending across the world." This, Pasuk and Baker note, suggests that for many Thais globalization was conceived of as an opportunity. However, it was a politically contested opportunity. According to Craig Reynolds, Thai writers took advantage of "the *lokanuwat* currency by exploiting the word's resonances with similar-sounding coinages," with meanings such as "global catastrophe," "greed," and "unbridled consumerism."[15]

Indeed, a significant countercurrent to Thailand's headlong embrace of rapid growth, financial liberalization, and urbanization coalesced around the term "globalization." The content of normal political debate and NGO activism in a newly democratic country—poverty and distribution, environmental degradation, and social values—was cast in terms of conflict between "globalizers" and "communitarians," to use the words of Thai academic and writer Kasian Tejapira. Neither camp was unified. The globalizers included newly emergent commercial interests as well as the long-established, oligopolistic Bangkok business families, both with an eye to foreign opportunities and the benefits that foreign capital brought to the local stock market.[16] Also in this camp were Thailand's technocrats, mostly economics-trained civil servants in the finance ministry, central bank, and planning agency. On the other side of the debate, the opponents of globalization included former Marxist radicals, advocates of "community culture" worried about equity and local control, conservative nationalists concerned about Thai culture, and Buddhist monks concerned with the survival of spiritual values under an onslaught of materialism. In one sense, these critical voices were raised against the externalities of rapid growth rather than anything specifically related to economic internationalization. However, they phrased their arguments in terms of globalization, the two phenomena taken to be indistinguishable in the Thai context.

While conceived of primarily in terms of economic integration and market-driven change, the globalization debate brought to light concerns over the copying of foreign models that echoed cultural debates at the start of the century. In both eras, as Craig Reynolds argues, fears revolved around damage to Thai social institutions and the erosion of autonomy. In the 1990s, globalization was associated with the undermining of Thai cultural standards; in the 1910s, the mood was symbolized by a monograph titled *The Cult of Imitation,* written by the Thai monarch shortly after territorial losses to France and England.[17]

In the most recent boom, actors identified with the globalist agenda were dominant in policy terms, largely able to implement their agenda of liberalization and internationalization. They may, as Pasuk and Baker argue, have been unable to manage the consequences of the forces they unleashed, but their opponents on the localist or communitarian side of the debate were almost completely marginal.[18] While some developments, such as the yen revaluation and changing Asian production strategies, owed little to the actions of Thai policymakers, other aspects of Thailand's integration with world markets at this time were a direct product of national initiatives. Perhaps most significant—and, in view of later events, most costly—were Thailand's financial policies. The story is worth telling in some detail because of the role that finance played in Thailand's currency crisis and because interpretations of Thailand's crash bear directly on debates about globalization.

Thailand's financial system has always been relatively open. For a long time, banks and nonfinancial firms have been able to access foreign sources of finance, making use of informal ties among the region's ethnic Chinese as well as formal financial markets.[19] Banks often had significant recourse to borrowings from abroad, which were in fact higher in the 1970s than in the 1980s. Cognizant of this openness, the central bank generally set interest rates close to foreign rates, and "from time to time the bank rate has been adjusted either to induce capital inflow or prevent capital outflow."[20] However, certain indirect controls and structural features of the financial system meant that the capital account was not as open in practice as it was to become after reform in the 1990s.[21] In particular, limited competition among banks and minimal stock market activity curtailed the scope and need for foreign financial inflows. Entry was controlled, and interest rate regulations reduced price-based competition. Foreign banks were restricted in their ability to set up branches. Competition was also reduced by the oligopolistic structure of the industry and the lack of competition from the capital market or nonbank financial institutions.[22] As described in detail by Hewison, the market operated in the context of a cozy alliance of domestic bankers, industrialists, and a political–government elite.

Financial reforms in the early 1990s changed much of this picture. The extent of change should not be overstated, as prereform financial policy was unusually hands off for a developing country.[23] However, the changes were real. Interest rate controls were removed and controls on the capital account lifted. Officials promoted and subsidized an offshore banking system, the Bangkok International Banking Facility.[24] Partly because of promotional efforts and partly because of external interest, the stock exchange also experienced unprecedented growth in the 1990s. Both the relative size of the financial sector and a policy of developing finance qua finance were novel departures for Thailand. The increased competition and internationalization that this involved meant that banks were no longer protected by the patterns of informal collusion that had previously operated, and failures became much more costly.

Crisis

The unfolding of Thailand's currency and financial crisis in 1997 and 1998 is now a well-known story. After coming under pressure from late 1996, Thai authorities were forced to float the baht in July 1997. Thailand became the first domino to fall in a series of emerging market financial crises that spread through Asia, reached Latin America and Russia, and threatened Wall Street over the next year. Even after a rebound in 1998, Thailand's currency had devalued by 36 percent between the end of June 1997 and May 1998. The stock market index fell by 27 percent over the same period. Many banks and finance companies were either nationalized or closed under high levels of bad debt. The economy plunged into deep recession in 1998, with a contraction of 9 percent. The total costs of recapitalizing the banking system were expected to reach almost 1.5 trillion baht — about 30 percent of gross domestic product (GDP).[25] The controversy over the causes of the crisis continues.

If the crisis was sparked by currency pressure in the context of prior large-scale capital inflows, then it may seem obvious that Thailand's crisis was indeed a crisis of globalization. There are other explanations for the crisis, of course, such as declining productivity and domestic cronyism.[26] However, even assuming that the crisis was substantially a currency and financial crisis, it is not obvious that "globalization" can explain it. In short, this is because although large foreign capital inflows were a precondition for the kind of crisis that Thailand experienced, the inflows themselves and the way in which Thai policymakers responded to them had at least as much to do with domestic factors as the external forces of global financial markets. The inflows could not have occurred had Thailand not embarked on a policy of financial liberalization and aggressive financial development. Had Thai policymakers been less wedded to these goals, they would also have been better able to manage the pressures on domestic monetary policy that were apparent well before the crisis.

Bello describes the financial policy engineered by Thailand's technocrats in the years before the crisis as an "institutionalized pattern of development that was greatly dependent on huge infusions of foreign capital" (or, as he has written elsewhere, Thailand was "addicted to capital"). Such dependence was the choice of local elites, hence the need to avoid seeing Thailand and the rest of the region as simply falling victim to external forces with the onset of the currency crisis.[27] They were undoubtedly in a difficult position when they found themselves wrestling with capital inflows while attempting to avoid currency appreciation in order not to further undermine Thailand's export competitiveness and widen the current account deficit. However, it was the elite's commitment to financial and capital account liberalization that disposed the Bank of Thailand to costly and counterproductive sterilization policies rather than controls on capital inflows.[28]

Capital inflows fed the growth in financial assets, but it is arguable that it was the extraordinarily rapid growth of these assets as much as their foreign element that proved so destabilizing. Foreign funds continued to flow into the stock exchange even after the baht was floated on July 2, with record inflows recorded in the third quarter of 1997. Rather than leading the panic, foreign portfolio investors did not panic enough.[29] Table 8.1 gives indicators of financial development and internationalization in Thailand, with comparative figures for Malaysia (which also suffered a sharp recession in 1998) and for the Philippines (which merely recorded a slow-down in growth).

Not only are Thailand and Malaysia characterized by much higher levels of financial development than the Philippines, but these levels are exceptionally high for what are still developing economies. Some of this is masked in the table by the discrepancy in the Thai case between bank credit to the private sector and credit to the private sector by the financial industry as a whole, which increased from 72 percent of GDP in 1990 to 142 percent of GDP in 1995.[30] Thailand's economy was more internationalized than that of the Philippines—its foreign investment boom had endured longer, and its financial sector was more internationally exposed than that of the Philippines. For example, a factor that distinguished the Thai financial sector was that just 1 percent of total foreign-exchange liabilities of commercial banks in Thailand was owed to residents, as compared to about 52 percent in the Philippines, as of the first quarter of 1996.[31] This exposure, however, had a great deal to do with the deliberate development and subsidization of the Bangkok International Banking Facility by Thai authorities. It is also likely to have had something to do with the incentives for foreign-currency borrowing created by comparatively high domestic interest rates. Again, these were a function of domestic policy preferences as much as the inherent pressures of capital mobility.

Table 8.1.   Precrisis Financial and Economic Indicators

	GDP							
	Credit[a]	Stocks[b]	Capital[c]	Trade[d]	CA[e]	$[f]	%[g]	Per cap.[h]
Thailand	100	77	10.5	38	-7.3	185	8.2	2,740
Malaysia	93	227	9.6	86	-6.5	98.7	8.9	3,890
Philippines	49	38	9.3	33	-3.6	82.6	2.7	1,050

a. Claims on private sector held by deposit money banks (as a percentage of GDP), end 1996.

b. Stock market capitalization (as a percentage of GDP), December 1995.

c. Net inflows of capital: financial and capital account of the balance of payments (as a percentage of GDP), 1996.

d. Exports of goods and services (as a percentage of GDP), annual average 1991-1996.

e. Balance of current account (as a percentage of GNP), annual average 1991-1996.

f. GDP in billions of U.S. dollars, 1996.

g. Real GDP growth, annual average 1991-1996.

h. Per capita income in U.S. dollars, 1995.[30]

THAILAND AND GLOBALIZATION AFTER 1997

Policy Responses to the Crisis

For those who interpreted the crisis as a crisis of globalization, the reforms undertaken by Thailand in its aftermath provide further evidence of the constraints imposed by a global economy. Thailand had little choice but to accept the $17 billion in rescue funds coordinated by the International Monetary Fund (IMF) and in the short run to comply with the conditionalities attached to these funds. Although the IMF reversed its initial directive on contractionary fiscal policy, it maintained pressure for a range of policy and institutional reforms: privatization, increased access for foreign investors, new laws on bankruptcy and foreclosure, and other efforts to provide Thailand with what it was deemed to have lacked prior to the crisis: good governance. These reforms were drawn up and implemented with the close involvement of personnel from international agencies such as the IMF and large numbers of foreign consultants. A local analyst could fairly write that Washington was now a player in Thai politics.[32] The judgment that Korea's reform program, instituted largely as a result of IMF demands and direct American pressure, entailed "a remolding of the Korean economy in the image of a Washington economist's idea of a free-market economy" can just as easily be applied to Thailand.[33]

Thailand did not leap at the opportunity to implement the reform program, but at the end of 1997 a new government headed by Chuan Leekpai came to power. In its first months of office, Chuan's administration proved much readier to adopt IMF policies, and by early 1998 Thailand was perceived to be "on track" in meeting its commitments under the IMF packages.[34] The thrust of the reform program was that, as a complement to economic openness, Thailand should adopt international standards in areas such as corporate governance, prudential regulation, and financial supervision. Ostensibly technical in nature, these standards, as interpreted by both international agencies and local players, have the potential to alter key features of the domestic political economy of countries such as Thailand. Transparency can be a reason for reducing the government's direct economic activity as well as for stepping up its monitoring functions in unprecedented ways. "Responsible" macroeconomic policy can mean institutionalizing changes in organizations such as the central bank. "International standards" can thus become "the wedge with which a broader set of policy and institutional preferences . . . will be imparted to recipient countries."[35]

What is interesting about Thailand's moves to adopt such standards, however, is that despite Thailand's limited bargaining leverage to resist reform, implementation has been very partial. For example, despite calling for privatization and a reduced direct government role in the economy, the crisis has involved public bailouts of financial institutions and the nationalization of three banks. With signs of recovery and reduced IMF leverage, privatization moved from being "one of the main buzzwords of Thailand's economic reforms" to being eliminated as an official part of the government's short-term plans for recovery. The country's liberal and internationalist finance minister, Tarrin Nimman-haeminda, stated that "the Government has no need or desire to sell assets cheaply to foreign investors."[36]

Despite new bankruptcy laws, many of the corporate restructuring deals brokered by the banks have in fact circumvented the bankruptcy code.[37] The most obvious result of the drive to adopt international standards in the areas of corporate restructuring and bankruptcy (as well as government regulation) has been the arrival of hundreds of foreign specialists in Thailand. The new bankruptcy laws were cited as having led a top New York law firm to boost its presence in Bangkok to over sixty lawyers. Foreign corporate recovery specialists and auditors have found business aplenty in Thailand after the crisis, their interest undiminished by the contract killing of an Australian auditor investigating possible corrupt practices. This influx of foreign specialists was not unique to Thailand. As noted in the press, "Asia's financial meltdown created a new breed of jet-setting corporate recovery specialists sent to administer the last rites over bankrupt companies and to put ailing regional banks, multinationals and state monoliths back on track. The opportunity for teams of bankers, lawyers, auditors, accountants and valuation experts to make vast fees out of Asia's corporate misery was viewed as one of the few upsides of the economic crisis." This foreign presence prompted criticism in Thailand, where concerns were voiced over U.S. merchant banks that the opposition believed had "trodden a thin line in balancing roles as corporate advisers and vulture funds picking over the leftovers of corporate failures."[38]

Despite liberalizing rules on foreign ownership, new foreign investment has been quite limited. Foreign investment in Thai banks increased significantly after the crisis, with investors from Taiwan, Singapore, the Netherlands, and the United Kingdom acquiring majority shares or significant equity positions in six Thai commercial banks. American investment firms acquired a large part of the discounted assets of closed Thai financial institutions—with the result that GE Capital now reportedly owns one in ten cars in Thailand and that Lehman Brothers has become a significant holder of Thai property. In another high-profile case, Merrill Lynch acquired a controlling share in a Thai securities company, one of about eighty deals concluded between foreigners and Thai firms since July 1997.[39] Nonetheless, overall, private capital continued to flow out of the country, with the balance of payments recording a net outflow of $12.2 billion in 1999 and $15.6 billion (over 10 percent of GDP) in 1998, almost twice the size of the outflow in 1997. During 1998, the foreign share of trading on the stock exchange decreased from 40 to 30 percent.[40]

Perhaps significant for assessments as to how much policy is becoming more market based, interest among foreign investors in the Thai finance sector was not stimulated only by the low prices of Thai assets. The government also announced it planned to give foreign investors a five- to seven-year guarantee on nonperforming loans of the nationalized Thai banks they buy into.[41] The weakness in Thailand's capital account monitoring regime is also a significant factor in light of the belief—endorsed by institutions such as the IMF—that "good governance" in an age of capital mobility requires more and better capital-account monitoring. Limited controls to monitor capital flows were imposed in mid-1997, but these were removed a few months later in an effort to boost investor confidence. This is reportedly in line with the preferences of Thailand's most important foreign portfolio investors, the Taiwanese, who contribute 25 to 30 percent of total trading volume on the Stock Exchange of Thailand. According to the press, "Taiwanese investors have an affinity for the Thai market mainly because Thai regulations allow easy repatriation of funds unlike Hong Kong where money flows are monitored and recorded."[42]

Globalists, Localists, and Others: Shifting Ground

Rather than simply interpreting Thailand's crisis as an example of a common phenomenon—mania followed by panic, magnified many times by the internationalization of financial markets—the public discussion among both globalists and their critics has tended to unearth Thai origins for the crisis. This emphasis naturalizes the domestic focus to reform efforts that has characterized Thailand's postcrisis policy. An emergent regionalist agenda may have been strengthened by the crisis, but this remains largely in the background.[43] Thailand ran a highly publicized and keenly fought campaign to have one of its cabinet ministers take over the top job at the World Trade Organization, but negotiations over the development of a "new international financial architecture" have received relatively little attention in Thailand, and Thai leaders have not pressed for a seat at the table in these negotiations.

A few Thai groups or individuals have revised their views on the benefits of globalization since the crisis. Some domestic businesses, for example, are less enthusiastic supporters of globalization, and the Ministry of the Interior adopted the principles of self-sufficiency and self-reliance in 1998. However, government policy remains for the most part committed to a proglobalization stance, albeit one that has been slightly modified in ways that are described later in this chapter. The debate between globalists and localists that began in the boom years has continued since the crisis, drawing in figures from official and private spheres. Both globalists and localists have interpreted the crisis in ways that support their earlier positions, and most have emphasized deficiencies in Thailand's domestic political economy. For example, a Thai writer at a liberal think tank prefaced her discussion of a conference on the crisis with the observation that the crisis was "a manifestation of deeper problems long suppressed in Thai society."[44] Localist or communitarian critics of globalization, while on the one hand seeing the crisis as an inevitable part of global capitalism, also frequently interpret it as "a symptom of the long-standing and deep-seated problem of unequal development." According to a Thai senator and social critic, the financial meltdown was highly visible, like a fire that erupts in a house, but "the heat and thick smoke obscure the fact that this old house of ours had already been eroded by many social problems and might as well fall apart under its own weight anyway."[45] Of course, globalizers and localists differ markedly in their assessment of what Thailand's "deep-seated problems" are.

For those on the globalist side, a range of good-governance desiderata now constitute an additional set of reforms to be undertaken in conjunction with liberalization. Not only is the aim to make Thailand more firmly "globalized," globalization is frequently referred to as the reason why both types of reform cannot be avoided. For example, in the months after the baht was floated, the Stock Exchange of Thailand announced that it aimed to become one of the most attractive capital markets in Asia. Its oversight body, the Securities and Exchange Commission, reaffirmed its commitment to capital market liberalization—for which it received a $300 million loan from the Asian Development Bank, part of Thailand's "rescue" package coordinated by the IMF. A senior official of the commission said that "because of globalisation, this country must continue opening its capital markets . . . we must compete with everyone all over the world for funds."[46] Charoen Pokphand, an executive of one of Thailand's largest (and most internationalized) companies, endorsed this attitude, maintaining that Thailand's primary goal must be to restore private capital flows to the country. He, like other advocates of continued openness after the crisis, also emphasized the need for adequate prudential regulation, better conditions in the civil service to eliminate corruption and attract talent, and other institutional reforms associated with the new catchphrase of good governance—and, in typical fashion, this agenda was presented as part of the demands of globalization: "it behooves the Asian countries to try to adjust the railway gauge of their respective economies to conform to the standard gauge of the globalised economies, so that the train of development may run on one harmonised track."[47]

The chairman of the Thailand Development Research Institute, a basically internationalist and liberal think tank, summarized this logic, stating that "nothing can obstruct the market . . . the market can wipe out whatever stands in its way . . . the globalisation impact has come suddenly to Thailand and has wreaked havoc." The appropriate response, however, is far from laissez-faire: "international rules are coming in to replace old rules that were not designed for globalisation . . . the government will have to change from being a patron to supervisor of regulations and to act as an inspector/auditor. It must create laws and regulations which are impartial so that the market can work to its fullest capacity."[48]

The logic of globalization presented by the other side of the debate takes market forces no less seriously but interprets them much more negatively. The social actors occupying different positions on the broad "localist" platform have been described by Pasuk Phongpaichit as combining elements of traditional left-wing politics concerned with equity and poverty, Buddhist thought on ethics and economics, and pro-agrarian, village-based ideas of community organization. Their concerns gained a new level of prominence and legitimacy in 1997 when the King's annual birthday speech took up the theme of self-sufficiency. His speech linked the crisis, the principle of self-sufficiency, and the idea of going back to a simpler economy rather than pursuing "tiger" status. It was widely reported, quoted, and officially adopted as policy by parts of the government.[49]

Other new variants and personalities have joined what was already a loose and diverse set of antiglobalist positions. Some of Thailand's established bankers—actors with considerable political and economic weight—are less-than-enthusiastic supporters of the globalist agenda as interpreted by technocrats. Thailand's largest and most internationalized bank, the Bangkok Bank, carried the slogan "A Self Sufficient Economy"—a reference to the King's speech—on the cover of its 1998 annual report. Senior executives from the Bangkok Bank as well as other Thai banks have voiced support for what was identified in the press as a Japanese idea to control short-term capital flows.[50] Taken together, the antiglobalist position cuts across left-right political cleavages: "self-sufficiency is a polysemic text that has been embraced across the political spectrum."[51] At least in some versions, however, the debate over globalization is portrayed as a stark contest between "on the one side, the markets. On the other, the poor . . . this is the key axis of the age of globalisation."[52]

The antiglobalist position has also, in some quarters, developed a new intensity, using terms such as "slave society," "white power," and "IMF invasion" to describe the consequences of globalization and its attendant crisis. Globalization and the crisis have also been depicted as manifestations of a distinctly Western capitalism that now has the destruction of Asian variants in its sights. Particularly in the works of Japanophile economist and prolific popularizer of economic and social ideas Suvinai Pornavalai, Japanese investment, culture, and spiritual values are depicted as offering a desirable alternative development path to that of Western-style capitalism and materialism.[53]

Thailand's earlier experience with foreign powers and foreign commercial interests has also surfaced in debates over the crisis. Globalizers are said to have "drawn a comparison with the colonial crisis a century ago. After opening up to trade with the West, Siam was threatened with colonial takeover. The rulers responded by becoming modern and civilised as quickly as possible. Similarly today, if foreigners say Thailand is backward/corrupt/lax in the way it runs its economy and government, then the solution must be to reform."[54] A former deputy prime minister stated at a seminar that "there is little difference between the 19th-century European traders who demanded Siam open up its markets, and the World Trade Organisation's current demands for liberalisation." (The newspaper report of the meeting carried the title "Lessons from History: Globalisation Revisited.") If Thai history is interpreted as a series of clever internal adjustments that secured the country's independence, the corollary for the present is, as argued

by the globalist camp, to adopt appropriate "good governance" reforms. However, the real parallel with the past may be somewhat different. Thai historian
Thongchai Winitchakul has argued that the parallel

> lies in the elite's tendency to chase after rainbows. In the late 19th century, the
> Siamese elite felt threatened not just by gunboats but by the cultural aggression of
> western Europe which made them feel inferior. Siamese aristocrats wanted to be *sivi-
> lai*—a term adapted from "civilised," expressing a yearning to be accepted as full
> members of the modern world. But being *sivilai* was not the same as being Western-
> ised. It was being what the Siamese elite thought being Westernised might be. In
> other words, an illusion. By definition, an illusion is unattainable. The quest is bound
> to be unsuccessful. The inevitable result is failure and disappointment. Today the
> idea of globalisation plays the same role as *sivilai* a century ago.[55]

The fragmented groups making such criticisms offer no real challenge to the
current policy direction taken by the Thai government. The "*ideas* of localism
have assumed a higher profile in the crisis," but "the *impact* of those ideas has
possibly diminished." Some precrisis concessions to localist agenda were reversed by the onset of the crisis and IMF conditionalities. The ruling Democrat
Party, "although officially adopting the King's self-reliance policy, stands clearly
for urban liberal progressivism."[56]

An internationalist, liberal, and good-governance agenda may be dominant,
but, as suggested here, Thai practice has qualified this agenda. These reforms
also rest on narrow political foundations. If, as a critic of globalization puts it,
the push for change is coming from "a band of so-called 'Wall Street gangsters'
who are foisting reforms in governance and transparency around the world,"[57]
the prospects for Thailand persisting with such reforms are highly contingent.
Thai entrepreneurs are being squeezed by the crisis, and the Democrat Party's
adoption of the IMF program meant that "the government grew increasingly re-
mote from the business community, in a way which was absolutely unique in
Thai political history since the late 1950s." Eventually, local capital will regroup
and press its case politically.[58] Local business has pressed, in some cases successfully, for greater government responsiveness to its concerns. This means de-
viating from the original reform agenda—or seeing it rest on the limited support
base of Bangkok professionals, foreign investors, and international technocrats.
This coalition owed much of its current degree of influence to the circumstances
of economic crisis. Its reforms will not be sustainable unless it can gain the support, or at least acquiescence, of a broader section of Thai society. This in turn
will depend on whether the reform program is consistent with rewards that have
domestic political salience. To date, Thailand's economic recovery has been
modest (the economy grew by 4 percent in 1999), private investment has yet to
be restored, and the stock exchange index lost 37 percent in the first six months
of 2000.

CONCLUSION

Globalization has become a powerful symbol in Thailand, representing the nation's reduced sphere of choice in the face of external forces. For those on the globalist side of politics, this is all to the good or, in any case, not something that can be resisted without incurring even higher costs. All sides would identify with the idea (if not the language) that "in this globalised age we are operating within the context of a hegemonic power structure dominated by very powerful MNCs and by the neo-liberal creed of free markets."[59] In contrast to the predictions of some academic theorists of globalization, however, the reforms associated with globalization in Thai public debates do not spell retreat or a diminished regulatory role for the state but a strengthening of its reach, particularly in the provision of the legal and institutional infrastructure required for markets to operate efficiently and with some stability. As publicly interpreted by both Thai technocrats and international agencies such as the World Bank, the state functions that globalization makes necessary also include the provision of "social safety nets" to protect the human casualties that may arise as the by-product of adjustment to economic forces. The good-governance and social agendas mark a significant addition to, rather than retreat from, the more uniformly deregulatory policies perceived, before the crisis, to be requisites in an age of global markets.

This assessment may capture something of the flavor of Thai discourses on globalization, but it leaves open a significant question: In what sense did globalization impel either the earlier neoliberal or later modified-neoliberal policies? As summarized at the start of this chapter, it is theoretically possible that globalization produces constraints on policy in two ways. The first is through the incentives created by "market forces" in an era of economic openness. The second is through the more direct agency of political actors in pursuit of their interests. This concluding section examines both possibilities in light of Thai experience over the last decade.

Regarding the structural constraints imposed by market forces in the context of globalization, the Thai case supports the view that these constraints bear little relation to much government policy. The liberalizing financial reforms undertaken before the crisis were "rewarded" by a massive inflow of capital, which then reversed direction. Thai policymakers could justifiably be confused by the signals emanating from global financial markets. It is revealing in this respect that sharp gains in many regional stock markets in 1999 raised the disturbing prospect that recovery would occur without reform.[60] During a crisis, market forces are possibly even less determinate. The question of how to restore market confidence does not have any obvious or consistent set of answers. Governments that take their cues directly from financial markets in their pursuit of confidence risk doing more harm than good.[61]

It is also relevant that although Thailand's ill-fated financial policy in the 1990s was clearly made in anticipation of market rewards, it was in no sense impelled by a structural need to change policy in the face of pressures emanating from globalized financial markets. Few scholarly studies have attempted to establish a causal relationship between globalization and the policy changes in Thailand during the boom years of the 1980s and 1990s. One of those to do so argues that central bank independence (operationalized as influence to maintain domestic price stability) can be related to a country's need to attract investment under conditions of capital mobility.[62] However, the fact that the central bank's influence was consolidated in a decade when Thailand was awash with foreign capital directly contradicts that author's main hypothesis. Somewhat ironically, the study ignores the most obvious constraint on policy imposed by capital mobility, namely, the costs it imposes on independent monetary policy. These costs are quite evident in the Thai case but do not bring with them any guarantee that policy will adjust appropriately.

This leads us to consider the second transmission mechanism through which globalization may affect policy: the agency of purposive economic and political actors. Thailand's precrisis financial reforms were brought about and consolidated by actors in both the government and the private sector. Their preferences were clearly influenced by opportunities presented by the internationalization of finance and the interests that they then developed in what proved to be rather perverse financial and monetary policy. However, their ability to translate preferences into policy was not based on any newfound influence related to the possibility of withholding investment. Neither do external political or market players have much of a role in Thailand's precrisis reforms. Agencies such as the World Bank did support Thailand's program of financial liberalization, but the technocrats who led the reform effort were largely self-motivated. To be sure, liberalizers in this period often stated that their policies were impelled by Thailand's need to compete in a globalized world economy, but structural pressure in the form of declining investment or capital outflows was completely absent. Foreign players are far more significant in Thailand's recent reforms. Not only have international agencies taken lead roles, but there is evidence that U.S. politicians and officials in particular have been the main force behind the conditionalities attached to IMF funds. Influence may extend to American financial interests, an instance of what Wade and Veneroso have termed the "Wall Street-Treasury-IMF Complex" at work.[63] Jeffrey Garten, undersecretary of commerce in President Bill Clinton's first term, gave perhaps unwitting support for this view when he argued that while Asian countries were going through "a deep and dark tunnel . . . on the other end there is going to be a significantly different Asia in which American firms have achieved much deeper market penetration, much greater access."[64]

This kind of involvement points to the political nature of the "demands of globalization." It also suggests that there may be some contradiction between the requirements of stable integration into the world economy and the actual preferences of powerful actors. How useful is it to analyze the preferences and influence of such players through the lens of globalization? Such a perspective reminds us that there is dynamic interplay between domestic and foreign politics and national and external forces. Small players generally make more concessions than do powerful ones, but only to the extent that the costs of doing so do not outweigh the benefits. Theories of globalization, however, are unlikely to shed much light on the domestic political and institutional factors that condition responses to openness. Unlike the British and French gunboats of the nineteenth century, the IMF can only threaten withdrawal. This is a crucial difference for Thai politicians making an assessment of the costs and benefits of complying with outside demands. Another factor that will enter their cost–benefit calculations is that, unlike the Bangkok monarchs of the nineteenth century, they operate in a democratic political system in which social forces are mobilized and cognizant of national identity in ways that were inconceivable in the past.

NOTES

1. See, for example, Robert Wade, "Globalization and Its Limits: Reports of the Death of the National Economy are Greatly Exaggerated," in Suzanne Berger and Ronald Dore, eds., *National Diversity and Global Capitalism* (Ithaca, N.Y.: Cornell University Press, 1996), 60–88.

2. The different schools of thought on globalization are identified by David Held, Anthony McGrew, David Goldblatt, and Jonathan Perraton, *Global Transformations: Politics, Economics, and Culture* (Stanford, Calif.: Stanford University Press, 1999), 3–10.

3. Michael Mann, "Has Globalization Ended the Rise and Rise of the Nation-State?," *Review of International Political Economy* 4, no. 3 (1997): 472–96.

4. Held et al., *Global Transformations*, 3–10.

5. The incompatibility of simultaneously maintaining a fixed exchange rate and monetary policy autonomy under conditions of capital mobility is a virtual truism, the force of which was well understood from the early nineteenth century, if not before. Often referred to as the Mundell–Fleming thesis, the model's simplicity is tempered by introducing risk factors.

6. David Andrews, "Capital Mobility and State Autonomy: Toward a Structural Theory of International Monetary Relations," *International Studies Quarterly* 38, no. 2 (1994): 193–218.

7. The case for the continued relevance of the state and national political choices has been argued, for example, by Linda Weiss, *The Myth of the Powerless State: Governing the Economy in a Global Era* (Cambridge: Polity Press, 1998); Ethan Kapstein, *Governing the Global Economy: International Finance and the State* (Cambridge, Mass.: Harvard University Press, 1994); Dani Rodrik, "Why Do More Open Economies Have Bigger Governments?," *Journal of Political Economy* 106, no. 5 (October 1998): 997–1032; and David Vogel, *Trading Up: Consumer and Environmental Regulation in a Global Economy* (Cambridge, Mass.: Harvard University Press, 1995). Those asserting the demise, retreat,

or dysfunctionality of the state include Philip Cerny, "Globalization and the Changing Logic of Collective Action," *International Organization* 49, no. 4 (1995): 595–625, and Susan Strange, *The Retreat of the State* (Cambridge: Cambridge University Press, 1996).

8. Such arguments are implicit in most studies of globalization. On the underlying theory, see Helen Milner, "Trading Places: Industries for Free Trade," *World Politics* 40, no. 3 (1988): 350–76, and Jeffrey Frieden, "Invested Interests: The Politics of National Economic Policies in a World of Global Finance," *International Organization* 45, no. 4 (1991): 425–51. Ideas about the influence of mobile investors generally draw on the work of Albert Hirschman, *Exit, Voice, and Loyalty* (Cambridge, Mass.: Harvard University Press, 1970), and Charles Lindblom, *Politics and Markets: The World's Political-Economic Systems* (New York: Basic Books, 1977).

9. Cited in Craig Reynolds, "Globalization and Cultural Nationalism in Modern Thailand," in Joel Kahn, ed., *Southeast Asian Identities: Culture and the Politics of Representation in Indonesia, Malaysia, Singapore, and Thailand* (Singapore: Institute of Southeast Asian Studies, 1998), 128. See also Wang Wen-liang, "An Observation of Thailand's Opening to the Outside World in the Age of Globalization from a Historical Perspective," in *Globalization: Impact on and Coping Strategies in Thai Society* (Proceedings of the 6th International Conference on Thai Studies, Chang Mai, October 1996), 301–8.

10. The metaphor is from Joseph Stiglitz, "The Role of International Financial Institutions in the Current Global Economy" (address to the Chicago Council on Foreign Relations, Chicago, February 1998), available at <http://www.worldbank.org/html/extdr/jssp022798.htm>.

11. Reynolds, "Globalization and Cultural Nationalism in Modern Thailand," 121–22. Intra-Asian regional trade was also active at this time, loosely organized around a Sinocentric tributary system; see Takeshi Hamashita, "The Intra-Regional System in East Asia in Modern Times," in Peter Katzenstein and Takashi Shiraishi, eds., *Network Power: Japan and Asia* (Ithaca, N.Y.: Cornell University Press, 1997), 113–35. Thailand was known as Siam until 1932 and for a brief period after World War II.

12. See, in particular, Lysa Hong, *Thailand in the Nineteenth Century: Evolution of the Economy and Society* (Singapore: Institute of Southeast Asian Studies, 1984).

13. On state development, see Carl Trocki, "Political Structures in the Nineteenth and Early Twentieth Centuries," in Nicholas Tarling, ed., *The Cambridge History of Southeast Asia*, vol. 2 (Cambridge: Cambridge University Press, 1992), 79–130. On the creation (but only partial rationalization) of the Ministry of Finance, see Ian Brown, *The Creation of the Modern Ministry of Finance in Siam, 1885–1992* (London: Macmillan, 1992). On the use of foreign advisers, see William Siffin, *The Thai Bureaucracy: Institutional Change and Development* (Honolulu: East-West Center Press, 1966), 95–99.

14. Richard Stubbs, "War and Economic Development: Export-Oriented Industrialization in East and Southeast Asia," *Comparative Politics* 31, no. 3 (April 1999): 337–55.

15. Reynolds, "Globalization and Cultural Nationalism in Modern Thailand," 125–26; Pasuk Phongpaichit and Chris Baker, *Thailand's Boom!* (St. Leonards, New South Wales: Allen and Unwin, 1996), 52.

16. On new business interests and their support for financial liberalization and internationalization, see Pasuk Phongpaichit and Chris Baker, "The Political Economy of the Thai Crisis," *Journal of the Asia Pacific Economy* 4, no. 1 (1999): 193–208.

17. Reynolds, "Globalization and Cultural Nationalism in Modern Thailand," 119, 132.

18. Pasuk and Baker, "The Political Economy of the Thai Crisis."

19. Robert Muscat, "Thailand," in Stephan Haggard and Chung H. Lee, eds., *Financial Systems and Economic Policy in Developing Countries* (Ithaca, N.Y.: Cornell University Press, 1995), 113–39.

20. Bhanupong Nidhiprabha, "Monetary Policy," in Peter Warr, ed., *The Thai Economy in Transition* (Cambridge, Mass.: Cambridge University Press, 1993), 172–98.

21. Peter Warr and Bhanupong Nidhiprabha, *Thailand's Macroeconomic Miracle: Stable Adjustment and Sustained Growth* (Washington, D.C.: World Bank and Oxford University Press, 1996), 169–71.

22. See Danny Unger, *Building Social Capital in Thailand: Fibers, Finance, and Infrastructure* (Melbourne: Cambridge University Press, 1998), 84, and Kevin Hewison, *Bankers and Bureaucrats: Capital and the Role of the State in Thailand* (New Haven, Conn.: Yale University, Department of Southeast Asia Studies, Yale Center for International and Area Studies, 1989), 197.

23. Richard Doner and Danny Unger, "The Politics of Finance in Thai Economic Development," in Stephan Haggard, Chung H. Lee, and Sylvia Maxfield, eds., *The Politics of Finance in Developing Countries* (Ithaca, N.Y.: Cornell University Press, 1993), 93–122.

24. On financial reform, see Unger, *Building Social Capital in Thailand*, 83–108.

25. Stock market and currency devaluations are from Morris Goldstein, *The Asian Crisis: Causes, Cures, and Systemic Implications* (Washington, D.C.: Institute for International Economics, 1998), 2–3. Costs of bank recapitalizations and bailouts are from *Business Times* (Singapore), August 12, 1999.

26. A comprehensive review of explanations for the Asian financial crisis is given by Stephen Radelet and Jeffrey Sachs, "The East Asian Financial Crisis: Diagnosis, Remedies, Prospects," *Brookings Papers on Economic Activity*, no. 1 (1998), 1–90. They find little support for the idea that domestic governance factors were pivotal. The case for seeing the crisis in Thailand, in origin as well as manifestation, as a financial one is made by Laurids Lauridsen, "Thailand: Causes, Conduct, Consequences," in K. S. Jomo, ed., *Tigers in Trouble* (London: Zed Books, 1998), 137–61.

27. Walden Bello, "East Asia: On the Eve of the Great Transformation?," *Review of International Political Economy* 5, no. 3 (1998): 424–44.

28. For a discussion on sterilization and other policy responses, see William Dean, "Recent Capital Flows to Asia Pacific Countries: Trade-Offs and Dilemmas," *Journal of the Asia Pacific Economy* 1, no. 3 (1996): 287–317.

29. William Overholt, *Asia's Bubble Crisis: No Instant Cure* (Hong Kong: Nomura International, 1999), 15.

30. Montes, *The Currency Crisis in Southeast Asia* (Singapore: Institute of Southeast Asian Studies, 1983), 12–13.

31. Ponciano Intal et al., "The Philippines," in Ross McLeod and Ross Garnaut, eds., *East Asia in Crisis: From Being a Miracle to Needing One?* (London: Routledge, 1998), 145–61.

32. Chris Baker, "Politics of Crisis: Failure, Reform, and Division" (paper presented to the National Thai Studies Centre and APSEM 1999 Thai Update Conference, Australian National University, Canberra, April 1999), 20.

33. Dani Rodrik, "Governing the Global Economy: Does One Architectural Style Fit All?" (paper prepared for the Brookings Institution Trade Policy Forum Conference on Governing in a Global Economy, April 1999), 6.

34. On the adoption of IMF reforms, see Stephan Haggard and Andrew MacIntyre, "The Political Economy of the Asian Economic Crisis," *Review of International Political Economy* 5, no. 3 (1998): 381–92. On the concurrent political changes and alliances, see Baker, "Politics of Crisis."

35. Rodrik, "Governing the Global Economy," 4.

36. *Australian Financial Review* (Sydney), August 25, 1999.

37. *The Nation* (Bangkok), June 9, 1999, B12.

38. Bruce Cheesman, *Australian Financial Review,* March 13–14, 1999, 6. On the arrival of New York lawyers, see *Australian Financial Review,* April 24, 1999.

39. *Business Times,* December 7, 1998.

40. Bank of Thailand, "Balance of Payments," *Monthly Statistical Data,* available at <www.bot.or.th> (March 1, 2000); *Thailand: Economic Performance in 1998 and Outlook for 1999* (Bangkok: Bank of Thailand, n.d.), 45, 52.

41. *Business Times,* November 3, 1998.

42. *Business Times,* August 12, 1999.

43. The need for greater regional cooperation has been raised by both globalists and localists. For example, a former finance minister and Bangkok Bank director argued that regionalism will become more important in a globalized world (quoted in *The Nation,* February 6, 1998). A former senior economic bureaucrat has said that Asian authorities should join forces to establish regional regulatory responses to investments by hedge funds; see *The Nation,* October 27, 1997.

44. Ryratana Suwanraks, "Summary of Discussion and Recommendations: The 1998 TDRI Year-End Conference, from Crisis to Sustainable Development," *TDRI Quarterly Review* 14, no. 1 (March 1999): 10–20.

45. Quoted in *Thai Development Newsletter,* no. 33 (July–December 1997): 29.

46. *The Nation,* November 19, 1997.

47. *The Nation,* June 5, 1998.

48. *The Nation,* February 6, 1998.

49. On the King's speech, see Pasuk Phongpaichit, "Developing Social Alternatives: Walking Backwards into a Klong" (paper presented to the National Thai Studies Centre and APSEM 1999 Thai Update Conference, Australian National University, Canberra, April 1999), 1–2. This paragraph draws on the paper's discussion of localist discourses in the wake of the crisis.

50. *The Nation,* October 2, 1998.

51. Craig Reynolds, "East Asian Identities in Southeast Asian Contexts: Self Cultivation and Homo Excellens" (unpublished paper, Asian History Centre, Australian National University, Canberra, 1999), 3.

52. Chang Noi, *The Nation,* June 4, 1998.

53. On Suvinai, see Reynolds, "East Asian Identities." On the construction of reforms as the triumph of Western over Asian capitalism, see Pasuk Phongpaichit and Chris Baker, *The Nation,* April 20, 1998. On the use of the term "slave society" by prominent social critic Saneh Chamarik, see Pasuk, "Developing Social Alternatives," 12. Saneh is also one of many Thais to criticize globalization and the official response to the crisis as having subjected Thailand to Western influence; see *The Nation,* November 19, 1998. I thank Chris Baker for the observation that the term "white power" has begun to feature in discussions of the crisis and globalization in the Thai-language press.

54. *The Nation,* April 20, 1998.

55. *The Nation,* December 26, 1997.

56. Pasuk, "Developing Social Alternatives," 14.

57. Chang Noi, *The Nation,* October 5, 1998.

58. Baker, "Politics of Crisis," 20, 32.

59. Pasuk Phongpaichit, "The Economic Crisis and the Way Ahead," *Thai Development Newsletter,* no. 35 (July–December 1998): 35–39.

60. Comments from market players such as "we all wanted a recovery but not before they had solved their deeper problems" were sometimes reported without a hint of irony (e.g., *Asian Wall Street Journal,* April 29, 1999, 1).

61. See Rodrik, "Governing the Global Economy," 10–14, and Stiglitz, "The Role of International Financial Institutions," 6–7.

62. Sylvia Maxfield, *Gatekeepers of Growth: The International Political Economy of Central Banking in Developing Countries* (Princeton, N.J.: Princeton University Press, 1997).

63. Robert Wade and Frank Veneroso, "The Asian Crisis: The High Debt Model vs. the Wall Street-Treasury-IMF Complex," Russell Sage Foundation, available at <http://epn.org/sage/imf24.html> (March 1998). On U.S. pressure and the IMF-mandated reforms, see Martin Feldstein, "Refocusing the IMF," *Foreign Affairs* 77, no. 2 (1998): 20–33, esp. 26, and Bello, "East Asia," 435–44.

64. Quoted in Bello, "East Asia," 435–36.

9

Indonesia and Globalization

Ann Marie Murphy

Whether we like it or not, whether we are prepared for it or not, we will be drawn into that implacable arena of global competition. We must prepare for the inevitable.

—Former president Suharto[1]

The deepening of Indonesia's incorporation into the world economy means that the state can no longer be the ever reliable benevolent patron to favorite cronies.

—Ariel Heryanto, sociologist[2]

GLOBALIZATION: AN INESCAPABLE FORCE

Indonesia has benefited tremendously and suffered severely from globalization. The New Order policy of integrating Indonesia into the global economy and progressively liberalizing its domestic market produced spectacular economic growth of almost 7 percent per annum for over thirty years, quadrupling the average annual income in one generation. However, globalization struck back during the Asian financial crisis (AFC), when the rupiah nose-dived and the economy contracted by almost 14 percent, the sharpest decline of any economy since the Great Depression. The economic crisis triggered a political one, toppling President Suharto after thirty-two years in power and elevating his longtime protégé, Vice President B. J. Habibie, to the nation's highest office. Habibie's refusal to prosecute political allies accused of corruption led the International Monetary Fund (IMF) and the World Bank to stop aid disbursements and the Indonesian public to demand his removal. The recent election of prominent reformers

Abdurrahman Wahid and Megawati Sukarnoputri opens the door to a new era of political reform in Indonesia and a new policy toward globalization. This chapter explores Indonesia's often testy reaction to globalization. In the next section, Indonesian perceptions of globalization are discussed. In Indonesia, globalization is viewed largely as an economic phenomenon, a seemingly inexorable process from which it cannot escape. Globalization is therefore perceived as an objective condition of international life that structures the policy choices facing Indonesian state and societal actors.

Indonesians may view globalization as an inescapable force, but they differ over whether it is a positive or a negative one. Globalization enthusiasts argue that opening and deregulating Indonesia's economy will spur efficiency, promote economic growth, and raise living standards. Critics of globalization dispute this and argue that the costs associated with globalization—the loss of state sovereignty and an economy dominated by foreigners and Indonesians of Chinese descent—are too high for Indonesia. Given these differences, it is argued that the best way to understand Indonesian perceptions of globalization is to analyze Indonesian responses to global pressure on the three key values promoted during the current era of globalization: economic liberalism, democracy, and human rights. The chapter then reviews the responses of Indonesian state and civic leaders to global pressures for economic liberalization, democracy, and human rights during the Suharto, Habibie, and Wahid administrations.

The chapter concludes that Indonesia's policy response to economic globalization has been largely defensive.[3] This should not be surprising. The essence of liberal capitalism is increased competition, and, as the data from table 1.2 in chapter 1 make clear, Indonesia is not well positioned to meet the challenges of the global marketplace. Indonesia achieved its strong economic growth largely by following the liberal prescriptions of global economic institutions, such as the IMF and World Bank. However, these policies tended to be adopted in times of economic crisis when Indonesia was dependent on external aid. Indeed, the strongest policy link between the Suharto, Habibie, and Wahid administrations is a reluctant acceptance of the need to bow to global pressures by signing IMF agreements.

If the Suharto, Habibie, and Wahid administrations share a common perspective toward economic globalization, they differ greatly in their responses to global pressures for democracy and human rights. Suharto strongly rebelled against such pressures, condemning them as unwarranted interference in Indonesia's domestic affairs. Habibie enacted significant reforms in the areas of democracy and human rights in an attempt to distance himself from Suharto and legitimize his regime domestically and internationally. However, Habibie's unwillingness to prosecute those accused of corruption in the Baligate scandal led the IMF and World Bank to suspend aid disbursements to Indonesia, and his inability to halt the Indonesian military's rampage in East Timor led the United Nations and most of the international community to condemn Indonesia. By the end of Habibie's presidency, his attempts to resist globalization in the economic and human rights areas had led to Indonesia's estrangement from key global actors and institutions.

In late October 1999, Abdurrahman Wahid was elected Indonesia's fourth president. A longtime champion of democracy and human rights, President Wahid has made a commitment to clean government—the rallying cry of his administration—and signed a new letter of intent with the IMF. It now appears that Indonesia is in congruence with the values of liberal capitalism, democracy, and human rights embodied in globalization. However, domestic support for democracy and human rights is much stronger than support for economic liberalism. Most Indonesians find liberal economics unappealing and have blamed globalization for the country's economic suffering. To date, the need to abide by the IMF agreements has limited Indonesian ability to craft its economic policy. In the future, however, anticapitalist sentiment, combined with the upsurge in Indonesian nationalism triggered by the international condemnation of Indonesian actions in East Timor, may lead to greater Indonesian resistance to globalization.

GLOBALIZATION IN THE INDONESIAN CONTEXT

Threat or Promise?

Globalization may be the defining feature of the 1990s, but it remains a much-contested subject. This is particularly true in Indonesia, where globalization raises issues, such as the proper role of the state in the economy and the potential loss of sovereignty, that arouse deeply held feelings among many Indonesians.

As Prawiro notes, globalization in Indonesia is not a well-defined phenomenon.[4] Much of the domestic literature on globalization attempts to clarify what it means and what the implications are for Indonesia's state and society. For the most part, however, Indonesians tend to view globalization mainly as "an economic phenomenon."[5] Globalization is conceived as the increasingly deep integration of national economies through the spread of market capitalism. Indonesians perceive globalization largely as an inevitable process from which Indonesia cannot escape. As a result, Indonesia has no alternative but to attempt to cope with or "survive" globalization.[6] Globalization, therefore, is viewed largely as an objective condition of international life that structures the policy choices facing Indonesian state and societal actors.

As to whether globalization benefits or hurts Indonesians, proponents, mostly Western-trained economists, argue that deregulating and opening Indonesia's economy will spur efficiency, promote economic growth, and raise living standards. Elite opponents of globalization warn, however, that

> globalization is a commercially driven process that tramples over national sovereignty and cultural norms . . . if Indonesia opens the economy to free trade and

investment, the whole country will be watching American videos on Japanese tele-vision while wearing Italian shoes as they eat food imported from Australia.[7]

Nonelite critics of globalization express their opposition differently. According to Keliat, the majority of Indonesians on the street have always viewed globaliza-tion with skepticism. This skepticism manifests itself not in public debate but in the fact that the term "*gombal*ization" has long been used in place of "globaliza-tion." *Gombal* refers to a piece of old cloth that is no longer used except to dust shoes or clean cooking utensils. The wide usage of this term can be seen as an act of silent protest against globalization by the masses that could trigger a future po-litical backlash against it.

Between the proponents and the critics is a large group that neither embraces nor resists globalization but reluctantly attempts to face its challenges. The main challenge is global economic competition. As the data in table 1.2 of chapter 1 make clear, Indonesia is the least competitive of the Asian countries surveyed. In-donesians across the political spectrum realize that the gains from trade flow dis-proportionately to countries producing high-technology goods. Indonesia, how-ever, is connected to the global economy largely as a producer of agricultural commodities and low-technology manufacturers, placing it at the bottom of the international economic hierarchy.

Indonesians are keenly aware that globalization produces winners and losers not only between nations but also within them. Many Indonesians, including De-fense Minister Juwono Sudarsono, fear that globalization will lead to greater in-equality between nations. Juwono contends that the United States, Japan, and Germany will dominate an increasingly globalized economy because of their ad-vantages in science and technology as well as their access to capital.[8] Juwono's concern regarding globalization's effects on Indonesia's international standing is seconded by former Indonesian foreign minister Ali Alatas, who contends that "the negative aspects of globalization" include the "marginalization of develop-ing countries from economic decision-making."[9]

Indonesian fears that globalization will produce greater inequality between na-tions is reinforced by fears that globalization will lead to a similar inequality within the country. Within Indonesia, those best equipped to compete in an open, liberalized economy are the ethnic Chinese. Chinese Indonesians account for ap-proximately 3 percent of Indonesia's population but are believed to control ap-proximately 70 percent of its wealth. Many in Indonesia fear that increased com-petition at home would lead to an even greater concentration of wealth and power, which in turn would lead to social unrest.

Globalization as Economic Policy

Partly as a result of divergent opinions over whether globalization is a positive force to be embraced or a pernicious one to be resisted, Indonesia lacks a coherent globalization policy. As Rinakit and Soesastro observe, globalization is "pretty much a matter of rhetoric."[10] Unlike South Korea's well-defined *segyehwa* policy, the Indonesian government "has not gone beyond rhetoric in defining its responses to the challenge of globalization."[11] Instead, Indonesia's policy response to globalization is viewed as an extension of its economic reform and liberalization policies.

Many Indonesians would like to respond to the challenge of globalization by changing the country's comparative advantage and restructuring its domestic economy. Economic nationalists argue for state intervention in the economy to protect strategic industries from foreign domination and promote industrialization so that it can leapfrog up the technology ladder. Much of the literature on globalization in Indonesia identifies a long list of issues that Indonesia must address in order to enhance its competitiveness. That literature also includes a long list of complaints directed at the government for failing to take such steps. Furthermore, many Indonesians reject further opening and liberalization of the economy without some plan to redress the growing inequality of wealth within the country. Economic populists demand greater government involvement in the economy on behalf of small businesses and rural workers so that the poor underclass has a better chance of meeting Chinese competition.

However, the dilemma for many Indonesians is that at the same time that state action is viewed as necessary for Indonesia to meet the challenges of globalization, the process of globalization erodes the power of the state. Juwono Sudarsono claims that in this era of globalization, "market authority has challenged state power for the high ground to determine public policy."[12] Even a staunch proponent of globalization concedes that the conflicting demands of the global marketplace and domestic constituents lead the Indonesia government to regard globalization with a fair degree of ambivalence. Prawiro describes this dilemma by noting that the duty of a government is to the nation; however, globalization requires that nations conform to global conventions that may conflict with their domestic interests. These issues are "particularly sensitive" in Indonesia since many worry that "opening the economy too widely could lead to foreign domination."[13]

Although globalization tends to be viewed primarily in economic terms, the loss of sovereignty believed to occur as a result of globalization raises concerns in the security field as well. Globalization is viewed as a challenge to national integration, a major concern given Indonesia's extremely heterogeneous population. Indonesia's current defense minister outlines the globalization challenge in this way:

Indonesians are concerned that intense regionalization and globalization can inflame fragmentation within regions as well as within nation-states: ethnic animosity, racial antagonism, religious exclusiveness, narrow provincialism. These tensions, especially if linked to the control and distribution over economic resources and strategic minerals, can lead to the rekindling of mutual suspicion, outbreaks of violence and mindless killings of innocent people in civil war. That is why Indonesians remain convinced that whatever the arguments in favor of intense regionalization and of globalization, government intervention and the regularity structures of the nation-state remain indispensable authority template to accommodate and resolve differing priorities among contending ethnic, religious, and provincial groups.[14]

The fear that globalization makes it easier for separatist movements to tap into global networks for support of their cause has been heightened by the decision of East Timor to secede from Indonesia and demands by Aceh and Irian Jaya for referenda in which they would be given a similar option.

No Consensus

As the previous discussion makes clear, there is no single Indonesian perspective of globalization. As a result, it is difficult to place Indonesia easily into one of the contending schools of thought outlined in chapter 1. Like the hyperglobalists, Indonesians tend to view capitalism and technology as the driving forces of globalization and the erosion of sovereignty as one of its consequences. However, Indonesians certainly do not agree with the hyperglobalist view that globalization portends the end of the nation-state. Instead, they believe that globalization means enhanced competition between states.

However, Indonesians also subscribe to a number of the skeptic's views. Although Indonesians tend to see the expansion of capitalism as a driving force of globalization, many also see the visible hand of the United States, the leading proponent of globalization, behind this expansion. Moreover, Indonesia agrees with the skeptics' contention that globalization is a process that will lead to the increased marginalization of the South. Those Indonesians who view globalization as nothing but Westernization would agree with the skeptics that it could lead to a clash of civilizations, but it would be difficult to find an Indonesian who agrees with the skeptics that globalization is nothing but "globaloney."

Given the lack of consensus within Indonesia over the merits of globalization and the proper response to it, what is the best way to analyze Indonesian perceptions and policies toward globalization? I argue that it is to recognize that globalization is not simply a process of increasing global integration but is also a transmitter of values, ideology, and organizing principles. Globalization promotes the economic benefits of liberal capitalism, the political virtues of democracy, and the moral imperative of respect for human rights. All three of these values privilege the rights of individuals. If incorporated into government policy, they limit the power of state authorities to make decisions regarding the structure of their economy, the nature of their political regime, and their relationship to society. In Indonesia, some government leaders have rebelled against globalization precisely because they fear this potential loss of sovereign control.

SUHARTO'S NEW ORDER: DEFENSIVE POLICY RESPONSES TO GLOBALIZATION

Economic Nationalists and Populists versus Liberals

When Suharto came to power in 1966, Indonesia was politically unstable, diplomatically isolated, and an economic basket case. Suharto was determined to reverse course. As the name "New Order" implies, the new regime defined itself in contradistinction to the old: Economic autarchy would be replaced by integration into the global economy, political order would replace political instability, and left-wing allies would be replaced with more conservative ones. Lacking Sukarno's nationalist credentials, Suharto set out to legitimize his regime through economic development. Unschooled in economics, Suharto turned to a group of Western-trained economists dubbed the "technocrats" who served as his interlocutors with international donors. The technocrats favored liberal economic policies and became the leading proponents of globalization in Indonesia.

The technocrats dismantled many of the government regulations of the Sukarno era and replaced them with the market mechanism to stimulate trade and production. A strong commitment to orthodox monetary policies brought inflation down quickly. In desperate need of capital and technology, Indonesia lifted restrictions on foreign investment. The policies implemented by the technocrats and their close working relations with the IMF and the World Bank reassured investors. Grateful that Indonesia had not been lost to communism, Western governments created the Inter-Governmental Group on Indonesia (IGGI) to coordinate the large amounts of economic assistance that were critical in helping the Suharto government survive until the economy revived. The economic results were spectacular. By the late 1960s, the economy was growing, inflation had dropped substantially, and foreign investment had increased sharply. Since the early 1970s, economic output grew 7 percent annually, and the average Indonesian's annual income more than quadrupled.[15] Social indicators likewise showed remarkable improvement. The percentage of Indonesians living in poverty fell from 61 percent in the mid-1960s to approximately 10 percent in the early 1990s.[16] Infant morality dropped sharply while life expectancy and literacy increased sharply. This development gave the Suharto regime a high degree of performance legitimacy.

Despite Indonesia's economic success, capitalist ideology was never widely embraced in Indonesia. Most Indonesians tended to equate capitalism with exploitation as a result of Indonesia's experience under Dutch colonialism, when Indonesia provided 30 percent of Dutch gross national product (GNP) while the majority of Indonesians remained impoverished. This anticapitalist attitude is enshrined in Article 33 of Indonesia's Constitution, which declares that "branches of production important for the State and of dominating interest to the livelihood of the masses of the people have to be controlled by the State."[17] Even today, according to Sjharir, "there is virtually no political or economic literature that could be categorized as being in favor of capitalism—or even competition, for that matter."[18]

This antipathy toward capitalism meant that the technocrats often faced competition in policy circles from proponents of economic nationalism and economic populism who greatly outnumber advocates of free-market capitalism in Indonesia. Suharto, dependent on economic development to legitimize his rule, followed the technocrats' liberal economic policies in times of economic crisis when Indonesia was dependent on foreign aid. Once the technocrats had restored the Indonesian economy to economic growth, however, policy decisions tended to shift in favor of the economic nationalists and populists.

During the mid-1980s, a sharp drop in oil prices meant that Indonesia had lost its most important revenue base and could no longer afford the economic nationalist strategy of import substitution to promote industries such as steel, petrochemicals, cement, and automobiles. The balance of power shifted toward the technocrats, who proposed an export-led strategy emphasizing low-wage and low-technology industries such as textiles. This was accompanied by measures to liberalize trade, investment, industry, and the financial sector.

However, these liberal polices were vehemently opposed by a number of groups. Ginandjar Kartasamita, an economic nationalist who would become the economic coordinating minister under President Habibie, represents a wide spectrum of Indonesian opinion when he portrays globalization as a threat to Indonesia:

> there is rapid technological development as countries compete to outdo each other. Other countries are traveling with the speed of a car, but our technology is moving like a tri-shaw [*becak*]. . . . This situation will leave us far behind, and if it persists our nation will have little resilience in international affairs. . . . We will be vulnerable to political, economic, and cultural penetration by other countries. . . . If we allow it [to happen], our sovereignty will come under threat. Our rights as an independent nation able to decide what is best for ourselves will cease to exist because we will be dependent on what other people decide.[19]

Populist critics often portrayed economic liberalization as something imposed on Indonesia by the West. According to one such critique, "Economic liberalization became a precondition imposed by those who provided aid. Essentially, the aid thus obtained from the IMF, IGGI, and World Bank during the New Order period has been a subtle from of foreign capitalist intervention in the Indonesian economy."[20]

Opposition to the liberalization measures of the late 1980s was so strong that in his 1990 state-of-the-nation speech, Suharto felt compelled to respond to anti-capitalist critics that the deregulation policies would reduce the role of the state:

> The measures of deregulation and de-bureaucratization are designed to put the . . . state in its most appropriate place for development. They are certainly not measures to abolish the role of the state. It is definitely not a step towards liberalism.[21]

Economic Openness and Political Centralization

Policy debates of the late 1980s were difficult for the technocrats, but they were vindicated by the results. The Indonesian economy boomed, gross domestic product (GDP) grew an average of 8 percent a year between 1990 and 1996, exports grew at 12.7 percent over the same period, and investment growth averaged 16.4 percent. Foreign direct investment poured in, and the banking system was awash in liquidity. However, these figures masked problems that would manifest themselves during the AFC. The deregulation of the banking industry, without the institution of strong regulatory mechanisms, meant that many Indonesian companies went on a borrowing binge. In less then ten years, Indonesia's private banking and corporate sector would borrow $80 billion. Despite the export boom, imports grew at an even faster rate, and Indonesia's trade dependency ratio rose.[22]

The major political effects of globalization were a perception of widening income inequality and a greater ethnic imbalance of wealth. Ironically, confirmation of long-standing suspicions of the degree of income inequality was made possible by the growth of the Jakarta Stock Exchange (JSE). As more Indonesian companies went public, they were forced to disclose their financial statements, which allowed others to calculate the new worth of many of Indonesia's top businessmen. The fact that an estimated 80 percent of the companies listed on the JSE were owned by Chinese Indonesians only reinforced popular perceptions of economic domination by the Chinese and gave rise to more vocal demands for government action to redress it.

In the end, it was neither the economic nationalists nor the economic populists who posed the greatest challenges to the technocrats' liberal economic policies but, rather, Suharto's family and cronies. Suharto's children came of business age in the 1980s, just as the economy was being liberalized. They used their political connections to secure business licenses, access to state credit, tax breaks, and the right to run government monopolies. When the financial crisis hit, Suharto would be forced to choose between protecting his family or Indonesia's economic progress.

Indonesia's economic opening was not accompanied by a political one. Indonesia willingly enmeshed itself in the global economy during the Suharto years, but it fiercely resisted global pressure in the area of democracy and human rights. Indeed, the New Order regime often linked the two: Economic development required stability, which necessitated a tightly controlled political system and social mores that privileged the community over the individual. During his tenure, Suharto strengthened the state while emasculating most civic organizations. Relying on economic incentives to coopt regime supporters and military power to coerce regime opponents, Suharto created a patrimonial authoritarian regime that bore little resemblance to a democracy and had little respect for human rights.

During the Cold War, Western governments overlooked Indonesia's political repression. With its end, many Western countries pressured Indonesia to open up politically. This pressure was portrayed as a Western plot to undermine the country's economic and political development. According to Foreign Minister Ali Alatas, linking "extraneous issues such as the environment, labor laws, human rights" in trade and economic cooperation agreements was simply a "new and insidious" way by which Western countries were undermining the economic potential of developing countries.[23]

Not only did Indonesia reject external pressure as unwarranted intrusion into its domestic affairs, it also was one of the chief proponents of the "Asian values" movement, a collective effort by some Asian countries to resist globalization in the areas of democracy and human rights. Proponents of "Asian values" argued that the Western emphasis on civil and political rights focused too much on the individual while ignoring economic and community rights. Like its response to economic globalization, Indonesia's "Asian Values" policy was clearly defensive: Absent Western pressure, it is highly unlikely that Indonesia would have devoted the significant amount of time to the issue that it did.

If the Suharto administration resisted global pressure on democracy and human rights issues, many opposition leaders welcomed it. According to human rights activist T. Mulya Lubis, "The government's distinction between universal human rights and indigenous human rights is dangerous and false."[24] Similarly, Mochtar Pakpahan, an opposition labor leader, diametrically opposes the government's contention that economic development requires constraints on individual liberty: "Globalization will continue. If a country [is] without democracy, without the principle of justice and without human rights, I think the country will fail to face the globalization."[25]

By the mid-1990s, Indonesia's political structure was the antithesis of that demanded by the logic of globalization: An open, deregulated economy coexisted not with open, transparent, and accountable domestic institutions but with a closed, patrimonial system. The combination of an open economy and closed polity created enormous opportunity for graft. During the Suharto era, Indonesia consistently ranked among the world's most corrupt countries. Corruption raised the transaction costs of doing business in Indonesia and was one of the reasons that Indonesia ranked so poorly in the international competitiveness ratings cited in table 1.2 in chapter 1.

CRISIS AND RESPONSE: SUHARTO IS TOPPLED BY GLOBALIZATION

Suharto and the IMF

On July 2, 1997, Thailand abandoned its long-standing foreign currency peg, triggering a crisis throughout the region as speculators dumped Asian currencies. As in past economic crises, Suharto turned to the technocrats. The technocrats allowed the rupiah to float freely on August 14, earning widespread praise for not wasting the country's valuable foreign-exchange reserves in a futile effort to defend the currency. The technocrats then proposed a wide-ranging package of reforms. In contrast to previous crises when Suharto followed the technocrats' advice, he rejected the reform package. As the rupiah continued to slide in international markets, Indonesian firms, which collectively owed approximately $80 billion of corporate debt to foreign banks, frantically bought the dollars needed to repay that debt. This panic buying only pushed the rupiah lower. At the end of October 1997, Indonesia turned to the IMF.

At the time, Indonesian technocrats approached the IMF less for its money than for the market confidence that they believed would come as a result. They also sought IMF support for their efforts to enact liberal economic reforms that Suharto had previously rejected. The IMF proscribed a policy of fiscal tightening, a reduction of food and fuel subsidies, the closure of sixteen private banks, and the maintenance of high domestic interests rates to make the rupiah attractive to international investors.

Suharto signed the IMF agreement, but many questioned his commitment to implementing it. Two banks with ties to the Suharto family were reopened days after they had been closed under the IMF agreement. Such incidents were taken by observers as evidence that in the inevitable battles between the IMF and his family, Suharto would side with the latter. On January 6, 1998, Indonesia presented a budget that was based on assumptions that many considered unrealistic. Viewing this as proof that Suharto was unwilling to respond effectively to the crisis, investors abandoned Indonesian assets. The rupiah lost half its value in five days, and panicked Indonesians rushed to purchase food, leaving grocery shelves bare. Fears that Indonesia's problems would deepen and spread throughout the region galvanized outsiders to take action. On January 8, 1998, President Bill Clinton telephoned Suharto and made it "quite clear that the IMF program has to be followed."[26] Clinton's message was reinforced by similar ones from the Japanese prime minister and German chancellor.[27] The IMF drafted a new fifty-point reform package. Addressing criticism leveled at its earlier package, the second IMF agreement eased fiscal conditions and demanded a host of structural reforms that struck at the heart of Suharto's patronage machine.

Under pressure from foreign leaders and financial markets abroad as well as businessmen at home, Suharto signed a second letter of intent with the IMF as its managing director, Michel Camdessus, stood over him with arms folded across his chest like a stern schoolmaster. As John Bresnan has correctly observed, the photograph of this scene, which was printed repeatedly in the Indonesian press, "became a symbol of the charged issue at the heart of the negotiation—whether the IMF and through it the United States, had the right to dictate terms to the Indonesian government in return for help in restoring confidence in the economy."[28]

Suharto signed the second IMF agreement in an attempt to restore confidence in Indonesia. However, his announcement five days later that he was ready to serve a seventh five-year term as president and that his preferred candidate for vice president was B. J. Habibie, an economic nationalist who had clashed repeatedly with the technocrats in the past, had the opposite effect. The markets reacted to the prospect of a Habibie vice presidency by sending the rupiah down to 17,000 to the dollar compared with 2,500 in August 1997.[29]

External Pressure and Internal Dissension Mount

The market's reaction to Habibie was reinforced by the actions of American and IMF officials who feared that Suharto was underestimating the seriousness of the situation. They went to great lengths to ensure that Suharto clearly understood their preferences and the potential costs to Indonesia if they were not reflected in Indonesian policy. Officials of the U.S. Treasury threatened to cut off aid if Habibie was appointed vice president. Clinton telephoned Suharto twice in one week to reiterate the message and dispatched former vice president Walter Mondale to carry it personally to Suharto.[30] During his March 3, 1998, meeting with Mondale, Suharto complained that he was being "victimized" and that implementing the IMF agreements would be "suicide."[31]

At the same time that Suharto appeared ready to defy proponents of globalization on the vice president issue, his very public discussion of instituting a currency board indicated that he was ready to resist them on economic issues as well. Camdessus publicly announced that he would recommend terminating the IMF bailout if Indonesia moved forward with the currency board.[32]

In the end, Suharto acceded to global demands by dropping the currency board proposal, but he defied them on the issue of Habibie. On March 11, 1998, Indonesia's rubber-stamp parliament reelected Suharto and dutifully named Habibie vice president. However, Suharto still had an opportunity to restore global confidence in Indonesia by appointing economic and political reformers to his new cabinet. Instead, Suharto did the opposite, appointing a cabinet full of politically connected but poorly respected figures. Suharto's eldest daughter, Tutut, was appointed minister of social affairs, while his golfing buddy and head of the plywood cartel, Mohammad "Bob" Hassan, was appointed minister of trade and industry. The cronies were in, and the technocrats were out.

By March, the cost of Suharto's global brinkmanship to the average Indonesian was high. Annual inflation was running at 47 percent. Over five and a half million workers had lost jobs since the crisis began, joining the ranks of underemployed that were estimated at 41 percent of the workforce before the crisis hit.[33] As it became clear that, in contrast to previous economic crises, Suharto was unwilling to swallow the liberal economic medicine required to cure Indonesia's ills, the economic crisis became a political one. Shorn of the legitimacy previously provided by thirty years of economic growth, the man who billed himself as the father of Indonesian development was now politically vulnerable.

Amien Rais, the leader of Muhammadiyah, a modernist Muslim organization that claims over 20 million members, was the first mainstream leader to blame the crisis on Suharto and call for his removal. Students and other activists began calling for political change. On the same day that Suharto took his oath as president, over 25,000 students demonstrated in Gajah Mada University. The economic crisis provided an opening for democratic reformers to attack the Suharto regime for *korupsi, kolusi, nepotisme* (KKN)—corruption, collusion, and nepotism—which they contended had led to the crisis. The eradication of KKN "has become a shorthand for demanding good governance" and the rallying cry of Indonesia's *reformasi,* or democratic, movement.[34]

Faced with an economy that continued to deteriorate and political protests that continued to rise, Suharto agreed to a third IMF package on April 8, 1998. The IMF agreement obligated Indonesia to reduce government subsidies of gasoline by October. Rather than lift the subsidies gradually, it was announced on May 4 that subsidies were being cut immediately and would result in a 70 percent increase in the price of gasoline. The announcement triggered large-scale rioting and looting. Student activists, who had previously obeyed laws that restricted their protests to university campuses, now took to the streets. Three days later, troops fired on a group of students returning to Trisakti University, killing four. The funeral for the slain students on May 13 attracted a huge procession that degenerated into riots and looting. Over the next three days, mobs burned hundreds of homes and looted shops, targeting those owned by ethnic Chinese. As Jakarta went up in flames, an estimated 150,000 people, mostly Chinese Indonesians and foreigners (including the IMF team), left the country. By the time order was restored, over 1,000 Indonesians were dead and thousands of shops and houses destroyed.

By this point, even those most loyal to Suharto realized that he was the problem, not the solution. On Monday, May 18, Harmoko, the speaker of parliament and a longtime Suharto ally, shocked the nation when he called on Suharto to resign by Friday or face impeachment. With pressure mounting outside in the streets and support eroding from within, Suharto resigned on May 21, 1998. Suharto had battled against globalization and lost.

THE HABIBIE ADMINISTRATION

Suharto's resignation opened the door to a new political era in Indonesia, but the country's severe political and economic problems remained unsolved. Indonesia's economy was in a shambles at the time that Suharto fell in May 1998. Inflation was running at 80 percent, output was down, the rupiah hovered at one-third its precrisis value, and the price of rice had tripled.[35] By the end of 1998, the Indonesian economy had contracted by almost 14 percent, the sharpest decline of any economy since the Great Depression of the 1930s. Given the severity of the economic crisis, the new administration felt that it had little choice but to renew Indonesia's commitment to the IMF agreement even though Habibie was Indonesia's leading economic nationalist and economic populists were well represented in his cabinet.

It is one of the great ironies of the current era of globalization that Indonesia's adherence to IMF policies has resulted in the de facto nationalization of most of the country's banking system and much of its corporate sector. By the end of 1998, nearly all of Indonesia's banks were bankrupt, and an estimated two-thirds of all outstanding loans were thought to be nonperforming. Unable to collect their debts, banks stopped new lending, starving even viable companies of working capital. In an effort to recapitalize the banking system, the government followed the advice of the IMF and created the Indonesian Bank Restructuring Agency (IBRA). Banks failing to meet a capital adequacy ratio of 4 percent are subject to takeover by IBRA. IBRA then assumed the debts of the banks under its control, thereby providing a government guarantee to bank creditors. The cost of bailing out Indonesia's banks is estimated at approximately $80 billion.[36]

With more than $60 billion of assets under its control, IBRA has become Indonesia's economic colossus. According to IMF plans, IBRA's dominance of the Indonesian economy is only temporary. Over time, IBRA will sell the assets that it has acquired to generate the income needed to finance at least part of the bailout. According to the liberal economic logic underlying the IMF plan, IBRA should sell the assets under its control to the highest bidder in order to maximize its return and reduce the cost of the bailout to the Indonesian taxpayer. However, with much of corporate Indonesia bankrupt, the likely buyers will be foreigners or Chinese Indonesians, two politically unpalatable scenarios to any Indonesian administration.

The logic of market efficiency at the heart of the IMF plan runs counter to popular opinion, which views IBRA's current control of many Chinese conglomerates as a once-in-a-generation opportunity to redress the ethnic imbalance of wealth. Economic nationalists can be divided into two groups on this issue. First, proponents of Muslim business interests, often represented politically by the PPP and Islamic factions of PAN and Golkar (the ruling party in the Suharto era), want the government to retain ownership of many Chinese-owned businesses and use them to create a series of state enterprises that would foster the growth of a *pribumi* business class. This group points to the success of Malaysia's New Economic Policy (NEP) in creating a Malay business class and argues that the assets currently held by IBRA could form the core of an Indonesian NEP. A second group advocates the retention of some of IBRA's assets. It consists of secular nationalists associated with Megawati's PDI-P party who advocate greater state control of the economy. Economic populists, such as Adi Sasono, minister of cooperatives under Habibie, would like to use IBRA's assets to support a larger role for cooperatives and to subsidize credit and training to small businesses and the agricultural sector.

In the political arena, Indonesian reformers and external advocates of globalization such as the IMF both wanted to eradicate the arbitrary political and economic practices of the Suharto era and replace them with clean, transparent, and accountable government institutions. Vice President Habibie's elevation to the presidency was acknowledged as constitutional. However, as Suharto's longtime protégé, Habibie was considered an illegitimate leader by many reformers. Habibie attempted to shore up his democratic credentials by enacting a series of reforms unthinkable during the Suharto era. He freed the press, released political prisoners, lifted restrictions on labor organizations, and promised free elections. Parliamentary elections, held on June 7, 1999, were the first free and fair elections held in Indonesia since 1955. Over 100 million Indonesians voted in an election contested by forty-three political parties. In a stark contrast to elections held under Suharto, the ballots were opened and counted at the polling stations in full view of the voters, a great victory for democracy.

The PDI-P, led by Megawati Sukarnoputri, daughter of Indonesia's first president, Sukarno, emerged as the front-runner with 33.7 percent of the votes. Golkar came in second with 20 percent of the vote. This meant that four out of five Indonesians voted against the status quo represented by Golkar, a clear victory for reformers. PKB, the party of Abdurrahman Wahid, won 12.6 percent of the vote, while PPP, the Suharto-era Islamic party, won 10.7 percent, and PAN, the party of Amien Rais, won 7 percent. No party achieved a victory sufficiently decisive to govern on its own. In the four-month period between the elections and the convening of the parliament, the need to form a coalition combined with Indonesia's arcane political rules produced backroom political dealings that contrasted sharply with the openness of the elections.

Under Indonesia's complex indirect presidential system, the electorate voted for 462 of parliament's 500 members; the military appoints the remaining thirty-eight members. However, Indonesia's president is chosen not by parliament but by the People's Consultative Assembly, which includes the 500 members of parliament and 200 members appointed by regional parliaments and "functional groups," such as women, farmer, and workers' organizations. Therefore, 30 percent of the members of the Consultative Assembly are not directly elected and are under no obligation to choose a president who reflects the desires of the Indonesian electorate. Many reformers feared that the status quo forces would engineer the reelection of President Habibie by reverting to KKN practices. In the end, however, the publication of precisely such an attempt as revealed in the Baligate scandal doomed Habibie's hopes of becoming more than a transitional president.

Baligate: KKN Challenges to Political and Economic Reform

Just as the strongest challenge to the technocrats in the Suharto era came from Suharto's family and cronies, the strongest challenge to IBRA's ability to function, according to liberal economic logic, came from Habibie's political cronies.

The Baligate saga clearly illustrates the tension between global institutions and Indonesian reformers, who demand open, transparent, and accountable practices, and the status quo forces resisting them to protect the corrupt system from which they have long benefited.

The Baligate scandal arises out of a 546-billion-rupiah fee that Rudy Ramli, managing director of Bank Bali, paid to a company named Era Giat Prima for assistance in helping Bank Bali collect the 904 billion rupiah owed to it from three banks that had been taken over by IBRA. At the time, Ramli was struggling to collect these debts in order to meet IBRA's capitalization requirements and to forestall Bank Bali's takeover by IBRA. IBRA claims that the transaction was illegal since it guaranteed the funds to Bank Bali. Ramli claims that repeated pleas to IBRA to make good on its guarantee went unheeded, and he agreed to pay the fee—which amounted to over 50 percent of the original debt—in a desperate attempt to save his bank. Ramli was ultimately unsuccessful, and Bank Bali was taken over by IBRA. The transaction came to light in August 1999, when Britain's Standard and Charted Bank was conducting a due-diligence report after agreeing to acquire an ownership stake in Bank Bali. The economic scandal turned into a political scandal when it was revealed that Era Giat Prima is controlled by Setya Novanto, deputy treasurer of Golkar and a close Habibie associate. Ramli has alleged that Golkar officials pressured him into agreeing to the deal and that the funds were to be used to buy votes for Habibie in the presidential election. Novanto was part of an informal group of Habibie allies dubbed *Tim Sukses* ("Team Success") in charge of Habibie's reelection campaign. Ramli's accusation is supported by former IBRA chairman Glenn Yusuf. Testifying before a parliamentary panel on September 13, he said that Baramuli, chairman of the Supreme Advisory Council and close Habibie ally, met with him on July 30, shortly before the scandal broke, and pressured him to assist in a cover-up, threatening that "if you don't, Tanri could become involved, I could become involved and the president could be dragged in."[37]

Under strong pressure from the IMF, Habibie agreed to an investigation of the Bank Bali case and hired PriceWaterhouseCoopers (PWC) to conduct the audit. On September 7, PWC submitted a 123-page report to head of the State Audit Agency, Satiro Joedono. The report was damning, naming officials and linking close aides of President Habibie to the illegal transition. Joedono instructed PWC to prepare a shorter version that omitted names, and this sanitized thirty-six-page report was made public. The report said that it found "preferential treatment, concealment, bribery, corruption, and fraud" in connection with the Bank Bali transaction and that "ministers, senior officials, and members of parliament" appear to be involved."[38]

The release of the sanitized report triggered demands by Indonesian reformers and the IMF that the full report be released. The IMF declared that it would not resume lending until the full report was made public.[39] Hubert Neiss, the IMF's director for the Asia-Pacific region, argues that the solution to Baligate is prompt and total transparency and believes that "eventually, this audit will go on a Web site."[40]

The Baligate scandal riveted Indonesia. What was most shocking was not necessarily the revelations themselves, which confirmed long-standing suspicions of corrupt ties between business and government, but the fact that Habibie refused to accede to public demands for accountability. Habibie took no action against government officials accused of wrongdoing. He not only rebuffed calls to suspend Baramuli, the chairman of the Supreme Advisory Council who is deeply implicated in the Baligate scandal, but also ensured that he was elected to the People's Consultative Assembly. Habibie's action created a groundswell of opposition and ultimately contributed to his downfall.

The Nationalist Backlash against Global Pressure on East Timor

President Habibie's attempt to remove East Timor as an irritant in the country's foreign policy had the unintended consequence of leading to widespread condemnation of Indonesia by the international community. The attempts by foreign countries and international organizations to condition their policies toward Indonesia on changes in its policy toward East Timor had long frustrated Indonesia. Indonesia opposed the UN votes on East Timor and U.S. congressional restrictions on military assistance to Indonesia. In 1992, Suharto responded to strong Dutch criticism over East Timor by borrowing a refrain from Sukarno and telling the Dutch to "go to hell with your aid."

In early February 1999, Habibie shocked Indonesia and the international community when he announced that he would permit a referendum offering the East Timorese independence from Indonesia. Habibie apparently made the decision alone, in a fit of pique after receiving a letter from Australian prime minister John Howard urging Habibie to reconsider Indonesian policy. The Indonesian military (TNI) was furious at Habibie's decision. Not only was it opposed to the potential loss of sovereign control over East Timor, but it also feared that the referendum could serve as a precedent for other restless provinces and ultimately threaten the territorial integrity of the Indonesian state that the military is sworn to uphold.

On August 30, 1999, the citizens of East Timor voted overwhelmingly in favor of independence from Indonesia in a referendum conducted by the United Nations. In the aftermath of the vote, pro-Indonesia militias and members of the Indonesian military unleashed a wave of terror: attacks on UN personnel, attacks on religious leaders and institutions, the burning of houses and public buildings, the forced movement out of East Timor of tens of thousands, and the systematic execution of suspected independence sympathizers.

The Indonesian military attempted to prevent news of these actions from reaching the outside world. The TNI destroyed the territory's telephone system, threatened journalists, and refused to protect the UN compound in an attempt to force a UN evacuation. However, TNI could not control the satellite communications systems that connected a number of journalists and UN workers to the outside world through their cellular phones. Throughout the crisis, they bore witness to the events in East Timor, frustrating TNI's attempts to deny the atrocities. "The army has been using tactics lately that are 15 or 20 years out of date," commented one senior ambassador in Jakarta. "It will have to learn that these tactics are unsuitable for an era of globalization when you've got a free press and the world is watching."[41]

The atrocities in East Timor were swiftly condemned by the international community. Under intense foreign pressure that included threats to cut off economic aid, Indonesia agreed to permit a foreign peacekeeping force authorized by the United Nations into East Timor to restore order.

Most Indonesians were stunned at how quickly foreigners, particularly westerners, were to treat Indonesia as a pariah state. An area of 800,000 people in a country of 210 million, East Timor had never received much attention in Indonesia. Moreover, until Habibie lifted restrictions on the press, all news from East Timor came via state-controlled agencies. Largely unaware of the true history of East Timor, most Indonesians accepted the official version of events and expected that the referendum would prove favorable to Indonesia. International condemnation of Indonesia, therefore, came as a shock to many Indonesians and triggered a rise in nationalism. Prior to events in East Timor, blatant anti-Westernism tended to be confined to the radical fringe in public. Fadli Zon presented the radical Muslim worldview of the IMF agreement in March 1998, when he argued that the "IMF provisions are impossible. They make everything cheap for foreigners. Suharto only signed the agreement because it was a crisis situation, but most Indonesians do not agree with the IMF package. The IMF does not want to help us. It would be better for us to close the country like Myanmar."[42]

These sentiments may have been radical in mid-1998, but they have now entered mainstream discourse. *Kompas,* an influential Indonesian-language daily, expressed the views of many when it accused the West of double standards:

> The presence of a UN peacekeeping force in East Timor is the result of continuous pressure against us. The international reaction to East Timor's problems has removed the mask of Western governments. Previously they supported invasion, now they threaten us. In the past, they sent war arms to fight the Timorese. Now they have stopped.[43]

Top political leaders have contributed to this discourse, which paints Indonesia as the victim of hostile external forces. Prior to his election as president, Abdurrahman Wahid called for an "anti-UN jihad."[44] Megawati, who owes much of her political support to the popularity of her father's staunch nationalism, had initially opposed the East Timor referendum. She laid the blame for strained relations between Indonesia and the outside world on unwarranted global pressures. Discussing ways to repair Indonesia's relations with the international community at the height of the crisis over East Timor in September 1999, Megawati declared, "First, the international community should halt the demonization of the Indonesian people. We know too well about violence and human rights, but as victims, not perpetrators."[45]

The rise of nationalism in Indonesia has taken on an anti-Western tone. The backlash began as anti-Australian, then became anti-West and now is becoming antiwhite. According to Dewi Fortuna Anwar, former presidential adviser on foreign affairs under Habibie,

> People are no longer focusing on what happened in East Timor, but on how Indonesia has been insulted. . . . There's always been a suspicion of white people in general. . . . The feeling is always there. Indonesia has always been very touchy about being pushed around by outside countries.[46]

In short, Habibie's attempt to remove Western pressure on East Timor by holding a referendum went horribly awry. In large part this was because of Habibie's failure to appreciate the depth of TNI's opposition to any action that threatens Indonesian sovereignty over its current territory. The fallout from events in East Timor also illustrates that Indonesia's progress toward democracy has not changed its defensiveness toward undesired pressure, particularly when it comes from the West.

THE WAHID ADMINISTRATION

In October 1999, the People's Consultative Assembly met in the aftermath of the Baligate scandal and the East Timor debacle to choose a new Indonesian president. Habibie, required to give an accountability speech, was humiliated when it was rejected. He was blamed for Baligate, the loss of East Timor, and his failure to bring corruption charges against Suharto. Although no constitutional provision required him to do so, Habibie withdrew from the presidential race. The Consultative Assembly's censure of Habibie and Habibie's acknowledgment of this censure represented a significant empowerment of Indonesia's traditionally weak Consultative Assembly and an important step toward creating an accountable political system.

Habibie's withdrawal paved the way for the election of Muslim cleric Abdurrahman Wahid as Indonesia's fourth president on October 20. The next day, Megawati was chosen vice president. The election of two popular, reformist leaders not only heralded a new chapter in Indonesian domestic politics but also created an opportunity to restructure Indonesia's badly damaged relationships with international organizations and foreign governments. At the time of this writing, the Wahid administration is four months old, and although it is far too early to make any definitive conclusions, the reform agenda pursued by the new government to date is fully congruent with the values embedded in globalization.

Wahid, long a leading advocate of religious tolerance, protection of minority rights, and democratic values, has appointed like-minded officials to key cabinet positions. Top government officials have pledged to conduct government policy in an open and transparent manner and to reject KKN. Wahid has created a new Human Rights Ministry, and the government has discussed establishing a Truth and Reconciliation Commission on the South African model to deal with Suharto-era abuses. The new government has begun corruption proceedings against Suharto, a step viewed by many as a litmus test for the new government. The TNI doctrine of *dwi fungsi,* or dual function, has traditionally proscribed an active military role in political affairs and reducing the military's political influence is necessary for democratic consolidation. The removal of General Wiranto from the cabinet in late February 2000 is a significant step toward establishing the supremacy of civilian rule.

In his quest to entrench democracy and respect for human rights in Indonesia, Wahid must be careful not to trigger a backlash from status quo forces. He must also avoid giving the impression that he is bowing to foreign pressure. The prosecution of TNI abuses in East Timor is the political issue on which status quo forces could most easily harness nationalism in their battle against the reformist Wahid government. Many in the international community demanded that the United Nations establish an international war crimes tribunal to prosecute those responsible for atrocities in East Timor. Realizing that the prospect of watching Indonesian generals hauled before an international tribunal would create a surge of nationalism that could scuttle the reform agenda, the Wahid administration argued that Indonesia should try the perpetrators itself. In February 2000, UN Secretary-General Kofi Annan agreed to hold off on the tribunal if Indonesia would "hold those responsible" for their misdeeds.[47] Wahid's ability to keep international pressure at bay is critically important because "nationalist resentment of the U.N. is rife among supporters of both Wahid and Wiranto."[48] Just as the corruption trial of Suharto is viewed as a litmus test of the Wahid administration by domestic reformers, the trial of those responsible for the atrocities in East Timor is viewed as a litmus test by the international community. Rendering a verdict that satisfies the international community without triggering a nationalist backlash against globalization will be a key test for the new government.

Indonesia has moved quickly to repair its relations with the IMF and international donors. Wahid has spent much of his first months in office traveling abroad to secure international political and economic support for the new regime. He has been extremely successful: The IMF and World Bank quickly resumed the lending that they had halted in the wake of the Baligate affair, the Consultative Group on Indonesia pledged almost $5 billion in aid, and the United States named Indonesia one of four key countries undergoing democratic transitions that would receive an increase in American aid. The change in international perceptions of Indonesia from a pariah state in September 1999 to a struggling democracy worthy of significant international support in February 2000 is stunning.

A Questionable Commitment

The Wahid administration signed a new letter of intent (LOI) with the IMF in January 2000. The IMF went to great lengths to consult with Indonesian officials on the LOI. When Wahid indicated a desire to see greater attention paid to small business and agriculture, the IMF was quick to announce that "the request to place emphasis on small and medium size companies and agriculture can be accommodated."[49] Despite these efforts, few Indonesians believe that the LOI reflects Indonesian preferences. According to one member of Indonesia's Council of Economic Advisers, "there is no sense of ownership over the LOI. The Indonesian people do not see the LOI as their own policy to cope with the problem. Instead, they see it as something imposed on Indonesia from Washington."[50]

Furthermore, some of the government officials responsible for implementing the LOI have advocated radically different policies in the past. Kwik Kian Gie, Indonesia's top economic official, is a longtime critic of Suharto's economic policies and a key Megawati adviser known for his nationalist views. In the past, Kwik advocated a fixed exchange rate and capital controls. If Kwik represents a secular-nationalist position on the economy, Wahid himself embodies the economic populist perspective.

Furthermore, prominent voices have advocated policies that are popular in Indonesia but not with global markets and institutions. Sri Mulyani Indrawati, a respected economist, has argued that Indonesia should not be responsible for repaying that portion of the country's public debt that international lenders knew would be lost to corruption. Internal World Bank documents leaked in 1998 included the "estimate that at least 20–30 percent of GOI [government of Indonesia] development budget funds are diverted through informal payments to GOI staff and politicians and there is no basis to claim a smaller 'leakage' for Bank projects as our controls have little practical effect on the methods used."[51] Sri Mulyani contends that this 20 to 30 percent is "criminal debt" that should be written off by international lenders rather than burden Indonesian taxpayers who did not benefit from the proceeds.

During the Suharto era, liberal economic policies were adopted during economic crises and abandoned when the economy had improved. Given that Wahid's cabinet is populated largely with economic nationalists and populists, a similar pattern of policy shifts may occur in the future.

CONCLUSION

This chapter has attempted to illustrate that in Indonesia globalization is viewed neither as the wholly progressive force portrayed by globalization enthusiasts nor as the pernicious force described by its critics. Instead, government and societal actors have welcomed globalization when it supported their pursuit of wealth,

power, or a just society and resisted it when it did not. Indonesia's future responses to globalization will be determined by a number of factors. First, there is
an increasing tendency in Indonesia to view globalization as Westernization. As
this chapter makes clear, the "global" actors in the Indonesian drama—Michel
Camdessus, President Clinton, or Australian prime minister Howard—have
mostly been Western. This tendency to view globalization as Westernization,
combined with the rise of Indonesian nationalism, means that periods of tension
in Indonesia's relationship with the West could affect its globalization policies.

Second, Indonesia's new political openness will probably make it more difficult for proponents of liberal policies to win policy debates. Under the New Order
regime, Suharto could shield the technocrats from their critics when he chose to
do so. That is no longer possible today. Liberal capitalism attracts few followers
in Indonesia outside technocratic circles, and as economic policy becomes an
issue in election campaigns, it is likely that economic nationalists and populists
will increasingly come out on top in policy debates.

Finally, the speed with which Indonesia's economy recovers will be a key factor determining Indonesia's future policy toward globalization. The longer and
more arduous the recovery, the greater the potential for bitter policy disputes between Indonesia and global actors. Policy disputes could trigger a vicious circle
in which Western pressure heightens Indonesian perceptions of "victimization"
and ultimately leads its leaders to conclude that globalization is a pernicious force
to be resisted.

Given Indonesia's sensitivity to outside pressure, its antipathy to liberal capitalism, and the perception among many Indonesians that globalization caused the
AFC, it is unlikely to ever embrace globalization as a wholly progressive force.
Nevertheless, Indonesia's reluctant acceptance of globalization could still produce a healthy policy response to its challenges. Key global actors have demonstrated an understanding of the domestic obstacles facing the Wahid administration and have taken steps to support it: President Clinton changed his schedule to
meet Wahid, the IMF has agreed to accommodate Wahid's preferences for greater
attention to agricultural policies, and the United Nations has given Indonesia
breathing space to try the perpetrators of violence in East Timor. The more Indonesia is treated with the respect that it seeks from Western countries and global
institutions, the more likely it is to trigger a virtuous circle of Indonesian policy
responses toward globalization.

NOTES

The author would like to thank John Bresnan, Bridget Welsh, and Sam Kim for comments on an earlier version of this chapter.

1. President Suharto, Speech at the Summit of the D-8, Istanbul, Turkey, June 15, 1997
(available at <www.dfadeplu.go.id.english/ralatril.htm>).

2. Ariel Heryanto, "Indonesia: Towards the Final Countdown?" in *Southeast Asian Affairs* (Singapore: Institute of Southeast Asian Studies, 1997): 109.

3. Throughout this chapter, "economic globalization" will be used interchangeably with "demands for the adoption of liberal economic policies."

4. Radius Prawiro, *Indonesia's Struggle for Development* (Kuala Lumpur: Oxford University Press, 1998), 312.

5. Sukardi Rinakit and Hadi Soesastro, "Indonesia," in Charles Morrison and Hadi Soesastro, eds., *Domestic Adjustments to Globalization* (Tokyo: Japan Center for International Exchange, 1998), 199.

6. Rinakit and Soesastro, "Indonesia," 193.

7. Prawiro, *Indonesia's Struggle for Development,* 321.

8. Cited in Prawiro, *Indonesia's Struggle for Development,* 328–29, n. 11.

9. Ali Alatas, Speech to the Group of 77, January 13, 1998.

10. Rinakit and Soesastro, "Indonesia," 193.

11. Rinakit and Soesastro, "Indonesia," 194.

12. Cited in Rinakit and Soesastro, "Indonesia," 202.

13. Prawiro, *Indonesia's Struggle for Development,* 315.

14. Juwono Sudarsono, *The Challenges to Indonesia's Resilience* (Jakarta: National Resilience Institute, 1996), 5.

15. Hal Hill, *The Indonesian Economy since 1966* (New York: Cambridge University Press, 1996), 4.

16. Hill, *The Indonesian Economy since 1966,* 5.

17. Prawiro, *Indonesia's Struggle for Development,* 301.

18. Sjharir, "The Struggle for Deregulation in Indonesia," in Ian Chalmers and Vedi R. Hadiz, eds., *The Politics of Economic Development in Indonesia* (New York: Routledge, 1997), 155.

19. Ginandjar Kartasamita, "To Build Economic Resilience," in Chalmers and Hadiz, eds., *The Politics of Economic Development in Indonesia,* 169.

20. Enin Supriyanto, "Growth-Oriented Development Strategies and Authoritarianism," in Chalmers and Hadiz, eds., *The Politics of Economic Development in Indonesia,* 197–98.

21. Suharto, "The State of the Nation," in Chalmers and Hadiz, eds., *The Politics of Economic Development in Indonesia,* 185.

22. These figures are from the charts in Ross H. McLeod and Ross Garnaut, eds., *East Asia in Crisis* (New York: Routledge, 1998), 23-27.

23. Ali Alatas, Speech to the Group of 77, January 13, 1998.

24. Adam Schwarz, *A Nation in Waiting* (Boulder, Colo.: Westview, 1999), 257.

25. Cited in the Public Broadcasting Stations (PBS) series "Globalization and Human Rights" (available at <www.pbs.org.globalization/role of.html>).

26. John Bresnan, "The United States, the IMF, and the Indonesian Financial Crisis," in Adam Schwarz and Jonathan Paris, eds., *The Politics of Post-Suharto Indonesia* (New York: Council on Foreign Relations Press, 1999), 93.

27. Bresnan, "The United States, the IMF, and the Indonesian Financial Crisis," 93.

28. Bresnan, "The United States, the IMF, and the Indonesian Financial Crisis," 93.

29. Bresnan, "The United States, the IMF, and the Indonesian Financial Crisis," 94.

30. Bresnan, "The United States, the IMF, and the Indonesian Financial Crisis," 93–95.

31. Bresnan, "The United States, the IMF, and the Indonesian Financial Crisis," 95.

32. Bresnan, "The United States, the IMF, and the Indonesian Financial Crisis," 95.

33. Bresnan, "The United States, the IMF, and the Indonesian Financial Crisis," 96.

34. Hadi Soesastro, *Globalization, Governance, and Sustainable Development* (Jakarta: CSIS, 1999), 2.

35. Soesastro, *Globalization, Governance, and Sustainable Development,* 100.

36. Dan Murphy, "Standard Treatment," *Far Eastern Economic Review,* December 2, 1999, 48.

37. Dan Murphy and John McBeth, "Follow the Money," *Far Eastern Economic Review,* September 23, 1999, 12.

38. Murphy and McBeth, "Follow the Money," 12.

39. Murphy and McBeth, "Follow the Money," 11.

40. Press release, *Far Eastern Economic Review,* September 23, 1999.

41. Seth Mydans, "Army Pullout Shows Indonesia Fault Lines," *New York Times,* September 19, 1999.

42. Schwarz, *A Nation in Waiting,* 348.

43. Derwin Pereira, "Jakarta Cave-in Sparks Anger," *Straits Times* (Singapore), September 14, 1999.

44. Keith Richburg, "Humiliated Indonesians Direct Anger at the West," *Washington Post,* September 19, 1999.

45. "MEGAWATI: I Am Saddened, Ashamed, Concerned," *Newsweek International,* September 20, 1999.

46. Richburg, "Humiliated Indonesians Direct Anger at the West."

47. Nisid Hajari, "Victory Signs," *Time,* February 28, 2000, 26–27.

48. Hajari, "Victory Signs," 26.

49. "Indonesia's Wahid Wants IMF Program to Include Agriculture, Small Business," *Dow Jones Newswires,* November 3, 1999.

50. "Interview with Sri Mulyani," *The Van Zorge Report,* February 2000.

51. Schwarz, *A Nation in Waiting,* 316.

10

Malaysia and Globalization: Contradictory Currents

Bridget Welsh

> Globalization, liberalisation and deregulation might bring many benefits to us, but this new thinking could destroy us too.
>
> —Prime Minister Dr. Mohamad Mahathir, July 1998

THE CONTRADICTORY QUALITY OF "GLOBALIZATION" IN MALAYSIA

No state in the post–Cold War world has attacked globalization as publicly as Malaysia. From attacks on currency speculators to the implementation of capital controls, Malaysia's leadership has challenged what analysts have labeled the process of "globalization." The focus of this criticism has centered on the global integration of the world economy through the expansion of portfolio capital. A closer study of the history of globalization in Malaysia, however, reveals a more complicated picture.

From the mid-1980s on, the relationship between Malaysia and globalization has been contradictory. Malaysia has embraced, redefined, and rejected globalization. These contradictory currents are clearly evident in economic policy and domestic politics, where the government has encouraged capital, labor flows, information technology, and the more open political dialogue only to limit the scope of these exchanges in recent years. To make matters more confusing, the consequences of policies tied to globalization for Malaysia are also contradictory. On the one hand, globalization has made Malaysia more integrated into the international economy, expanded its domestic economy, and fostered the creation of new political forces. On the other hand, globalization has increased its vulnerability to the international environment, leading to domestic political challenges and greater susceptibility to changes in the international economy. While the long-term consequences of globalization for Malaysia are not clear, the events of the past two years show that globalization has evoked extensive changes. The Asian financial crisis and the resulting political crisis between Prime Minister Mahathir Mohamad and his former deputy, Anwar Ibrahim, have contracted the country's economy, redefined its relationship with international capital and the United States, and undermined support for Malaysia's leaders, particularly among the country's largest ethnic group, the Malays. It remains to be seen whether Malaysia can address these short-term consequences and return to conditions before 1997 in which the Malaysian leadership was able to effectively harness globalization to promote growth and political stability in a semidemocratic environment.

This chapter discusses the relationship between globalization and Malaysia, focusing on the contradictory currents in the approaches and consequences of globalization. I address a number of issues associated with globalization, including capital flows, labor migration, use of information technology, and expansion of democracy. In light of the recent controversies over capital controls and the Mahathir–Anwar conflict, the emphasis is on economic policy and domestic politics. Because of the importance of Mahathir's leadership in Malaysia since 1981, I concentrate on his role in defining policies and globalization in Malaysia. It becomes clear that globalization in Malaysia is riddled with contradictions, some of which the Malaysian state played a large part in creating.

"GLOBALIZATION" IN THE MALAYSIAN CONTEXT

Within Malaysia, "globalization" has become a catchphrase. It is used by politicians to woo constituents and investors alike, debated by academics in annual conferences and journal articles, and included in the latest annual reports of leading companies.[1] Yet, despite its frequent usage, the main protagonist who has defined globalization is Mahathir. While his attitude toward globalization has changed over time, he views globalization as both a process and as an ideological label.

His main view of globalization is that of a process of transformation that extends and intensifies global interconnectedness, similar to the definition used in this volume.[2] As such, "globalization" serves as an umbrella term that captures a broad range of changes in Malaysia. "Globalization" explains the widespread use of the Internet, the popularity of Astro satellite television, the closer connection of Malaysian Muslims to Mecca and international Islamic movements, the rising significance of international actors such as nongovernmental organizations (NGOs), increased economic expansion, and Malaysia's high vulnerability to changes in the flow of foreign labor and capital, among other developments. Mahathir, like other Malaysians, recognizes that the effects of globalization are extensive; the "global" environment has become a greater part of everyday life in a manner never encountered in the country's history.

While he acknowledges the cultural changes associated with abandoning parochial concerns and adopting a more cosmopolitan worldview, Mahathir concentrates on two dimensions of global interconnectedness: economic ties and the expansion of information technology. He associates these changes with Malaysia's national development, which has been one of his main concerns in office. For Mahathir, states and markets drive the changes induced by globalization. He acknowledges the importance of neoliberal views of competition, free enterprise, and limited government regulation as sources of development. Yet he sees the state as a main factor in filtering globalization. The state can promote the Internet in Malaysia through the Multimedia Super Corridor, distribute the contract for satellite television, encourage the hajj, cooperate with NGOs, and reap the benefits and pitfalls from closer economic connections through policies to attract or regulate capital flows. He sees leaders of small states as active participants in globalization.

On the other hand, globalization has also become an ideological label. With his emphasis on national interests, Mahathir sees globalization as leading to clashes between regions and the power of states. As such, there are ideological overtones embedded in this process. For Mahathir, globalization is a process advocated explicitly by Western financial capitalists and implicitly by the U.S. government to promote the expansion of markets and their form of democratic government. These prodemocratic, neoliberal, or market-oriented policies are seen to be advocated by multinational companies and Western dominated international financial institutions such as the International Monetary Fund (IMF) and international or foreign-funded domestic NGOs to benefit Western states and their financial interests.[3] Interpreted in this form, globalization is an ideological construct reflecting a skeptical, if not negative, view of the effects of the globalization process.[4] The role of globalization as an ideological construct is particularly important in Malaysia, where Mahathir has challenged the West in shaping "universal" values and promoting the adoption of neoliberal economic policies to undermine developing countries.

Mahathir's conceptualization of globalization as both a process and an ideological construct reflects a combination of the three different theoretical orientations outlined by Kim in chapter 1. On the one hand, Mahathir, corresponding to the view of the "hyperglobalists," recognizes the role of the market as an agent of change and the promise of global interconnectedness for economic development. On the other hand, with his skepticism and criticism of the process, his views correspond to that of the neorealist and dependency schools. His view of globalization remains state-centric; he explicitly rejects the hyperglobalists view of the demise of the nation-state. In the words of David Held, skeptics, like Mahathir, hold that "internationalization depends on state acquiescence and support" and results in the creation of "regional blocs" and "clashes of civilizations."[5] Following the *dependencistas,* he highlights the importance of conflict between the powerful developed countries and weaker developing countries. He understands that globalization can promote inequalities, at least on an interstate level. The fact that

Mahathir's view fits into all three schools illustrates the embedded contradictions in his conceptualization of "globalization." Overall, the dominant theme is state-centrism and, of late, skepticism, but at times he has dampened these views in favor of a more positive interpretation. The reasons for these different perspectives lie with Mahathir's pragmatism and the changing international and domestic conditions in Malaysia.

SWIMMING IN A DEEP OCEAN: EMBRACING GLOBALIZATION

While Malaysia had traditionally been open to international capital and allied with the West, the Malaysian government initiated a series of steps toward deepening its integration into the international environment in the 1980s, thus beginning the process of globalization. The first changes were political. In the beginning of the decade, Mahathir opened up the political system by encouraging debate among groups, in forums such as budget dialogues, and meetings with Islamic groups in the country.[6] While he controlled the scope of these exchanges, Mahathir set in place the conditions that would contribute to the rise of a domestic NGO community and rising Islamic fundamentalism within Malaysia.[7] These changes at home coincided with increased involvement in international organizations, including the United Nations and the Association of Southeast Asian Nations (ASEAN).[8] Politically, Malaysia became more democratic and internationally prominent.

Economic Liberalization

By 1985, the major changes toward the global environment were economic. In 1986, the state implemented a series of liberalizing measures in the country's economy, including the privatization of the electricity and telephone companies. The government also introduced sweeping changes in tax policy that reduced direct taxes. The aim was to make Malaysia more attractive to foreign capital. This was followed by a reduction in tariffs and a wider tax incentive scheme for foreign investors. The market was accepted as the engine of economic growth, as the scope of public spending was reduced. By 1990, Malaysia had embraced the globalization process in economic policy.

These changes in policy coincided with the adoption of new, grander goals in economic development. Malaysia's leadership began to adopt and promote many of the ideas associated with neoliberal proponents of globalization as its own. The new direction of economic policy was laid out by Mahathir in the Sixth Malaysian Plan, or "The Way Forward," known as Vision 2020. Here, he outlined his aim to make Malaysia a developed country:

> Our economic objective should be to secure the establishment of a competitive economy. . . . It must mean, among other things: a diversified and balanced economy with

a mature and widely based industrial sector, a modern and mature agriculture sector and an efficient and productive and equally mature services sector; . . . an entrepreneurial economy that is self-reliant, outward-looking and enterprising; . . . an economy that is subjected to the full discipline and rigour of market forces.[9]

Malaysia's leadership explicitly stated its commitment to the private sector, market forces, and integration into the international economy:

> No nation can afford to abandon a winning formula. And this nation will not. For the foreseeable future, Malaysia will continue to drive the private sector, to rely on it as the primary engine of growth.[10]
> Entry into the world market pits our companies against all comers and subjects them to the full force of international competition. This is a challenge we must accept not simply because the domestic market is too small but because in the long run it will actually enrich our domestic market and reduce our dependence on export.[11]

Mahathir's plan also called on Malaysia to stand up to the challenge of greater global integration: "When the going is tougher, we must not turn inward. We simply have no choice but to be more lean, more resourceful, more productive and generally more competitive, more able to take on the world."[12] By 1990, Malaysia's leadership had deepened many of the policies associated with globalization, namely, privatization and liberalization. He opened up the telecommunications sector and privatized road construction. Mahathir believed that these policies would further economic development.

There were four major consequences of broadening globalization in the economic realm for Malaysia. First, the relationship between the state and society changed, particularly the relationship between the state and its Malay constituents. In the 1970s, the government had increased patronage to the Malay community through the New Economic Policy (NEP). The government continued to distribute benefits to the Malay community, but the scope and the form of those benefits changed. A smaller group of supporters received a larger percentage of the benefits from the state.[13] They were known as Mahathir's closest allies, selected on the basis of their loyalty and perceived capacity to generate economic growth. They received their connection through personal ties to the leadership. Today, these people are known as Malaysia's "cronies" and make up a small circle of businessmen, including Vincent Tan, who is involved in the hotel industry and the monorail project, and Halim Saad, who is the director of Malaysia's largest conglomerate, Renong.[14] The process of deregulation opened up the way for a handful of individuals to gain sizable fortunes.

Second, the ethnic alliances supporting the regime shifted. This was due to the fact that the pro-*bumiputera* (largely Malay) affirmative action program (NEP) was cut back. With the introduction of a new policy, National Development Policy (NDP) in 1990, the emphasis was placed on growth rather than equality.[15] The government encouraged the development of domestic Chinese capitalists in small and medium-size industries and relied more on their support politically.

Third, foreign investment rose significantly. As Greg Felker points out,

> In 1985 and 1986, FDI approvals in Malaysia were RM 325 million and RM 525 million. Approved foreign investment rocketed to RM 2 billion in 1988, RM 3.4 billion in 1989 and RM 6.2 billion in 1990.[16]

Japanese and Taiwanese investment more than tripled during the 1980s.[17] Finally, and perhaps the most important result, the economy expanded. The growth rate increased after 1986, up from 7 percent annually to 8 to 9 percent. In short, globalization had significant implications, contributing to political realignments, increased dependence on foreign capital, and economic growth.

Promoting Competitiveness

With record levels of economic expansion, the process of globalization intensified in the 1990s. As the economy expanded, it soon became apparent that there was a shortage of labor in Malaysia. From 1987 to 1993, labor demand increased 3.9 percent per year, while the labor supply increased only 3.1 percent per year.[18] To compensate for this shortage, the Malaysian government initiated a series of measures that encouraged labor from neighboring countries, particularly Muslim countries. Malaysia had to maintain its competitiveness for foreign capital. A recruitment program was set in place to attract labor from Bangladesh to work mainly in the manufacturing sector.[19] Immigration controls were relaxed at the borders to facilitate the flow of labor from Indonesia, Thailand, and the Philippines. In 1991, official statistics reported that there were 1.2 million foreign laborers. By 1995, estimates put that figure at close to 2.5 million.[20] Most of these workers were employed in low-paying jobs in construction and agriculture, yet they played a large part in the economic expansion of Malaysia. They filled jobs that Malaysians were not willing to do. Their role in the construction sector was particularly important since the Malaysian leadership placed increasing emphasis on building large projects (such as the Petronas Twin Towers) for Malaysia's economic development.[21] Openness to foreign labor signaled Malaysia's deep commitment to broader global integration.

In another effort to maintain their competitiveness as an attractive site for foreign capital and further economic development, the government liberalized the regulations governing portfolio capital and projected itself as a financial center. The aim was to open up Malaysia's capital markets in order to make these markets more competitive and foster investor confidence in Malaysia.[22] The most public measure involved the promotion of the island of Labuan as an offshore financial center in 1990. In that same year, the government set up a Ratings Agency that was geared to inspire confidence in the Malaysian markets. This was followed by the establishment of a Securities Commission in 1993, the Kuala Lumpur Options and Financial Futures Exchange in 1995, and the Malaysian Monetary Exchange in 1996. These last two institutions facilitated the use of hedging in equity markets and derivatives, practices that are associated with high-risk speculative investment. While the Malaysian portfolio markets were used primarily by local investors, these measures encouraged more foreign involvement in Malaysia's economy and further integrated Malaysia into the international economy.

The final initiative that illustrates Malaysia's adoption of globalization measures involves the creation of the Multimedia Super Corridor (MSC). This plan was launched with fanfare in 1996 with the aim of making Malaysia a regional center for information technology. Even as far back as 1990, Mahathir had highlighted the importance of technology in his Vision 2020 memorandum:

> [Malaysia faces] the challenge of establishing a scientific and progressive society, . . . one that is not only a consumer of technology but also a contributor to the scientific and technological civilization of the future.[23]

Technology transfers had been part of the arrangements with foreign investors in the electronic and automobile industries in the 1980s. As Greg Felker points out, the Malaysian government introduced a wide series of measures to attract technology, including tapping into the regional integration of Northeast and Southeast Asian economies.[24] Yet with the introduction of the MSC, Malaysia took a step to connect itself to what was perceived as the most cutting-edge industry in economic development.[25] The aim was to create a "multimedia utopia" in which the flow of foreign investment into this high-tech community would foster the creativity of Malaysia's skilled workers and move the country into the millennium as part of the information age. Tim Bunnell points out that this plan was closely tied to the ideas associated with globalization.[26] The MSC would operate in a world in which "borders are disappearing due to ease of global communications, capital flows, the movement of goods and people and the location of operational headquarters." Accompanying measures, foreign capital, labor, and technology transfers supported the closer interconnectedness between Malaysia and the global economy. Each of these three deepening measures— labor flows, portfolio capital liberalization, and the creation of the MSC— represented a diversification of the economy and a stronger tie to the process and neoliberal ideas supporting globalization. The bond between the Chinese Malaysians and the regime strengthened even further. In 1995, the UMNO-led government received record support from Chinese Malaysians.[27] The prominence of cronies also persisted, although the benefits were distributed more widely.[28] The policies continued a trend of openness to and dependence on foreign capital. By 1995, foreign capital became the most important factor contributing to growth in Malaysia, even greater than in the neighboring countries of Thailand and Indonesia. The 1995 *World Investment Report* showed that the ratio of foreign investment to gross capital formation in Malaysia was very high, 24.6. In Thailand and Indonesia, the ratio was 4.7 and 4.5, respectively. Greg Felker's study provides a concrete example of this transformation:

> In the late 1980s, Matsushita selected Malaysia as its chief off-shore production platform in Asia for global and regional markets. . . . From 1987 to 1995, Matsushita established thirteen new wholly-owned subsidiaries. These included enormous aircondition and color television complexes; a range of components plants, including scroll compressors, condensers, and television cathode ray tubes; a mold and die design unit; and a separate R&D facility for the air conditioner complex. By the late 1980s, the Matsushita group's turnover accounted for an estimated 4 percent of Malaysia's entire GDP, and by 1995, it employed 23,500 staff and produced 25 percent of its parent company's overseas production and the same proportion of its total global output of air conditioners and televisions.[29]

This investment was accompanied by economic expansion. Through 1996, the growth rate averaged 8 percent annually. With its developed infrastructure, political stability, and impressive record of economic performance, Malaysia was one of the most attractive countries for investment in Asia.

PREFERRING AN ASIAN SEA: PRIORITIZING "ASIAN VALUES" AND REGIONAL ALLIANCES

While Malaysia reached out widely to the international community, there was a change in its relationship with the West that coincided with increased globalization. The most obvious change involved rising conflict between the U.S. policy of democratization and Malaysia's articulation of semiauthoritarian rule. In 1987, under Operation Lalang, Malaysia arrested over 100 political activists, effectively closing the door on the political openness that Mahathir had introduced in 1981.[30] The arrests represented a marked change in the political context in which the government would increase its monitoring of the NGO sector and articulate an "Asian values" defense in the face of rising criticism over human rights abuses.[31] The government began to identify itself with "Asia," as opposed to the Western powers, and attempted to limit the political influence from the West in order to protect the government from criticism. The globalization of political dialogue was allowed to extend only to the point that it did not threaten the Malaysian leadership.

This anti-Western attitude also translated into economic policy. With the adoption of the "Look East" and "Buy British Last" policies in the 1980s, the Malaysian government signaled that it began to look toward a new regional hegemon, Japan, for economic leadership.[32] Japan's economic success served as model for Malaysia's economic development and its capital underscored Malaysia's economic expansion.[33] The government began to form trade zones with its neighbors in the late 1980s. In 1989, the government introduced its own regional trading bloc, East Asian Economic Cooperation, that excluded the United States. The Malaysian government allied itself with China and Japan in an effort to curb American influence in the region. By 1995, the relationship with the West had changed. Despite the shift toward a more autonomous position, the economic tie between Malaysia and the West remained strong. American companies were the main investors in the semiconductor industry, which remained the main source of industrial expansion in Malaysia.[34] The political relationship was clearly not as warm as it had been in the Cold War era. Mahathir was seen to hamper American interests on trade liberalization, and his government was seen as increasingly undemocratic. These changes had broader significance for understanding Malaysia's current relationship with globalization; Malaysia's leaders were willing to distance themselves from the West and Western models of development for their own perceived interests.

STRUGGLING IN THE SURF: REDEFINING GLOBALIZATION

Losing Control

Although not explicitly stated as such, the Malaysian government has adopted policies to foster globalization since the 1980s. By 1996, Malaysia was ranked the tenth most competitive economy by the World Economic Forum. The changes had occurred in a highly extensive and intensive manner. These policies continued the early adoption of orthodox ideas to promote economic development that began even before the globalization measures were implemented in Malaysia in the mid-1980s; they have a distinctly Asian regional focus. It is important to note, however, that throughout the years of embracing globalization, the timing and scope of globalization initiatives were controlled by the Malaysian state; from 1981 through 1996, the Malaysian state, led by Mahathir and the technocrats around him in the Economic Planning Unit, selected which policies to promote and when. They strategically reacted to the international environment to address their goal of economic development and made adjustments to correspond to the perceived importance of regional ties. The Malaysian state was in control and able to filter globalization to meet its own goals.

With the onset of the financial crisis in the summer of 1997, the Malaysian state was no longer in control of global forces; it could not channel capital, labor, technology, or political criticism effectively. The rapid devaluation of the Malaysian ringgit in a contagion effect that swept through Southeast Asia undercut the expansion of the country's economy and threatened to undermine years of successful economic development. The immediate reaction on the part of Malaysia's leadership was to redefine "globalization," to abandon the neoliberal ideas that had served as the foundation of Vision 2020 and the MSC, and to reinterpret the term in a different form.[35]

The word "globalization" had become a common part of Malaysian political discourse in the mid-1990s. Mahathir first used the term in his published speech in 1994 (ironically) to promote the expansion of capital markets.[36] In that speech, he focused on globalization as a process that involved opening the economy to the global environment. It was not until 1996, however, in a speech titled "Globalization—What It Means to Small Nations," that he began to redefine the term. There he identified with the view that held that globalization was tied to the decrease in power of nation-states and posed a threat to developing countries. He viewed the process of globalization as one dominated by the West. In his words,

> The breaking down of borders will result in the powerful truly dominating the weak. . . . A globalised world is not going to be a very democratic world. A globalised world is going to belong to the powerful dominant countries.[37]

For Mahathir, "globalization" now posed a potential threat to Malaysia. This sharply contradicted his previous policies fostering greater global interconnectedness and his speeches in favor of the MSC.

The Attack on Globalization

After the onset of the Asian financial crisis, Mahathir built on his concerns about inequality in the international community and the importance of regional autonomy and further developed his own interpretation of "globalization." He labeled globalization as "unfettered" and associated globalization with currency traders. In two publications—*In the Face of Attack: Currency Turmoil* and *Hidden Agenda*—and nearly fifty speeches, Mahathir used the term "globalization" as criticism of the events that occurred from July 1997 onwards.[38] With speeches titled "Market Forces Are Sacrosanct," "Massive Loss of Wealth," "Currency Manipulation," and "Free Market Ideology," the attack on neoliberal ideology of globalization and emergence of a unique conceptualization of globalization rhetoric had arrived. He said, "Globalization is a great idea whose time has come. But it must be interpreted correctly if it is going to bring about a better world."[39]

This new interpretation of globalization had three distinct elements. First, he challenged the role of the market as an unchecked force:

> Market forces are not meant to bring benefits, to improve governments, financial management and practices of the countries under attack. Market forces are driven ultimately by huge profits. It is all right if something favorable happens. But benefits, if they do occur, are merely side issues.[40]

Moreover, he emphasized inequality in the international capitalist system:

> The net result of the globalised, deregulated world would be the emergence of huge corporations and banks with branches in every country in the world. Their numbers

would not be too big as all the small companies and banks would have been acquired or absorbed in one way or another. . . . Today it is not the exploitation of local labour that is the focus of new capitalists. It is the exploitation of the poor countries world-wide that promises unlimited gains.[41]

The third dimension of his rhetoric is anti-Western and perceived Western domination. Again, in his own words,

Do remember, those who created the economic turmoil that we are facing now are just like the colonialists who once colonised us. Do not think their behavior has changed.[42]

Globalization more than anything means Westernisation and the acceptance of Western business standards and political systems around the world.[43]

As Philip Kelly points out, Mahathir evoked images of warfare.[44] He focused his attack on the West. He blamed the Western media and currency speculators, notably Hungarian businessman George Soros, for Malaysia's economic difficulties. In his view, the Western media portrayed Malaysia negatively, while currency traders exploited Malaysian capital markets for their own gains.[45] While the rhetoric echoes back to the dependency era, Mahathir's new view of globalization formed a unique interpretation of globalization that emerged from local and international conditions, namely, a previous loosening of ties with the West and the Asian financial crisis.

The reasons for this ideological interpretation of globalization are complex, yet two stand out.[46] By redefining globalization in a new form, he could distance himself from the problems that he had initiated as the leading advocate for embracing globalization. Recall that Malaysia had liberalized its own portfolio market to encourage foreign investment. This is not to say that Mahathir was willing to accept any culpability in contributing to the crisis, but rather the new form of rhetoric gave Mahathir more space to direct blame on external actors. In this regard, "globalization" as redefined by Mahathir became an "escape valve" for dissatisfaction with the changes in Malaysia. As recently as October 1999, Mahathir blamed "globalization" for undercutting the benefits of the Malay community.[47] External threats rather than domestic choices were undermining the welfare of Malaysia. The new interpretation of globalization protected the existing Malaysian leadership.

The second reason for the redefinition of globalization involved a growing political conflict within Malaysia that was triggered by the Asian financial crisis. Different views of "globalization" became intertwined in Mahathir's political battle with then–Deputy Prime Minister Anwar Ibrahim for leadership of the Malay community.[48] In the UMNO General Assembly in July 1998, supporters of Anwar called on Mahathir to increase transparency in the government and address corruption. These themes were perceived to be linked to the neoliberal ideas supported in the West and international lending institutions, notably the IMF. In

Mahathir's response, he explicitly called for Malaysians to be "suspicious" and "beware" of globalization. He implicitly called his challenger (Anwar Ibrahim) an "agent of foreign powers" and used the themes he developed in his own view of globalization to discredit Anwar.

> Irrespective of who is successful, the attack on the country will continue until a leader is chosen, one who will submit to the wishes of the foreign powers, that is prepared to have his country once again recolonised.[49]

In February 2000, he continued tying globalization to his attack on domestic challenges to his leadership when he reminded civil servants that a potential tie with the West would undermine the future of Malaysia. He added, "I'm not saying this to frighten you into giving the government political support. What I'm saying is really happening."[50] The different views of globalization—one seen allied to neoliberal ideas and the other redefining globalization as a threatening force—underscored the ideological differences between the two men in a domestic power struggle.

GETTING OUT OF THE WATER: REJECTING GLOBALIZATION?

Mixing Globalization and Politics

The move from redefining "globalization" as a threat paved the way for the rejection of globalization in economic policy and even stronger rejection of political challenges. More than any other nation in Asia, with perhaps the exception of North Korea, Malaysia has attempted to carve out an independent position that rejects many of the ideas and policies associated with globalization. This change in attitude toward globalization was best illustrated with the domestic political crisis within the Malay leadership and the implementation of capital controls in September 1998. Yet the rejection of globalization began earlier and included reversing the flow of foreign labor into Malaysia. The rejection of globalization is not complete, however, and is riddled with contradictions. Like the previous policy choices, however, it seems that the rejection of globalization has benefited the Malaysian leadership, especially Mahathir, at least in the short term.

The political crisis and the corresponding implementation of capital controls evolved slowly. For one year after the financial crisis occurred, Malaysia struggled to find a solution to its deepening economic problems. In the first few months of the crisis, Malaysia denied the existence of a problem and focused its criticism on external actors, especially currency traders. It was at this time, in the summer and fall of 1997, that Mahathir redefined "globalization" to challenge the attacks on Malaysia. In December 1997, the government introduced a series of reforms that increased interest rates and curtailed credit.[51] The package, introduced by then–Finance Minister Anwar Ibrahim, also involved cutting spending and followed the recommendations of international lending institutions. While not as comprehensive as the IMF-supported packages introduced in Korea and Thailand since it did not include financial restructuring, it followed the accepted international norms of what to do when faced by economic difficulties. The response tied into many of the ideas favoring globalization: Improve your economic management and this will, in turn, improve investor confidence and attract foreign capital. In January 1998, the government created the National Economic Recovery Council, chaired by former finance minister Daim Zainuddin, which implemented the plan.

Unfortunately, the reform package did little to stop the decline of the economy. In fact, by the middle of the summer of 1998, conditions were worse in Malaysia than they were the year before. In 1997, the economy contracted by 6.7 percent, and unemployment increased. Malaysians were tapping into their savings, and the banking sector was in deep trouble as a result of domestic debt.

At this time, the economic crisis transformed itself into a political crisis. It is important to understand that earlier policies that promoted globalization and Malaysia's economic difficulties significantly contributed to this crisis. Anwar had been coopted into the government in 1983 as part of Mahathir's increased political openness. He also was closely tied into increasing Islamization in Malaysian society as a result of wider global exchanges. Finally, Anwar as finance minister was closely allied with international institutions (the IMF) and had a better relationship with the United States. He gained influence as a result of global interconnectedness and being an advocate of neoliberal policies promoted by the West. Mahathir, in contrast, had limited political openness from 1987 onward and had challenged the West and Islam at home.[52] Moreover, he used the difficulties brought about by changes in the global environment to support his leadership challenge.

The brewing differences between Mahathir and Anwar came to the surface in the heated UMNO general assembly meeting in July 1998. Anwar's push for power coincided with Daim's introduction of a National Economic Recovery Plan (NERP), which had a slightly different emphasis than the reforms promoted by Anwar in that NERP focused on currency stabilization and did not advocate spending reductions. Anwar recognized that his own policy prescriptions, supported by the IMF, were not in favor. The deepening crisis gave Anwar the chance that he had been looking for. The May resignation of Suharto in Indonesia convinced Anwar that a leadership challenge was viable. With Anwar's arrest in late September 1998, the Malaysian government showed that it had categorically rejected what Anwar had come to represent: a close tie to the West, deepening of Islam, greater transparency, and more political openness. Mahathir had moved from redefining globalization to rejecting it.

Economic Policy Changes

The attack on globalization moved beyond Anwar and translated into economic policy. Malaysia's capital controls, introduced shortly before Anwar's arrest, placed restrictions on the flow of money in and out of the country. The focus was on short-term capital or portfolio capital. The Malaysian government pegged the exchange rate and tightened its regulations of the flow of investment and portfolio capital.[53] The policy was widely seen as a challenge to the market and international financial institutions such as the IMF that advocated a more transparent and open financial sector, both measures that were deemed as "Western." The policy was based on the premise that consumption in the domestic market would stabilize the economy. The capital control policy reversed a long-standing tradition of openness to foreign capital and threatened to undermine future economic growth; by sending out a loud signal that the country was restricting the flow of capital, the Malaysian government potentially undermined future foreign investment in Malaysia. This was particularly precarious since so much of the economy depended on foreign investment for expansion. Yet, as it had earlier, the Malaysian state defined its relationship with the global economy on its own terms, choosing to buffer itself from the volatility of fickle international investors.

The world's reaction to this measure was mixed. In the West, capital controls were widely criticized as foolhardy, leading to short-term benefits at best. *Time* magazine, for example, in an article titled "Moving in the Wrong Direction," called the policies "capital isolationism" that was "nothing short of disaster."[54] Others were more hopeful, believing that the measures might protect the Malaysian economy from the regional downslide and offer a respite from the close scrutiny of foreign investors. Within Malaysia, the measures received broad support since they allowed Malaysians to recoup their losses and lowered inflation. There were, however, some serious concerns about whether the measures were introduced to bail out Malaysian companies tied to the country's leaders, namely, Renong.[55]

In the last year, the effect of this policy has been generally positive, contributing to lower inflation, comparatively lower unemployment, and a seeming economic recovery. Paul Krugman argues that this policy has promoted investor confidence in Malaysia and dampened the social costs of the financial crisis.[56] Malaysia's economy did bounce back and was projected by the World Bank to achieve over 3 percent economic growth in 1999. In the fall of 1999, both the World Bank and the IMF publicly acknowledged that capital controls had worked. In the course of 1998–1999, the government began to relax some of the restrictions on capital controls. By September 1999, the government had removed all the regulations on investment capital and severely reduced the restrictions on portfolio capital. Malaysia's global competitiveness ranking by the World Economic Forum increased to sixteen (from seventeen) in 1998, making it the highest-ranked Southeast Asian economy.

A closer look at capital controls reveals that the measures did seem to work, but for reasons that were unanticipated.[57] In the few months of capital controls, Malaysia's economy expanded as a result of agricultural exports, notably palm oil. The prices for these goods were set in U.S. dollars. The lower exchange rate for the Malaysian ringgit brought in unanticipated profits. In the second half of 1999, the Malaysian economy expanded through growth in industry. Companies in Malaysia streamlined and expanded production. Manufacturing grew by 14 percent in the first three quarters of 1999. The rejuvenation of the electronics sector was particularly important. Consumption in the domestic market was incidental to the success of these measures.

The rejection of globalization went beyond capital controls and included the repatriation of foreign labor. In the early months of the economic crisis, the Malaysian government opted to repatriate over 500,000 Indonesian workers. Many of the Indonesian workers were forced to leave when their jobs were removed. This was particularly evident in the construction sector, which virtually dried up with the withdrawal of government support. The forced repatriation followed a trend set earlier of repatriation of Bangladeshi workers in the mid-1990s, when there were slowdowns in the semiconductor industry. The Malaysian economy's use of foreign labor gave it a buffer that the other Southeast Asian economies lacked. The retrenchment of the manufacturing sector in Malaysia did not lead to a significant increase in Malaysian unemployment. The majority of workers who lost their jobs were foreign laborers.

The repatriation of foreign labor was widely accepted in Malaysia. Foreign workers faced difficult conditions in the country. In the construction of the Petronas Twin Towers, for example, over twenty Indonesian workers died. Safety standards were not as tightly regulated in industries hiring non-Malaysians. Many workers were also heavily indebted to the agents who brought workers into the country, often illegally. Foreign migrants lacked the ability to reach out to the authorities for protection. In Malaysian society, foreign workers became the scapegoat for rising crime. The rise in robberies was attributed to the increase in foreign migration. Malaysian society as a whole accepted the forced return of the workers without protest. Like the policy of capital controls, the government chose to reject a critical dimension of the globalization process to meet its own domestic interests.

Lingering Questions

It should be noted that the adoption of these three measures should not be equated with a complete rejection of globalization. The Malaysian government reiterated its commitment to the MSC and offered a new set of incentives in its 1999 and 2000 budgets to attract foreign capital. With the onset of the financial crisis, the government pursued new avenues to attract investors into information technology, including an investment of $790 million on infrastructure and a commitment of five to ten years of tax breaks for companies.[58] The government has also walked a fine line in its censorship of the Internet and recently allowed a Web site critical of the government (malaysiakini.com) to continue to operate, even as it censored other forms of the media.[59] Recent reports suggest that these measures have paid off; according to *FEER,* the MSC is comprised of 187 companies (34 percent foreign owned) that employ over 9,000 people and have invested over half a billion dollars in the MSC.[60] The Malaysian government remains open to elements of the globalization process that it perceives as vital to its future economic growth.

This effort to maintain a commitment to information technology stands in stark contrast to the imposition of capital controls and foreign labor repatriation. There seems to be a deep contradiction in Malaysia's economic policy. Capital controls have led to a downturn in foreign direct investment, contributing to a 27 percent reduction in the inflow of foreign capital between 1997 and 1998.[61] Capital controls have eroded investor confidence, especially new sources of capital. Yet Malaysia's economic development remains highly dependent on foreign capital. There are real concerns whether capital controls will be successful over the long term. Similarly, Malaysia's economy also relies on cheap labor, which cannot be sustained without opening the country to the external environment. The country will need to allow foreign migration to maintain its competitiveness. The long-term rejection of globalization in the form of capital controls and labor repatriation will undermine the future growth of the economy.

Beyond the issues of attracting foreign capital and labor, the government has made some choices in its adoption of an independent course that may threaten confidence in the economy. The government has carried out bailouts to address domestic debt. Lacking access to IMF funds, the government has used public funds from oil revenue and spent billions to bail out Renong and Bank Bumiputra, among others. For some analysts, the rejection of globalization through capital controls is seen as a strategic effort to benefit his closest allies. This has created a moral hazard that may undermine international credibility, especially if there is a reversal in Malaysia's economic fortunes.

The rejection of globalization embedded in the Anwar–Mahathir conflict has also had political costs. From police brutality to sodomy charges and reports of arsenic poisoning, the conflict between Mahathir and Anwar Ibrahim has severely damaged Malaysia's international reputation and the credibility of the leadership. Internationally, the relationship with the West has cooled. Mahathir has become the "pariah" of Southeast Asia. The comments of U.S. Vice President Al Gore at the Asian Pacific Economic Council (APEC) summit of November 1998 in support of pro-Anwar protesters were widely criticized in Malaysia but praised in the United States. Recently, tensions between Malaysia and the United States have increased. The 1999 *U.S. Department of State Report* was highly critical of the rising human rights violations in Malaysia, which include the arrest of leading opposition figures.[62] In March 2000, the U.S. government indicated that relations with Malaysia were not going to improve until its leadership had addressed concerns about the judiciary and human rights violations. These developments indicate a brewing conflict with Western nations that extends to include Britain and

Australia as well.[63] Malaysia is likely to focus its international ties on developing regional links, probably in the form of a regional trading bloc, such as that proposed in the November 1999 ASEAN meeting. Current international conditions will make Malaysia more dependent on its authoritarian allies, especially China. At home, Mahathir has lost support among the Malay community. A political movement inspired by Anwar's arrest, known as "Reformasi," formed a political party called Keadilan. In existence less than nine months, this party won five seats in Malaysia's tenth general election on November 29, 1999. Anwar's wife won her seat decisively. At the same time, the support among Malays for Mahathir's own party, UMNO, decreased. The other Malay opposition party, PAS (the Islamic party), gained control over the oil-rich state government of Trengganu and picked up seats in other Malay areas. While Mahathir won the election, he lost significant Malay support. He has had to make new allies. He is now more dependent on Chinese Malaysians, who continued to support him in record numbers. This support is an extension of earlier policies initiated in the early 1990s and Malaysia's economic recovery since 1997. Yet the new political alignments in Malaysia point to potential problems. Traditionally, the leadership is dependent on Malays, who make up 60 percent of the population, for political legitimacy. Mahathir lacks the legitimacy that he once had among the majority of the population. Moreover, he will have to initiate policies to appease the Chinese Malaysians, which may further undermine his support among Malays. All of this will threaten political stability and, if current indicators continue, suggest a greater reliance on coercion and increasing authoritarian rule to maintain his leadership.

The 1999 elections hide a deeper issue in Malaysian politics: generational conflict. The new generation of Malaysians, newly registered under twenty-five (especially Malays who have a higher birthrate) and largely excluded from voting in November, are increasingly dissatisfied with the government and want a more open political environment. Having grown up with economic prosperity, their attention is focusing on opening the political environment and, with the pervasiveness of Islamic thought, on concerns of morality, which the current government is seen to undermine. Their views are different than older Malaysians. Without the support of younger voters, the government will lack the stability of earlier years. It remains to be seen whether Malaysia can address the contradictions it has created in its own economy and political system and reconcile different approaches to globalization.

REFLECTIONS

Over the last twenty years, the Malaysian state has adopted very different approaches to globalization. From 1981 through 1997, Malaysia became the "poster country" for globalization. The country opened up politically and privatized and liberalized its economy. These changes led to a variety of consequences within Malaysia, including short-lived political openness, new political alliances, and impressive economic growth, and deepened the country's dependence on foreign capital. Throughout there was an Asian regional bias in the policies promoting globalization. With the Asian financial crisis, Malaysia's strategy changed, first ideologically and then with a political crackdown on a leadership challenge and policy reversals. Ironically, the rejection of globalization has continued the domestic political realignments and buttressed Malaysia's economic growth, at least in the short term. To date, Malaysian leaders have reacted to international conditions in ways that protect their own interests. More than anything, the Malaysian experience illustrates that small states can adapt to the pressures of an interconnected world.

Recent changes in the attitude and policies toward globalization have created many contradictions and costs. The long-term consequences of these are not clear. In the short term, these consequences are mixed. Domestically, the political landscape has changed. With a fragmented Malay community and cronyism, Malaysia is not as stable or democratic as it once was. Over 40 percent of Malaysians voted against the current leadership in the November 1999 election. The government did not receive an overwhelming new mandate. Internationally, the country has gained both respect and disdain. If the Malaysian leadership is able to address the domestic turmoil and continue to react to international conditions strategically, it may become a model for other developing countries. The real test will be whether Mahathir is a strong enough swimmer to resolve the political and economic contradictions. As it stands now, the current contradictions may yet sink a small state trying to float in an increasingly globalized world.

NOTES

1. For example, "globalization" was debated at a conference sponsored by the National University of Malaysia in the spring of 1998 and is the subject of a forthcoming edited volume from that conference.

2. See James Mittelman, ed., *Globalization: Critical Reflections* (Boulder, Colo.: Lynne Rienner, 1996).

3. For example, this view was incorporated in the widely debated 1993 World Bank study, *The East Asian Miracle: Economic Growth and Public Policy* (New York: Oxford University Press, 1993).

4. See Abdul Rahman Embong, "Pembinaan Bangsa Dalam Arus Persejagatan," *Pemikir* (January–March 1997): 53–69.

5. David Held and Anthony McGrew, eds., *Global Transformations: Politics, Economics, and Culture* (Stanford, Calif: Stanford University Press, 1999), 10.

6. See Bridget Welsh, "The Political Economy of the Malaysian Tax Regime of the 1980s" (paper presented at the Southeast Asia in the Twentieth Century conference, University of the Philippines, Quezon City, January 28, 1998).

7. See D. Mauzy and R. S. Milne, "The Mahathir Administration: Discipline through Islam," *Pacific Affairs* 56, no. 4 (1983–1984): 617–48, and R. S. Milne and D. Mauzy, *Malaysian Politics under Mahathir* (New York: Routledge, 1999), 28–49.

8. See Murugesu Pathmanathan and David Lazarus, eds., *Winds of Change: The Mahathir Impact on Malaysia's Foreign Policy* (Kuala Lumpur: Eastview Productions, 1984), and J. Saravanamuttu, "Malaysia's Foreign Policy in the Mahathir Period, 1981–1995: An Iconoclast Comes to Rule," *Asian Journal of Political Science* 4, no. 1 (1996): 1–16.

9. Government of Malaysia, "The Way Forward: Vision 2020," Sixth Malaysia Plan (1990), 3.

10. Government of Malaysia, "The Way Forward: Vision 2020," 5.

11. Government of Malaysia, "The Way Forward: Vision 2020," 9.

12. Government of Malaysia, "The Way Forward: Vision 2020," 154.

13. K. S. Jomo, *Privatizing Malaysia: Rents, Rhetoric, Realities* (Boulder, Colo.: Westview, 1995).

14. See Edmund Terence Gomez and K. S. Jomo, *Malaysia's Political Economy: Politics, Patronage, and Profits* (New York: Cambridge University Press, 1997).

15. See D. Geoffrey and S. D. Stafford, "Malaysia's New Economic Policy and the Global Economy: The Evolution of Ethnic Accommodation." *Pacific Review* 10, no. 4 (1997): 556–80.

16. Greg Felker, "Globalization and the State in Late Industrialization: The Malaysian and Thai Cases" (paper presented at the annual meeting of the American Political Science Association, Boston, September 3–6, 1998), 17.

17. See K. S. Jomo, ed., *Japan and Malaysian Development: In the Shadow of the Rising Sun* (New York: Routledge, 1994).

18. See K. S. Jomo and Patricia Todd, *Trade Unions and the State in Peninsular Malaysia* (Kuala Lumpur: Oxford University Press, 1994).

19. See Anja Rudnick, *Foreign Labor in Malaysian Manufacturing* (Kuala Lumpur: INSAN, 1996).

20. Lee Hong Min, "Foreign Labor in Malaysia" (master's thesis, University of Wales, 1999).

21. The construction sector grew at a rate of 15 percent per year in the early 1990s.

22. Ong Hong Cheong, "Evolution of the Malaysian Financial System beyond the Financial Crisis," in S. Masutama et al., eds., *East Asia's Financial Systems: Evolution and Crisis* (Singapore: ISEAS Institute of Southeast Asian Studies, 1999), 144-65.

23. Government of Malaysia, "The Way Forward: Vision 2020," 27.

24. Felker, "Globalization and the State in Late Industrialization," 18–20.

25. Tim Bunnell, "Multimedia Utopia? A Geographical Critique of IT Discourse in Malaysia" (paper presented at the Second International Malaysian Studies Conference, University of Malaya, Kuala Lumpur, Malaysia, August 2–4, 1999).

26. Tim Bunnell points to the close connection in the early 1990s between Mahathir and Kenichi Ohmae, who is a leading advocate of the "borderless" exchange of information technology and an important advocate of neoliberal globalization ideas.

27. UMNO is the dominant Malay party that has led the coalitions that have governed Malaysia since independence.

28. See Gomez and Jomo, *Malaysia's Political Economy*.

29. Felker, "Globalization and the State in Late Industrialization," 24.

30. See Harold Crouch, *Government and Society in Malaysia* (Ithaca, N.Y.: Cornell University Press, 1996).

31. J. Bauer and D. Bell, *The East Asian Challenge for Human Rights* (New York: Cambridge University Press, 1999).

32. See Kit G. Machado, "Malaysian Cultural Relations with Japan and South Korea in the 1980s: Look East," *Asian Survey* 27, no. 6 (1987): 638–60.

33. See Jomo, *Japan and Malaysian Development*.

34. See Rajah Rasiah, *Foreign Capital and Industrialization in Malaysia* (London: Macmillan, 1995).

35. For this section, I examined Mahathir's published works written in the 1990s, including, most recently, *The New Deal for Asia* (Petaling Jaya: Pelanduk Publications, 1999). His speeches were compiled from the Prime Minister's Department Web site (<http://www.smpke.jpm.my>) and published versions in two of Malaysia's leading newspapers, the *New Straits Times* and *Berita Harian*. Mahathir has made over 2,000 speeches in his political career. I found over 150 speeches that used the term "globalization" or "globalisasi" in Bahasa Malaysia. All these speeches were written in the 1990s.

36. Speech by Mahathir, "The Opening of the Asian Capital Markets: Growth Frontiers Conference," Kuala Lumpur, Malaysia, June 20, 1994.

37. Speech by Mahathir, "Globalization—What It Means to Small Nations," July 24, 1996.

38. Mahathir Mohamad, *In the Face of Attack: Currency Turmoil* (Kuala Lumpur: Limkokwing Integrated, 1998), and *Hidden Agenda* (Kuala Lumpur: Limkokwing Integrated, 1998).

39. Speech by Mahathir, "Unfettered Globalization," in *In the Face of Attack: Currency Turmoil* (Kuala Lumpur: Limkokwing Integrated, 1998), 117.

40. Mahathir Mohamad, *The Challenges of Turmoil* (Petaling Jaya: Pelanduk Publications, 1998), 31.

41. Speech by Mahathir, "Future Asia in a Globalized and Deregulated World," in *In the Face of Attack*, 111.

42. Mahathir, *The Challenges of Turmoil*, 33.

43. Mahathir, *New Deal for Asia*, 40.

44. Philip Kelly, "Metaphors of Meltdown: Political Representations of Economic Space in the Asian Financial Crisis" (paper submitted to *State and Society* for review, 1999), 13–16.

45. See Mahathir, *Hidden Agenda*, 96–97.

46. See Bridget Welsh, "Globalization as Rhetoric: Malaysia's 'Political Discourse from Above'" (paper presented at the meeting of the Second International Malaysian Studies Association, Kuala Lumpur, August 1999).

47. "Shrinking Malay Benefits," *Star,* October 4, 1999.

48. See Sherri Prasso, "The Anwar-Mahathir Conflict," *Business Week,* February 1998.

49. Mahathir, *The Challenges of Turmoil*, 19.

50. "Globalization Makes West Richer, Poor Nations Poorer, says Dr. M." *Business Times,* February 25, 2000.

51. *Managing Economic Crisis: The Malaysian Experience* (Kuala Lumpur: Dato' Abdul Rashid Mahmud, 1999).

52. Through 1995, the government continued to encourage connections to the Islamic world, but this changed as well in 1995 with the arrest of the Al-Arqam group, which was

seen as threatening the leadership of the government. The government tried to limit international sources of local dissent.

53. See S. Haggard and L. Low, "The Politics of Capital Controls in Malaysia" (unpublished manuscript, 1999), and Prema-chandra Athukorala, "Swimming against the Tide: Crisis Management in Malaysia," in H. W. Arndt and H. Hill, *Southeast Asia's Economic Crisis: Origins, Lessons, and the Way Forward* (1999), 28-40.

54. D. Roche, "Moving in a Wrong Direction," *Time,* December 21, 1998.

55. K. S. Jomo, "Malaysia Props up Crony Capitalists," *Asian Wall Street Journal,* December 21, 1998.

56. Paul Krugman, "Capital Control Freaks: How Malaysia Got Away with Economic Heresy," *Slate,* September 27, 1999.

57. Comments by K. S. Jomo at the Second International Malaysian Studies Conference, August 4, 1999.

58. Simon Elegant and Murray Hiebert, "Tech Mecca," *Far East Economic Review,* March 16, 2000. See also "The Tiger and the Tech," *Economist,* February 5, 2000.

59. Robin Paul Ajello, "Politics.Com—Dr. M Meets New Media" *Asiaweek,* February 18, 2000.

60. Simon Elegant and Murray Hiebert, "Tech Mecca," *Far East Economic Review,* March 16, 2000.

61. *World Investment Report,* 1999. The inflow of foreign capital went from $5,106 million in 1997 to $3,727 in 1998.

62. U.S. Department of State, *1999 Country Reports on Human Rights Practices* (Washington, D.C.: Bureau of Democracy, Human Rights, and Labor, February 25, 2000).

63. "Learning to Live with Mahathir: Australia and Asia—At Peace or Adrift," *Australian,* March 4, 2000.

11

Globalization and Security in East Asia

Peter Van Ness

The objective of this chapter is to describe in broad-brush terms the main impacts of globalization on security issues in East Asia during the 1990s. Since this topic is much too large for a single chapter, I have restricted myself to discussing what seem to be the most important changes, since the collapse of the Soviet Union, among three major actors (the United States, Japan, and China) and the member countries of the Association of Southeast Asian Nations (ASEAN). I will also briefly mention Korea, Taiwan, and the South China Sea as the three geographic areas where most analysts believe interstate conflict is most likely to break out. I have excluded Russia from this discussion solely in order to narrow the topic to a more manageable size. Russia is clearly a major power in East Asia, but since the collapse of the Soviet Union, it has been playing a much diminished role.

I begin by defining the two key terms: "globalization" and "security." In short, I understand globalization as a multifaceted, structural phenomenon that has progressively intensified since the collapse of the Soviet Union and that appears to be reshaping understandings of security in the region. Among several important results is the emergence of new, essentially nonmilitary threats to regime survival and changing strategies to enhance security.

Following the discussion of definitions, I address, in turn, security in the region, old and new security threats, alternative security strategies, and implications for the future. The period under investigation is the 1990s, or what is usually called the post–Cold War era. Our story begins after the breakup of the Soviet Union, but we should keep in mind the events that led to its collapse. Was the Soviet Union the first major victim of globalization? Does the fall of the Suharto regime in Indonesia show similar features? Does the Chinese Communist Party (CCP) leadership, for example, infer that this is one of the main threats to its hold on power?

Clearly, one lesson that security policymakers should have learned from the events of the past decade is to expect the unexpected. Our old ways of thinking about security have not prepared us for unexpected events such as the collapse of the Soviet Union, the East Asian financial crisis, India's and Pakistan's nuclear tests that Western intelligence services failed to anticipate, and the fall of Suharto, previously thought to be one of the most firmly entrenched leaders in the region. Environmental disasters, such as the Taiwan earthquake of September 1999, reemphasize the general point: Expect the unexpected.

DEFINITION OF KEY TERMS

"Globalization"

I conceive of globalization as those "human activities that have a reshaping planetary impact." I have in mind a combination of historical, economic, military, environmental, and technological factors. Let me briefly introduce each category and then attempt to weave them into a more integrated whole.

History. Indispensable to this concept of globalization is an understanding that contemporary global relationships have their roots in the 500-year history of Western expansion and conquest of the world. The interstate and transnational relations of today have been shaped by the history of imperialism, colonialism, wars of national liberation, and struggles for self-determination between what Kishore Mahbubani has called "The West and the Rest." In my opinion, it is not possible to understand contemporary debates about human rights, economic inequality, national security, or global power relationships without placing the analysis firmly in the context of this history.

Economics. All analysts agree that globalization is an economic phenomenon. Most analyses describe globalization as essentially the result of increasing market participation by virtually all countries in the world plus the growing impact of rapidly changing information technologies.[1] International trade, investment, foreign aid, and technological transfer within an international division of labor increasingly shaped by the power of multinational corporations (MNCs) and liberalized capital and currency markets have made economic competitiveness a universal concern. For any country that wants to modernize and increase its material standard of living, there now appears to be no alternative but to join the cutthroat competition of the global capitalist market—to put on what Thomas L. Friedman calls "the golden straitjacket" of economic reforms to make its economy as competitive as possible.[2]

Military. The nuclear age began with the atomic bombings of Hiroshima and Nagasaki in August 1945, but it was not until the United States and the Soviet Union achieved a capacity to destroy each other completely that it could accurately be said that nuclear weapons had a planetary impact. Often today, nuclear weapons are lumped together with chemical and biological weapons in a category of "weapons of mass destruction." However, although chemical and biological warfare can cause terrible casualties, it is only the quality and quantity of nuclear weapons, so far, that have the capacity to destroy civilizations. Fear of the destructive power of nuclear weapons has altered global strategic calculations, making the Cold War unique when compared to earlier military confrontations.[3] The global "peace" maintained by the strategic standoff among the world's nuclear powers is also a key element of what we call globalization.

Ecology. Rapid industrialization has begun to affect the capacity of the global ecological system to support human life on the planet. Evidence of the planetary effects of pollution and other forms of ecological deterioration, such as species elimination, the greenhouse effect, global warming, and ozone depletion, all contribute to the realization by inhabitants of the planet that we share a common fate and future. Regional events, such as air pollution from the Indonesian forest fires in 1997 that affected public health and economic enterprises in neighboring Malaysia, Singapore, and Brunei, demonstrate the limits of self-help strategies by individual countries in attempting to deal with these environmental dangers. Increasingly, it has become clear that the world cannot forever seek to solve problems of material sufficiency and equity by encouraging more and more economic growth. There are ecological limits to what the planet can bear.

Science and technology. The driving force behind all these factors is the power of modern science and technological development. Friedman points especially to changes in "how we communicate, how we invest, and how we learn about the world."[4] All analysts acknowledge the significance of information technology in reshaping how we live, and Bill Gates of the Microsoft Corporation predicts that the pace of change in information technologies will further increase in the future.

David Held and his colleagues argue that "far from this being a world of 'discrete civilizations,' or simply an international society of states, it has become a fundamentally interconnected global order, marked by intense patterns of exchange as well as by clear patterns of power, hierarchy, and unevenness."[5] The United Nations Development Program (UNDP), in its understanding of globalization, emphasizes who gets what ("global progress" versus "global deprivation").[6] In this analysis, I understand globalization as a particular context in which states, social organizations, and individuals seek to enhance their security.

Clearly, globalization is controversial, as the demonstrations against the 1999 Seattle meeting of the World Trade Organization (WTO) illustrated. There are winners and losers in this new globalized environment. On balance, it would seem that the most powerful, the most internationalized and innovative, and the most competitive in world markets gain the most. However, globalization has a variety of impacts through different levels of society right down to the individual (including influences on sexuality, marriage, and the family), as Anthony Giddens has shown in his 1999 Reith Lectures.[7]

"Security"

Defining "security" is even more problematic. Muthiah Alagappa, in his edited volume *Asian Security Practice,* suggests a typology for analyzing security comprised of five key elements: referent (whose security are we talking about?), core values to be protected, types of threats, nature of the security problem, and approaches to enhancing security.[8] Making decisions about the first is probably the most difficult, and choices made about whose security is at stake obviously shape the other key elements. Is the principal task to protect the security of the individual citizen, the national society, the regime in power, or the state?

Denny Roy has shown how each of these four different referents can threaten the security of the others:

> Individuals may endanger the state (via treason, sabotage, espionage, and fifth column activities), the regime (through dissent, agitation, insurrection, and assassination), or the nation (via hate crimes). Nations may be a threat to individuals (such as cases of persecution of minorities), the state (via separatism and ethnic nationalism), or the regime (when an ethnic minority controls the government—to the objection of the majority). The regime is often a threat to individuals (extrajudicial detention, execution, torture, or poor social or economic policies that cause the masses to suffer) and occasionally to a nation (genocide) as well. The state can threaten individuals (through a system of government that restricts civil liberties) or even nations (by boundaries that create multistate nations or isolated ethnic minorities).[9]

Since in most studies of security issues, the subject of analysis becomes the decisions made by national policymakers, almost inevitably the implied referent for those studies is regime security, the policymakers' preoccupation. In this analysis, I also focus mainly on the problems of regime security. During the decade of the 1990s, however, policymakers everywhere in East Asia became aware that regime security was in turn dependent on their fulfilling certain requirements for individual citizens and the national society. The UNDP has specified these requirements in terms of a concept of "human security."[10]

For the UNDP, human security essentially means individual "freedom from fear and freedom from want." They argue that conventional concepts of security must be changed from "an exclusive stress on territorial security to a much greater stress on people's security" and from "security through armaments to security through sustainable human development." The UNDP's list of component needs includes economic security, food security, health security, environmental security, personal security, community security, and political security.[11] Agreeing, Chung-In Moon draws the following lesson from his analysis of South Korean security: "The existence of military tensions does not necessarily justify the primacy of the military security. Military threats are always prominent. But economic, ecological, and social security concerns can be just as pressing and vital as the military issue."[12]

Emphasis on human rights in the foreign policies of Western countries, especially since the Tiananmen student-led demonstrations in China in 1989 and the Beijing massacre, has pressed authoritarian governments in East Asia to give greater priority to the "human security" of their citizens. After the collapse of the Soviet Union, the Cold War enemy, anticommunist authoritarian governments in the region found that their claims to serving as bulwarks in defense of the "Free World" no longer made them immune from criticism for domestic human rights atrocities. Their support was no longer seen to be indispensable in the global anticommunist crusade. On the contrary, as we will see, for some East Asian governments Western emphasis on democracy and human rights began to be perceived as an ideological threat to their regime security.

Finally, at the level of state security, the breaking apart of Yugoslavia and of the Soviet Union has raised fears about the territorial integrity of other multiethnic nations. The vote by the people of East Timor for independence in August 1999, the subsequent Indonesian military-led scorched-earth policy, and the UN decision to support a multinational intervention force to establish order and defend the survivors have made the territorial integrity of the state yet another important security concern in the region.

In sum, for the purposes of this chapter, "security" will be defined principally in terms of regime survival. An effort is made, however, to incorporate the security concerns of other referents where feasible.

SECURITY IN EAST ASIA

East Asia is strategically important from a global perspective because of the interests that major powers (the United States, China, Japan, and Russia) have identified in the region. It is often understood to be especially volatile because of the number of wars that have been fought there during the last century and because of the lack of multilateral institutions in the region designed to enhance cooperation. However, interstate relations in East Asia over the past two decades, and especially since 1989, have been quite stable and basically cooperative. Stability and cooperation in the region have been maintained, I argue, by two interlinked structures: the U.S. hegemonic security regime and deepening economic interdependence. Each country is enmeshed in these structures to varying degrees, including those countries very much on the periphery, such as North Korea and Myanmar. Individual East Asian states design and operationalize their security strategies within the structural constraints of hegemony and economic interdependence. For the countries of the region, there is no such thing as a completely autonomous security strategy—not even for China.

U.S. Hegemony

The United States today plays the role of the ultimate guarantor of the strategic stability of East Asia. The most recent statement by the Department of Defense of its strategic doctrine immodestly describes three key U.S. responsibilities: "to shape the international environment; respond to the full spectrum of crises; and prepare now for an uncertain future."[13] Committing 100,000 military personnel to the region for the foreseeable future, the United States seems prepared for any eventuality.

This is not just talk. When major crises have occurred (e.g., the fear that North Korea would go nuclear in 1994, the threat by the People's Republic of China [PRC] to use force against Taiwan in 1996, or the 1999 East Timor crisis), the United States has either directly intervened or indirectly brokered a solution. The U.S. capacity to project power into the region is built on an infrastructure of bilateral security ties, most importantly with Japan, South Korea, and Australia but also including a wide diversity of security understandings with countries such as the Philippines, Singapore, and Taiwan—including the "three communiqués" relationship with China.

Current U.S. strategic doctrine has its roots in the thinking of Richard Nixon and Henry Kissinger thirty years ago about a post-Vietnam design for U.S. policy in East Asia. The Nixon Doctrine, announced in July 1969, articulated a strategy for continued U.S. involvement that insisted on more self-reliant Asian efforts to deal with their own domestic security and development problems. The Nixon opening to China provided an opportunity for the United States to play communists against communists while withdrawing from Vietnam "with honor." Finally, the establishment of formal diplomatic relations with China in 1979, in combination with Deng Xiaoping's decision to open China to the global capitalist system as the best way to achieve wealth and power, turned China into a reluctant but fairly consistent supporter of the regional status quo. When the Soviet Union still existed, China enjoyed some strategic leverage on the United States in the triangular relations among the three major powers, but after the general collapse of the communist world, China was less able to exact a price for its strategic collaboration.

The U.S. strategic role in East Asia is best understood as one of "hegemony" in the Gramscian sense of "consensus protected by the 'armor of coercion.'"[14] Robert Cox spells out the implications of the Gramscian concept:

Hegemony at the international level is thus not merely an order among states. It is an order within a world economy with a dominant mode of production which penetrates into all countries and links into other subordinate modes of production. It is also a complex of international social relationships which connect the social classes of the different countries. World hegemony can be described as a social structure, an economic structure, and a political structure; and it cannot be simply one of these things but must be all three. World hegemony, furthermore, is expressed in universal norms, institutions, and mechanisms which lay down general rules of behavior for states and for those forces of civil society that act across national boundaries, rules which support the dominant mode of production.[15]

For Gramsci, "ideas and material conditions are always bound together, mutually influencing one another, and not reducible one to the other." The state "maintains cohesion and identity within the bloc through the propagation of a common culture."[16]

In sustaining the U.S. role as hegemon in the East Asian region, then, the propagation of human rights, democracy, and other liberal values by the United States is as important as the maintenance of its military bases. Another way of putting the same point is the distinction that Joseph Nye makes between what he calls "soft power" (values, norms, and ideology) and "hard power" (economic and military capabilities). Both together are vital to maintaining hegemony. Among the more serious problems for those countries living under the U.S. hegemonic regime are, paradoxically, a lack of strategic autonomy from the United States on the one hand and worries about the sustainability of the American hegemonic regime on the other. For example, even a country as powerful as Japan, having successfully built the second-largest economy in the world, is nonetheless dependent on U.S. commitments under the U.S.–Japan security treaty to guarantee its national security. China, too, is in some respects a strategic dependent of the United States. For example, it is the United States that guarantees the strategic stability of the region, thus facilitating the free flow of investment, foreign aid, trade, and technology transfer so vital to China's economic modernization and to maintaining the high rate of economic growth that the PRC has achieved.

Sustainability is a different matter. The literature on the American role in East Asia written by analysts from the region is one deeply concerned about the question of how long the United States will be willing to remain as guarantor of strategic stability in the region and under what circumstances it is most likely to withdraw. Especially for those countries most dependent on the United States, such as Japan, this is a topic prompting some anxiety. The U.S. Senate's rejection of the Comprehensive Test Ban Treaty and the rise of isolationist sentiment among right-wing Republicans in the U.S. Congress heighten these concerns. Moreover, judging from the 500-year history of Western expansion, it would seem that the hegemony of any Western state over significant portions of the non-Western world is not sustainable for the long term. Contemporary American critics, such as Chalmers Johnson, employ concepts from Paul Kennedy's *The Rise and Fall of the Great Powers,* such as "imperial overstretch," to characterize U.S. power today in East Asia.[17]

Economic Interdependence

On the other hand, economic interdependence as a basis for interstate cooperation, if supported by strategic stability, does appear to be indefinitely sustainable.

The absolute gains from economic relationships based on mutual benefit appear sufficient to encourage interstate cooperation over the long term.

In 1991, I interviewed former foreign minister Okita Saburo in Tokyo. Wondering about the feasibility of certain kinds of multilateral institutions for the region, I asked Okita whether he thought that an institution such as the Conference on Security and Cooperation in Europe (CSCE, now OSCE) would be a good idea for East Asia. "No," he replied, "but it already exists. It is economic." What he was referring to was the structure of foreign trade, aid, investment, and technology transfer between Japan and the rest of East Asia that had been carefully constructed in the post–World War II period by the Japanese. Some wag once labeled it "Greater East Asian Co-Prosperity Sphere II," suggesting a comparison with Japan's World War II policies. Many of the objectives were indeed the same: gaining access to vital natural resources and markets for Japan's industrialization. Obviously, however, the means are quite different. This time Japan's relations with Asia have been built on voluntary cooperation rather than enforced compliance, and the result has had substantial benefits for all parties. Building relationships of economic interdependence based on mutual benefit has been a key dimension of Japan's Asian policy now for decades.

The security regime in East Asia, maintained by a combination of U.S. hegemony and economic interdependence, has facilitated the growing impact of globalization on the region.

SECURITY THREATS: OLD AND NEW

It is sometimes said that after the collapse of the Soviet Union, the Cold War ended in Europe but not in Asia. Since a communist China still exists, the argument goes, as well as Communist Party states in North Korea, Vietnam, and Laos, the Cold War continues in East Asia, and that is the reason why so many of the security ties between the United States and countries in the region, established many decades ago, remain intact today. As a means of understanding the hostility between North and South Korea, this argument may be somewhat useful, but more broadly in the region, it would be a mistake, I think, to understand contemporary relationships with China, Vietnam, and Laos as a continuation of the Cold War.

All three countries have gradually established formal diplomatic relations with their neighbors in the region, and each is becoming progressively more integrated into the global capitalist system. Both Vietnam and Laos have joined ASEAN, and China has joined the ASEAN Regional Forum security dialogue. Communism is not perceived as a security threat in the region as it was during the decades of Cold War, and East Asia is no longer ideologically polarized as it was in the past. If anything, communism has now become something of an embarrassment for those Communist Party leaders who still feel compelled to invoke it to defend their claims to monopoly power.[18]

Problems from the Past

Yet many of the most serious security problems of the past persist. The most important are problems of divided nations, territorial disputes, and nuclear proliferation.

Divided nations. Most analysts agree that tensions between North and South Korea and between China and Taiwan remain the most potentially serious sources of interstate military conflict in the region. The United States still maintains a military force of more than 37,000 personnel in South Korea, fifty years after the outbreak of the Korean War. The Democratic People's Republic of Korea (DPRK) is perhaps the most isolated regime in the world today, a dynastic communist dictatorship ruled by Kim Jong Il, son of the founder, Kim Il Sung. The four major powers in the region (Russia, China, Japan, and the United States) appear to favor the status quo over the prospect of a reunified Korea, but meanwhile there is the danger of renewed military conflict between North and South or the implosion of the DPRK state, resulting in anarchy and problems associated with the escape of thousands of refugees to the shores of neighboring countries.

The possibility of North Korea becoming a nuclear power remains a serious concern, as do DPRK missile development and missile exports abroad. In August 1998, North Korea tested a three-stage *Taepodong-1* missile with a range of 1,500 to 2,000 kilometers that overflew Japan and landed in the Pacific Ocean. During the following year, there were reports that North Korea next intended to test the longer-range *Taepodong-2*.[19] As the result of negotiations with the United States in Berlin in September 1999, however, North Korea put those plans on hold. Nonetheless, Japanese reaction to North Korea's missile development prompted support for the U.S. theater missile defense initiative for the region.

Taiwan has been an issue of contention in Sino–American relations since the original Nixon–Mao accommodation of 1972. Officially, the United States has adopted a "one China" policy, but it continues informal relations with Taiwan, including sales of modern military equipment under the provisions of the Taiwan Relations Act. The United States has consistently opposed the use of force by the mainland as a means of reunifying the country but at the same time maintains a posture of purposeful ambiguity with respect to what it might do if the PRC were to launch a military attack on the island—for fear that any more forthright commitment would encourage Taiwan government formally to declare its independence from China.

Taiwan, in this sense, is a stage set for war by miscalculation. When in 1995–1996 the PRC carried out a series of "missile exercises" to intimidate the electorate on the island prior to their March 1996 presidential election, it was not clear until the last minute what the United States would do. Washington finally sent not one but two aircraft-carrier battle groups to the area to make the point that it would not tolerate use of force, but what will the United States do next time?[20] President Lee Teng-hui's rejection of a "one China" policy, insisting instead that relations with the PRC should be understood in terms of a "special

state-to-state relationship," plus Taiwan's continuous efforts to regain membership in the United Nations and other international institutions, has increased the
tension.[21]

Territorial disputes. East Asia is replete with territorial disputes from North to
South. Throughout history a main source of interstate conflict, the territorial disputes in the region have been contained largely as a result of the U.S. hegemonic
role. The different parties to the dispute are often closely linked to the United
States, thus providing Washington with a capacity to help meliorate the differences on both sides.

The most important territorial disputes range from the Northern Islands dispute
between Japan and Russia in the far north, to Takeshima/Tok Do between Japan
and Korea, to Senkaku/Diaoyu Dao between China and Japan, and finally to the
volatile South China Sea, where six countries have competing claims.[22] Globalization, so far, seems to have made no difference in either meliorating or exacerbating these conflicts. However, if joint development of the natural resources involved becomes a viable way to resolve some of these disputes, the role of MNCs
in implementing joint development plans may help to play a positive role.

Nuclear proliferation. One of the most serious threats to global security and yet
one of the most difficult to resolve is the proliferation of nuclear weapons. The
unexpected tests by India and Pakistan in May 1998 renewed fears of even more
extensive proliferation in Asia. North Korea had agreed under U.S. pressure in
1994 to give up its nuclear weapons program, and China had reluctantly agreed
to sign the Comprehensive Nuclear Test Ban Treaty in 1996. However, the nuclear weapons tests in South Asia once again raised the issue in the region. If, following the Indian and Pakistani tests, Japan, for example, were to decide that, in
order to become a "normal nation,"[23] nuclear weapons were an indispensable requirement to achieve the international status that it sought, the entire global nonproliferation regime would be in jeopardy.

These security threats from the past (divided nations, territorial disputes, and
nuclear proliferation) appear to have been little affected so far by globalization.
In some respects, they seem to have been held in abeyance while globalization
created both new opportunities for cooperation and new kinds of security threats.

New Security Threats

If there had been doubts earlier, the Asian financial crisis, which began with the
run on the Thai baht in July 1997, soon convinced everyone that, for good or ill,
the region was an integral part of a globalized economy. As Friedman put it,
"Globalization isn't a choice. It is a reality." Moreover, "No one is in charge."[24]
Environmental disasters in one country often had impacts in neighboring countries, such as the forest fires burning out of control in Kalimantan in 1997, and
what had earlier been understood to be exclusively domestic security issues, such
as East Timor for Indonesia, suddenly became internationalized. The Indonesian

army for the first time was being held to account for its twenty-four-year reign of terror in East Timor. "The army has been using tactics lately that are 15 or 20 years out of date," a senior ambassador to Indonesia commented. "It will have to learn that these tactics are unsuitable for an era of globalization when you've got a free press and the world is watching."[25]

Economic insecurities. After the financial crisis, few people in the region remain unconvinced that economic viability (or vulnerability) is a security issue. Virtually overnight, the currencies and equity markets of countries that had been previously identified as models of Third World development collapsed, forcing millions of people into unemployment, bankruptcy, and material hardship. In Indonesia, hardest hit by the crisis, the Suharto regime, thirty-three years in power, collapsed as a result. Comparing globalization to the Cold War period, Friedman talks about how globalization literally blew down the walls among the very different economies of the First, Second, and Third Worlds of that time:

> What blew away all the walls were three fundamental changes—changes in how we communicate, how we invest and how we learn about the world. These changes were born and incubated during the cold war and achieved a critical mass by the late 1980s, when they finally came together into a whirlwind strong enough to blow down all the walls of the cold war system and enable the world to come together as a single, integrated, open plain.[26]

Among those countries hardest hit by the crisis, Thailand, Indonesia, and South Korea have all accepted the IMF's advice to more substantially liberalize and to open up their economies to foreign competition—in effect, making them in some respects even more vulnerable than before to the impact of globalization. Malaysian prime minister Mahathir bin Mohamad's unorthodox decision in September 1998 to impose currency and capital controls appears now only to have been a temporary measure. All the countries of the region appear to be faced with the imperative of putting on what Friedman calls "the golden straitjacket"—the definition of capitalist economics popularized by Margaret Thatcher in England and Ronald Reagan in the United States in the 1980s. Friedman wants us to believe that there is no alternative: "Globalization has only the Golden Straitjacket. If your country has not been fitted for one, it will be soon."[27]

Whether or not Friedman's analysis is correct, it has become clear that economic competitiveness has become a security requirement in today's globalized world. Unlike the days of the Cold War, today there is only one international economic system. Autarky, or attempting to be economically self-sufficient apart from the global economy, would condemn any country to permanent poverty and material hardship.

Environmental threats. The damaging impact on the environment of virtually universal efforts by countries to industrialize is nothing new. Problems of ozone depletion, species elimination, and global warming have been identified before.

During the 1990s in East Asia, however, it became increasing clear that ecological damage in one country could have serious impacts in neighboring countries. Acid rain, produced by air pollution in China, was a serious problem in South Korea and Japan, while the forest fires burning out of control in Indonesia in 1997 created public health hazards in Singapore and Malaysia.[28]

These problems cannot be controlled simply by any individual country's self-help strategies. Environmental threats have become regional and global problems, requiring a cooperative response by the affected countries. The UN environment program's GEO-2000 report, published in September 1999, has added water shortage and nitrogen pollution to the growing list of imminent dangers to the survival of the human species and emphasized the need for immediate action.[29] Disasters such as China's 1998 Yangtze River floods, which reportedly cost China 2,100 lives and some $30 billion, might be controlled in part by reforesting the watersheds upstream, but the broader problems of environmental security require regional and global cooperation. Environmental threats generally present no enemy in the conventional "national security" sense except ourselves. Sending in the military will not help.

Ideological threats. In many East Asian countries, governments have for many years been as much or more concerned about domestic security as they had security from foreign military attack. In fact, some armed forces, such as the Indonesian TNI, have been principally organized, both in their overt and covert operations, as a coercive weapon to ensure domestic stability. During the Cold War, they fought against communism, but after the collapse of the Soviet Union, everything changed. Authoritarian governments in the region that had received Western support and training to fight communism in the past increasingly now felt themselves under ideological threat, especially from the U.S. insistence on human rights and democracy. Allen Whiting, reporting on his research on security issues in ASEAN during 1995–1996, found that, "on human rights and democracy, ASEAN stands on the side of China insofar as the question involves interference in domestic affairs and the imposition of predominantly Western values. . . . However, when faced with the threatened Chinese use of force, ASEAN sides with U.S. policy as the mainstay of peace and stability in East Asia."[30]

It is not surprising that communist governments such as China's and Vietnam's would perceive an ideological threat from Western criticism of their human rights practices, but analysts report a similar concern on the part of the governments of Singapore, Malaysia, Myanmar, and Indonesia.[31] Typically, it is those governments, both communist and noncommunist, that conflate the security of the state, their regime, and their ruling party, that perceive ideological threats from the West.

The perception of ideological threat among governments in East Asia is directly a result of globalization, I would argue, in the sense that Giddens sees globalization producing "global cosmopolitan society" committed to universal values. He asks,

Can we live in a world where nothing is sacred? I have to say . . . that I don't think we can. Cosmopolitans, of whom I count myself one, have to make plain that tolerance and dialogue can themselves be guided by values of a universal kind. All of us need moral commitments that stand above the petty concerns and squabbles of everyday life. We should be prepared to mount an active defence of these values wherever they are poorly developed, or threatened. None of us would have anything to live for, if we didn't have something worth dying for.[32]

For Giddens, globalization contains this moral imperative that cannot be ignored. Concepts of state sovereignty and noninterference in the internal affairs of other countries are increasingly contested in the era of globalization. Priorities are shifting toward human rights and humanitarian intervention.[33] The NATO intervention in Kosovo and the UN decision to support an Australian-led international force to intervene, however belatedly, in East Timor are setting new precedents. Human rights atrocities, broadcast worldwide by CNN, are helping to mobilize citizens and human rights NGOs to pressure governments to take action.

STRATEGIES TO ENHANCE SECURITY

Changing perceptions of threat are causing the governments of East Asia to design new strategies to enhance the security of their countries. Giddens, again, gives us his tentative understanding of what the new global order might look like:

Although this is a contentious point, I would say that, following the dissolving of the cold war, nations no longer have enemies. Who are the enemies of Britain, or France, or Japan? Nations today face risks and dangers rather than enemies, a massive shift in their very nature. . . . As the changes I have described in this lecture gather weight, they are creating something that has never existed before, a global cosmopolitan society. We are the first generation to live in this society, whose contours we can as yet only dimly see. It is shaking up our existing ways of life, no matter where we happen to be. This is not—at least at the moment—a global order driven by collective human will. Instead, it is emerging in an anarchic, haphazard, fashion, carried along by a mixture of economic, technological and cultural imperatives.[34]

This vision may appear utopian for East Asia, a region still confounded by divided countries, territorial disputes, and fears of nuclear proliferation; however, notable in East Asia is a gradual erosion of realist thinking and a new emphasis on cooperative security strategies. Perhaps most striking is the absence of the classic security dilemma in relations among the major powers in the region, a decade after the breaching of the Berlin Wall.

Erosion of Realist Thinking

Kenneth Waltz, a leading realist theorist, describes the security dilemma as "the condition in which states, unsure of one another's intentions, arm for the sake of security and in doing so set a vicious circle in motion. Having armed for the sake of security, states feel less secure and buy more arms because the means to anyone's security is a threat to someone else who in turn responds by arming." Waltz himself is convinced that there is no way in international politics to avoid the security dilemma: "Whatever the weaponry and however many states in the system, states have to live with their security dilemma, which is produced not by their wills but by their situations. A dilemma cannot be solved; it can more or less readily be dealt with."[35]

However, Waltz may be wrong about that. In the decade of post–Cold War politics to date, the major powers have thus far avoided creating a new security dilemma among themselves. Despite the many problems in the U.S. relationship with China, for example, Beijing so far has not sought to "balance" the United States, to ally with other major powers (such as Russia, India, or Japan) against the United States, or to provoke the United States into a new arms race. Part of the reason is the magnitude of the U.S. predominance of power: militarily (in both the nuclear and the "conventional" areas), economically, and technologically. As the U.S. National Security Adviser Samuel R. Berger, has put it, "Our military expenditures are now larger than those of all other countries combined, [and] our weaponry is a generation ahead of our nearest potential rival."[36] Another part of the reason is that the PRC, like virtually all other developing countries, would much prefer to allocate scarce resources to economic and technological modernization rather than to unproductive military expenditures. A final reason why they have avoided a security dilemma so far is that the world has changed: Globalization has transformed the way that states connect with each other—in Waltz's terms, "the situation" has changed.

In the realist understanding of international politics, the condition of anarchy (i.e., the lack of an authoritative global government) produces the necessity for self-help strategies on the part of state actors. The security dilemma is produced in turn by the reliance on self-help. Waltz says that it cannot be avoided because of this situation that states find themselves in. However, the situation that Waltz describes, which he understands to be anarchy, is being daily transformed by the forces of globalization.

One of the important benefits from globalization for security relations is that, in a globalized world, there are already established patterns of cooperation in trade and investment relationships and well-used channels of communication, especially among the major powers. All parties have become accustomed in the use of these globalized relationships to working together on the basis of mutual benefit. Governments have become accustomed to focusing on the absolute benefits for all participants derived from cooperation rather than on the relative benefits that realists insist must be the focus of strategic relations. Moreover, the destructive power of nuclear weapons and the extensive character of growing ecological problems have shown the world the extent to which all countries share a common fate.

Self-Help: An Illusion?

In the ten years since the fall of the Berlin Wall, we have all become much more aware of new kinds of security problems for which self-help by individual countries is totally inadequate, for example, the economic insecurities so well demonstrated by the recent East Asian financial crisis and the various threats to environment security that require at least regional and often global remedies. To deal effectively with these kinds of security threats, cooperation among states would seem to be imperative. Can any country in today's globalized world ensure its own security (military, economic, environmental, or human) exclusively through self-help? The interconnected nature of our globalized world makes going it alone increasingly impracticable.

Even for the United States, self-help alone is not sufficient. In August 1998, when the financial crisis that had begun in Asia reached global proportions, Russia defaulted on its domestic bonds, and many analysts worried that the United States and Europe might be drawn into a global economic meltdown if the United States could not resolve the situation by itself. Despite *Time* magazine's billing of the combined forces of U.S. Treasury Secretary Robert Rubin, his deputy Lawrence Summers, and U.S. Federal Reserve Bank Chairman Alan Greenspan as "The Committee to Save the World,"[37] the policies proposed by the Clinton administration could not have been implemented without the cooperation of the other G-7 rich capitalist countries. Not even the United States, the sole remaining superpower, enjoying the world's largest economy, was powerful enough to defend its own economic security without the collaboration of other world powers.

From Zero-Sum to Positive-Sum Thinking

Over the past two decades, the governments of East Asia have taught one another the benefits of cooperation rather than war and confrontation—first by means of trade, investment, and foreign aid and later by participating in multilateral forums associated with ASEAN. The mutual benefit that they have derived from relationships of economic interdependence serves as a model for the kinds of strategic relations that they want to build for themselves. Their common enemy is not some other country, such as the Soviet Union during the Cold War, but rather instability and possible military conflict. Remarking on ASEAN and the 1976 Treaty of Amity and Cooperation in Southeast Asia, Dewi Fortuna Anwar observes, "Although many bilateral disputes have remained unresolved, it is now becoming unthinkable that an ASEAN country would go to war against a fellow ASEAN member for any reason."[38]

Compared to the previous 150-year history of endless warfare in the region, dating from the first Opium War in 1839 to the withdrawal of Vietnamese troops from Cambodia in 1989, this is a magnificent achievement. All countries in East Asia (including those most apparently left out of the present cooperative arrangements, such as North Korea and Myanmar) have a fundamental interest in deepening these patterns of cooperation in order to help minimize the probability of interstate conflict in the future. As Kofi Annan has argued, "In the context of many of the challenges facing humanity today, the collective interest *is* the national interest."[39] Realists may condemn the ASEAN Regional Forum as "just a talking shop," but the talking has produced the beginnings of a demonstrable change in security behavior among the participants. For the ASEAN member countries, in varying degrees membership has contributed to a growing sense of regional stability, if not yet to any greater tangible security.

EAST ASIAN SECURITY AT A CROSSROADS

"In the globalization system," Friedman writes, "the United States is now the sole and dominant superpower and all other nations are subordinate to it to one degree or another."[40] Globalization in the region has strengthened U.S. predominance, and East Asian economic interdependence has been reshaped as the result of the financial crisis in accordance with American notions of economic liberalization, principally as a result of U.S.-influenced IMF conditions imposed on the most affected countries. From each of the recent crises in the region (North Korea in 1994, Taiwan in 1996, the financial crisis from 1997, and East Timor in 1999), American power has emerged enhanced. In Washington's view, the United States is "the indispensable country."

The U.S. relationship with China is perhaps the most important one in the region, especially regarding security policy. Unilateral decisions taken by the American hegemon have the power either to increase cooperation in the region or to disrupt it. Two issues high on the U.S. foreign policy agenda appear likely to shape future security relationships in East Asia. They are the issue of "China threat" and the U.S. decision whether to deploy ballistic missile defenses. Ironically, it is precisely at the peak of U.S. global power that insecurities in the United States appear to be prompting decisions in the country that could polarize the region politically and even begin a new Cold War.

"China Threat"

Since the establishment of formal diplomatic relations with Washington twenty years ago, the Chinese have argued that a peaceful and stable international environment is absolutely indispensable for their efforts to modernize their country. On balance, they have practiced what they preached, gradually participating more fully and cooperatively in international institutions and resolving problems with their neighbors.[41] Taiwan and the competing claims in the South China Sea have been the main exceptions, but in even 1995–1996, when Beijing attempted to use "missile exercises" to intimidate the citizenry of Taiwan, the PLA backed off when the United States intervened to make the point that use of force would not be tolerated. The PRC's declaratory policy promotes "a new security concept" and invokes the Five Principles of Peaceful Coexistence and the UN Charter. The core values of this new concept, according to Beijing, are mutual trust, mutual benefit, equality, and cooperation.[42]

China has a huge stake in the status quo. No non-Western country has gotten more of what it needed from the global capitalist system for its economic modernization at less cost. China has been even more successful in exploiting the international system during the past twenty years than Japan was during the Meiji era. By itself, the training of PRC students and scholars abroad in Western countries and Japan over the past two decades constitutes the most significant case of technology transfer to one country in a short period of time that the world has ever seen.

On the U.S. side, six American administrations, from Richard Nixon to Bill Clinton, have pursued essentially the same "engagement" strategy toward the PRC, working to coopt China and to encourage the PRC to behave like a "responsible power." However, in the final years of the Clinton administration, a strange coalition of conservative Republicans on the political right and human rights activists on the political left has become vocal in calling for a harsher policy toward China. Meanwhile, the list of problems in the Sino–American bilateral relationship has grown. The human rights agenda (political repression, Tibet, abortion, and religious freedom), an ever increasing bilateral trade deficit, NATO's Kosovo intervention that China opposed, charges of illegal PRC contributions to Clinton's presidential election campaign in 1996, the Cox Report alleging Chinese theft of U.S. nuclear weapons secrets, and then the NATO bombing of the Chinese embassy in Belgrade in May 1999 all contributed to heightened tensions. By the end of 1999, the "constructive strategic partnership" promised during the earlier exchange of summit visits by Presidents Clinton and Jiang Zemin was in tatters.

The November 1999 agreement on China's WTO membership gave some hope for a renewal of close Sino–American cooperation, but hard-liners on both sides have pressed for confrontation in the new, globalized world. For example, in February 1999, two PLA senior colonels from the air force published a book called *Unlimited War: Explorations on War and Tactics in an Era of Globalization,* in which they examined a wide range of methods for doing harm to adversaries in unconventional ways (e.g., cyberwar and economic warfare),[43] while on the American side hard-line authors have focused on the theme of "China threat."

Despite the fact that in measurable military, economic, and technological capabilities, China's power constitutes only a small fraction of U.S. might,[44] these authors insist that China is a threat to American national security. Analyses have ranged from the more measured assessment by Bernstein and Munro of future dangers to the United States[45] to charges by Timperlake and Triplett that President Clinton had betrayed American national security by appeasing China and cooperating with the PLA.[46]

Ballistic Missile Defenses

Citing fears of ballistic missile attack from terrorists or so-called rogue states (usually thought to mean North Korea, Iran, or Iraq), the United States plans to build and to deploy both a national missile defense (NMD) system and a theater missile defense (TMD) system in East Asia. The decision to revive Ronald Reagan's "Star Wars" concept has received relatively little debate in the United States so far,[47] but if these systems are deployed, the strategic implications in East Asia will be serious. For many supporters of the initiative, the target is not so much terrorists as China.

Both China and Russia have opposed the plan as strategically destabilizing. All agree that deployment would violate the 1972 Anti-Ballistic Missile Treaty, long thought to be a foundation stone of the global nuclear arms control regime. The Clinton administration has approached Russia about revising the treaty, but Moscow has refused. On November 5, 1999, Russian won support from many U.S. allies and friends when the First Committee of the UN General Assembly voted overwhelmingly in favor of a resolution to preserve the ABM Treaty.[48] If unilateral deployment by the United States were to provoke a classic security dilemma and a new arms race, everyone's security would be diminished.

In contrast with perceptions by some American analysts of a military threat from China, it is the small size of China's nuclear weapons capability that would make U.S. deployment of ballistic missile defenses such a serious problem for China. The International Institute for Strategic Studies (IISS) notes that "China's strategic capability is composed of less than 200 nuclear warheads, of which only perhaps 20–30 would be operational at any given time."[49] Russia still has the capacity to overwhelm any conceivable ABM system, but for China, the deployment of an NMD would threaten its basic nuclear deterrent. The IISS concludes that if the United States decides on deployment, a "head-on collision with China will be difficult to avoid."[50]

After the August 1998 North Korean *Taepodong-1* missile shot that passed through Japanese airspace, Tokyo agreed to joint research with the United States on a TMD system that may, at some future time, also include South Korea and Taiwan. Chinese analysts have characterized stated Japanese fears of North Korean missile attack as "an excuse" for participating in a TMD arrangement that is obviously aimed at China.[51] Seen from Beijing, an East Asian TMD looks like a new multilateral security alliance against China. If it were to include Taiwan, obviously that would make things much worse.[52]

American policy toward China is at a crossroads. At stake is the strategic stability of the region. Globalization in the variety of its many influences on East Asia has, on balance, helped to provide a sense in the region of a common fate and to establish patterns of cooperation among governments. Nonetheless, the hegemon has the power either to disrupt or to encourage these tentative relationships of mutual benefit. Making an enemy of China would probably make all countries in the region less secure.

NOTES

1. See, for example, the best-selling book by *New York Times* columnist Thomas L. Friedman, *The Lexus and the Olive Tree: Understanding Globalization* (New York: Farrar Straus & Giroux, 1999). For a withering critique of Friedman ("a tone of arrogance so grandiose that one suspects the author has taken leave of his senses"), see Thomas C. Frank, "Paeon of Praise to Globalization: Creation Myth of the 'Geo-Architect,'" *Le Monde Diplomatique,* July 1999, 7.

2. Frank, "Paeon of Praise to Globalization," 86–88.

3. "The advent of nuclear weapons meant that a head-on war, of a classical type, between the two principal contestants would not only spell their mutual destruction but could unleash lethal consequences for a significant portion of humanity. The intensity of the conflict was thus simultaneously subjected to extraordinary self-restraint on the part of both rivals" (Zbigniew Brzezinski, *The Grand Chessboard: American Primacy and Its Geostrategic Imperatives* [New York: Basic Books, 1997], 6).

4. Friedman, *The Lexus and the Olive Tree,* 40.

5. David Held, Anthony McGrew, David Goldblatt, and Jonathan Perraton, *Global Transformations: Politics, Economics, and Culture* (Stanford, Calif.: Stanford University Press, 1999), 49.

6. United Nations Development Program, *Human Development Report 1999* (New York: Oxford University Press, 1999).

7. Anthony Giddens, "Family," Lecture 4, Runaway World, 1999 Reith Lectures/BBC Homepage. For more critical understandings of globalization, see, for example, John Gray, *False Dawn: The Delusions of Global Capitalism* (New York: New Press, 1998); Richard Falk, *Predatory Globalization: A Critique* (Cambridge: Polity Press, 1999); and Chalmers Johnson, *Blowback: The Costs and Consequences of American Empire* (New York: Henry Holt, 2000).

8. Muthiah Alagappa, ed., *Asian Security Practice: Material and Ideational Influences* (Stanford, Calif.: Stanford University Press, 1998), 17.

9. Denny Roy, "Human Rights and National Security in East Asia," *Issues & Studies* 35, no. 2 (March/April 1999): 134–35.

10. United Nations Development Program, *Human Development Report 1994* (New York: Oxford University Press, 1994), chap. 2.

11. United Nations Development Program, *Human Development Report 1994,* 24–25.

12. Chung-In Moon, "South Korea: Recasting Security Paradigms," in Alagappa, ed., *Asian Security Practice,* 287.

13. Office of International Security Affairs, U.S. Department of Defense, *The United States Security Strategy for the East Asia-Pacific Region* (Washington, D.C.: U.S. Dept of Defense, November 1998), 8.

14. William I. Robinson, *Promoting Polyarchy: Globalization, U.S. Intervention, and Hegemony* (Cambridge: Cambridge University Press, 1996), 22.

15. Robert W. Cox, with Timothy J. Sinclair, *Approaches to World Order* (Cambridge: Cambridge University Press, 1996), 137.

16. Cox, *Approaches to World Order,* 132.

17. Chalmers Johnson, "In Search of a New Cold War," *Bulletin of the Atomic Scientists,* September/October 1999, 44–51. See also Paul Kennedy, *The Rise and Fall of the Great Powers* (New York: Vintage, 1987), 515.

18. Note, for example, the list of official slogans announced by the Chinese Communist Party to celebrate the fiftieth anniversary of the founding of the People's Republic of China. Erik Eckholm, "China Issues 50th Anniversary Slogans, and They're a Mouthful," *International Herald Tribune,* September 16, 1999, 1, 4.

19. International Institute for Strategic Studies, *Strategic Survey 1998/99* (London: Oxford University Press, 1999), 40–41.

20. John Garver, *Face Off: China, the United States, and Taiwan's Democratization* (Seattle: University of Washington Press, 1997).

21. Lee Teng-hui, "Understanding Taiwan: Bridging the Perception Gap," *Foreign Affairs* 78, no. 6 (November/December, 1999): 9–14. In this essay, Lee expands on his concept of special state-to-state relations, discussing Taiwan's "new sense of identity."

22. Mark J. Valencia, "China and the South China Sea Disputes," Adelphi Paper 298, International Institute for Strategic Studies, October 1995.

23. Ichiro Ozawa, *Blueprint for a New Japan: The Rethinking of a Nation* (Tokyo: Kodansha International, 1994).

24. Friedman, *The Lexus and the Olive Tree,* 93.

25. Quoted in Seth Mydans, "A Military Humiliated by Debacle in Timor," *International Herald Tribune,* September 16, 1999, 1, 4.

26. Friedman, *The Lexus and the Olive Tree,* 40

27. Friedman, *The Lexus and the Olive Tree,* 86.

28. David Glover and Timothy Jessup, *Indonesia's Fires and Haze: The Cost of Catastrophe* (Singapore: Institute of Southeast Asian Studies, 1999).

29. Paul Brown, "UN Report Warns of Environmental Crisis," *Guardian Weekly,* September 23–29, 1999, 7.

30. Allen S. Whiting, "ASEAN Eyes China: The Security Dimension," *Asian Survey* 37, no. 4 (April 1997): 301.

31. See the individual country chapters in Alagappa, ed., *Asian Security Practice.* See also Roy, "Human Rights and National Security"; Denny Roy, "Human Rights as a National Security Threat: The Case of China," *Issues & Studies* 32, no. 2 (February 1996): 65–81; and Peter Van Ness, "Unconventional Threats to China's National Security: A Teaching Note," *Journal of Contemporary China* 9, no. 23 (March 2000).

32. Anthony Giddens, "Tradition," 1999 Reith Lectures, BBC Homepage, May 1999. It is interesting, I think, to compare Giddens's view on these questions with the very different perspective of George Kennan, author more than fifty years ago of the U.S. containment policy toward the Soviet Union; see George Kennan's interview with Richard Ullman in *New York Review of Books,* August 12, 1999, 6.

33. See, for example, UN Secretary-General Kofi Annan's important essay on competing concepts of sovereignty, "Two Concepts of Sovereignty," *The Economist,* September 18, 1999.

34. Anthony Giddens, "Globalization," 1999 Reith Lectures, BBC Homepage, May 1999.

35. Kenneth N. Waltz, *Theory of International Politics* (Reading, Mass.: Addison-Wesley, 1979), 186–87. Waltz, in turn, draws his understanding of the security dilemma from the original essay by John H. Herz, "Idealist Internationalism and the Security Dilemma," *World Politics* (January 1950).

36. Quoted in Flora Lewis, "Isolationism in America? Another Ruckus That Will Pass," *International Herald Tribune,* November 2, 1999, 8.

37. "The Three Marketeers," *Time,* February 15, 1999, 46–54.

38. Dewi Fortuna Anwar, "Indonesia: Domestic Priorities Define National Security," in Alagappa, ed., *Asian Security Practice,* 508.

39. Kofi Annan, "Two Concepts of Sovereignty," *Economist,* September 18, 1999.

40. Friedman, *The Lexus and the Olive Tree,* 11.

41. Yong L∍ng, "The Chinese Conception of National Interests in International Relations," *China Quarterly,* no. 154 (June 1998): 308–29.

42. Foreign Minister Tang Jiaxuan's address to the UN General Assembly in September 1999 is a good example. For the complete text, see *Beijing Review,* October 11, 1999, 9–11.

43. Qiao Liang and Wang Xianghui, *Chaoxian zhan* (Beijing: People's Liberation Army Cultural Press, 1999).

44. Samuel S. Kim, "China as a Great Power," *Current History,* September 1997, 246–51; Sheng Lijun, "China and the United States: Asymmetrical Strategic Partners," *Washington Quarterly* 22, no. 3 (summer 1999): 147–63.

45. Richard Bernstein and Ross H. Munro, *The Coming Conflict with China* (New York: Knopf, 1997).

46. Edward Timperlake and William C. Triplett II, *Red Dragon Rising: Communist China's Military Threat to America* (Washington, D.C.: Regnery, 1999).

47. See, for example, George N. Lewis, Theodore A. Postol, and John Pike, "Why National Missile Defense Won't Work," *Scientific American,* August 1999, 22–27, and Michael O'Hanlon, "Star Wars Strikes Back," *Foreign Affairs* 78, no. 6 (November/ December 1999): 68–82.

48. Some of the questions that the advocates of ballistic missile defenses have not answered are the following: Can an "upper tier" ABM system really be made to work, especially against countermeasures? Why would deterrence *not* work against potential attackers as it has in the past? Does a system with, at best, such a limited capability justify the immense cost? Would not deployment give the American public a false sense of safety when the real threat from terrorists and rogue states is not ballistic missile attack but the so-called suitcase bomb? Finally, why is it in the American national interest to deploy a system that has a high probability of causing a security dilemma that would make everyone less secure?

49. International Institute for Strategic Studies, *The Military Balance 1999–2000* (London: Oxford University Press, 1999), 171.

50. International Institute for Strategic Studies, *Strategic Survey 1998/99* (London: Oxford University Press, 1999), 50.

51. Interviews in Beijing, May 1999.

52. Hong Yuan, "The Implication of the TMD System in Japan to China's Security" (paper presented at the Sixth ISODARCO Beijing Seminar on Arms Control, October 29–November 1, 1998, Shanghai [from npp@nautilus.org Nuclear Policy List]; Yan Xuetong, "Theater Missile Defense and Northeast Asian Security," *Nonproliferation Review* 6, no. 3 (spring–summer 1999): 65–74.

Bibliography

Abbas, Ackbar. *Hong Kong: Culture and the Politics of Disappearance*. Minneapolis: University of Minnesota Press, 1997.

Alagappa, Muthiah, ed. *Asian Security Practice: Material and Ideational Influences*. Stanford, Calif.: Stanford University Press, 1998.

Amsden, Alice H. *Asia's Next Giant: South Korea and Late Industrialization*. New York: Oxford University Press, 1989.

Andrews, David. "Capital Mobility and State Autonomy: Toward a Structural Theory of International Monetary Relations." *International Studies Quarterly* 38, no. 2 (1994): 193–218.

Annan, Kofi. "Two Concepts of Sovereignty." *Economist,* September 18, 1999, 49–50.

Appadurai, Arjun. *Modernity at Large: Cultural Dimensions of Globalization*. Minneapolis: University of Minnesota Press, 1996.

Appiah, Kwame Anthony. "Cosmopolitan Patriots." In *Cosmopolitics: Thinking and Feeling beyond the Nation,* edited by Pheng Cheah and Bruce Robbins. Minneapolis: University of Minnesota Press, 1998.

Baker, Chris. "Politics of Crisis: Failure, Reform and Division." Paper presented to the National Thai Studies Centre and APSEM 1999 Thai Update Conference, Australian National University, Canberra, April 1999.

Baldwin, Richard E., and Philippe Martin. "Two Waves of Globalization: Superficial Similarities, Fundamental Differences." National Bureau of Economic Research Working Paper no. 6904, January 1999.

Barber, Benjamin. *Jihad vs. McWorld*. New York: Times Books, 1995.

Beinart, Peter. "An Illusion for Our Time: The False Promise of Globalization." *New Republic,* October 20, 1997, 20–24.

Bello, Walden. "East Asia: On the Eve of the Great Transformation?" *Review of International Political Economy* 5, no. 3 (1998): 424–44.

———. "The Answer: De-Globalize." *Far Eastern Economic Review,* April 29, 1999, 61.

Bello, Walden, and Shea Cunningham. "Trade Warfare and Regional Integration in the Pacific: The USA, Japan, and the Asian NICs." *Third World Quarterly,* no. 3 (1994): 445–58.

Berger, Suzanne, and Richard K. Lester, eds. *Made by Hong Kong*. Hong Kong: Oxford University Press, 1997.

Brecher, Jeremy, and Tim Costello. *Global Village or Global Pillage: Economic Reconstruction from the Bottom Up*. Boston: South End Press, 1994.

Brown, Ian. *The Creation of the Modern Ministry of Finance in Siam, 1885–1910*. London: Macmillan, 1992.

Brunhes, Bernard. "Labor Flexibility in Enterprise: A Comparison of Firms in Four European Countries." In *Labor Market Flexibility: Trends in Enterprises*. Paris: Organization for Economic Development, 1989.

Bunnell, Tim. "Multimedia Utopia? A Geographical Critique of IT Discourse in Malaysia." Paper presented at the Second International Malaysian Studies Conference, University of Malaya, Kuala Lumpur, Malaysia, August 2–4, 1999.

Chalmers, Ian, and Vedhi R. Hadiz, eds. *The Politics of Economic Development in Indonesia*. New York: Routledge, 1996.

Chang, Ha-Joon, Park Hong-Jae, and Yoo Chul Gyue. "Interpreting the Korean Crisis: Financial Liberalization, Industrial Policy, and Corporate Governance." *Cambridge Journal of Economics*, no. 6 (November 1998) 735–46.

Cho, Dong Seok. *The South Korean Chaebol*. Seoul: Maeil Kyungje Shinmunsa, 1997.

Choi, Seoung-No. *The Analysis of the Thirty Korean Big Business Groups for 1996*. Seoul: Korea Economic Research Institute, 1996.

Chu, Hun-han. "Social Protests and Political Democratization in Taiwan." In *The Other Taiwan: 1945 to the Present*, edited by Murray A. Rubinstein. Armonk, N.Y.: M. E. Sharpe, 1994.

Chu, Yun-han. "The Realignment of Business-Government Relations and Regime Transition in Taiwan." In *Business and Government in Industrializing Asia*, edited by Andrew MacIntyre. Ithaca, N.Y.: Cornell University Press, 1994.

Clough, Ralph N. *Cooperation or Conflict in the Taiwan Strait?* Lanham, Md.: Rowman & Littlefield, 1999.

Cohen, Benjamin. "Phoenix Risen: The Resurrection of Global Finance." *World Politics* 48, no. 2 (1996): 268–96.

Cohen, Eliot. "A Revolution in Warfare." *Foreign Affairs* 75, no. 2 (1996): 37–54.

Contemporary Taiwan. Special issue of *China Quarterly*, no. 148 (December 1996).

Cox, Robert. "Democracy in Hard Times: Economic Globalization and the Limits to Liberal Democracy." In *The Transformation of Democracy? Globalization and Territorial Democracy*, edited by Anthony McGrew. Cambridge: Polity Press, 1997.

Crane, George T. "Imagining the Economic Nation: Globalization in China." *New Political Economy* 4, no. 2 (July 1999): 215–32.

Crouch, Harold. *Government and Society in Malaysia*. Ithaca, N.Y.: Cornell University Press, 1996.

Dean, William. "Recent Capital Flows to Asia Pacific Countries: Trade-Offs and Dilemmas." *Journal of the Asia Pacific Economy* 1, no. 3 (1996): 287–317.

Deng, Yong. "The Chinese Conception of National Interests in International Relations." *China Quarterly*, no. 154 (1998): 308–29.

Dickenson, Donna. "Counting Women In: Globalization, Democratization, and the Women's Movement." In *The Transformation of Democracy? Globalization and Territorial Democracy*, edited Anthony McGrew. London: Polity Press, 1997.

Dittmer, Lowell, and Samuel S. Kim, eds. *China's Quest for National Identity*. Ithaca, N.Y.: Cornell University Press, 1993.

Doremus, Paul N., William W. Keller, Louis W. Pauly, and Simon Reich. *The Myth of the Global Corporation*. Princeton, N.J.: Princeton University Press, 1998.

Eichengreen, Barry. "The Asian Financial Crisis: The IMF and Its Critics." In *Great Decisions 1999*. Washington, D.C.: Foreign Policy Institute, 1999.

Elegant, Simon, and Murray Hiebert. "Tech Mecca." *Far Eastern Economic Review,* March 16, 2000, 48–50.

Emmerson, Donald K. "Americanizing Asia?" *Foreign Affairs* 77, no. 3 (May–June 1998): 46–56.

Falk, Richard. "Resisting 'Globalization-from-above' through 'Globalization-from-below.'" *New Political Economy,* no. 2 (1997): 17–24.

——. "State of Siege: Will Globalization Win Out?" *International Affairs* 73, no. 1 (1997): 123–36.

——. *Law in an Emerging Global Village: A Post-Westphalian Perspective*. Ardsley, N.Y.: Transnational Publishers, 1998.

Fang Ning, Wang Xiaodong, and Song Qiang. *Quanqiuhua yinying xia de Zhongguo zhilu* [China's road: Under the shadow of globalization]. Beijing: Zhongguo shehui kexue chubanshe, 1999.

Felker, Greg. "Globalization and the State in Late Industrialization: The Malaysian and Thai Cases." Paper presented at the annual meeting of the American Political Science Association, September 36, 1999.

Feng Hua-nong. *Taiwan de zhongji mingyun* [The determinative fate of Taiwan]. Taipei: Shengzhi, 1996.

Findlay, A. M., F. L. N. Li, A. J. Jowett, and Ronald Skeldon. "Skilled International Migration and the Global City: A Study of Expatriates in Hong Kong." *Transactions— Institute of British Geographers* 21, no. 1 (1996): 49–61.

Fine, Robert. "Civil Society Theory, Enlightenment and Critique." *Democratization* 4, no. 1 (1997): 7–28.

Frank, Thomas C. "Paeon of Praise to Globalization: Creation Myth of the 'Geo-Architect.'" *Le Monde Diplomatique,* July 1999.

Frenkel, Stephen J., and David Peetz. "Globalization and Industrial Relations in East Asia." *Industrial Relations* 37, no. 3 (July 1998): 282–310.

Frieden, Jeffrey. "Invested Interests: The Politics of National Economic Policies in a World of Global Finance." *International Organization* 45, no. 4 (1991): 425–51.

Friedman, Thomas L. *The Lexus and the Olive Tree*. New York: Farrar, Straus & Giroux, 1999.

Garg, Ramesh, Suk H. Kim, and Eugene Swinnerton. "The Asian Financial Crisis of 1997 and Its Consequences." *Multinational Business Review* 7, no. 2 (fall 1999): 32–36.

Geoffrey, D., and S. D. Stafford. "Malaysia's New Economic Policy and the Global Economy: The Evolution of Ethnic Accommodation." *Pacific Review* 10, no. 4 (1997): 556–80.

Gerardo, R. Ungson, Richard M. Steers, and Seung-Ho Park. *Korean Enterprise: The Quest for Globalization*. Boston: Harvard Business School Press, 1997.

Gereffi, Gary, and Miguel Korzeniewicz, eds. *Commodity Chains and Global Capitalism*. Westport, Conn.: Greenwood Press, 1994.

Giddens, Anthony. BBC Reith Lectures 1–5. Available at <http://www.news.bbc.co.uk/hi/english/static/events/reith_99>.

Gills, Barry, K. "Korean Capitalism and Democracy." In *Low Intensity Democracy: Political Power in the New World Order,* edited by Barry K. Gills, J. Rocamora, and R. Wilson. London: Pluto Press, 1993.

———. "The International Origins of South Korea's Export Orientation." In *Transcending the State/Global Divide: A Neo-Structuralist Agenda in International Relations,* edited by R. Palan and Barry Gills. Boulder, Colo.: Lynne Rienner, 1994.

———. "Economic Liberalization and Reform in South Korea in the 1990s: A 'Coming of Age' or a Case of 'Graduation Blues?'" *Third World Quarterly* 17, no. 4 (1996): 667–88.

———. "The Crisis of Postwar East Asian Capitalism: American Power, Democracy, and the Vicissitudes of Globalization." *Review of International Studies* 26 (July 2000): 381–403.

———. *Globalization and the Politics of Resistance.* London: Macmillan/St. Martin's, 2000.

Ginsberg, Faye D., and Rayna Rapp, eds. *Conceiving the New World Order: The Global Politics of Reproduction.* Berkeley: University of California Press, 1995.

Goldblatt, David, et al. "Economic Globalization and the Nation-State: Shifting Balances of Power." *Alternatives* 22, no. 3 (1997): 269–85.

Goldstein, Morris. *The Asian Financial Crisis: Causes, Cures, and Systemic Implications.* Washington, D.C.: Institute for International Economics, 1998.

Gomez, Edmund Terence, and K. S. Jomo. *Malaysia's Political Economy: Politics Patronage and Profits.* New York: Cambridge University Press, 1997.

Government of Malaysia. *Sixth Malaysia Plan: "The Way Forward: Vision 2020."* Kuala Lumpur: Government of Malaysia, 1990.

Haggard, Stephan. *The Pathways from Periphery: The Politics of Growth in the Newly Industrializing Countries.* Ithaca, N.Y.: Cornell University Press, 1990.

Han, Sung-Joo. *Korea in a Changing World: Democracy, Diplomacy, and Future Developments.* Seoul: OREUM, 1995.

———. *Segyehwa sidae ui Hankuk oyekyo* [Korean diplomacy in an era of globalization: Speeches of Foreign Minister Han Sung-Joo, March 1993–December 1994]. Seoul: Chisik samopsa, 1995.

Han, Xiuchen, and Zhou Yongsheng. "Shijie jingji geju de bianhua jiqi dui woguo de yingxiang yu duice" [The transformation of world economic order: Implications to the Chinese economy and suggested responses]. *Shijie jingji wenhui* [World Economic Forum], no. 5 (1995): 10–15.

Hartmann, Betsy. *Reproductive Rights and Wrongs: The Global Politics of Population Control and Contraceptive Choice.* Rev. ed. Boston: South End Press, 1995.

Hasegawa, Keitaro. *Ajia daitenkan to Nippon* [The shift of the Asian MEGA trend]. Tokyo: Kobun-sha, 1997.

Hatch, Walter, and Kozo Yamamura. *Asia in Japan's Embrace: Building a Regional Production Alliance.* Cambridge: Cambridge University Press, 1996.

Held, David. *Democracy and the Global Order.* Stanford, Calif.: Stanford University Press, 1995.

———. "Democracy and Globalization." *Global Governance* 3 (1997): 251–67.

Held, David, Anthony McGrew, David Goldblatt, and Jonathan Perraton. *Global Transformation: Politics, Economics and Culture.* Stanford, Calif.: Stanford University Press, 1999.

Higgot, Richard. "The Asian Economic Crisis: A Study in the Politics of Resentment." *New Political Economy* 3, no. 3 (November 1998): 333–56.

Hirst, Paul, and Grahame Thompson. *Globalization in Question?* Cambridge: Polity Press, 1996.

Hong, Yuan. "The Implication of the TMD System in Japan to China's Security." Paper presented at the Sixth ISODARCO Beijing Seminar on Arms Control, October 29–November 1, 1998. From npp@nautilus.org_npp@nautilus.org Nuclear Policy List.

Hood, Steven J. *The Kuomintang and the Democratization of Taiwan*. Boulder, Colo.: Westview, 1997.

Hoogvelt, Ankie. *Globalization and the Postcolonial World*. London: Macmillan, 1997.

Hsiao Hsin-Huang. *Social Transformation, Nascent Civil Society, and the Taiwanese Capital in Fujian*. Hong Kong: Institute of Asia-Pacific Studies, August 1998.

Hsiung, Ping-Chun. *Living Rooms as Factories: Class, Gender, and the Satellite Factory System in Taiwan*. Philadelphia: Temple University Press, 1996.

Hughes, Christopher. "Globalization and Nationalism: Squaring the Circle in Chinese International Relations Theory." *Millennium: Journal of International Studies* 26, no. 1 (1997): 103–24.

———. *Taiwan and Chinese Nationalism: National Identity and Status in International Society*. London: Routledge, 1997.

Huntington, Samuel P. *The Third Wave: Democratization in the Late Twentieth Century*. Norman: Oklahoma University Press, 1991.

———. *The Clash of Civilizations and the Remaking of World Order*. New York: Simon & Schuster, 1996.

International Institute for Management Development. *World Competitiveness Yearbook 1998*. Lausanne: International Institute for Management Development, 1998.

———. *World Competitiveness Yearbook 1999*. Lausanne: International Institute for Management Development, 1999.

International Institute for Strategic Studies. *The Military Balance, 1997/98*. London: Oxford University Press, 1997.

International Monetary Fund. *Direction of Trade Statistics Yearbook, 1999*. Washington, D.C.: International Monetary Fund, 1999.

———. *World Economic Outlook*. Washington, D.C.: International Monetary Fund, October 1999.

Jackson, Karl, ed. *Asian Contagion*. Boulder, Colo.: Westview, 1999.

Jacobs, Jane. *Cities and the Wealth of Nations: Principles of Economic Life*. New York: Random House, 1984.

Japanese Ministry of Foreign Affairs. *1998 Diplomatic White Paper*. Available at <http://www.mofa.go.jp/policy/other/bluebook/1998>.

Johnson, Chalmers. "In Search of a New Cold War." *Bulletin of the Atomic Scientists* 55, no. 5 (1999); 44–51.

Jomo, K. S. *Privatizing Malaysia: Rents, Rhetoric, and Realities*. Boulder, Colo.: Westview, 1995.

———, ed. *Tigers in Trouble*. New York: St. Martin's, 1998.

Kang, In Duk. "South Korea's Strategy toward North Korea in Connection with Its 'Segyehwa' Drive." *East Asian Review* 7, no. 1 (spring 1995): 55–70.

Kang, Jun-man. *Kim Young-sam ideologi* [Kim Young-sam's ideology]. Seoul: Kaimagowon, 1995.

Keller, William W., and Janne E. Nolan. "The Arms Trade: Business as Usual?" *Foreign Policy,* no. 109 (winter 1997–1998): 113–25.

Keohane, Robert O., and Helen Milner, eds. *Internationalization and Domestic Politics.* Cambridge: Cambridge University Press, 1996.

Keohane, Robert O., and Joseph S. Nye, Jr. "Power and Interdependence in the Information Age." *Foreign Affairs* 77 (September–October 1998): 81–94.

Kim, Dae-jung. *Daejung Kyungjaeron* [Mass-participatory economics]. Seoul: Cheongsa, 1986.

Kim, Eun Mee. *Big Business, Strong State: Collusion and Conflict in South Korean Development, 1960–1990.* Albany: State University of New York Press, 1997.

———. "Crisis of the Developmental State in South Korea." *Asian Perspective* 23, no. 2 (1999): 35–55.

Kim, Samuel S. "Taiwan and the International System: The Challenge of Legitimation." In *Taiwan in World Affairs,* edited by Robert Sutter and William Johnson. Boulder, Colo.: Westview, 1994.

———. "The Impact of the Division of Korea on South Korean Politics: The Challenge of Competitive Legitimation." In *Korean Democracy toward a New Horizon.* Seoul: Korean Political Science Association, 1995.

———, ed. *China and the World: Chinese Foreign Policy Faces the New Millennium.* Boulder, Colo.: Westview, 1998.

———, ed. *Korea's Globalization.* New York: Cambridge University Press, 2000.

Kim, Seung Kyong. *Class Struggle or Family Struggle? The Lives of Women Factory Workers in South Korea.* Cambridge: Cambridge University Press, 1997.

Kim, Yong Cheol. "The State and Labor in South Korea." In *The Rush to Development: Economic Change and Political Struggle in South Korea,* edited by Martin Landsberg. New York: Monthly Review Press, 1993.

King, Ambrose. "State Confucianism and Its Transformation: The Restructuring of the State-Society Relation in Taiwan." In *Confucian Traditions in East Asian Modernity,* edited by Tu Wei-Ming. Cambridge, Mass.: Harvard University Press, 1996.

Kitamura, Kayoko, and Tsuneo Tanaka, eds. *Examining Asia's Tigers: Nine Economies Challenging Common Structural Problems.* Tokyo: Institute of Developing Economies, 1997.

Klare, Michael, and Yogesh Chandrani, eds. *World Security: Challenges for a New Century.* New York: St. Martin's, 1998.

Korea International Labor Foundation. *Handbook of the Social Agreement and New Labor Laws of Korea.* Seoul: Korea International Labor Foundation, 1998.

———. *Labor Reform in Korea Toward the Twenty-first Century.* Seoul: Korea International Labor Foundation, 1998.

Korean Overseas Information Service. *The Segyehwa Policy of Korea under President Kim Young Sam.* Seoul: Korean Overseas Information Service, 1995.

Krugman, Paul. "Capital Control Freaks: How Malaysia Got Away with Economic Heresy." *Slate,* September 27, 1999.

Kuwahara, Yasuo. "Japanese Industrial Relations." In *International and Comparative Industrial Relations: A Study of Developed Market Economics,* edited by Greg J. Bamber and Russell D. Lansbury. London: Allen & Unwin, 1987.

Lai, Kon S., Dong-Woo Lee, Jean Loo, and Jong-Hwan Yi. "Asian Financial Crisis Shows Globalization Can Promote Risks as Well as Opportunities." *Business Forum* 23, nos. 1–2 (winter–spring 1998).

Lee, Hong-koo. "Attitudinal Reform toward Globalization." *Korea Focus* 2, no. 2 (March–April 1994): 85–94.

Lee, Hye-kyung. "The Employment of Foreign Workers in Korea: Issues and Policy Suggestions." *International Sociology* 12, no. 3 (1997): 353–71.

Lee, Kyu Uck, and Jae Hyung Lee. *Business Group (Chaebol) in Korea: Characteristics and Government Policy*. Seoul: Korea Industrial Economics and Trade, 1996.

Lee Teng-hui. *The Road to Democracy: Taiwan's Pursuit of Identity*. Tokyo: PHP Institute, 1999.

Leipziger, D. M. "Public and Private Interests in Korea: Views on Moral Hazard and Crisis Resolution." EDI Discussion Paper. Washington, D.C.: World Bank, May 1998.

Leng Tse-kang. *The Taiwan-China Connection*. Boulder, Colo.: Westview, 1996.

Lett, Denise Potrzeba. *In Pursuit of Status: The Making of South Korea's "New" Urban Middle Class*. Cambridge, Mass.: Harvard University Press, 1998.

Leung, Beatrice, and Joseph Cheng, eds. *Hong Kong SAR: In Pursuit of Domestic and International Order*. Hong Kong: Chinese University of Hong Kong Press, 1997.

Lewis, George N., Theodore A. Postol, and John Pike. "Why National Missile Defense Won't Work." *Scientific American* 281, no. 2 (1999): 36–41.

Li, F. L. N., A. M. Findlay, and H. Jones. "A Cultural Economy Perspective on Service Sector Migration in the Global City: The Case of Hong Kong." *International Migration* 36, no. 2 (1998): 31–58.

Lin Cheng-yi. "The Taiwan Factor in Asia-Pacific Regional Security." In *North-East Asian Regional Security: The Role of International Institutions,* edited by T. Inoguchi and G. Stillman. Tokyo: United Nations University Press, 1995.

Lloyd, P. J. "Globalization, Foreign Investment, and Migration." In *International Trade and Migration in the APEC Region,* edited by P. J. Lloyd and Lynne S. Williams. New York: Oxford University Press, 1996.

Lo, Fu-Chen, and Yue-man Yeung, eds. *Emerging World Cities in Pacific Asia*. Tokyo: United Nations University Press, 1996.

Lü Ronghai. *Zhonghua Taiwan guolian* [United Republics of China and Taiwan]. Taipei: Shinian hui, 1995.

Lu Yi et al., eds. *Qiuji: Yige shijiexing de xuanze* [Global citizenship: A worldwide choice]. Shanghai: Baijia chubanshe, 1989.

Machado, Kit G. "Malaysian Cultural Relations with Japan and South Korea in the 1980s: Look East." *Asian Survey* 27, no. 6 (1987): 638–60.

Magretta, Joan. "Fast, Global, and Entrepreneurial: Supply Chain Management, Hong Kong Style." *Harvard Business Review* (September/October 1998): 102–14.

Mahathir, Mohamad. *The New Deal for Asia*. Kuala Lumpur: Pelanduk Publications, 1999.

Management Efficiency Research Institute. *Analysis of Financial Statements—Thirty Major Business Groups in Korea*. Seoul: Management Efficiency Research Institute, 1985–1996.

Managing Economic Crisis: The Malaysian Experience. Kuala Lumpur: Dato' Abdul Rashid Mahmud, 1999.

Mann, Michael. "Has Globalization Ended the Rise and Rise of the Nation-State?" *Review of International Political Economy* 4, no. 3 (1997): 472–96.

Mansbach, Richard W., and Dong Won Suh. "A Tumultuous Season: Globalization and the Korean Case." *Asian Perspective* 22, no. 2 (1998): 243–68.

Mauzy, D., and R. S. Milne. "The Mahathir Administration: Discipline through Islam." *Pacific Affairs* 56, no. 4 (1983–1984): 617–48.

McGrew, Anthony, ed. *The Transformation of Democracy? Globalization and Territorial Democracy*. Cambridge: Polity Press, 1997.

McLeod, Ross, and Ross Garnaut, eds. *East Asia in Crisis*. New York: Routledge, 1998.

McNally, David. "Globalization on Trial." *Monthly Review* 50, no. 4 (September 1998).

Meyer, D. R. "Expert Managers of Uncertainty: Intermediaries of Capital in Hong Kong." *Cities* 14, no. 5 (1997): 257–64.

Milne, R. S., and D. Mauzy. *Malaysian Politics under Mahathir*. New York: Routledge, 1999.

Ministry of Finance and Economy, Overall Economic Policy Division. *Challenge and Chance: Korea's Response to the New Economic Reality*. Seoul: Ministry of Finance and Economy, 1998.

Ministry of Foreign Affairs and Trade. *1998 Oyekyo paekso* [1998 diplomatic white paper]. Seoul: Ministry of Foreign Affairs and Trade, 1999.

Ministry of National Defense. *Defense White Paper 1999*. Seoul: Ministry of National Defense, 1999.

Mittelman, James H., ed. *Globalization: Critical Reflections*. Boulder, Colo.: Lynne Rienner, 1997.

Mo, Jongryun, and Chung-in Moon, eds. *Democracy and the Korean Economy*. Stanford, Calif.: Hoover Institution Press, 1999.

———. "Korea after the Crash." *Journal of Democracy* 10, no. 3 (July 1999): 150–64.

Montes, Manuel. *The Currency Crisis in Southeast Asia*. Singapore: Institute of Southeast Asian Studies, 1998.

Moon, Chung-in. "Changing Patterns of Business-Government Relations in South Korea." In *Business and Government in Industrializing Asia,* edited by Andrew MacIntyre. Ithaca, N.Y.: Cornell University Press, 1994.

———. "Globalization: Challenges and Strategies." *Korea Focus* 3, no. 3 (May–June 1995): 64–67.

Moon, Chung-in, and Kim Yong Cheol. "A Circle of Paradox: Development, Politics, and Democracy in South Korea." In *Democracy and Development: Theory and Practice,* edited by Adrian Leftwich. London: Polity Press, 1996.

Moon, Chung-in, and Jongryun Mo, eds. *Democratization and Globalization in Korea: Assessments and Prospects*. Seoul: Yonsei University Press, 1999.

Moore, Thomas G. "China as a Latecomer: Toward a Global Logic of the Open Policy." *Journal of Contemporary China* 5, no. 12 (summer 1996): 187–208.

Moore, Thomas G., and Dixia Yang. "Empowered and Restrained: Chinese Foreign Policy in the Age of Economic Interdependence." In *The Making of Chinese Foreign and Security Policy in the Era of Reform, 1978–2000,* edited by David M. Lampton. Stanford, Calif.: Stanford University Press, in press.

Morrison, Charles, ed. *Asia-Pacific Security Outlook*. Honolulu: East-West Center, 1997.

Morrison, Charles E., and Hadi Soesastro, eds. *Domestic Adjustments to Globalization*. Tokyo: Japan Center for International Exchange, 1998.

New Industry Management Academy. *Financial Analysis of the South Korean Thirty Chaebol*. Seoul: New Industry Management Academy, 1998.

Noland, Marcus, Li-Gang Liu, Sherman Robinson, and Zhi Wang. *Global Economic Effects of the Asian Currency Devaluations*. Washington, D.C.: Institute for International Economics, 1998.

Nye, Joseph, and William Owens. "America's Information Edge." *Foreign Affairs* 75, no. 2 (1998): 20–36.

O'Hanlon, Michael. "Star Wars Strikes Back." *Foreign Affairs* 78, no. 6 (1999): 68–82.

Ohmae, Kenichi. *The Borderless World: Power and Strategy in the Interlinked Economy.* New York: HarperBusiness, 1990.

———. "The Rise of the Region State." *Foreign Affairs* 27, no. 2 (spring 1993): 78–87.

Oka, Takashi. *Prying Open the Door: Foreign Workers in Japan.* Washington, D.C.: Carnegie Endowment for Peace, 1994.

Okura, Masanori. "The Asian Currency Crisis and Future Policy Problems." *Social Science Japan* 13 (August 1998): 13–15.

Oman, Charles. *Globalization and Regionalization: The Challenge for Developing Countries.* Paris: Organization for Economic Cooperation and Development, 1994.

Ong, Aihwa. *Spirits of Resistance and Capitalist Discipline: Factory Women in Malaysia.* Albany: State University of New York Press, 1987.

———. "'A Better Tomorrow'? The Struggle for Global Visibility." *Sojourn* 12, no. 2 (1997): 192–225.

Ong Hong Cheong, "Evolution of the Malaysian Financial System beyond the Financial Crisis." In *East Asia's Financial Systems: Evolution and Crisis,* edited by S. Masutama et al. Singapore: ISEAS Institute of Southeast Asian Studies, 1999.

Organization for Economic Cooperation and Development. *Trade, Employment, and Labor Standard: A Study of Core Workers Rights and International Trade.* Paris: OECD, 1996.

Pang, Zhongying. "Globalization and China: China's Response to the Asian Economic Crisis." *Asian Perspective* 23, no. 1 (1999): 111–31.

Pasuk Phongpaichit. "Developing Social Alternatives: Walking Backwards into a Klong." Paper presented at the National Thai Studies Centre and APSEM 1999 Thai Update Conference, Australian National University, Canberra, April 1999.

Pasuk Phongpaichit and Chris Baker. "The Political Economy of the Thai Crisis." *Journal of the Asian Pacific Economy* 4, no. 1 (1999): 193–208.

Pempel, T. J., ed. *Politics of the Asian Economic Crisis.* Ithaca, N.Y.: Cornell University Press, 1999.

Perraton, Jonathan, et al. "The Globalization of Economic Activity." *New Political Economy* 2, no. 2 (1997): 257–77.

Peterson, V. Spike. "The Politics of Identification in the Context of Globalization." *Women's Studies International Forum* 19, no. 1–2 (1996): 5–15.

Pettway, Richard H. "Asian Financial Crisis: The Role of China and Japan in the Post-Asian Crisis Era." *Multinational Business Review* 7, no. 2 (fall 1999): 13–21.

Postiglione, Gerard A., and James T. H. Tang, eds. *Hong Kong's Reunion with China: The Global Dimensions.* Armonk, N.Y.: M. E. Sharpe, 1997.

Prasso, Sherri. "The Anwar-Mahathir Conflict." *Business Week,* February 1998.

Prema-chandra Athukorala. "Swimming against the Tide: Crisis Management in Malaysia." In *Southeast Asia's Economic Crisis: Origins, Lessons, and the Way Forward,* edited by H. W. Arndt and H. Hill. 1999.

Presidential Segyehwa Promotion Committee. *Segyehwa ui pichon kwa chonryak* [Globalization vision and strategy]. Seoul: Presidential Segyehwa Promotion Committee, August 1995.

Qiao Liang and Wang Xianghui. *Chaoxian Zhan* [Unlimited war]. Beijing: People's Liberation Army Cultural Press, 1999.

Radelet, Steven, and Jeffrey Sachs. "The East Asian Financial Crisis: Diagnosis, Remedies, Prospects." *Brookings Papers on Economic Activity*, no. 1 (1998): 1–90.

———. "The Onset of the East Asian Financial Crisis." National Bureau of Economic Research Working Paper no. 6680 (August 1998).

Rasiah, Rajah. *Foreign Capital and Industrialization in Malaysia*. London: Macmillan, 1995.

Reich, Robert. *The Work of Nations*. New York: Vintage, 1992.

Reinicke, Wolfgang. "Global Public Policy." *Foreign Affairs* 76, no. 6 (1997): 127–38.

Reynolds, Craig. "Globalization and Cultural Nationalism in Modern Thailand." In *Southeast Asian Identities: Culture and the Politics of Representation in Indonesia, Malaysia, Singapore, and Thailand*, edited by Joel Kahn. Singapore: Institute of Southeast Asian Studies, 1998.

Rigger, Shelley. *Politics in Taiwan: Voting for Democracy*. New York: Routledge, 1999.

Risse, Thomas, Stephen Ropp, and Kathryn Sikkink, eds. *Power of Human Rights: International Norms and Domestic Change*. Cambridge: Cambridge University Press, 1999.

Robertson, Roland. *Globalization: Social Theory and Global Culture*. London: Sage, 1992.

Robison, Richard, and David S. G. Goodman, eds. *The New Rich in Asia: Mobile Phones, McDonald's, and Middle-Class Revolution*. New York: Routledge, 1996.

Rodrik, Dani. *Has Globalization Gone Too Far?* Washington, D.C.: Institute for International Economics, 1997.

———. "Sense and Nonsense in the Globalization Debate." *Foreign Policy*, no. 107 (summer 1997): 19–37.

———. "Why Do More Open Economies Have Bigger Governments?" *Journal of Political Economy* 106, no. 5 (October 1998): 997–1032.

———. "The Asian Financial Crisis and the Virtues of Democracy." *Challenge* 42, no. 4 (July–August 1999): 44–59.

———. "Governing the Global Economy: Does One Architectural Style Fit All?" Paper prepared at the Brookings Institution Trade Policy Forum Conference on Governing in a Global Economy, Washington, D.C., April 1999.

Rosenau, James N. "The Dynamics of Globalization: Toward an Operational Formulation." *Security Dialogues* 27, no. 3 (1996): 247–62.

———. *Along the Domestic-Foreign Frontier: Exploring Governance in a Turbulent World*. New York: Cambridge University Press, 1997.

Roy, Denny. "Human Rights as a National Security Threat: The Case of China." *Issues & Studies* 32, no. 2 (1996): 65–81.

———. "Human Rights and National Security in East Asia." *Issues & Studies* 35, no. 2 (1999): 132–51.

Ruggie, John G. "At Home Abroad, Abroad at Home: International Liberalization and Domestic Stability in the New World Economy." *Millennium: Journal of International Studies* 24, no. 3 (1994): 507–26.

Sachs, Jeffrey. "International Economics: Unlocking the Mysteries of Globalization." *Foreign Policy*, no. 110 (spring 1998): 97–111.

———. "Ten Trends in Global Competitiveness in 1998." In *Global Competitiveness Report 1998*. Available at <http://www.weforum.org/publications/GCR/sachs.asp>.

Sassen, Saskia. *The Global City: New York, London, Tokyo*. Princeton, N.J.: Princeton University Press, 1991.

———. *Losing Control? Sovereignty in an Age of Globalization*. New York: Columbia University Press, 1996.

Schwarz, Adam, and Jonathan Parris, eds. *The Politics of Post-Suharto Indonesia*. New York: Council on Foreign Relations Press, 1999.

Sharma, Shalendra. "Bitter Medicine for Sick Tigers: The IMF and Asia's Financial Crisis." *Pacific Rim Report*, no. 8 (June 1998).

Shen Min. *Taihai zhanzheng da yuyan* [Predictions about war in the Taiwan Strait]. Taipei: Dujia, 1997.

Sheng Lijun. "China and the United States: Asymmetrical Strategic Partners." *Washington Quarterly* 22, no. 3 (1999): 147–63.

Short, John Rennie, and Yeong-Hyun Kim. *Globalization and the City*. New York: Longman, 1999.

Silliman, G. Sidney, and Lela Garner Noble. *Organizing for Democracy: NGOs, Civil Society, and the Philippine State*. Honolulu: University of Hawaii Press, 1998.

Simon, Denis Fred. "Charting Taiwan's Technological Future: The Impact of Globalization and Regionalization." *China Quarterly* (December 1996): 1196–1223.

———, ed. *Techno-Security in an Age of Globalization*. Armonk, N.Y.: M. E. Sharpe, 1997.

Singh, Ajit, and Bruce A. Weisse. "The Asian Model: A Crisis Foretold?" *International Social Science Journal* (June 1999): 203–15.

Skeldon, Ronald, ed. *Reluctant Exiles? Migration from Hong Kong and the New Overseas Chinese*. Armonk, N.Y.: M. E. Sharpe, 1994.

Soesastro, Hadi. *Globalization, Governance, and Sustainable Development*. Jakarta: Center for Strategic and International Studies, 1999.

Song, Qiang, et al. *Zhongguo haishi shuo bu: Zhongguo keyi shuo bu xupin: Guoji guanxi bianshu yu women de xianshi yingfu* [China still can say no: The sequel to China can say no: The variables in international relations and our realistic handling]. Beijing: Zhongguo wenlian chubanshe, 1996.

———. *Zhongguo keyi shuo bu: Lengzhanhou shidai de zhengzhi yu qingnan jueze* [China can say no: The political and emotional choice in the post–Cold War era]. Beijing: Zhongguo gongshang lianhe chubanshe, 1996.

Steven, Rob. *Classes in Contemporary Japan*. Cambridge: Cambridge University Press, 1983.

Strange, Susan. "The Defective State." *Daedalus* 124, no. 2 (1995): 55–74.

———. *The Retreat of the State: The Diffusion of Power in the World Economy*. New York: Cambridge University Press, 1996.

Tabb, William K. "The East Asian Financial Crisis." *Monthly Review* 50, no. 2 (June 1998): 24–38.

Talbott, Strobe. "Globalization and Diplomacy: A Practitioner's Perspective." *Foreign Policy*, no. 108 (fall 1997): 69–83.

Tanzer, Andrew. "Silicon Valley East." *Forbes,* June 1, 1998: 122–27.

"Thinking about Globalization: Popular Myths and Economic Facts." *Economist* (London). Available at <http://www.economist.com/editorial/freeforall/18-1-98/sb0225.html>.

Timperlake, Edward, and William C. Triplett II. *Red Dragon Rising: Communist China's Military Threat to America*. Washington, D.C.: Regnery, 1999.

Transparency International. *Bribe Payers Index*. Berlin: Transparency International, 1999.

———. *Corruption Perceptions Index*. Berlin: Transparency International, 1999.

Tu, Wei-ming. "Cultural China: The Periphery as the Center." *Daedalus* 120, no. 2 (spring 1991): 1–32.

Unger, Danny. *Building Social Capital in Thailand: Fibers, Finance, and Infrastructure.* Melbourne: Cambridge University Press, 1998.

Ungson, Gerardo, Richard M. Steers, and Seoung-Ho Park. *Korean Enterprise: The Quest for Globalization.* Cambridge, Mass.: Harvard Business School Press, 1997.

United Nations Conference on Trade and Development. *World Investment Report 1997.* New York: United Nations, 1997.

———. *World Competitiveness Report 1998.* New York: United Nations, 1998.

United Nations Development Program. *Human Development Reports 1995–1999.* New York: Oxford University Press, 1995–1999.

United States Department of Defense, Office of International Security Affairs. *The United States Security Strategy for the East Asia–Pacific Region.* Washington, D.C.: November 1998.

Van Ness, Peter. "Unconventional Threats to China's National Security: A Teaching Note." *Journal of Contemporary China* 9, no. 23 (2000): 127–39.

Wade, Robert. *Governing the Market: Economic Theory and the Role of Government in Asian Industrialization.* Princeton, N.J.: Princeton University Press, 1990.

Wade, Robert, and Frank Veneroso. "The Gathering Support for Capital Controls." *Challenge* 41, no. 6 (November–December 1998): 14–26.

Wang, Gungwu, and Wong, Siu-lun, eds. *Hong Kong in the Asia-Pacific Region: Rising to the New Challenges.* Hong Kong: Center for Asian Studies, University of Hong Kong, 1997.

Wang, Hexing. "Quanqiuhua dui shijie zhengzhi, jingji de shida yingxiang" [Ten influences of globalization on world politics and economies]. *Guoji wenti yanjiu* [International Studies], no. 1 (1997): 10–15, 33.

Wang Wen-liang. "An Observation of Thailand's Opening to the Outside World in the Age Globalization from a Historical Perspective." *Globalization: Impact on and Coping Strategies in Thai Society.* Proceedings of the Sixth International Conference on Thai Studies, Chang Mai, October 1996.

Wang, Yizhou. *Dangdai guoji zhengzhi xilun* [Analysis of contemporary international politics]. Shanghai: Renmin chubanshe, 1995.

———. "New Security Concept in Globalization." *Beijing Review* 42, no. 7 (February 15–21, 1997): 7.

Warr, Peter, and Bhanupong Nidhiprabha. *Thailand's Macroeconomic Miracle: Stable Adjustment and Sustained Growth.* Washington, D.C.: World Bank and Oxford University Press, 1996.

Watson, Justin. *The Christian Coalition: Dreams of Restoration, Demand for Recognition.* New York: St. Martin's, 1997.

Weber, Steven, ed. *Globalization and European Political Economy.* New York: Columbia University Press, 2000.

Welsh, Bridget. "The Political Economy of the Malaysian Tax Regime of the 1980s." Paper presented at the Southeast Asia in the Twentieth Century Conference sponsored by the University of the Philippines, Quezon City, January 28, 1998.

White, Lynn, and Li Cheng. "Elite Transformation and Modern Change in Mainland China and Taiwan." *China Quarterly,* no. 121 (March 1990): 1–35.

——. "China's Coast Identities: Region, Nation, and World. In *China's Quest for National Identity,* edited by Lowell Dittmer and Samuel S. Kim. Ithaca, N.Y. Cornell University Press, 1993.

Wickramasekara, Piyasiri. "Recent Trends in Temporary Labur Migration in Asia." In *Migration and the Labor Market in Asia.* Paris: Organization for Economic Cooperation and Development, 1996.

Wolf, Diane. *Factory Daughters: Gender, Household Dynamics, and Rural Industrialization in Java.* Berkeleys: University of California Press, 1994.

Wong, Siu-lun, and Janet W. Salaff. "Network Capital: Emigration from Hong Kong." *British Journal of Sociology* 49, no. 3 (September 1998): 358–74.

Wong, Siu-lun, and Toyojiro Maruya, eds. *Hong Kong Economy and Society: Challenges in the New Era.* Hong Kong: Center of Asian Studies, University of Hong Kong, 1998.

World Bank. *The East Asian Miracle: Economic Growth and Public Policy.* New York: Oxford University Press, 1993.

——. *World Development Indicators 1998 CD-ROM.* Washington, D.C.: World Bank, 1998.

——. *World Development Report 1991.* New York: Oxford University Press, 1991.

——. *World Development Report 1997: The State in a Changing World.* New York: Oxford University Press, 1997.

——. *World Development Report 1998/99: Knowledge for Development.* New York: Oxford University Press, 1998.

Wu Naiteh. "Social Attitudes of the Middle Classes in Taiwan." In *East Asian Middle Classes in Comparative Perspective,* edited by Hsin-Huang Michael Hsiao. Taipei: Institute of Ethnology, Academia Sinica, 1999.

Yan Xuetong. "Theater Missile Defense and Northeast Asian Security." *Nonproliferation Review* 6, no. 3 (1999): 65–74.

Yeung, Yue-man. "Planning for Pearl City: Hong Kong's Future, 1997 and Beyond." In *Strategic Alliances: An Entrepreneurial Approach to Globalization,* edited by Michael Y. Yoshino and Srinivasa U. Rangan. Boston: Harvard Business School Press, 1995.

Index

ABM. *See* Anti-Ballistic Missile Treaty
Adi Sasono, 222
AFC. *See* Asian financial crisis
Agreement on Information Technology
 (tariff reduction pact), 117
Alagappa, Muthiah, 258
Ali Alatas, 212, 218
Altman, Roger, 176
AMF. *See* Asian Monetary Fund
Amien Rais, 221, 223
Amity and Cooperation in Southeast Asia,
 Treaty of (1976; ASEAN), 269
Annan, Kofi, 228, 270
Anti-Ballistic Missile Treaty (1972), 272
antiglobalization, 4, 10, 11. *See also*
 localism, localization
Anwar, Dewi Fortuna, 227, 269
Anwar Ibrahim, 20, 49, 234, 243, 244,
 245, 248, 249
APEC. *See* Asian Pacific Economic Co-
 operation
ASEAN. *See* Association of Southeast
 Asian Nations
Asian Development Bank and Institute,
 45, 198
Asian financial crisis (AFC), 2, 22–24, 25,
 26, 264, 265; analysis of, 36–41,
 46–50, 269; origins and events of,
 32–36, 48, 51n9. *See also* International
 Monetary Fund; *individual countries*

Asian model of developmental capitalism,
 24, 25, 37, 38, 39, 40, 41, 44, 47–48
Asian Monetary Fund (AMF), 45, 71, 72
Asian Pacific Economic Co-operation
 (APEC), 45, 46, 53n34, 120, 248
Asian Regional Forum, 46
Asian Security Practice (Alagappa), 258
Asian values, 13, 19, 24, 25, 38, 39, 48; in
 Indonesia, 218; in Malaysia, 240
Association of Southeast Asian Nations
 (ASEAN), 32, 45, 46, 47, 97, 161, 173,
 236, 262, 266, 269; Regional Forum,
 46, 262, 270
Australia, 35, 225
authoritarianism, 48, 49, 96
auto industry, 23, 35, 57–58

Baker, Chris, 191
ballistic missile defenses, 272
banking: and Asian financial crisis, 35, 36,
 37, 39, 40–41, 44, 52n26; BIS
 standards for, 63–64, 68. *See also*
 individual countries
Baramuli, 224, 225
barter, 162
baseball, 165
Basle Accord, 63
Beinart, Peter, 152
Bello, Walden, 4, 193
Berger, Samuel R., 268

291

About the Volume and the Editor

This volume presents the first sustained and structured analysis of globalization in the East Asian context as well as various strategies for coping with the forces of globalization, especially in eight countries that have been selected as representative of the region. Eschewing both neoliberal "hyperglobalization" chant and neorealist "globaloney" castigation, the contributors integrate a broad synthetic analytic framework with region- and country-specific case studies. Specifically, this volume poses and addresses three major questions about East Asia's globalization. First, it identifies the range of contending conceptualizations of globalization, albeit with some overlapping characteristics, that have underpinned East Asia's changing and contradictory views and attitudes toward globalization in the 1990s. Second, it critically probes the discrepancy between promise and performance—the myths and realities—of East Asia's globalization and the complex interaction of globalization challenges and East Asian responses. Finally, it evaluates the impacts and consequences of globalization for East Asia's political, economic, social, cultural, ecological, and security development. These questions, which examine in particular the nature, challenges, responses, impacts, and consequences of East Asia's globalization, provide the focus and theme that the volume seeks to address, with special attention to the developments after the onset of the Asian financial crisis in July 1997.

Samuel S. Kim teaches in the Department of Political Science and is a senior research associate at the East Asian Institute, Columbia University. He is the author or editor of sixteen books on East Asian international relations and world-order studies, including most recently *Korea's Globalization* (New York: Cambridge University Press, 2000).

About the Contributors

Samuel S. Kim is an adjunct professor of political science and a senior research associate at the East Asian Institute, Columbia University. He is the author or editor of sixteen books on East Asian international relations and world-order studies, including most recently *Korea's Globalization* (New York: Cambridge University Press, 2000).

Lowell Dittmer is a professor of political science at the University of California at Berkeley. Among his many books are, as author, *Liu Shaoqi and the Chinese Cultural Revolution* (Armonk, N.Y.: M. E. Sharpe, rev. ed., 1998) and *Sino-Soviet Normalization and Its International Implications* (Seattle: University of Washington Press, 1992) and, as coeditor, *Informal Politics in East Asia* (Cambridge: Cambridge University Press, 2000) and *China's Quest for National Identity* (Ithaca, N.Y.: Cornell University Press, 1993).

Barry K. Gills teaches in and directs the postgraduate programs in international political economy and transnational development at the Department of Politics, University of Newcastle upon Tyne, United Kingdom. He is a founding editor of the *Review of International Political Economy* and a frequent guest editor for *Third World Quarterly*. His latest works include *Korea versus Korea: A Case of Contested Legitimacy* (New York: Routledge, 1996) and *The World System* (coedited with A. G. Frank), reprinted in paperback in 1996.

Dong-Sook S. Gills teaches sociology and international development at the School of International Studies, University of Sunderland, United Kingdom. A specialist on women and development, her latest work is *The Forgotten Workers: Rural Women and Triple Exploitation in Korean Industrialization* (New York: Macmillan, in press).

William W. Grimes is an assistant professor of international relations at Boston University. He is the Reischauer Institute Visiting Assistant Professor of Government at Harvard University for 1999–2000 and has written *Unmaking the Japanese Miracle: Macroeconomic Politics since 1985* (Ithaca, N.Y.: Cornell University Press, in press). His current research project is on the internationalization of the yen.

Natasha Hamilton-Hart is a postdoctoral fellow in the Department of International Relations, Research School of Pacific and Asian Studies, the Australian National University. She received her Ph.D. from Cornell University in 1999. Her most recent publication, concerning the Singapore state, will appear in a year 2000 issue of *Pacific Review*.

Thomas G. Moore is an assistant professor of political science at the University of Cincinnati, where he teaches courses on Asian politics, U.S. foreign policy, and international political economy. His most recent publication, on China and APEC, appears in the *Journal of East Asian Affairs,* and he has written *China in the World Market: International Sources of Reform and Restructuring in the Deng Xiaoping Era* (Cambridge: Cambridge University Press, in press).

Ann Marie Murphy is an adjunct professor at the School of International and Public Affairs, Columbia University, and a junior research fellow at the East Asian Institute. Her current research focuses on international politics of Southeast Asia and political change in Indonesia.

Peter Van Ness is a visiting fellow at the Contemporary China Centre and lectures on security in the Department of International Relations at the Australian National University. He is the editor of his latest book, *Debating Human Rights: Critical Essays from the United States and Asia* (New York: Routledge, 1999).

Hongying Wang is an assistant professor of political science at the Maxwell School of Citizenship and Public Affairs, Syracuse University. She has written *Weak State, Strong Networks: The Institutional Dynamics of Foreign Investment in China* (New York: Oxford University Press, in press).

Bridget Welsh is a lecturer in the Department of Political Science at Hofstra University in New York. Her current research focuses on democracy, state formation, and political economy in Malaysia and Guyana. She has published a number of articles on these themes and is currently working on a study of the 1999 Malaysian elections.

Lynn T. White III is a professor of politics and international affairs at Princeton University. He has worked at the Centre of Asian Studies of Hong Kong University and the Institute of Sociology at the Academia Sinica. His most recent book is *Unstately Power: Local Causes of China's Intellectual, Legal, and Governmental Reforms* (Armonk, N.Y.: M. E. Sharpe, 1998).